HELLFIRE

HELLFIRE

The Story of Australia, Japan and the Prisoners of War

CAMERON FORBES

MACMILLAN
Pan Macmillan Australia

First published 2005 in Macmillan by Pan Macmillan Australia Pty Limited
This Macmillan edition published in 2013 by Pan Macmillan Australia Pty Limited
1 Market Street, Sydney

CIP details for this book are available from the National Library of Australia.

ISBN: 9781742613123

Cover photographs courtesy of the Australian
War Memorial (P1502.003/P02443.013)
Maps by Laurie Whiddon, Map Illustrations

Typeset in 12/16.5 Sabon by Midland Typesetters, Australia
Printed by McPherson's Printing Group

For Anne

Contents

List of maps

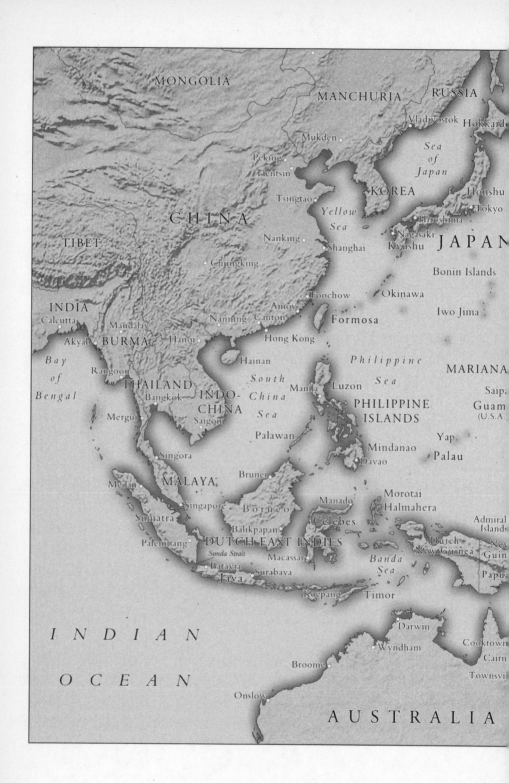

CHAPTER 1

A different courage

[Men] will sacrifice occupations and other things to go to war where they can fight as soldiers and gain a little of the glory of war.

General Gordon Bennett

Nightjars call. It is the changing of the guard for jungle creatures and soon there are new bird songs. Pale light touches the tops of teak trees and giant bamboo but in the cutting it is dark still. Candlelight plays on the old faces of men and on rocks rough-hewn by hand. Kevin Ward is here. It is April 25, Anzac Day, 2003. Ward tasted a little of what some generals like to call the glory of war, saw blood on the bayonet, bodies tattered and battered by machine-gun bullets and mortar bombs, saw mates and enemy die for distant king and emperor in ambush at Gemas on the Malayan peninsula in 1942. Brief glory quickly became inglorious defeat in Singapore, Britain's greatest military humiliation. Kevin Ward was transformed from Australian front-line soldier to prisoner of war.

On this day in 1943, a batch of Australians stood in a jungle clearing on the first day of a new phase of their lives as slaves of their Japanese captors. They would clear jungle along this

1

mountainside in Thailand, gnaw through limestone ridges, pile up embankments and build bridges. They would be part of an army of 61,000 Allied prisoners – British, Australian, Dutch, a handful of Americans – and 250,000 Asian labourers carving a railway to Burma as Japan desperately tried to hold the ground it gained in its amazing blitzkrieg and to push the war into the huge prize of India.

Hellfire Pass, 60 years on: Ward, other survivors, widows, friends, young regular soldiers who were at Anzac Cove, Gallipoli, the previous year and who have found a new place of pilgrimage, await the Dawn Service. In 1943 for months there was no night in Hellfire Pass. Flares, carbide lamps and bamboo fires lit workers, men near naked and skeletal, and guards with bamboo staves. Elongated shadows twisted and danced up rock faces and into the jungle. There were shouts of *speedo* and screams. But now a minister breaks the hush: 'We are assembled here in the presence of Almighty God to remember before Him, with thanksgiving, the honoured dead who gave up their lives for their country.' Later the Last Post sounds. The dead were many; the railway was built to the sound of the Last Post.

The bugle sang to rest Wally Mulvena, father of eight, released from the agony of cholera, and Mickey Hallam, punched, kicked, beaten with bamboo staves and with wooden clogs, pulped by Japanese engineers. More than 12,000 Allied prisoners died along with a guessed-at 90,000 Asian impressed labourers, brutalised and betrayed by the Japanese who boasted that they would liberate them from the European imperialists and embrace them in the Greater East Asia Co-Prosperity Sphere.

The Thai–Burma railway stretched 415 kilometres, built north-west from Nong Pladuk in Thailand and south-east from Thanbyuzayat in Burma to link the existing systems in the two countries. Only a short section still operates. Irresistible monsoons tore down embankments. Konkoita, where the line was joined, lies under the surface of man-made Khao Laem lake and the jungle has obliterated much of the path of misery and death. Yet the memory of the railway burns and it binds Australia and Japan in a fraught relationship. Hellfire Pass has been reclaimed from the jungle and is a memorial not only to those who suffered and those who died along the railway but to all the men and women held in the diaspora of Japanese prisoner-of-war camps: on Ambon and Sandakan, most of them doomed; in Java, Sumatra and Hainan, and in Japan itself as mine and factory fodder; senior officers in Taiwan and Manchuria; and the nurses in Sumatra, only a third of whom would survive the sinking of their ship, massacre, disease and maltreatment.

Wally Mulvena died on May 23, 1943 at a camp known as Shimo Songkurai, 20 kilometres from the crossing to Burma at Three Pagodas Pass. He was 45. Cholera kills quickly, draining body and spirit. It was the most feared of the diseases that preyed on the prisoners of war and Mulvena spent his last night isolated on a small rise called Cholera Hill. Now the view from Cholera Hill is across paddy fields and the serene waters of Khao Laem lake to spectacular saw-toothed mountains along the Thai–Burma border. In the foreground, the railway embankment on which he worked briefly is clearly discernible under a cloak of grass and small shrubs as it emerges from the lake. It loses shape further up the valley.

While Mulvena was a prisoner momentous things were happening. On the seas in May and June in 1942, Japanese naval superiority was shattered in the battles of the Coral Sea and Midway. On land in the last months of the year, at Milne Bay, along the Kokoda Trail and at Buna, Australians were proving that Japanese soldiers were not invincible. New legends of the digger were being created. But Mulvena and his mates were fighting a different war with a different courage.

For Australians, Gallipoli the defeat is the defining element of World War I. Young men from a young country showed such spirit and bravery under fire that they helped build a nation. As the old soldiers have faded away the myth has grown and the Anzac Day crowds have swollen. In World War II there was much battlefield bravery too, even during the debacle that was the struggle to save Singapore.

Here is the story of Charles Anderson. He started the war a decorated hero. Born in South Africa, he won the Military Cross fighting with the King's African Rifles against German-led Askari natives. He migrated to Australia and joined the Citizen Military Forces and, in combat against the Japanese in the Battle of Muar in January 1942, won the Victoria Cross, the Empire's highest award for bravery. The citation reads, in part:

> During the operations in Malaya from the 18th to the 22nd of January, Lieutenant-Colonel Anderson, in command of a small force, was sent to restore a vital position and to assist a brigade. His force destroyed 10 enemy tanks. When later cut off, he defeated persistent attacks on his position by ground and air forces, and forced his way through the enemy lines to a depth of 15 miles. He was again surrounded and subjected to very heavy and frequent attacks resulting in severe casualties to his force. He personally led an attack with great gallantry on the enemy who were holding a bridge and succeeded in destroying four guns. Lieutenant-Colonel Anderson, throughout all this fighting, protected his wounded and refused to leave them ... Throughout the fighting which lasted for four days, he set a magnificent example of brave leadership, determination and outstanding courage.

But now consider this story from the Thai–Burma railway, told by Ray Parkin. Parkin had been steering the Australian light cruiser *Perth* at crucial stages in the gallant battle against a Japanese invasion fleet in the Java Sea on March 1, 1942. The *Perth* sank, 352 of the crew died and Parkin was one of the 320 survivors. After capture, he was sent to work on the railway.

It was July 1943 at Hintok, not far from Hellfire Pass. Two men on a work party had collapsed with malaria, another with cholera. Parkin eventually persuaded a petulant, brutal Japanese guard to allow the two men with malaria to help the man with cholera to the shelter of a cave 450 metres away. He managed to get the three standing up in a wobbly tripod.

> I watched them go – the two malarias with the cholera about their necks. They were bowed and sweating with pain and concentration, trying not to collapse. The man with cholera was limp between them with his head lifelessly on his chest, hanging like a crucified man. His knees were buckled and his feet dragged. His trousers, which were ripped across in two places revealing his skinny, fouled buttocks and stringy thighs, were unbuttoned at the waistband, and, as the others dragged him with slow and shambling gait, his pants kept falling about his knees. The two men had to stop and pull them up before they could go on. One of the malarias reached over and pulled them up: they wobbled, then they all fell over. Slowly they dragged themselves up again and staggered along the cutting until they came to the cave. Later the stretcher party, making their fourth trip, came out and picked up the cholera.

And so, step by step and day by day, the prisoners of war fought their battles for survival; often, most of them, in ignorance of what was happening in the wider world, trapped in a terrible cocoon of pain, boredom and sometimes shame and sometimes guilt. Back in Australia, many of the families of the prisoners lived in ignorance too. Letters went into the void; rare, cryptic messages came out, so delayed that there was no way of knowing whether the senders were alive or dead. In 1942 Doris Mulvena received word that Wally was missing, believed prisoner of war. Then nothing, but through those long years, she always believed he would come home. He would see Gwen, last born, for the first time. Then in June 1945 she was told he had died two years before. And with peace only a month away, six words, just six, from poor dead Wally, a postcard the Japanese allowed him to write, undated: 'I am well. We have concerts.'

They did have concerts and mock Melbourne Cup horse races. They practised graveyard humour in the face of oppression and the tyranny of dragging time. They survived as an act of will. Like foot soldiers down the ages, they had suffered at the hands of their military and political leaders. Generals had plotted against fellow generals; Allied leaders squabbled. Blunders, jealousies and, of course, the great lie – that Britannia ruled the waves and Singapore, her splendid naval base, was an impregnable fortress – helped deliver them into captivity. There they died in tragic numbers. In World War II, 550,000 Australians served in the different theatres. Nineteen thousand – 3 per cent – were killed in action. Of the 22,000 taken prisoner by the Japanese, 8000 died, 36 per cent of them.

When the survivors blinked their way into freedom after the atomic bombs had done their work, they found there had been seismic shifts. Australia, having seen its duty and security in fighting Britain's battles on veldts, Flanders fields and Middle Eastern deserts, had turned to fight for its survival in the region in which it lived. It had attached itself to a new great and powerful friend. The long-feared thrust by the yellow hordes to the north had been faced and overcome but the days of White Australia were numbered. Old empires were giving their death rattles and a new Asia was emerging. But Australia would be no more comfortable and relaxed in the new order than it was in the old.

The returning prisoners of war had to make sense of an Australia that had changed while they had been away. Some didn't know whether wives, fiancées or girlfriends had waited for them. Some tried to make sense of their POW experience. Some wrote memoirs, some kept silent, even to their wives.

For some the railway is more than memory. 'A day wouldn't pass when I wouldn't revisit it,' Kevin Ward says, 'but I like to keep it to myself. Every time I talk to anyone, it's like exposing your soul and you pay the penance afterwards.'

The general who led Australia's ill-fated 8th Division, who left them on the day of surrender – deserted them, so his critics charged – spent the rest of his war defending himself, as generals often must. Henry Gordon Bennett saw the war through his favourite prism: himself. This is how he began his memoirs:

> I will take you from an older Australia, through the burning sands of Egypt to the fatal Hellespont, and then through muddy Flemish trenches and the sloughs of civic intrigue and rivals' jealousy, to the jungles of Malaya and the last, despairing days before the fall of Singapore. After a voyage which equals that of Ulysses, we shall come back to face disillusion and deceit such as seldom has fallen to the lot of any man. Yet, on the way, we shall catch glimpses of the peaks of splendour rising through the murk.

There is a telling photograph as frontispiece of A. B. Lodge's book *The Fall of General Gordon Bennett*. Aged 31 and at the dizzy young career height of brigadier general at the end of World War I, Bennett sits on a marvellous white horse, a perfect vantage point from which to spy peaks of splendour. For many prisoners of war in the worst of times, during 1943, the only peak on the horizon was Cholera Hill. This second world war, as close as anything in history to that rarest of animals, a just war, was as brutal and wicked in its way as those fought for greed, enslavement or for no better reason than that the aggressor had the power to crush. Civilians were targeted in the Blitz, cities in Europe and Japan were surveyed for their burnability and the attempted extermination of a people was conducted like an industry.

On battlefields soldiers killed one another, which is what soldiers do. But it was not often in a contest conducted to the warrior code. Prisoners are a problem for a modern, mobile army, particularly when the soldiers are strangers in a strange land, and lines of supply are extended. Away from textbooks and drills, war is fast-moving confusion, death an instant away and the Geneva Convention on the treatment of prisoners of war an interesting theory even for those armies bound by it. And Japan's was not. In August 1943, death was having its best time along the Thai–Burma railway, helped by Japanese camp commanders like Lieutenant Tsuneo Fukuda at Shimo Songku-rai, where Mulvena died. In a confrontation with Australian doctor Major Bruce Hunt, Fukuda said: 'You have in the past spoken somewhat boastfully of the Geneva Convention and humanity. You must remember that you are our POW; you are in our power; and that in the present circumstances these things do not apply. International law and the Geneva Convention do not apply if they are in conflict with the interests of the Japanese army.'

IN MALAYA IN January 1942 Lieutenant Colonel Anderson, having fought bravely with pistol and grenade, eventually had to order the withdrawal through jungle and swamps of the remnants of his men capable of it. He was forced to the bitter decision to leave the more seriously wounded behind at Parit Sulong. One hundred and ten Australians and 40 Indians were taken prisoner by the Japanese, among them Lieutenant Ben Hackney. They would face hours of torment, kicked and prodded, herded together into confined agony, taunted, denied water or aid. Hackney pretended death. That was easy enough: his leg was shattered and he had been stabbed with a bayonet 52 times. At dusk the killing began. Some were machine-gunned then doused with petrol and set alight, others beheaded. A few survived, but most of those perished later. Hackney, after desperate weeks at large, was again captured. Parit Sulong was brutality in cold blood, and the Japanese commander, Lieutenant General Takumo Nishimura was hanged as a war criminal.

But no armies are pure. Sparrow Force, Australia's sacrificial offering on Timor, had its reality check in its brief battle with Japan's 228th Regiment. The Japanese invaded on February 20, 1942. Australia's official historian, Lionel Wigmore, recorded the 'savagery of the Japanese' revealed two days later when Australian troops entered the village of Babau: 'It was found that several Australians, including a medical orderly, had been tied to trees, and their throats cut. One man, forced by the para-troopers to carry a wireless set, had been bayoneted when he collapsed of exhaustion.'

On the same day Bombadier Tom Uren, who would later become deputy leader of the Australian Labor Party, had volun-teered to carry ammunition to companies of Sparrow Force's 2/40th Battalion attacking Usau ridge. 'The taking of that ridge,' he would write, 'was the only time I have personally witnessed a bayonet charge. With the Japanese entrenched on the ridge with their machine guns, the men of the 2/40th walked steadily up the slope, cool as cucumbers. They eventually overran the Japanese position, and bayoneted those in the trenches.'

R Company, operating on the flank, had captured one wounded Japanese soldier. He was not securely guarded. This is what follows, recorded in the 2/40th's history, *Doomed Battalion*: 'He managed to get control of an automatic weapon, "jumped into a trench and opened fire". The Japanese was killed, and the incident prompted R Company troops to make sure all Japanese in the area were dead. Reg Farquhar, a C Company sergeant, wrote, "I still squirm when I think of those raw R Company blokes arriving at the finish to continually bayonet Japanese bodies".'

What happened at Usau is perhaps understandable under the rough rules of war. Imagine being there, particularly as, say, an 18-year-old, barely trained in battle craft and having to learn the hardness that might mean survival. But Australians also slaughtered the helpless and at times joined the Japanese in a moral no-man's land.

It was Australian policy to take prisoners and to encourage surrender. Leaflets in Japanese were dropped claiming to give the testimony, some of it poetic, of captives to the kindness of their captors.

In a white cot in the hospital
Those who came to comfort me
Were men of a strange country.
Who made me weep? A tear fell on my knees.

The reality was frequently different. There is considerable anecdotal evidence of the reluctance of Australian soldiers to bring Japanese in alive, despite the value officers placed on interrogation. There are also official records. In July 1943, official war artist Ivor Hele produced a graphic charcoal sketch of an incident at Salamaua, in New Guinea. It shows a digger, pistol in hand, looking down at a cluster of bodies and it is titled 'Shooting Japanese wounded, Timbered Knoll'. In January 1944 a tank commander in New Guinea reported on the use of tanks north of Finschhafen:

> At Lakona 'A' Sqn employed five tanks in line against a coconut plantation where they succeeded in driving 40 Japs over a cliff into the sea when the infantry did the rest by playfully tossing hand grenades as if on a fishing expedition with dynamite.

Hate comes easily in war. It came easily too when the principle of White Australia encouraged short steps from feelings of distinctiveness to feelings of superiority and when the homeland itself was seen as under direct threat. This is what one Australian private, who had fought in Libya and Greece, and then in the bitterness of Sanananda in New Guinea, wrote in December 1942: 'My regard for Tony [the Italian] was always impersonal and for Fritz . . . tinged with admiration, but none of us know anything but vindictive hatred for the Jap.' And another: 'If an Italian or German were running away, one might let him go, but never a Japanese.' And another: 'Out foraging this morning I came across the head of a good Jap – for he was dead – like a damned baboon he was; this is not murder killing such repulsive looking animals.' Dr Mark Johnston, who made this study of attitudes, says that ironically, in their brutal treatment of each other, Australians and Japanese had something in common.

Sometimes it is easy to judge when the blurry line between terrible imperative and senseless atrocity has been crossed. Then guilt can be apportioned. It could be at Banka Island, when Australian nurses were forced to walk into the sea and were then machine-gunned. The killers were never found. It could be at Parit Sulong. It could be along the Thai–Burma railway and in some camps in the diaspora.

KEVIN WARD HAS returned several times to Hellfire Pass. He ties a poppy to a tree branch. 'I do it every time I go back,' he says. 'I go quietly and I think my thoughts deep. The poppy touches the tree and the tree touches the earth. My mates died here and we buried them around here. I'm happy with the serenity of it. I take comfort.'

Others have come too and walked along the scar of the railway. The rails have long gone but the gravel ballast remains, and an occasional sleeper. Sometimes the monsoon washes out a spike. The three-tiered bridge has disappeared but bomb craters straddle its path. Takashi Nagase has come. He was an interpreter for the *kempeitai*, the Japanese military police. He turned the torturers' questions into English. His have been journeys in search of reconciliation, driven by remorse (though some Australian survivors flinch at the mere thought of taking his hand). Renichi Sugano has come. He looks at the path of the railway with an engineer's eye and pride. He was one of the senior officers in charge of the construction. He goes to cemeteries and shrines, carrying flowers and prayers, he says, for all the railway dead. But there is no doubt that first in his thoughts is his young friend and protégé, Eiji Hirota. Hirota was the engineer in charge of the section of railway north of Hellfire Pass which was worked by Edward (Weary) Dunlop's men. He was executed as a war criminal in Singapore on January 21, 1947, found guilty of, among other crimes, responsibility for the fatal beating of Mickey Hallam. Weary Dunlop had kept his word. In his *War Diaries*, Dunlop recorded a confrontation with Hirota on March 22, 1943: 'I invited him to make good his threat to shoot me (rifles were trained on me). "You can shoot me, but then my 2 I/C is as tough a man as me, and after him you will have to shoot them all. Then you will have no workmen. In any case, I have taken steps to one day have you hanged, for you are a black-hearted bastard." '

'No, no, no,' Sugano says. 'Hirota was a gentle man and a caring man. For example, when he told prisoners of war to do certain work in a day, he himself carefully checked how hard the rock was and how hard the task was and he would make an assessment of how difficult it was to complete the task in such and such a time. He never set workers an impossible task. He was reliable. I believe Hirota's execution was attributable to hatred by the other side. Hirota was executed as a revenge, as a sacrifice.'

There is no doubt that Australia sought revenge, executing Nishimura and 136 other Japanese as war criminals, and angry about the ones that got away. Now Australia and Japan are trading partners, Australian gardens are props for Japanese wedding photos and the Returned Services League leadership has reached out to the Japanese. But there is unfinished business. The prisoner-of-war survivors are fading away but there still has not been a fulsome Japanese apology and the loser has written a skewed history.

Gallipoli has been transformed from history to myth. It is a folk festival and the Turks are almost honorary mates. Yet few wounded Anzacs left with the Turks survived, Patsy Adam-Smith reports in her study of Australian prisoners of war from Gallipoli to Korea. Charles Bean, the official historian, wrote: 'Some were shot or bayoneted. A German officer, seeing the Turkish soldiers kicking a number of wounded men and preparing to roll them over a cliff on the hillside, stepped in and saved their lives.' Leslie Duncan Richardson, a 1st Light Horse signaller, captured in August 1916 as the Turks advanced towards the Suez Canal, wrote of his experiences as prisoner. Change the war, change the captors, change the climate from tropical heat to snow chill. Richardson is forced to help lay a railway. He has malarial fever and dysentery (though he is allowed to live in a tent and then in a hospital for 14 days). The men live in bitterly cold mud houses where the vermin carry typhus. They walk 5 miles to and from the railway and work on 1 pound of black bread a day.

But that was another war half a world away. Japan and Australia share a region and a long past of racial tension which began to grow even in the late nineteenth century, as the British colonies were forming the small fledgling Australian nation, a defiantly White Australia and proudly British. Around the time Japan was asserting itself, crushing Chinese forces in the first Sino-Japanese War fought in 1894 and 1895 in Korea over competing interests there, the *Illustrated London News* commented: 'The spectacle of this Eastern nation fighting and manoeuvring and organising with a nerve and intelligence worthy of a first-class European war has sent a thrill of admiring wonder through the military world.' Half a century later, in Hellfire Pass the prisoners looked at their captors with hate, fear and puzzlement. Questions linger for both sufferers and persecutors. Was the Japanese behaviour an aberration? If there is such a thing as a national psyche is there at the heart of Japan's a rough force that could be awakened again?

Was a prisoner, forced to work for the enemy's war effort, a soldier still? Kevin Ward carries his wounds. He is near blind and his leg has been reconstructed, a gaping hole filled with plastic surgery. These things happened on the railway which for Ward was just as much a battlefield as Gemas, with its shot and shell. He had put his age up to enlist and he was 18 years old when he first went into battle. He turned 21, the prime rite of passage in those days, in a prisoner-of-war camp. 'Why don't you tell the Nip?' a mate said. 'He might give you the key to the gate and then we can all go.'

As he walks along Hellfire Pass, he walks among the ghosts of fighting men and fighting leaders. Scattered there are the ashes of Weary Dunlop, tallest tree among equals in the band of medical officers. 'We were soldiers,' Ward says. 'I still am a soldier and always will be.'

CHAPTER 2

A pestiferous varmint

Something world-shaking is happening in the Palace of Versailles. Here's a procession of statesmen walking into the Hall of Mirrors, the grand monument that Louis XIV, King of France, the Sun King, built to his perception of his own magnificence. Seventy metres long, with the Salon of War at one end and the Salon of Peace at the other, the hall has 17 giant windows on one side and 17 mirrors on the other, reflecting the sweeping gardens. It is June 28, 1919 and this solemn occasion is about peace and a treaty to end the war to end wars. The representatives of Germany, heavy with defeat and humiliation, have trudged to put their signatures on parchment first. Then there is Woodrow Wilson, President of the United States, who had swung American power into the war to make the world safe for democracy and America, and his delegation. He is followed by Britain's great wartime leader, Lloyd George, and his colleagues. Next come the representatives of Canada, led by Minister of Justice, Charles Doherty. And who's this now? The smallest man at the conference. Surely he can be forgiven if he tries to catch a glimpse of himself in the mirrors: sharp nose, big ears, a face begging to be caricatured. It's William Morris Hughes, the Prime Minister of Australia, the Little Digger. Waiting behind him are the Japanese representatives, Prince

Saionji and Baron Makino. They have found the Little Digger a massive, immovable obstacle to one of their major ambitions at the peace conference.

Small man, small nation, but Hughes had a huge, silent army behind him: Australia's 59,000 war dead, a terrible toll for a country with a population of four million. He was always ready to invoke their sacrifice to Australia's advantage. Born in England and bred in Wales, as was Lloyd George, Hughes migrated to Australia aged 22 and worked first as an itinerant rural labourer. But politics became his life. He was 90 when he died and still a parliamentarian after 58 years. A biographer described him as an illusionist, an orator and a writer who summoned up magical shapes, an epic enough liar to play some part in the making of his own legend. He emerged from World War I a hero to many Australian soldiers, and a villain to the Labor Party from which he split over his support for conscription. The party coined for him its blackest epithet: Labor rat. He went to Paris on a mission which was bound to bring him into conflict with the Japanese.

Japan began the twentieth century as it had ended the nineteenth, with a military triumph, this time not over an Asian neighbour, but over Russia. It was on the side of the Allies in World War I, though a bit player. Japanese forces confronted the Germans in their colony on China's Shantung peninsula and the Japanese battle cruiser *Ibuki* helped escort Australian troops sailing towards Gallipoli.

Woodrow Wilson came to Paris determined that 'the world be made safe and fit to live in'. He carried with him his plan to achieve this, the Fourteen Points, the last being that 'a general association of nations must be formed under specific covenants for the purpose of mutual guarantees of political independence and territorial integrity to great and small states alike'. Everyone came to the conference with their own agendas, many elements being selfish, self-interested or self-serving. Billy Hughes wanted

New Guinea as Australia's safety barrier, arguing that 'whoever controls the islands within the Australian waters also controls Australia'. As a prop for his presentation he had a map which his principal adviser Robert Garran had scoured London for: it showed the hemisphere centred on Australia. In comparison, Japan's major proposal seems marvellously universal and imbued with admirable idealism – from the vantage point of the twenty-first century, that is. Baron Makino had been effusive when the first draft of the League of Nations covenant had been tabled. 'Perhaps the most important document that has been compiled by man,' he said. But Japan had a proposal to make it even better. The prince and the baron argued that in the covenant of the League, fittingly for the body which was to build and guard peace, should be this proposition: 'The equality of nations being a basic principle of the League, the High Con-tracting parties agree that concerning the treatment and rights to be accorded to aliens in their territories they will not discrimi-nate, either by law or in fact, against any person or persons on account of his or their race or nationality.'

Who could disagree with this? Billy Hughes, the Little Digger, Prime Minister of Australia, for one. He faced formidable oppo-nents. Both of the principal Japanese negotiators were former premiers. And Prince Saionji was more than that. He was a *genro,* a member of an inner circle of elder statesmen, survivors of the original Meiji ruling elite and now special advisers to the emperor. He had a unique base for his personal influence. As a child he was playmate of a god, the young Emperor Meiji, and later in the dangerous world of the Japanese court, he developed sword-sharp political skills. Hughes, a veteran of knockabout Labor Party internecine warfare, was undaunted.

Billy Hughes and his noble Japanese counterparts represented two profoundly racist and exclusivist nations. Japan's religion, Shinto, preached the people's unique, divine origins. The imperial line was descended from Amaterasu, goddess of the sun, and the whole Japanese race was of divine origin, though sprung from lesser deities. The corollary was superiority over all other races. Australians were proud, white and British, sons (and daughters) of the great Empire, and, as we shall see, regarded by Hughes as the purest of the heirs, indeed, purer than the inhabitants of the Mother country.

THE DIPLOMATIC CONFRONTATION in Paris had been waiting to happen since 1831 and the voyage of the whaling ship, *Lady Rowena*, home port Sydney. Neville Meaney relates the tale of this inauspicious first contact in his study of the first hundred years of Australia–Japan relations. The *Lady Rowena* was leaking after weathering a heavy storm off Hokkaido, Japan's northernmost island. Captain Bourn Russell sailed her into Hamanaka Bay hoping to career and repair her. This was a time when Japan was attempting to quarantine itself from the Western barbarians. There was one edict in force, *bakufu*, which forbade Japanese subjects, on pain of death, to leave their country and another, unknown to Captain Russell, designed to keep barbarian ships from Japanese shores. Under the 'No Second Thought' Expulsion Order foreign ships entering Japanese waters were to be destroyed and their crews arrested or put to death. Having been greeted with 'cold indifference', Russell led an armed party ashore and, in the absence of the inhabitants who had fled, took what he needed. And more, it seems, for in the logbook he said he had 'committed Sackarlige by Robbing their temple'. Armed, bloodless clashes followed, with the crew of the *Lady Rowena* carrying the day and a village being torched. Through a captured Japanese, Russell attempted to send a letter to the Emperor. In it he complained about the treatment of his ship in distress, urged the benefits of trade and asserted that Europeans were 'infinitely farther advanced in the Arts and Sciences and Civilisation' than the Japanese.

Commodore Matthew Perry's American 'black' ships permanently breached Japan's defences in 1853. Six years later, when Yokohama was opened to foreign trade, a young Melbourne merchant, Alexander Marks, was there to do the first deals between Australia and Japan in what would become a partnership worth billions of dollars between the two nations. In 1866, Japan repealed the *bakufu* edict and four years later Sukagawa Rikinosuke arrived in Australia. He was an acrobat, Australia's first recorded Japanese migrant. He married an Australian woman, became a naturalised citizen and purchased land. His was a success story: 46 years later he owned a circus which toured Queensland towns.

In 1877 the South Australian Government proposed a scheme, which it would fund, for the settlement of Japanese in the Northern Territory, empty except for its Aboriginal owners. An inward-turned Japanese Government aborted it. In 1901 there were nearly 4000 Japanese in Australia, but the doors would be slammed shut as the Australian federation was forged. Founding father Alfred Deakin told Parliament that year: 'The unity of Australia is nothing if that does not imply a united race. A united race means not only that its members can intermix, intermarry and associate . . . but implies one inspired by the same ideas . . . of a people possessing the same general cast of character, tone of thought, the same constitutional training and traditions . . . Unity of race is an absolute to the unity of Australia.' Japan lobbied London against Australia's Immigration Restriction Act, not mollified by Deakin's backhanded compliment when he said Japanese should be excluded 'because of their high abilities' and that (prescient prophecy) they 'would be our most formidable enemies'.

According to Fitzhardinge, Hughes's official biographer, the Australian Prime Minister had entered the Paris Peace Conference 'convinced that Japan intended, if not checked, to make some challenge to Australian immigration policy . . . In the long run he still believed war between Japan and Australia was inevitable, because of the pressure of population on Japan's resources.' Paranoia? Not if you listen to Kiyoshi Kari Kawakami, who was producing a running commentary on the negotiations called 'Japan and the Race Question at the Paris Peace Conference: a Japanese View in 1919'. Kawakami, making a plea for understanding of the intense feeling behind the desire of the Japanese people to have a racial equality clause in the covenant, outlined what he described as 'the population problem which has been harassing the Japanese': during the past half-century Japan's population had been increasing at an average rate of 400,000 a year, and the rate was increasing, 1917 witnessing a record-breaking increase of 800,000. In 50 years the population had increased from 33 million to almost 58 million with a density of 389 people per square mile. 'All European countries, at certain stages of their internal development,' Kawakami said, 'have alleviated the pressure of population at home by encouraging emigration. Moreover, most European countries have acquired vast overseas territories which have proved profitable to the mother countries either as colonies or as sources of raw materials.'

Kawakami quoted an editorial in the influential newspaper *Tokyo Asahi*, which would hardly have soothed Billy Hughes's fears. The *Asahi* said it did not recognise the justice of the exclusion policy of certain Western countries.

To the contrary, we believe that such sparsely populated countries as Australia, most sections of which have only one inhabitant to the square mile, should receive our emigrants. At the same time we realise that our insistence upon this point will disturb our amicable relationship with foreign nations. Wisdom dictates that we should not insist upon an absolute freedom of emigration for our people of the working class. But there is no reason why the exclusive or restrictive measures directed against our working men should also be applied to our merchants and travelers, who, small in number, seek to enter countries controlled by Western nations. For this class of our countrymen, we can reasonably demand an absolute freedom of travel and residence.

The *Asahi* appealed to 'the statesmen of the West who are championing the cause of humanity'. To this William Morris Hughes turned one large, deaf ear and raised his voice, a solo one for a time, against the racial-equality proposition. By now the conference knew what to expect.

According to Lloyd George, when Hughes was arguing with Woodrow Wilson that Australia should annex New Guinea, the former German colony, the exchange went like this:

Mr Hughes listened intently with his hand cupped around his neck . . . The President asked him slowly and solemnly . . . that 'if the whole civilised world asks Australia to agree to a mandate in respect of these islands, Australia is prepared to defy the appeal of the whole civilised world?' Mr Hughes answered 'that's about the size of it, President Wilson'.

Hughes finally compromised, but the trusteeship system settled upon gave Australia the control over New Guinea it wanted. He was not about to back down on the racial-equality clause. He was fighting for the White Australia policy and he was willing to use any weapon. He wrote on a British Empire delegation paper giving notice of Japan's proposal that 'sooner than agree to it I would walk into the Seine – or the Folies Bergère with my clothes off', something that would certainly frighten the horses or the chorus line. He met with the Japanese in private twice, later writing that Baron Makino persisted in 'beslobbering me with genuflections and obsequious deference'. Face to face he was more diplomatic, saying that Australia recognised the Japanese as friends and equals 'but the history of your people has its roots in far different soil. I hope they will always be our friends and allies. But in ordinary, everyday life, men do not invite all their friends into their houses, nor even when they invite them into their houses do they make them permanent residents therein.' Hughes was determined to keep the door closed.

American foreign correspondent and former diplomat Stephen Bonsal, who had privileged access to both the American and Japanese camps, wrote that 'little Hughes from Australia . . . morning, noon and night bellows at poor Lloyd George that if race equality is recognised in the preamble or any of the articles of the covenant, he and his people will leave the conference bag and baggage. Even the President, usually so restrained, not to say formal in his language, says Hughes is "a pestiferous varmint" – but still he represents a continent.' [Shades of Labor rat.]

Eventually on April 11 the Japanese delegation insisted that the racial-equality clause be put to the vote. The proposal won a comfortable majority but the motion was declared lost. Woodrow Wilson, visionary and idealist, had ruled the decision must be unanimous, surely knowing that he had doomed the Japanese cause. In the real world of 1919, America was not ready for racial equality, not for the blacks of the South or the Japanese living in the West. Nor were European colonial powers such as Britain. Delegation member and former prime minister

Arthur James Balfour told the Americans that the doctrine that all men are created equal was an eighteenth-century idea which he did not believe to be true. There might be some sense in which all people of one country were equal but he did not think that a man in central Africa was created equal to a European.

Following a grand ball in Paris to mark the signing of the Treaty of Versailles, Hughes crossed the English Channel for a reunion with his wife and four-year-old daughter Helen. At Victoria Station some diggers mobbed him, lifted him shoulder high, put a slouch hat on his head and carried Prime Minister and child down to the Anzac Buffet where their mates were celebrating.

Billy Hughes would sum up the Paris Peace Conference to the Australian Parliament in November 1919 with a flourish of racist triumphalism:

> We went into this conflict to maintain those ideals which we have nailed to the very top of our flagpole – White Australia and those other aspirations of this young democracy. I venture to say, therefore, that perhaps the greatest thing we have achieved, under such circum-stances and in such an assemblage, is the policy of White Australia . . . Remember that this is the only community in the Empire, if not, indeed, in the world, where there is so little admixture of race . . . We are more British than the people of Great Britain, and we hold firmly to the great principle of White Australia, because we know what we know . . . The White Australia policy is yours. You may do with it what you please, but at any rate, the soldiers have achieved the victory and my colleagues and I have brought that great principle back to you from the conference, as safe as it was on the day it was first adopted.

There were more sober assessments. Australia's Governor-General, Ronald Munro-Ferguson, sent Hughes a note expressing the hope that as a result of the conference Australia would not be 'inscribed permanently . . . in the Black Book of the little brown men of Japan'. In 1921 Hughes told Parliament: 'For us the Pacific problem is for all practical purposes the problem of Japan. Here is a nation of nearly 70 million people crowded together in narrow islands; its population is increasing rapidly and is already pressing on the margin of subsistence. She wants both room for her increasing millions and markets for her manufactured goods.' He spoke of Japan's desire to exploit China's 400 million market as a special right coming up against the desire of other nations for an open door and their own share. 'This is the problem of the Pacific – the modern riddle of the Sphinx,' he said, 'for which we must find the answer'.

There was not much enigmatic about Kawakami's Japanese view of the League of Nations without a racial-equality clause in the covenant.

The Far Eastern peoples then must not, under the new world regime, expect much brighter days, but must be prepared to trudge along the same thorny path as heretofore, making the best use of their own resources, and endeavoring not to trespass upon the domain monopolised by the great powers of the West, even if they have to trample upon one another within their own sphere in the sheer struggle for existence.

Germany was unhappy. Japan was unhappy, though while it failed in its pursuit of the racial-equality clause, it did not come away from Paris empty-handed. Australia had New Guinea; Japan had the German Pacific island territories, the Marshalls, the Marianas and the Carolines. They would come in very handy.

After the war to end wars and the signing of the Treaty of Versailles, the next world war was only 20 years away. In that period there seems to have been little dulling of the hard edge of racism in Australia. Perhaps the Depression even sharpened attitudes to race and immigration. In his speech to the nation in December 1941 after the Japanese launched the Pacific war, Labor Prime Minister John Curtin predicted that Australians would 'hold this country, and keep it as a citadel for the British-speaking race and a place where civilisation will persist'. It was an appeal to defend the White Australia policy, a founding principle of the nation. It could have been Billy Hughes speaking. However, being pure had its problems. America was in the war, which Curtin and Churchill had desperately desired, but America had black troops. Curtin's biographer David Day relates that the Advisory War Council on January 14, 1942 had decided that no black troops could be allowed in the country since it could affect 'the maintenance of the White Australia policy in the post-war settlement'. Curtin overruled this, assured that the troops would be used for construction purposes in tropical Australia and that America would show sensitivity on the numbers sent.

Hughes and Curtin, the two old White Australia warriors, were on their way to defeat. In Nagasaki on August 9, 1945 Allan Chick, cray-fisherman from the east coast of Tasmania turned prisoner-of-war, had a miraculous escape when the second atom bomb dropped. He later served in the occupation forces and eventually returned home with his Japanese bride. Chick was an unlikely agent of one of Australia's great social changes, the overthrowing of White Australia.

Winning a war can have unintended consequences.

CHAPTER 3

Troops of God

Corpses drifting swollen in the sea-depths,
Corpses rotting in the mountain-grass –
We shall die, by the side of our lord we shall die
We shall not look back.

Japanese soldiers' instruction pamphlet

It is a sunny autumn day in Tokyo. The Japanese family man is wearing a T-shirt which proclaims proudly 'Been there, drunk that'. Drinking in Japan is bonding with co-workers and with friends. But today he is holding the hand of his young daughter, who is in pretty pink. It is a steady climb up the highest natural point in central Tokyo, Kudan Hill. They walk under the imposing *torii*, the gate that marks the entrance to a Shinto shrine, and past the giant bronze statue of Masujiro Omura, nineteenth-century Vice-Minister of War, in heroic samurai pose. On the right of the path is a screen. From behind it comes indrawn-breath silence, then a zinging sound, then a thud and then a guttural exchange of chants. This is a *kyudo* competition, with men and women firing arrows at the stuffed figure of a deer. Like many things Japanese, the complex, slow-motion ritual surrounding archery is as important as the moment of pure action.

Man and daughter watch for a while then go to the *temi-ausha*, the font for ablutions. Rinse hands and face with water from the stone basin; do not touch the dipper directly with lips: this is a cleansing process. They are approaching one of the most sacred places in Japan, and the most controversial. Yasukuni Shrine is not the most popular shrine in Tokyo. This would be Asakusa Kannon, in a lively district, the centre for *kabuki* and other entertainments. The approach to Asakusa Kannon shrine is through a long gauntlet of stalls, gaudy with souvenirs or selling Japanese fast food. A dog performs acrobatics for yen in the forecourt of a Buddhist garden. Thousands press through the Kaminarimon Gate, drawn to the statue of Kannon, the Buddhist goddess of mercy, found, according to legend, by two fishermen brothers in 628 in the nearby Sumida River. A sutra touts Kannon's powers: 'As soon as people's cries of agony reach Kannon, the bodhisattva takes pity on them and saves them from the tortures of hell. If people offer sincere prayers to Kannon, even fire cannot burn them and water cannot drown them.'

Asakusa Kannon is the comforting face of Buddhism; Yasukuni Shrine is the confronting, militaristic mask of Shinto. The family man is going there to pray, perhaps to a grandfather in an act of love and remembrance. 'I am here', he will call, as he enters the inner shrine. Emperors have been there to give thanks and to pray for the wellbeing of the nation. For many Japanese soldiers the thought of Yasukuni was a solace as they went into battle and faced death. 'We'll meet at Yasukuni,' they called to one another. There was a popular song in World War II: 'You and I are cherry blossoms of the same year. Even if we are apart when our petals fall, we'll bloom again in the treetops of the Capital's Yasukuni Shrine.' Yet Yasukuni is also the symbol of the new nationalism and rampant militarism, born in the nineteenth century, that roared out of Japan to devastate the region.

Yasukuni represents suffering, bravery and sacrifice, but it also represents the dark side of the Japanese spirit and the perversion of the code of *bushido*, the code by which Japan's warrior class, the samurai, lived.

Yasukuni is the home of the divine spirits, the more than two and a half million Japanese war dead since the restoration to power, at least titular, of the imperial line in 1868. Their names are recorded, the dates and location of their deaths in battle and their birthplaces. The noticeboard outside the shrine says that the name Yasukuni, which means 'peaceful country', was bestowed by the Emperor Meiji in 1879 'implying that owing to the meritorious services of the spirits of the deities worshipped, the nation enjoys peace and security'. Banned from the world of the divine spirits are those Japanese who fought against Emperor Meiji's forces in the civil war of 1868 that gave him control of the state; included are the 14 Japanese military and political leaders, including Hideki Tojo, who were executed after World War II as class A war criminals. They were secretly enshrined in 1979 and designated Martyrs of the Showa Era, the reign of Emperor Hirohito.

No emperor has visited Yasukuni since 1977. To do so would send a tsunami of outrage across the region. It is bad enough when a Japanese prime minister bows and claps his hands before the divine spirits. Old angers and old fears get new life. It is not the honouring of the battle dead that offends; Yasukuni symbolises the stubborn refusal to acknowledge that some of these divine spirits were guilty of atrocities, that Japanese militarism brutalised the nation and the region.

Many of the millions enshrined at Yasukuni are members of what Keith Rossi, an Australian World War II veteran who also served in Vietnam, calls a great freemasonry of soldiers. 'I saw the contents of German and Italian soldiers' pockets,' Rossi says. 'Pictures, identical pictures with those you'd see on the bodies of Australians: wives, children, loved ones. After the war when I got access to translations of diaries, no matter what the bloody nationality, Japanese, German, they all write the same things, miss the same things, have the same hopes. And that's when it comes to me that the soldiers are the same. You go off and fight and the enemy are demonised and we were told we were fighting for right. They were too.'

Each month at Yasukuni, a priest selects the name of one of the two and a half million who left a last message, posting it on the shrine noticeboard and on its website. This is what pilot Mikoto Kanji, 23, on his last day on earth, wrote: 'The verdure is so beautiful that one could forget about having to die today. The deep blue sky with a white cloud floating idly by. June in Chiran, where the cicadas are already singing, is almost like summer. The little bird sings so happily. The next time I will be reborn as a little bird. This is what Sugimoto says while lying in the sun on the grass. Don't make me laugh. Today at 1455 hours I will take off from Chiran. Goodbye to the dear land of my ancestors. I send you my favourite pen as my keepsake.'

So Kanji flew fatalistically to his death, a *kamikaze*, cleverly named after the typhoons, the divine winds that twice destroyed the invading Mongol fleets of Kublai Khan. The *kamikaze* of World War II aimed their aircraft or submarines at combatants. In the new terrorist wars, the Tamil Tigers, Hamas, Al Qaeda and Chechen extremists, produced by the mating of nationalism and religious fanaticism, deliberately target civilian populations, men, women and children. Under Western eyes, this martyrdom is a wicked madness. Decades ago the *kamikaze* phenomenon was also looked at across a culture gap, with fear and puzzlement, but then the whole Japanese army appeared alien and inscrutable as it tramped into Asia on its war of expansion. At the start of World War II the Allies certainly did not know the enemy.

There had been warnings about the Japanese. Kipling, poet laureate to the Raj, described them as 'handy little men . . . with the easy lope of the rickshaw coolie' . . . 'If you meet Japanese infantry, led by a Continental officer, commence firing early and often and at the largest range compatible with getting at them. They are bad little men who know too much.' Australian soldiers like Kevin Ward went into battle with a composite image of their Japanese counterparts that was part propaganda, part wishful thinking. A small, stupid, bandy-legged man with glasses like Coke-bottle bottoms, afraid of the dark, scared easily by loud noises. From their supreme commander, Field Marshal Sir Thomas Blamey, Australians heard a comforting analysis: 'Your enemy is a curious race – a cross between the human being and an ape. And like an ape, when he is cornered he knows how to die. But he is inferior to you and you know it and that knowledge will help bring you to victory.'

Japanese soldiers were similarly reassured. Westerners, they were told, were 'very superior, very effeminate and very cowardly', with an intense dislike of fighting in the rain, mist, or at night. They were even more feeble than the Chinese and their tanks and aircraft a collection of rattling relics.

The war began with a blitzkrieg of Japanese successes throughout South-East Asia and the utter humiliation of Singapore. Prisoners were sent to work throughout the Japanese empire. A group of about 90 Australians was greeted by their camp commander, Colonel Noguchi, when they arrived in Seoul in September 1942. Noguchi thought Seoul part of Japan and this, in the words of his interpreter, is what he thought of the war, the Japanese army and its captives:

We are fighting for the emancipation of the nations of East Asia, firm and unshakable in our resolve that our enemy Britain and the U.S.A. should be crushed. Australia is on the verge of capture, India of rebellion. We have already sunk 2801 vessels and destroyed 4500 aircraft. The Nippon Army is under the Imperial command of the Emperor who is the personification of God, so that the Imperial troops are called the troops of God. Now you have become prisoners of war through struggling against God's army are you not feared to the marrow? Hostile feelings in your hearts against us cannot go permitted. We will punish you if you [sic] against our regulations or attempt to escape. According to your malice feelings, so shall we limit your freedom or treat you with severity or lenity. Sign parole as proof of your non-hostility or be placed under restraint. Grumbling against food, clothing or housing is strictly prohibited. You have come to Japan not as honoured guests – you must endure.

The troops of God could behave like troops of the devil. They were shaped by the nature of Japanese society and the psychological manipulations of the militarists.

MASUJIRO OMURA LOOKS out over modern Tokyo from Kudan Hill, with a stern bronze gaze. He was a samurai who moved with the times, a student of Confucian philosophy, Western thought, medicine and military tactics. On the plaque at the base of his statue he is described as playing a seminal role in the modernisation and Westernisation of Japan's military system. Omura died in 1869 at the hand of a samurai outraged by his suggestion that the samurai's skills were in decay and that the army rank and file should be conscripted from all classes of society.

Once before the samurai had stood against change and won. Introduced to guns by the Portuguese in 1543 AD, the Japanese refined the harquebuses, and according to one scholar, by the beginning of the seventeenth century had more and better guns than any other country in the world. For samurai this weapon, as deadly in the hands of a coarse peasant as in those of a skilled warrior, was a threat to their way of warfare with its ritualised single combat and, of course, to their prestige and power. So the government, under samurai control, restricted the production and licensing of guns until they virtually disappeared from armouries for a century or so.

The man who began moulding the modern army that Omura dreamed of was Major Jacob Meckel, who arrived in Japan in 1885. He has been described as the prototype Prussian, tall, stiff-backed, a holder of the Iron Cross from the Franco-Prussian War, interested in drinking and in German opera. Meckel was for an offensive army that could be quickly mobilised. He was for discipline and obedience. He was for the steady closed-rank advance under fire. He was against companies taking cover in undergrowth.

Meirion and Susie Harries, in their comprehensive study of the rise and fall of the Imperial Japanese Army, think Meckel's heart would have been gladdened by Japanese tactics in the first Sino-Japanese War (1894–95). The infantry advanced in perfect order, regardless of casualties, the officers, leading from the front, took the brunt, and the stronghold of Port Arthur was taken in a single day. This was the war in which the *Illustrated London News* had Japan's conduct of it sending an admiring thrill through the military world. But the process of the perversion of the *bushido* warrior code, described by the Harries, was already taking effect. The man from *The Times* was in Port Arthur when the troops of God entered and massacred soldiers and civilian men, women and children. He reported:

More of these piteous deaths we saw, unable to stay the hands of the murderers, until sick and saddened beyond the power of words to tell we slowly made our way in the gathering gloom to the headquarters. There at the Chinese General's pavilion, facing the spacious parade-ground, Field Marshal Oyama and all his officers assembled amid strains of strange music from military bands, now weird, now lively, and ending with the impressive national anthem, '*kimo gayo*', and a huge roar from 20,000 throats of *Banzai Nippon*. The contrast was horrible, insufferable.

Nations demand much of warriors. The soldiers' world is a world of paradoxes and tensions. They must be obedient, sometimes unquestioningly obedient, but they should show initiative. They must be brave, or at least able to overcome fear, but they should not be foolhardy. For the spectators at home, a little chivalry is good. But in essence they should be excellent killing machines. Back in the fourteenth century a Buddhist monk, Yoshida Kenko, pondered, with a deal of irony, on the contradictions. Kenko was born late in the thirteenth century, a decade after the *kamikaze* had blown away the Mongol menace. If he travelled in time he would recognise the patterns of Japan in the twentieth century easily enough: the insecurity, the tensions between militarists and the imperial court. If he came further forward, he would be pleased that today's Japanese students read with enthusiasm his *Essays in Idleness*. This is essay 80:

Every man likes doing things which are foreign to his calling. A priest learns the art of war, while soldiers on our frontiers do not know the way to draw a bow. They pretend to know the Buddhist law, they indulge in linking verses and playing music, although they are more despised for these accomplishments than for stupidity in their own profession.

And it is not only priests. Generally, among nobles and

courtiers up to the very highest, there are numbers who are fond of arms. 'You may fight a hundred battles, and win a hundred battles, but it is still hard to establish warlike fame.' For this reason: any man is soldier enough to crush the foe when fortune favours him, but war is a profession where he cannot make his name until, his forces exhausted, his weapons at an end, he seeks death at the hands of his foe rather than surrender. So long as he is living, he cannot boast of warlike fame.

What then does it profit, unless one is of a military family, to devote oneself to conduct removed from human principles and approaching that of beasts?

Warrior codes are an attempt to cope with contradictions. In Japan *bushido* was developed in the early twelfth century, unwritten laws that were the moral underpinnings for the *bushi*, the samurai warriors. Killing machines should have a spirit that will limit savagery.

In 1990 the Queensland Ex-Prisoner of War Association made a submission to the United Nations High Commissioner for Human Rights as part of a campaign for reparations from the Japanese Government. It was titled *Nippon very sorry – many men must die,* a reference to an announcement by a Japanese officer to British and Australian prisoners of war that the work rate on the Thai–Burma railway was to be dramatically increased without regard to the human cost. The submission included an analysis of *bushido* by Professor S. Adachi, of Japan's National Defence Academy. *Bushido* has seven essential doctrines. The first is righteousness which comprises the concepts of justice and duty. The second is courage, which emphasises moral courage rather than physical courage and is deeply rooted in honour. The third is humanity, which is specifically attributed to the ruling class. 'Therefore,' Professor

Adachi says, 'on the battlefield the spirit of humanity with regard to the inferior, the weak and the defeated was highly valued as the most suitable moral of the *bushi*.' The fifth is sincerity, the sixth honour and the seventh is loyalty. Loyalty, Adachi says, means obedience of one's superior, though not at the sacrifice to the samurai's conscience.

The code of *bushido* was incorporated in the 1882 Imperial Rescript to Soldiers and Sailors. A rescript was holy writ, though not necessarily solely the words of the Emperor. It instructed in traditional samurai values of obedience, fidelity to one's word, frugality and bravery of a rational and willed kind. The Rescript then gave a warning, an echo of Yoshida Kenko's, that went unheeded by many Japanese soldiers: 'To be incited by mere impetuosity to violent action cannot be called true valour. If you affect valour and act with violence, the world will in the end detest you and look upon you as wild beasts. Of this you should take heed.'

The massacre at Port Arthur in the first Sino-Japanese War was only a prelude to the behaviour of the Imperial Japanese Army at times during the second Sino-Japanese War (1937–45) as Japan's expansionism continued. What became known as the Rape of Nanking, which is what the Japanese forces did literally and figuratively to the Chinese city and its population over perhaps six weeks from November 1937, indelibly stained the army's reputation. To the crimes of looting, raping and slaughter would be added medical and biological warfare experiments on civilians and prisoners of war. Then in World War II came the litany of horrors: Banka Island, the Thai–Burma railway, Ambon, Sandakan . . .

The Rescript encouraged soldiers to look on death as something to be embraced. 'Duty is weightier than a mountain, while death is lighter than a feather.' As the army was preparing for World War II, soldiers had been schooled in this ethos and they were subject to a regulation which commanded death before surrender. The Field Service Code of January 15, 1941 instructed: 'Meet the expectations of your family and home community by making effort upon effort, always mindful of the honour of your name. If alive, do not suffer the disgrace of becoming a prisoner; in death, do not leave behind a name soiled by misdeeds.' They paid heed. Among Allied troops, one surrendered for every three dead while one Japanese surrendered for every 120 dead. This attitude to death and the disgrace of surrender would have a tragic impact on Allied prisoners of war.

Many of the Japanese soldiers who fought in South-East Asia had been hardened (and could there be a more apt term?) in the China campaign. Some of the officers had passed 'trials of courage' to fill a samarui with shame. Shozo Tominaga, an officer candidate, describes the final test. His instructor, Second Lieutenant Tanaka, takes the group to a place where 24 Chinese prisoners are squatting, blindfolded, hands tied behind their backs, beside a large trench. 'Heads should be cut off like this,' Tanaka says. He stands behind the prisoner, steadies himself, legs spread apart and cuts off the man's head with a shout, 'Yo!' Tominaga is appalled and feels he can't breathe. He is fourth to be called on and his only thought is 'Don't do anything unseemly'. He swings with one breath, the head flies away and the body tumbles down, spouting blood. 'At that moment I felt something change inside me. I don't know how to put it, but I gained strength somewhere in my gut.'

That was in the northern summer of 1941. It was 10 years since Japan grabbed Manchuria, rich in resources, renamed it Manchukuo and made it a puppet state. The costly war in China was entering its fifth year and Japan had paid a heavy price in its relations with America and Britain for its expansionism. America was supporting China and threatening Japan's access to essential oil and iron imports by cancelling the commercial treaty.

Takashi Nagase, 23 years old, was studying English at Tokyo University, expecting war and determined to fight in it. In November 1875, the Emperor Meiji had written about his vision for his new Japan: 'In the olden days of the throne there was no distinction between soldiers and citizen: every man was a soldier. This honour must be revived . . . for the future I wish the army to consist of the whole nation.' Nagase wanted to join the ranks. He was born in a small village, son of a country doctor. On the wall in his school, and in all schools in Japan, was a copy of the Imperial Rescript on Education, issued in the name of the Emperor Meiji in 1890. He bowed to it each morning.

'Know ye, our subjects,' the Rescript said:

Our Imperial ancestors have founded Our empire on a basis broad and everlasting, and have deeply and firmly implanted virtue; Our subjects ever united in loyalty and filial piety have from generation to generation illustrated the beauty thereof. This is the glory of the fundamental character of Our empire, and herein also lies the source of Our education. Ye, our subjects, be filial to your parents, affectionate to your brothers and sisters; as husbands and wives be harmonious, as friends true; bear yourselves in modesty and moderation; extend your benevolence to all; pursue learning and cultivate arts, and thereby develop intellectual faculties and perfect moral powers; furthermore, advance public good and promote common interests; always respect the Constitution and observe the law; should emergency arise, offer yourself courageously to the State; and thus guard and maintain the prosperity of Our Imperial throne coeval with heaven and earth. So shall ye not only be Our good and faithful subjects, but render illustrious the best traditions of your forefathers. The way set forth here is indeed the teaching bequeathed by Our imperial ancestors, to be observed alike by Their descendants and the subjects, infallible for all ages and true in all places. It is Our wish to lay it to heart in all reverence, in common with you, Our subjects, that we may all attain to the same virtue.

The young Nagase did indeed lay the Rescript to heart, with its Confucianist principles and high moral tone. He was obedient. His body belonged to the Emperor and he was instructed in a schoolbook to 'make it his duty to cultivate his body and mind from childhood so that he will be able to pass the conscription examinations and join the army and navy to perform the honorable duty of defending his country'. A dutiful death would bring a magnificent reward, he was taught. He, Takashi Nagase, would become a god. 'It is the desire of the Emperor that those loyal heroes who died for the country and him should be enshrined and be worshipped [at Yasukuni].' But he would come to see the Rescript and the other imperial pronouncements as instruments used by authorities to hold the individual and the nation in an iron grip. He would become a critic of Emperor Meiji's descendant Emperor Hirohito, who led Japan into World War II. After the war he would be haunted by the memory of the torture of a British prisoner of war and he would be driven by remorse to return again and again to the Thai–Burma railway.

But on December 8, 1941 he was exhilarated when news broke of the Japanese attack on Pearl Harbor. Emperor Hirohito's Imperial Rescript accused Britain and America of obstructing by every means Japan's peaceful commerce. Japan 'for its existence and self-defence has no other recourse but to appeal to arms and to crush every obstacle in its path', the

Rescript said, ordering that 'the entire nation with a united will shall mobilise their strength so that nothing will miscarry the attainment of our war aims'.

Nagase volunteered immediately. 'For many years the Japanese papers and radio had taught us that American, British, Chinese and Dutch, all were encircling Japan. I had no hesitation.' His was an army family. His uncle was an army doctor and his cousin a general but Takashi himself was slight, light, weighing only 45 kilograms. He was classified unsuitable to join the army. He tried again, and was accepted as an interpreter. 'I had been educated that the greatest thing was to die for the Emperor. All Japanese people were born to die for the Emperor. Now perhaps I would have my chance.' Nagase's war would be about words, and in its cruellest moments, about words accompanied by pain.

Renichi Sugano's war would be about building a railway. He was an engineer and for him the Thai–Burma railway was a triumph on the scale of the Panama Canal. Born in 1919, son of a salaryman, Sugano came to the Thai jungles by chance. He finished high school. Military school entrance examinations were held ahead of university entrance examinations. He sat and he passed. There was academic study in the mornings and military training in the afternoons. When we met in Tokyo he was president of the Burma ex-servicemen's association but he described himself not as a soldier but an engineer working on military tasks. 'But the defence of the nation, the defence of the Emperor, was a matter of course,' he said. 'That was given as a priority and so was dying for the Emperor. We had already been taught that. Everybody understood that.'

SOLDIERS BEGAN DYING for the Emperor and for the Japanese dream of securing its future by constructing the

Greater East Asia Co-Prosperity Sphere on December 8, 1941. The first blow, an hour and 20 minutes before the attack on Pearl Harbor (across the International Dateline), was struck at Kota Bharu, on the north-eastern coast of Malaya. In their packs as they waded through heavy fire to the beach was a pamphlet, *Read only this alone and the war can be won*, the work of the Taiwan Army Research Section, headed by Masanobu Tsuji. It is a handbook on jungle fighting, and much more. There are hints on hygiene, how to move through sugar cane plantations, encouragement to use the jungle because it 'is regarded by weak-spirited Westerners as impenetrable' and warnings about rape and mistreating the natives. Tossing about in the transport ships, they read the old poem, 'Corpses drifting swollen in the sea-depths . . .' in a chapter advising them, on the ship at the very latest, to make their wills, enclosing a lock of hair and piece of fingernail for return home. They were told to demonstrate to the world the true worth of Japanese manhood. And why must they fight? To realise the Emperor's desire for peace in the Far East; to liberate 100 million Asians tyrannised by 300,000 whites. The poem was repeated at the end of the pamphlet.

Tsuji is the most fascinating of the Japanese military figures, a Rasputin, the Harries call him, bobbing up in every theatre of war with his taste for violence and his capacity for escalating it unimpaired. A relatively junior officer, a colonel, he often infuriated his superiors but played a significant role in the preparations for and the waging of the Singapore campaign. He was not self-effacing. 'My body,' he once said, 'carried the bullets of five countries – Russian from Nomonhan, American from Guadalcanal, Chinese from Shanghai, British from Burma and Australian from the Philippines.' After the war, he was elected to the Diet and was a co-founder of the Liberal Democratic Party, the political arm of big business and the dominating force in national politics for decades. He became a popular author. Reading Winston Churchill's memoirs ('some regrettable mistakes; but they are small flaws in a gem . . .') prompted him to write *Singapore 1941-1942: The Japanese Version of the Malayan Campaign of World War II.* He stars, though he does reprimand himself: 'I even became conceited, feeling that it depended upon me whether we would win or lose the war which would determine the destiny of the State.'

Here's Tsuji, sitting on a rush mat, vowing to the gods that, day and night, he will abstain from wine and tobacco, forget instinctive desires and worldly passions, to say nothing of lust and appetite, forget life and death, his whole mind concentrated on gaining the victory. Here's Tsuji (and pilot) in an unarmed reconnaissance plane, dodging thunderheads, flying over Kota Bharu and returning to base in Saigon, the last drop of petrol gone. Here's Tsuji, on December 8, in Singora, Thailand, under fire from Thai police, the first shot of the entire Malayan campaign grazing his right arm, the next passing his hip.

Tsuji was good as Staff Officer in charge of 25th Army Military Operations; very good. He was also undoubtedly as much a war criminal as any of the Japanese executed, with his fingerprints on *sook ching,* the 'purification by elimination' campaign in which tens of thousands of Chinese were slaughtered after the fall of Singapore. He was probably saved by what he calls his 'period of penance' when he spent several years after the war wandering in disguise through Thailand, Indo-China and China, the claim being that he was under orders from the Japanese High Command to preserve himself for the reconstruction of the nation.

Ironically, *Read only this – and the war will be won* is clearly his handiwork and if the Imperial Japanese Army had absorbed its instructions they would have marched across the moral high ground. There was the great aim: as representatives of all peoples of the Far East, to deal a resolute and final blow to the centuries of European aggression in these lands. 'Hundreds of thousands of the heroic dead will be watching over us,' the soldiers were told. 'Officers and men, the eyes of the whole world will be upon you in this campaign and, working together in community of spirit, you must demonstrate to the world the true worth of Japanese manhood.' The pamphlet outlines pragmatic reasons for being 'strong, correctly behaved and self-controlled': 'If you look at the history of past campaigns you will see that troops who are really efficient in battle do not plunder and rob, chase after women, or drink and quarrel. Those who flee and hide in the midst of bullets are the great braggarts and the great tormentors of the weak.'

However, the reality was that the Imperial Japanese Army was an army built on codes of violence and the duty of sacrifice. The field service code, *senjinkun*, required soldiers to commit suicide rather than surrender. Discipline was physical. An officer struck a junior officer for his sins; a junior officer struck an non-commissioned officer; a non-commissioned officer struck a first-class private; and the blows went down to the lowest rank, the third-class private. In prisoner-of-war camps minor or perceived infringements, such as failing to bow, or to bow obsequiously enough, brought a bashing. The lowest ranked Japanese, or the even more lowly Korean guard, would take out anger on the prisoners.

Of course the troops of God were not all evil. Even in Outram Road jail in Singapore, the devil's playground of the *kempeitai*, the military police, there could be an act of kindness, a glimmer amid the pain and hate. Nor can a whole race be wicked though the question in Japan is, as in Germany, why militarism was allowed to take root and flourish. Masanobu Tsuji is scathing about those who claim, 'We were against the war at the time'. 'It is probably true,' he says, 'that there were many intellectuals who opposed the war, but they lacked the courage to risk their lives or their liberty by open opposition to the outbreak of hostilities.' The authorities had as a legal weapon the Peace Preservation Law, which targeted at first communists, labour organisers and members of allegedly radical groups. It was broadened in 1941 to cover liberals, independent intellectuals and people who held religious beliefs opposed to those propounded by Shinto, the state religion. Thousands were arrested and convicted in the lead-up to and during the war. Harbouring dangerous thoughts was a crime.

Militarists took as their manifesto the advice of Tadasu Hayashi, Vice-Minister of Foreign Affairs, writing in the late nineteenth century in a period of Japanese humiliation internationally:

At present Japan must keep calm and sit tight so as to lull suspicions nurtured against her. During this time the foundations of the national power must be consolidated, and we must watch and wait for the opportunity in the Orient that will surely come one day. When this day arrives, Japan will decide her own fate, and she will be able not only to put into their place the powers who seek to meddle in her affairs, she will even be able, should this be necessary, to meddle in their affairs.

The militarists pulled off a political coup in 1900: a new regulation required that the army minister be a serving general or lieutenant-general, basically the army's own creature. What is more, the army could decline to nominate a minister. This would bring the government down.

Emperor Hirohito was cloaked in divinity and myth, with an education system, the philosophy of Confucianism and the Shinto religion all working to give him an impregnable position at the peak of national life. The Japanese people had not even heard him speak until that day in August 1945 when he ended the war.

There were calls then for Hirohito to be tried as a war criminal, but the Allies needed him as a man and a symbol, though not as a god, to create a new Japan. There was always someone wanting to use an emperor for his own purposes. Prince Saionji, the last *genro,* apparently did. Certainly elements of the army tried to. But, according to the Harries, Hirohito disliked many of the leaders intensely as individuals and he personally believed that Japan was a constitutional monarchy and he himself merely an organ of state. He rarely acted independently, making his decisions only on the advice of government and court officials. This gave militarists an easy rationale for what should be described as acts of treason, if not impiety. They saw it as their duty to defend the Emperor from wrong-headed, if not evil advisers and on occasions they did this with sword and gun. In 1936 a group of young officers led a revolt, killing, among others, Finance Minister Korekiyo Takahashi and the Lord Keeper of the Privy Seal, Makoto Saito, in their bedrooms. They intended to isolate Emperor Hirohito in his palace and appeal for a wider uprising. The Emperor's aide-de-camp, General Shigeru Honjo, tried to argue that the young officers were acting out of esteem for Emperor and country. A furious Hirohito was not persuaded: 'Why should we forgive them when these brutal officers kill our right-hand advisers?' he said. 'All my most trusted retainers are dead and the mutineers' actions are aimed directly at me.' The revolt was put down, but grave damage was done to the Japanese polity. The Harries comment: 'The revolt not only changed the balance of power within the army, it also profoundly altered the balance between the army and its civilian antagonists. At a stroke, the rebels removed several of the leading proponents of constitutional monarchy in Japan, and provided a display of military brute force vicious enough to guarantee the cooperation of others who might otherwise have challenged the army . . . direct and overt opposition ceased after February 1936.'

Prince Saionji, humiliated internationally by his little nemesis, Billy Hughes, was destroyed politically by the young rebels. There was another victim, the man who would become the nemesis of the Allied generals in Malaya and Singapore, Tomoyuki Yamashita who in World War II would take only 70 days to turn himself into legend and the Tiger of Malaya. Yamashita had friends and protégés among the young radical officers. In 1936, he made a wrong call, listening to conspiracy plans but doing nothing, and worse, acting as a go-between, carrying the rebels' demands to the government. Perhaps it was remorse about the events of 1936 and remembrance of the lash of the Emperor's anger that drove Yamashita towards a redeeming victory to lay at the Emperor's feet.

SUCH A FRIENDLY country, modern Japan. All the staff shout a welcome as you bow your head and walk through the doorway of a sushi bar. One, two, three people gather round you and your map in Kyoto, helping you find the way to Eikan-do temple founded in 855. Must see famous Mikaeri Amida, Buddha Glancing Backwards. The country is fast-changing and changeless. Technology runs wild; the young in Tokyo's Roppongi are parodies of punk; the *shinkansen* bullets along the track past an immaculate Mt Fuji; down a cobbled Kyoto street totter young geisha, *maiko*, a dying breed, having to suffer brides being painted and wrapped in kimonos as pretend geisha; on Miyajima, high in the pine-clad peaks on the path to Misen-san, a monk runs, robe flapping around his knees, to a small shrine to stoke a dimming fire under a pot kept simmering since a Buddhist saint used it in the eighth century.

At Yasukuni Shrine and its museum wing, neighbouring Yushukan, one the home of the divine spirits, the other displaying the weapons the young soldiers used, the old arguments of the militarists are perpetuated. Kiyama Terumichi was an air force reserve officer during the war. He was stationed in Indonesia when the Imperial Rescript announcing the Japanese surrender came through by telegram. Decades later Terumichi spoke to the compilers of an oral history of Japan at war. By this time he was the *Gon-no-Guji*, the deputy high priest at Yasukuni. He remembered the shock of that day in August 1945. He drove his car to the top of the mountain at Bandung. He took his pistol with him. He thought Japan was done for. His life was over. He lay on the lawn. 'The stars were unbelievable, overwhelming,' he said. 'While I was looking at the Southern Cross, the image of the shrine at Ise appeared to me. Speaking religiously, I was saved by the gods. I came back down the mountain.'

Terumichi and his fellow students had never argued among themselves about the war. 'We accepted it as it was, part of one great flow.' Terumichi the priest said that since Meiji times Japan had been advancing in that direction. In order to enrich the nation, Japan had to strengthen the army. Population increased; the country had to expand. All nations of the world would have done this, he argued. Japan was not the only nation that expanded aggressively. The Yasukuni Shrine's favourite historian, Kenji Ueda (he is featured on the shrine's website) questions the introduction into schools of textbooks with the details of the forcing into prostitution of Korean 'comfort women' by the army. He questions whether Japan should have been charged with conducting a war of aggression. 'Isn't it a fact that the West with its military power invaded and ruled over much of Asia and Africa and that this was the start of East–West relations? There is no uncertainty in history. Japan's dream of building a

Great East Asia was necessitated by history and it was sought after by the countries of Asia. We cannot overlook the intent of those who wish to tarnish the good name of the noble souls of Yasukuni.'

Yasukuni continues to invoke the Emperor's name, clearly regretting the end of personal visits but pointing out that the Emperor dispatches an envoy to the spring and autumn festivals. At the entrance to the Yushukan displays there is a scroll with a version of the poem Masanobu Tsuji had soldiers read as they prepared to storm the Malayan beaches with its promise to die in the sea, in the mountains, beside the Emperor. There is a sword, 'a symbol of justice and peace, attributes of the samurai spirit, and a mirror of the Japanese soul'.

At the start of the modern section is a map of East and South-East Asia with large arrows showing the path of Western powers encroaching on Asia. In this version of history, the United States is the villain. As Japan searches for a peaceful resolution, the United States demonstrates its hostility by providing aid to Chiang Kai-shek; it imposes an embargo that threatens Japan's very survival; its plan to force Japan into war is set in motion.

Meanwhile, Asia awaits deliverance and a panel outlines the debt independence movements owe Japan.

Japan's victory in the Russo-Japanese war inspired other nations, particularly Asian nations, to dream of independence. Many future leaders visited Japan. But even when the turmoil of World War I subsided, the road to independence seemed endless to the peoples of Asia. Not until Japan began to accomplish stunning victory in the Great East Asia War did the idea of independence enter the realm of reality. Once the desire for independence had been kindled under Japanese occupation, it did not die, even though

Japan was ultimately defeated. After the war ended, Asian nations fought for their independence and won it.

Why spoil this version of history by acknowledging the trumped-up incidents that gave Japan the opening to press on with its resources grab in Manchuria and China? Why talk of atrocities?

The Thai–Burma railway is commemorated. In the entrance hall, fittings gleaming, paintwork a lustrous black with red trim, is locomotive C5631. Built in 1936, C5631 was first used in Ishikawa prefecture on Honshu, Japan's main island. It was shipped to Thailand early in the war and brought back in 1977 by former members of a Japanese field railway squadron. In 1979 it was dedicated at Yasukuni shrine. On October 25, 1943 crossed Thai and Japanese flags had been tied in front of its smoke stack. It towed three trucks which had been roofed with atap, a thatch covering. Protected from the tropical sun were senior Japanese officers, including the chief of staff of the Southern Army. It made its cautious way along the new-laid lines to the joining point at Konkoita for the official opening ceremony of the Thai–Burma railway. It was running on a railway built by hundreds of thousands of Allied prisoners of war and Asian labourers. Metaphorically and sometimes literally, it was built on the bones of the dead. There is not one mention in Yushukan Museum of their work or their suffering, of their lives or deaths.

THE JAPANESE TROOPS sent into action in Malaya had been taught in the pamphlet *Read only this — and the war will be won* how to hate the Allied soldiers who would become their prisoners. 'When you encounter the enemy after landing,' it said, 'regard yourself as an avenger come at last face to face with his father's murderer . . . Here at last is the man whose death will lighten your heart of its brooding anger. If you fail to destroy him utterly you can never rest in peace.'

CHAPTER 4

Heirs of the Anzacs

Colin Finkemeyer, enemy-to-be, prisoner of war-to-be, was born in 1920 in the Wimmera, a broad and sparsely settled swathe of western Victoria. Along its southern edge is the Little Desert, not a true desert, but a vibrant micro-environment of high beach-like dunes, the home of varied flora and the mound-building megapode, the mallee fowl. But unless you look with a farmer's eye, most of the Wimmera is monotony, with far, featureless horizons; which is how the intellectual elite saw between-the-wars Australia, a land where books were enthusiastically banned, there was no permanent, professional orchestra and little interest in the arts. Poet A. D. Hope was savage about Australia's five cities, teeming sores with their timid, second-hand Europeans. In the bush he saw the darkening spread of drab green and desolate grey trees.

> They call her a young country, but they lie:
> She is the last of lands, the emptiest,
> A woman beyond her change of life, a breast
> Still tender but within the womb is dry.
>
> Without songs, architecture, history [. . .]

Hope's Australia was not Colin Finkemeyer's Australia. Finkemeyer lived a good and simple life and held a simple patriotism that moved to the rhythm of Dorothy Mackellar's love poem to a sunburnt country. The Finkemeyers escaped the worst of the Great Depression which ravaged the nation from 1929 to 1932: half a million out of 6.5 million out of work, one million surviving on less than 20 shillings a week when the pre-crash wage had been almost five pounds; families walking off farms; dispossessions, shanty towns at Melbourne's Dudley Flats, on the banks of the Torrens and at Sydney's La Perouse, sardonically called Happy Valley. The Depression sapped bodies and souls. It shattered families. Men jumped the rattler or took to the roads and there was nothing jolly about the swagmen. 'There were unemployed dances,' Sylvia Wight reminisced, 'held in a shop in Ryrie Street, Geelong, and I remember as a small child playing a violin solo and being given a cauliflower as my first earnings. The entrance fee to the dance was three pence (if you had it). If not, come anyway. One elderly man always wore a scarf summer and winter, because he had no singlet or shirt. Another friend of ours wore ladies shoes issued to him at the self-help depot. Imagine what all this did to our feelings. We were called the "Susso kids", and the shame we felt at school when charity was dished out to us.' But the Finkemeyers could still put a leg of mutton on the table and feed a family of five from it over three meals.

For Colin Finkemeyer, the 1930s were uncomplicated times, with expectations low and enjoyment high. There were yabbies to catch and ducks, quail and rabbits to shoot. In winter they played football which in Victoria of course meant Australian Rules, and in summer, cricket. Sport was where legends and heroes lived, the arena of tragedy and drama. There was Phar Lap (yes, yes, he was actually bred in New Zealand) who won the Melbourne Cup and 38 other races, went to America to show the Yanks he was a champion and then died. Did they poison him? There was our Don Bradman, the greatest batsman ever. Finkemeyer was not much moved by the most inflammatory Anglo-Australian international incident of the time, bodyline bowling. The English arrived for the 1932–33 Test series with a great fast bowler, Harold Larwood; a driven and ruthless captain, Douglas Jardine; and tactics made for Australians to boo at. The third Test was played at the Adelaide Oval. It was a battlefield. Australia's Bill Woodfull was struck over the heart by a rising ball and collapsed. When the English manager 'Plum' Warner visited the Australian dressing room on a cheer-up mission, Woodfull's reaction severely strained imperial ties. 'I don't want to speak to you, Mr Warner,' Woodfull said. 'Of the two teams out there, one is playing cricket, the other is making no effort to play the game of cricket. It is too great a game to be spoiled by the tactics you are adopting. I don't approve of them and never will. If they are persevered in it may be better if I do not play the game. The matter is in your hands. I have nothing further to say. Good afternoon.' Finkemeyer and his mates were convinced that Bradman would come through bodyline; that he really was invincible. Naturally they booed Jardine and Larwood, but Finkemeyer got their autographs at the Boxing Day Test in Melbourne.

In the cities there was some political sound and movement. The right-wing New Guard hijacked the opening of the pre-Opera House icon, the Sydney Harbour Bridge. Communists marched in May Day parades, but while they followed huge banners of heroes-to-fall, Marx, Engels, Lenin and Stalin, they hardly looked like raging revolutionaries. Orderly ranks of men in suits, hats, ties and vests march in a photograph, one holding his small daughter's hand. In 1934 the vigilant government tried to keep out of Australia a left-winger, Egon Kisch, a Czech journalist and writer given to clenched-fist salutes and a shout of *Rotfront* (Red front). He had been invited to an anti-war, anti-fascism conference. His credentials were good. He had been arrested by the Hitler regime. Kisch's entry was barred when his ship berthed in Melbourne. He circumvented this briefly by jumping onto the wharf and breaking his leg. In Sydney he faced the weapon used by the Australian authorities against unwanted migrants and visitors. He was given a dictation test in a language of the authorities' choice to establish whether he was literate. The authorities got lucky. Gaelic was not one of the 11 or so languages Kisch spoke. As legal battles were waged, he remained in Australia for five months.

On the beaches, moral danger threatened. Right-thinking people prepared to avert their eyes when men were officially permitted to appear topless.

In the Wimmera, however, life moved with the seasons. The wheat and the boys grew tall. An improved strain, Federation, was boosting yields. The land had of course been stolen from the Aborigines, but the dark people barely flitted across Colin Finkemeyer's consciousness, or the nation's. His mother had told him of the last corroborees held at Jung Jung, he saw Aborigines staggering at some of the pubs and he knew they were the tough boxers in Jimmy Sharman's troupe. He also knew they had no recognised rights to the land. In January 1938, the Australian Aborigines Progressive Association announced that on Wednesday the 26th, the sesquicentenary of European settlement, a day of mourning and protest would be held in Elizabeth Street, Sydney, open only to Aborigines and people of Aboriginal blood. The following resolution would be moved:

> We representing the Aborigines of Australia assembled at the Australian Hall, Sydney – this being the 150th anniversary of the whitemen's seizure of our country, hereby make

protest against the callous treatment of our people by the whitemen during the past 150 years, and we appeal to the Australian nation of today to make new laws for the education and care of Aborigines, and we ask for a new policy which will raise our people to full citizen status and equality within the community.

And millions of ears, as deaf as Billy Hughes's, turned in the direction of the Australian Hall, Elizabeth Street, Sydney.

Deep in the Wimmera there was one matter of race that loomed large for Colin Finkemeyer. He went to high school in Horsham where he fell under the spell of a teacher, Hank Menadue. Menadue was a member of the Australian Natives' Association which, under the banner of 'Advance Australia', had in the late nineteenth century zealously promoted the uniting of the colonies into the Commonwealth of Australia. It was a friendly society which provided benefits to its native-born members and was also concerned with their moral, social and intellectual improvement. But alongside its belief in humanitarianism was its determination to restrict immigration.

Menadue would tell the boys that Australia was a beautiful country, the most beautiful in the world. Japan, he said, was only a little place, overpopulated. They had 100 million, Australia had seven. The Japanese saw this vast land, all this farmland, all this beautiful country. They had their eyes on Australia, the Yellow Perils, and some younger generation was going to have to look after it and defend it. On Monday mornings Finkemeyer and his classmates would take turns raising the flag. The assembly would salute flag, God and country. He grew up a strict Lutheran. He believed in God and he believed in the White Australia policy. Then he found it was his generation that would have to do the defending.

Towards the end of the 1930s there were some signs of a

slow, wider awakening to the realities and dangers of the world. The *Argus* in its 1939 New Year editorial, against the background of Hitler's rise and German and Japanese expansionism, said that:

> Until recent years, recent months, perhaps, there was little need in Australia to look ahead in a national sense. One year was much the same as another. Seasons and economic conditions fluctuated, of course; but taking the years and the decades by and large, Australia was steadily progressing towards the high destiny which Australians, assisted by the bounty of nature, had mapped out for her. The caprice of nature was the only factor outside the control of Australians, and as nature in the main was kind the only problem remaining was to make Australia a better and better paradise for her citizens. External interference was out of the question. Great Britain would smile indulgently as the grown-up daughter went her own way, and the British Navy would see to it that no other nation disposed to frown at Australia's doings would vent its displeasure actively. But those halcyon days are gone.

Aware of how divisive conscription had been as an issue during World War I, the *Argus* delicately brought up the question of a call-up for some form of national service.

> National unity implies a certain measure of national regimentation; yet regimentation is foreign to the Australian temperament. The lone bushman is accustomed to working out his own problems. The city young man believes in keeping fit in his own way. Neither has been accustomed to a regimen prescribed by authority for making and keeping all able-bodied Australians fit and

trained for a national emergency. Yet such a regimentation would impose on individual liberty very few restrictions additional to those which are accepted voluntarily as a matter of course.

There was never any doubt that Colin Finkemeyer would serve when called. In 1938 he went to work in the Defence Department in Melbourne. On September 3, 1939 he listened to Robert Menzies, the most Anglophile of Australian prime ministers, address the nation. 'Fellow Australians,' Menzies said in an accent 10,000 miles away from the country town of Jeparit, where he was born, 'it is my melancholy duty to inform you officially that in consequence of a persistence by Germany and her invasion of Poland, Great Britain has declared war upon her and that, as a result, Australia is also at war.'

The dead of the World War I killing fields of Europe haunted many Australian families and memorials to their sacrifice, the statue of a lone soldier with a multitude of names inscribed on the base, sprouted in stone throughout the land. Europe was where Finkemeyer expected to go.

Finkemeyer transferred from the civilian to the army ranks in 1940. Captain Cooper told him a great regiment was being formed, young fellows, great opportunities, mostly all farmhands, all in their eighteens, nineteens and twenties. He joined the 4th Anti-Tank Regiment and went, as Hank Menadue foretold, to fight the Japanese. His war started in the jungles of Malaya. His war ended during the last days of Singapore when he was shot in the shoulder by a Japanese soldier. On the Thai–Burma railway, he met the troops of God in all their brutality and he broke the ties with his own God.

Desmond Jackson, son of a Tasmanian bank manager and bored by bank work himself, was already a member of the militia when Menzies made his announcement. War was inevitable, he thought, war with Germany. The Treaty of Versailles might have delivered Billy Hughes all he wanted, but its punitive provisions would drive Germans into the grip of fascism. For Jackson, Japan was a vague threat in the back of his mind; it was overcrowded, lacking natural resources and looking for expansion. Hitler was the real danger. 'We still felt we were part of the British Empire. With Britain facing such terrible problems and fighting alone, she just had to be supported.' Jackson trained as a machine-gunner and on Good Friday, 1941 boarded the glamorous French liner *Isle de France*. It was supposed to be a secret departure, but a flotilla of small craft escorted the liner across sparkling Sydney Harbour and South Head was black with people waving goodbye. The shipboard rumour was that Nazi propagandist Lord Haw-Haw sent the troops a message as they sailed out: 'Hello Australians from the *Isle de France* now passing through Sydney Heads, make the most of the next couple of weeks because you will not reach your destination. You will be sunk and you will go to the bottom of the ocean.' Jackson's initial destination was Palestine. He became a foot soldier in Prime Minister John Curtin's battle with Winston Churchill and Australia's great strategic shift. He fought as a machine-gunner in Syria and then as a rifleman in Java.

Lance Gibson was a farmer in north-central Victoria. He and a cobber could see a war was coming and that Britain would be in trouble, so they joined the militia 'to learn a bit about soldiering'. Like Jackson, Gibson served in the 2/3rd Machine Gun Battalion. He did officer training in Jerusalem and joined as a replacement in Java where he played an important role in Jackson's survival. Lord Haw-Haw's prophecy would, in part, apply to him. Gibson was held in camps in Java until he was sent to Japan in 1944 as commander of a group of prisoners to be used as slave labour. The ship they were on, the *Tamahoko*

Maru, was torpedoed close to Nagasaki by the American submarine *Tang*, skippered by Captain Dick O'Kane. Only 212 of the 772 prisoners on board survived.

HITLER AND HERITAGE were catalysts in putting Australians into khaki, but there was also the fact that many of this generation were sons of soldiers. For Bill Dunn, tradition went back to the Boer War (1899–1902). His father Percy fought on the veldt. It's a long-ago and far-away war, with its popular Australian myth of brave Harry 'Breaker' Morant of the Bushveldt Carbineers, betrayed by the British, calling out to the British firing squad, 'Shoot straight, you bastards'.

Galloping across the veldt in that sad war was the man whose name, for many Australians, certainly for many of the Anzacs and many in the World War II prisoner-of-war diaspora, became synonymous with British betrayal, Winston Churchill. He was a dashing figure, a war correspondent. He was captured. He escaped. He was in the front rank during actions and his fame grew back home, ready to be used for the start of his political career, brilliant, at least in wartime.

The British set up concentration camps. For Boer women and children, it was as bitter an experience as that suffered by the Allied prisoners of war 40 or so years later. The innocents died in tens of thousands. Five hundred and eighteen Australians fell in battle, more than in the Vietnam War, and six were awarded the Victoria Cross. It was a war that had nothing to do with Australia but the newspaper headlines were proud:

THE ATTACK ON LADYSMITH
SEVENTEEN HOURS' FURIOUS FIGHTING
TRENCHES TAKEN AND RETAKEN
BOER REPULSED ON ALL SIDES

A FINAL BAYONET CHARGE
SPLENDID BEHAVIOUR OF TROOPS

Percy Dunn's family was not impressed. He had ridden away from the family farm. It was to have been left to him but he was struck out of the will and out of the family. In 1914 he joined up again, serving in the railway section in Belgium. Bill Dunn was born in 1920. His family life was only briefly happy. His mother died giving birth to his sister and his father remarried. His step- mother wouldn't accept him and he was sent to his grandmother in Western Australia. He couldn't remember how or why, but he was homeless at eight and the Salvation Army, or a church, sent him to a dairy farm. He had never been so happy, a roof over his head, three meals a day, and he helped the farmer with the bullock team, yoking the leaders, whipping and whistling them along to drag a chain and clear dairy land. He eventually finished up back with grandparents in Victoria, at work making coffins, then helping an uncle run a billiard saloon in a country town. A sense of adventure had probably taken Percy Dunn off the farm and away to the Boer War. He was a big, strong man. For Bill Dunn, enlisting was something that seemed right to do. Like Colin Finkemeyer, he became an anti-tank gunner and went to Malaya. On April 25, 1943, Anzac Day, Bill Dunn was one of those Australians standing in monsoon rain in the jungle close to the ridge through which Hellfire Pass would be carved.

Chilla Goodchap was born in 1923 in Brisbane. For a while the Goodchaps had been very rich. Chilla Goodchap's grandfather joined the Gympie gold rush in 1867. One afternoon grandfather and two partners had an early meal. By dusk they had a sugar bag full of pure gold. The Goodchaps became prosperous sawmillers in the region, employing 400, but the 1893 flood washed away the family mill and much of the fortune. Chilla's father, George, a gunsmith by trade, joined up the day World War I was declared. He was an Anzac, wounded at Gallipoli ('blown-up', according to Chilla), and the major figure in Chilla's life. Father took son to his first Dawn Service when he was three years old. George Goodchap was a light-horseman and in 1939, with the whiff of war in the air, 16-year-old Chilla put his age up and joined the 5th Light Horse. He liked horses. They didn't like him. One winter's morning in Gympie 320 horses being taken to water stampeded. There was panic in the small town. People huddled in doorways, thought the Germans were coming, Chilla said. Carnage. Dead horses littered the streets. Chilla decided that day to join the navy and he sailed to war on the ill-fated *Perth*.

Don Wall's father was at Gallipoli. Wall in World War II was part of F Force, the prisoner-of-war group that suffered particularly heavily on the Thai–Burma railway. Snowy Marsh, who worked in labour camps in Japan, buried his father aged 58. He had been gassed in France and Belgium. *Perth* survivor David Manning's father was a light-horseman at Beersheeba.

Ray Wheeler's father, Fred, missed World War I. He was in uniform just as it ended so he enlisted for World War II. Ray did too. He had just turned 17. He didn't think the war would last for many years and he remembered Fred Wheeler talking regretfully about World War I and how he should have been there. Ray needed his parents' permission. His mother sent his father a telegram saying, 'Ray's in the army. What will I do about it?' She showed Ray the reply: 'Let the young bugger do as he likes.' Fred Wheeler survived the war; Ray Wheeler survived the Thai–Burma railway and then six days in the sea after a Japanese cargo ship carrying prisoners of war to Japan had been sunk by an American submarine.

FOR PATRICIA GUNTHER, nursing was a delight after a
difficult childhood. It was a duty, too, and so was enlisting when
war broke out. Gunther was born in 1913. The family had
memories of grand days in Scotland. Her great-grandfather was
Baron Kenneth Munro McKenzie, Laird of Dundonald but the
Gunthers of Casino, New South Wales, lived in genteel poverty.
Gunther was posted to the 10th Australian General Hospital
and the nurses boarded the *Queen Mary* in Sydney Harbour.
They were farewelled by Lady Gowrie, wife of the Governor-
General, who said she couldn't tell them their destination but
that they were the luckiest nurses to leave Australia. Lady
Gowrie was wrong.

The *Queen Mary* sailed in convoy led by the four-funnelled
Aquitania. Crowds waved from the foreshore. Out of Fremantle, the *Queen Mary* dropped out of the convoy and the other
ships, with a band fore and aft, formed a line. To the strains of
the 'Maori's Farewell', she passed by then turned to starboard
and sailed at full steam to Singapore, carrying the nurses and
the 8th Division of the Australian Imperial Force towards the
disaster of Singapore. They landed on February 18, 1941. Less
than a year later, as the false fortress crumbled, 65 of the nurses
sailed out, this time on the *Vyner Brooke*, small, old, once the
private yacht of Sir Charles Vyner Brooke, the White Rajah of
Sawarak. Only 24 of them returned to Australia at war's end.

For Ron Wells, his short life a mess, enlisting for war was a
way out. Wells's mother had died when he was a baby. He had
no family life and he drifted into the world of racing, a tough
and often dirty world behind the Runyonesque façade and the
society glamour. He started riding at 14 on the New South
Wales country circuit. He was a big kid for a jockey and he got
used to wasting each week, missing as many meals as it took to
make the weight. Turned out it was great training for life as a
prisoner of war. Loved a game little mare called Cameltine; won

a lot on her. Then had winners in the big smoke, Randwick and Canterbury and Rosehill. At 17, he was a self-described little villain, in love with his boss's daughter, but then he found his boss was ripping him off. All the money had gone. He shot through to Melbourne, put his age up. Turned out, besides having a talent as a jockey, he had a talent to amuse. Both came in handy on the Thai–Burma railway.

Hitler, heritage, a chance to escape, thirst for adventure, a sense of duty, a beaten family path: but there was something else driving some Australians. Many of this generation were moulded by and many scarred by the Great Depression. In 1939, much of the nation was still doing it hard. Wally Mulvena was. When he enlisted for World War II, he knew about war. He had fought in the Great War, living in the trenches and slogging through the mud of France. Born in 1897, he had put his age up. He returned to country Queensland and when he was 29 met 18-year-old Doris at a dance in Tewantin. They took a liking to each other and married in 1928. They weren't Catholic but the babies just came, steadily. So did the Depression, tough years when Wally moved around, looking for work. When the war began, the roadwork Wally was doing had finished. Now 42, he said to Doris: 'That's a thing I can do, and if anything happens to me, the children will be looked after.' So he put his age down. He was officially 39 and he went away to war, leaving Doris pregnant with their eighth child, Gwen. He had expected to go to the Middle East to fight the Germans. Doris was in hospital with Gwen in August 1941 when her mother came with a letter from Wally. The address was Malaya. That's all right, Doris thought, there's no war in Malaya. That will be garrison duty. But Cholera Hill waited for him in a pretty valley in Thailand.

CHAPTER 5

John Curtin and the Former Naval Person

Desmond Jackson looks down from the escarpment. His Vickers machine gun is set up now, and he has time to take in what he sees: against a backdrop of barren red hills, a sprawling city sprinkled with shining white minarets like exclamation points. This is Damascus, a city built over the bones of its predecessors. Syrians say it is the oldest city in the world, settled maybe before 8000 BC, hub of a region which was the cradle of agriculture and metallurgy, where alphabets and religions were invented. It was also the cradle of wars. Over the millennia, many conquerors have taken the road to Damascus. Halfway through the second millennium BC, the start of the city's documented history, it was the centre of the Aramaean kingdoms. Then came the Assyrians, then the Neo-Babylonians under Nebuchadnezzar, then Alexander the Great, then the Romans. Saul of Tarsus was blinded on the road to Damascus, the city's Christians were saved and it became an important centre for the new religion. In the seventh century, regarded as a golden age, Muslims made Damascus capital of a sprawling empire. Crusaders came. Tamurlane's Mongols extracted a ransom of one million pieces of gold and left little but ruins behind. The Ottoman Empire stifled it. After World War I there was a short-lived Syrian kingdom, but France claimed it, under League of Nations mandate, as part of the spoils of victory. Which is why on the afternoon of June 20, 1941 Corporal Desmond Jackson, just 21 years old and citizen of one of the world's youngest nations, has followed in the footsteps of the ancients. C Company of the 2/3rd Australian Machine Gun Battalion has the task in this battle of supporting Free French infantry against the Vichy French forces allied to the Germans.

While Masanobu Tsuji and his Taiwan Army Research Section were gathering jungle lore in preparation for Japan's thrust into South-East Asia, the machine-gunners were hardening themselves on route marches up and down sandhills in preparation for Operation Explorer, the invasion of Syria. Battalion headquarters was Hill 95 in Palestine, a camp built north of Gaza city. It was in this area in World War I that General Chauvel's Australian Light Horse had fought the Turks. For Jackson, as for Chauvel's cavalry, the Middle East was a necessary battleground. Suppose the Germans crossed the Dardanelles from Greece then pushed through Syria, Lebanon and Palestine to take the Suez Canal. It would have been catastrophic.

This did not happen and perhaps the French could have been left to fight among themselves. Official Australian historian Gavin Long says that the Germans tried to avoid giving the British any excuse for the invasion. British intelligence summaries warning of a possible German assault on Syria ignored evidence that Germany was concentrating major forces against Russia and the intelligence summary of June 3, based on Enigma code intercepts, stated that the German air force was withdrawing from both Syria and Iraq.

THE VICKERS WAS a formidable infantry support weapon, descended from the Maxim that had been invented by American Hiram Stevens Maxim. In the gory, glory days of the Empire, the British slaughtered the Matabele in the 1893 uprising in southern Africa using Maxims and Lord Kitchener's Anglo-Egyptian force wiped out 11,000 charging Dervishes at Omdurman in the Sudan in 1898. Old machine-gunners speak fondly of the Vickers and its 'beaten zone' and discuss the relative virtues of Mark VII and Mark VIII ammunition. Mark VIII had a range of 4000 metres but it was too accurate, falling in a tight pattern; Mark VII only had a range of 2400 metres, but its 'beaten zone' was a large oval, a deadly place for troops. C Company had 12 Vickers. They took them to war from Hill 95 on a moonless night under blackout conditions, north through Palestine and crossed the Jordan River at the Jisr Bennt Jacub, the Bridge of Jacob's Daughters. At 7 pm on June 17, 1941 they fired their first shots, supporting an attack on Kuneitra, on the Golan Heights, by Britain's 2nd Queens. The Vickers were lined along a ridge, firing Mark VIII ammunition at Vichy French field guns and forward positions. They gave close cover to the advancing infantry. Nothing fell short. The 2nd Queens were pleased.

Two days later, C Company, with 6 Platoon from A company attached, received a curious order from the 2/3rd Battalion commander, Arthur Blackburn, Gallipoli veteran and Victoria Cross winner at Pozières. The Free French troops of wonderfully named General Legentilhomme had struck a problem along the road to Damascus. After 11 days of fighting in sand and heat, they had simply come to a standstill near Kiswe, 15 kilometres to the south. The machine-gunners were to 'inspire' the Free French to attack boldly. Company commander Captain Roy Gordon placed most of his men in the French line then sent 6 Platoon a thousand metres ahead.

All four platoons came under fire but suffered no casualties. Long reports that half an hour later the French commander Colonel Casseau and his troops began to advance, with Casseau himself driving his car slowly along the road, level with the leading men. (Here the battalion's historian disagrees. The claim is that the brave colonel was being driven by an attractive young woman in uniform.) But when the infantry drew up to the machine-gunners, they halted and it was not until the machine-gunners moved another 300 metres ahead and opened fire again that the Free French moved forward again. And so the progress continued until the Free French reached the outskirts of Damascus. The commander of 6 Platoon, Bronte Edwards, received the Military Cross for his actions.

The next day Damascus fell and Colonel Blackburn in the morning received the surrender of the city and its police force from the mayor. It was quite an Australian day. That afternoon the Free French's General Legentilhomme was entering Damascus, accompanied by the pomp of Circassian Cavalry, to be received by the Syrian Cabinet. As it happened, the machine-gunners' 11 Platoon had been ordered through Damascus to the north to guard that exit. They passed the French procession. Bernard Fergusson, professional soldier, then aide-de-camp to General Archibald Wavell and future leader of one of Britain's Chindit guerilla brigades in Burma and future Governor-General of New Zealand, watched. Fergusson grumbled that 'lorry after lorry of yelling Australians drove past covering it with dust'. Fergusson was also critical of Australian manners at the Cabinet reception. 'In the crowd cheering like mad and waving his hat was an Australian lieutenant colonel,' he wrote in his memoirs. 'He shook my hand saying, "I was first". My eyes fell on his 1914–1918 medal ribbons. Ragged as they were, the first was indubitably the Victoria Cross, the first I had ever encountered unexpectedly, so I choked back whatever it was I had in mind to say. He was Arthur Blackburn, in private life Coroner for the City of Adelaide.'

Fighting in Syria stopped in July and the battalion went on garrison duty. It had, Jackson remembered, funnily enough been a clean sort of warfare; there had been danger, but not danger that had anything really sinister about it. They knew if they were captured they would be looked after, and that was an important thing. On February 1, 1942 after a Christmas in the snow in the Syrian mountains and more training in the desert for jungle warfare, Jackson and his mates set sail on the *Orcades*, bound, as it turned out, for cruel captivity at the hands of the Japanese.

John Curtin had won the tug of wills with Winston Churchill over control of the defence of Australia. The diggers were returning to their home region.

They were an odd couple, Churchill and Curtin, emphatically different in some ways, strikingly similar in others. Churchill's ancestor was the Duke of Marlborough, his father Lord Randolph Churchill. He had a high-establishment education at Harrow and then at Sandhurst, training ground for the military elite. Curtin was the son of an Irish immigrant policeman who, after a blighted career, became a struggling publican. John left school at 14, trying to find work to help support his family. Biographer David Day charts the Curtins' descent into poverty, John sleeping in the same bed as brother George, the whole family retiring early during winter because they could not afford the firewood, a daily struggle for basic necessities.

Churchill was a conservative. Curtin abandoned first Catholicism and then the Salvation Army to embrace socialism. He wrote in the autograph book of Elsie Needham, who eventually became his wife:

Ye shall be one nation; ye shall know the truth and the
Truth shall set you free – Holy Writ.

Workers of the World Unite! You have a world to gain
and only your chains to lose – Karl Marx.

Let there be no fatalism in our counsels,
Let us look neither right nor left,
Nor to hell or heaven. But let us spend
Ourself in discovering the law of life and
Of society so that we may do wisely and justly –
And let it not be for the love of God nor the
Fear of hell – but because we are truthful and
Fear no evil.

Churchill was a great orator. Curtin had this reputation too, but he lacked the roundness and rhythm of Churchill. Wartime newsreels show him with stiff gestures and a strange flapping of the arms. His careful enunciation could slide into gravel. But there was steel as he addressed a crowd in Sydney's Martin Place: 'No longer shall this Government appeal. It will order and direct.' Yet as Churchill had his black dog, the recurring bouts of depression that attacked him through his political life, Curtin had his battle with the booze. He went on benders, once cadging a loan from a journalist so he could 'go on the scoot' with Frank Anstey, his mentor in socialism and politics. One time on the scoot he broke an engagement to speak at the Socialist Sunday School in Melbourne. He was drunk and unconscious and spent some time in hospital. Anstey preached to him, saying the 'man who has carried his crucifix and climbed his Calvary is a better man than he who never touched the stony road of suffering . . . Stand upright, proud of yourself, proud of the conquest that you are going to achieve, and the good that you yet will do.' However, he often broke his guarantee to Labor colleagues to stay sober as a condition of winning Labor leadership in 1935 though he claimed in 1940 he had 'wowsed' since his marriage in 1917. Day accepts that he had at least 'wowsed' by 1940 but says it was a daily battle. His new addiction was nicotine. He smoked 40 cigarettes a day.

During World War I, Curtin was the enemy of what he saw as capitalist-inspired militarism. In January 1915 he published in the *Timber Worker*, the union journal he edited, this attack: 'If you kill a man in a private quarrel you are called a murderer, and may be hung. If you put on a soldier's uniform and kill a hundred, you are a hero and are decorated. Patriotism glorifies wholesale murder.' In June, when the seeds of the Gallipoli myth had been planted in blood-soaked soil, Curtin, who clearly foresaw its potency, tried to harness it to his international socialist ends. He wrote:

> This horrible business of war! Our brothers displayed magnificent courage. This was to be expected, and it is a heritage that in years to come may help us to win to social emancipation. We mourned with those whose homes are desolate, whose hearts are anguished. Let the death of those who are of our blood move us to confront this mockery called civilisation and consecrate ourselves anew to the movement which builds for social justice and the world's peace.

At the start of World War II, Curtin was still an internationalist and a socialist, and he still recoiled from the horror of war. When he made his first wartime speech as opposition leader, when the fighting and dying was being done at a distance, he expressed 'the hope, however little there may be to justify it, that somehow, as early as possible, there will intrude into the councils of the countries at war those influences that persuade them to call a truce from warfare so that they may, even now, while the guns are flaring, sit down to discover where, after all, right cannot triumph without being backed by might'. As the Japanese stormed closer down the Malayan peninsula, it was Curtin, reconciled to war, speaking; utopia could wait: 'We have to concentrate on the one supreme task which the enemy has imposed on us. We have to defeat him or die. It is no use speculating at present on new orders to come, nor is it any use preaching the precepts of the Apostles to the enemy. The whine of bullets is the only precept he will understand.'

In 1941, like Churchill a year before, he was summoned to power as political warrior and national saviour. Conflict was inevitable. Churchill in 1940, making his first speech as Prime Minister, offered the British people his blood, toil, tears and sweat. The policy, he said, was to wage war against a monstrous tyranny. 'You ask, what is our aim? I can answer that in one word: it is victory, victory at all costs, victory in spite of all terror, victory, however long and hard it might be; for without victory, there is no survival.' In December 1941, the evening after the Japanese launched the Pacific war, Curtin told the men and women of Australia in a national broadcast that it was the nation's darkest hour. 'The call is to you for your courage, your physical and mental ability, your inflexible determination that we as a nation of free people will survive.'

Curtin and Churchill would argue about strategies, priorities and resources. There were spikes of anger in the exchanges of cables. Churchill had the ear and the sympathy of Franklin Roosevelt and that came through in the cables too. These were written with an eye to reputation and posterity. 'Prime Minister to President'; 'President to Prime Minister'. But there was also the personal touch. In his first letter, written in 1939,

Roosevelt, who had picked Churchill as a prime minister-in-waiting, mentioned their common interest in matters naval. He had been Assistant Secretary of the Navy in World War I; Churchill delighted in his role as First Sea Lord of the Admiralty. Churchill became 'Naval Person', and after he moved to 10 Downing Street, on occasions in wartime cables 'Former Naval Person'. That is how, with warmth, sympathy and informality, Roosevelt addressed him on February 19, 1942:

> President to Former Naval Person . . . I realise how the fall of Singapore has affected you and the British people. It gives the well-known back-seat driver a field day, but no matter how serious our setbacks have been – and I do not for a moment underrate them – we must constantly look forward to the next move that needs to be made to hit the enemy. I hope you will be of good heart in these trying weeks, because I am sure that you have the great confidence of the masses of the British people. I want you to know that I think of you often, and I know you will not hesitate to ask me if there is anything you think I can do . . . Do let me hear from you.

Churchill did not have the great confidence of the Australian Government and the matter of Singapore was at the hub of the dispute. On Christmas Day 1941 Curtin had received the worst present, a cable from V. G. Bowden, the Australian representative in Singapore which said: '. . . deterioration in our position in Malaya defence is assuming landslide proportions and in my belief is likely to cause a collapse in whole defence system . . . Present measures for reinforcing Malayan defences can from a practical viewpoint be regarded as little more than gestures . . . If Singapore and AIF are to be saved, there must be very radical and effective action immediately . . . plain fact

71

is that without immediate air reinforcements Singapore must fall.' Curtin that same day cabled Churchill and Roosevelt, who were meeting in Washington, criticising reinforcements earmarked by the United Kingdom Government as totally inadequate and stating that Australia would 'gladly accept' United States command in the Pacific Ocean area.

Then Curtin asked the *Melbourne Herald* to publish a New Year's message to the Australian people, many of whom still called Britain Home. It said:

We refuse to accept the dictum that the Pacific struggle must be treated as a subordinate segment of the general conflict. By that it is not meant that any one of the other theatres of war is of less importance than the Pacific, but that Australia asks for a concerted plan evoking the greatest strength at the Democracies' disposal, determined upon hurling Japan back.

The Australian Government therefore regards the Pacific struggle as primarily one in which the United States and Australia must have the fullest say in the direction of the Democracies' fighting plan.

Without any inhibitions of any kind, I make it quite clear that Australia looks to America, free of any pangs as to our traditional links with the United Kingdom.

We know the problems that the United Kingdom faces. We know the constant threat of invasion. We know the dangers of dispersal of strength. But we know too that Australia can go, and Britain can still hold on.

We are therefore determined that Australia shall not go, and we shall exert all our energies towards the shaping of a plan, with the United States as its keystone, which will give to our country some confidence of being able to hold out until the tide of battle turns against the enemy . . .

The Former Naval Person was not amused. He began the fourth volume of his Second World War series with a chapter headed 'Australasian Anxieties'. Winners get to write histories and settle scores. John Curtin did not survive the war, dying ill and exhausted in July 1945. It was not New Zealand that concerned Churchill; its Prime Minister Fraser received a pat for 'the well-balanced reasoning' with which he had presented his views. But, as for the Australians:

> It will always be deemed remarkable that in this deadly crisis, when it seemed to them and their professional advisers, destruction was at the very throat of the Australian Commonwealth, they did not all join together in a common effort. But such was their party phlegm and rigidity that local politics ruled unshaken. The Labor Government, with its majority of two, monopolised the whole executive power, and conscription even for home defence was banned. These partisan decisions did less than justice to the spirit of the Australian nation, and made more difficult our task in providing, so far as possible, for their security while observing a true sense of proportion in world strategy.

From the grave, Curtin's response would surely be that in leaving Singapore a false fortress and in building strategy round it, Britain had undermined Australia's security; that the ghost of the Gallipoli blunder walked the Malayan peninsula; that Churchill's sense of proportion was skewed, putting the Mediterranean, the Middle East and Russia ahead of the Pacific region; that Australia needed to deploy its own troops in defence of their homeland.

Churchill expressed regret, in *The Hinge of Fate*, at any traces of impatience his cables might bear and said that later in the war he formed a personal friendship with Curtin, 'this eminent and striking Australian personality'. But he said that Curtin's message to the Australian people produced the worst impression both in high American circles and in Canada. Indeed, the Former Naval Person's friend Franklin Roosevelt said that it smacked of 'panic and disloyalty'. Churchill said he had 'weighed painfully' in his mind the idea of making a broadcast direct to the Australian people, an outrageous suggestion. He was sure, he claimed, that 'these outpourings of anxiety' did not represent Australian feelings and he clearly took delight in what he described as a 'keen controversy' in Australia. He was right, to an extent. Curtin did not represent the views of conservatives and quickly on the attack was the Little Digger. Billy Hughes said it would be 'suicidal and dangerous to regard Britain's support as being less important than that of other great associated nations'. However, in a cable to his War Cabinet colleague Clement Attlee, Churchill said: 'If the Malay peninsula has been starved for the sake of Libya and Russia, no one is more responsible than I, and I would do exactly the same again.' On this statement Curtin could rest his case. He could call another witness. In 1912, a precocious British politician put down his thoughts in a memorandum: 'If the power of Britain were shattered upon the sea, the only course open to the 5,000,000 white men in the Pacific would be to seek the protection of the United States.' That was Winston Churchill in his role as First Lord of the Admiralty.

Thirty years later, exchanges of unpleasantries continued by cable. On January 18, Curtin charged that 'As far back as 1937, the Commonwealth Government had received assurances that it was the aim of the United Kingdom Government to make Singapore impregnable'. The next day Churchill received a cable from General Wavell, appointed Supreme Commander in the region, and what he described with understatement, 'a painful surprise'. In essence, the fortress of Singapore was most pregnable. The giant guns pointed south over the sea. There were no fortifications covering the northern landward side of the naval base and of the city. No field defences had even been constructed since the Japanese invasion of Malaya on December 8.

Churchill, the student of military history, had read of defences being improvised by the Turks in the teeth of a Russian assault at Plevna in 1877 and of a field army using detached forts gloriously at Verdun in 1917. Yes, he had had high hopes for Singapore but 'now, suddenly, all this vanished away, and I saw before me the hideous spectacle of the almost naked island and of the wearied, if not exhausted troops retreating on it'.

'I do not write this in a way to excuse myself,' he said. 'I ought to have known. My advisers ought to have known and I ought to have been told, and I ought to have asked. The reason I had not asked about this matter, amid the thousands of questions I put, was that the possibility of Singapore having no landward defences no more entered into my mind than that of a battleship being launched without a bottom.'

By now Churchill was turning his mind to Burma, important to America for a supply line to China to sustain Chiang Kai-shek's forces. He was resigned to the loss of Singapore; it was only a matter of time. Australia was not. A cable under Curtin's name was sent to Churchill on January 23. Historian Alan Warren says that in Curtin's absence, Dr Herbert Evatt, in the chair at the meeting of the Australian war council, had inserted the famous paragraph: '. . . Page had reported that the Defence Committee has been considering the evacuation of Malaya and Singapore. After all the assurances we have been given the evacuation of Singapore would be regarded here and elsewhere as an inexcusable betrayal . . . Even in an emergency diversion of reinforcements should be to the Netherlands East Indies and not to Burma. Anything else would be deeply resented, and might force the Netherlands East Indies to make a separate peace.' As it happened (and Day puts this down to Curtin's pressure) Churchill sent a division of British troops to Singapore instead of Burma, which was not a wise move. There they would swell the army of prisoners of war. Day claims Churchill never forgave Curtin for this.

As the Australian troops were returning from the Middle East, Churchill made one last cheeky attempt to have his way about Burma. He described it as a painful episode in relations between Britain and the Australian Government. He cabled Curtin, pointing out that the leading Australian division was the only force capable of reaching Rangoon in time to prevent its loss. In a 'Former Naval Person' cable to Roosevelt, he urged the American president to add his pressure. Roosevelt obliged.

Curtin was unmoved but Churchill had already turned the convoy northward to Burma. He told Curtin it had been sent towards Rangoon because 'we could not have contemplated that you would refuse our request, and that of the President of the United States for the diversion of the leading Australian division to save the situation in Burma'. Curtin remained unmoved, saying that a message from Wavell had revealed that Java faced imminent invasion, Australia's outer defences were now quickly vanishing and the government's primary obligation was to save Australia for itself and as a base for the war against Japan.

It was to Java that the *Orcades* had sailed, carrying Jackson and the 2/3rd Machine Gun Battalion, part of a mostly Australian force of 3400. The battalion's role in the army of occupation in Syria had not been arduous. Headquarters was the small mountain village of Fih, near Tripoli. There was a heavy fall of snow on Christmas Eve and Christmas Day was snowball fights with the villagers and a turkey dinner. They embarked in February. In one of the customary blunders of war, the *Orcades* was not carrying the company's kitbags, left in railway trucks on the wharf, or the Vickers machine guns and ammunition, which were to be sent on later but which were never seen again. The machine-gunners did not know their destination. Burma, perhaps; Australia, they hoped. A lecture on the Netherlands East Indies gave the clue.

CHAPTER 6

Twilight of the tuans

Once upon a time, a Chinese-Singaporean schoolboy, brought up in the Confucian way of filial obedience, believed these things: the Englishman was *tuan*, master; the superior status of the British in colonial government and society was simply a fact of life. The boy felt no resentment. After all, the British were the greatest people in the world. They had the biggest empire that history had ever known, stretching over all time zones, across four oceans and five continents. He learnt that in history lessons in school. Harry Lee, like his grandparents and his parents, accepted that the white man's supremacy was the natural order of things.

Modern Singapore glistens. Commercial towers soar and so do the apartment buildings of the affluent expatriates and the Singaporean working class. Cleanliness is a religion and the government punishes sinners. Social order is closely guarded. Blessed are the conformists. This city-state has been built on the ruins of the British colony and the defeat and disgrace of the tuans.

Central Singapore is a giant shopping mall. Long gone is the raffishness of one of the world's great seaports; gone is Bugis Street and the transvestites, but there are still some stubborn exotica, and swirls of spice perfume the Indian section along

Serangoon Road, the world's best fish-head curry is served in a small, laminated-table restaurant on Racecourse Road and chilli crabs are still an institution. In semi-jungle close to the new Singapore there are the former homes away from Home of the tuans, sprawling double-storey buildings, with marble floors and french doors, electric fans replacing the punkahs, and detached servants' quarters. I lived in one in the 1980s. During the war a senior Japanese officer would have enjoyed the rainbow of greens, the flame trees, the scampering squirrels and kept an eye out for pythons. Before him, a senior British colonial officer would have issued curt commands to the domestic staff. In the 1980s it was still a place where you could pretend. Asmah, the friendly amah, would only call me 'tuan'. Each morning, a squat middle-aged Chinese woman in conical hat would place a small, portable Buddhist shrine in a tree fork, light a candle and then, with langorous strokes, sweep leaves from the narrow road. Most of the distant neighbours had dogs, always large, Rhodesian ridgebacks and Dobermans preferred, patrolling high fences to protect tuans, mems, and children in one of the safest places on earth. These time warps still exist, but Singapore is fiercely, if defensively independent, an amalgam of Chinese, Malays and Indians, a multicultural, multi-religious island in a Malay-Islam sea. It is as close to a one-party state as a democracy can be and there is a whiff of authoritarianism in the tropical air.

Singapore has had to live on its wits, and it has prospered. It is overwhelmingly the work of Harry Lee Kuan Yew, a third-generation descendant of migrants from China's Guangdong province, raised in an extended family hurt financially as many families around the world were, by the Great Depression. The schoolboy tossed aside the name Harry and his sense of racial inferiority, became a steely politician, and despite his small power base, a world statesman. 'Harry' was suggested by his paternal grandfather Lee Hoon Leong, an Anglophile. A family friend, an expert on auspicious names, had urged 'Kuan Yew', the dialect rendering of the Mandarin *guang yao*, meaning 'light and brightness'. He got it right. Lee was a brilliant student, reading law at Cambridge, gaining a First and the only star for Distinction on his final honours list.

When his wife Kwa Geok Choo, an equally brilliant student, joined him to study in England, she found him a changed man, deeply anti-British, particularly regarding the colonial regime in Singapore and Malaya, which he was now determined to end. In his memoirs, he carries out self-analysis. There was no need to go very deep. He had seen the twilight of the tuans and when he got to their home country after the war, he had rubbed up against the colour prejudices of the British working classes, the bus conductors and conductresses, the salesgirls and barrow boys, and most of all the fearsome landladies who stood in front of the 'room vacant' sign and said all were taken.

Lee questioned the ability of the British to govern their colonies for the good of the locals: the administrators were only interested in high pay and positions; the colonial powers in exploitation. But that's how it had been in the region for centuries. The Arabs, the Portuguese, the Dutch and the British came, more on a mission for gain than on a mission from God, though the *Malay Annals* do record that the Prophet Muhammad appeared in a dream to Sri Majharaja, the ruler of Malacca, the port on the west of the Malayan peninsula. The Prophet predicted the imminent arrival of a missionary from Jeddah. When the King awoke, he found he had been circumcised. This could be described as a kind cut. The next day the ship and the iman arrived and so did Islam. The Arabs dominated Middle East trade routes and had a monopoly over the spice trade from the Far East in the fifteenth century. Then the

Portuguese muscled in, but as merchants rather than proselytisers. The great Jesuit missionary, St Francis Xavier, who lived in Malacca for two years, condemned them: 'There is a very rich merchandise which the traders regard of little account. It is called a man's conscience, and so little esteemed is it in these parts, that the merchants believe they will go bankrupt if they invest in it.' The British and the Dutch became the dominant powers and, as such colonial powers do, shuffled territory, peoples and destinies to their satisfaction and profit. This is what the Japanese would attempt to do in the Greater East Asian War, under the false banners of the Greater East Asia Co-Prosperity Sphere and helping the colonies to independence.

The Singapore of the tuans was created by Thomas Stamford Raffles, who in 1819 did a deal with a local chieftain on behalf of the East India Company. At that time it was the home of about 1000 poor villagers and, seasonally, of the *orang laut,* nomadic fishermen who had migrated to the region towards the end of the first millennium AD. Raffles wanted the projection of British commercial and naval strength. With the opening of the Suez Canal in 1869, Singapore became a pre-eminent pivot of international trade. And, if British propaganda was to be believed, in the early twentieth century it became a mighty naval base and an impregnable fortress, a check against an expansionist Japan and a shield for the loyal dominions, Australia and New Zealand, which were owed a blood debt. Unfortunately, many did believe the propaganda. Believers did not include Japan.

A prophetic Winston Churchill wrote in *The Hinge of Fate*: 'It may well be that we shall never have a formal pronouncement by a competent court upon the worst disaster and largest capitulation in British history.' While the Allies were hunting down Japanese war criminals, including General Tomoyuki Yamashita, the Tiger of Malaya, the British Chiefs of Staff were drawing up a report for postwar Prime Minister Clement Attlee arguing that it would be all too hard and much too risky diplomatically and politically, to find out what went wrong: why all those troops surrendered, why Wally Mulvena died, why all those men, women and children perished in prison camps. It would be impossible to discuss policy in the Far East in isolation, they said. True. There would be a need to review the whole question of the preparations that were carried out in the years between the two world wars. Of course. A worldwide inquiry would require evidence of states-men and military leaders, which would involve not just military matters, but a discussion of 'controversial and delicate political issues'. Oh dear. Attlee walked to the filing cabinet and put the inquiry out of sight and out of mind.

Indeed, these are awkward questions and more than 60 years on they are still being asked. For instance, in one of his snippy exchanges with John Curtin, Churchill was emphatic that he bore no responsibility for the neglect of defences in the decade or so before the war. He had been out of office for 11 years and had given ceaseless warnings for six years before the war began.

But the fatal flaw in the Singapore strategy went back further than that. In a 2002 conference of historians and defence academics in Singapore, the fall was revisited. Naval historian Malcolm Murfett 'reflected on an enduring theme' and, in passing, on Churchill: sapped economically by World War I, Britain did not have the funds to base a permanent battle fleet in the Far East; in the Admiralty's opinion, as long as the British Government could always send the main fleet from home or Mediterranean waters to Singapore on the outbreak of war, the Japanese would not have sufficient time to mount a credible military threat to the security of the base, let alone the crown colony itself. The British Treasury, looking at meagre coffers after World War I, refused to fund the Admiralty plan for the Singapore base, known as the Green Scheme, and providing facilities for 19 capital ships. The cut-price Red Scheme which replaced it was inadequate.

Enter, says Murfett, the 'insouciant' Churchill in his unlikely guise as Chancellor of the Exchequer in Baldwin's government of 1924–29. He sabotaged the scheme still further, demanding cost-cutting economies in the construction phase of the base, eliminating repair facilities. 'It is manifestly clear that he took this decision with few, if any qualms since he felt, both at the time and later, that Singapore's sheer geographical distance from Tokyo – which he equated as being similar to that from Southampton to New York – made it invulnerable to a surprise attack launched by the Japanese either by sea or by land.'

There was insouciance among Australian politicians too. Consider Prime Minister Stanley Bruce's statement after the Imperial Conference of 1923 which reviewed the Singapore strategy: '[W]hile I am not quite clear as to how the protection of Singapore is to be assured, I am quite clear on this point, that apparently it can be done.'

John Lavarack, a young army officer, became the Australian voice of opposition to the strategy. He had been commissioned by the Chiefs of the General Staff in 1929 to prepare plans to deal with a possible Japanese invasion of Australia. The danger was underestimated, he found, and then forecast that Japan might exploit a British Empire involvement in Europe which substantially diminished its capacity to respond to a threat in the Far East.

In 1930, as chairman of a Defence sub-committee examining spending cuts as the Great Depression bit, Laverack wrote:

The despatch of the British battle fleet to the Far East for the protection of Imperial (including Australian) interests cannot be counted on with sufficient certainty, and the risk that it will be withheld, added to the risk of non-completion, capture or neutralisation of Singapore, results in a total risk that no isolated white community such as Australia would be justified in taking.

It was the theme too of criticisms of the imperial defence strategy, based on the Royal Navy and Singapore, by other military men, most prominently Lieutenant Colonel Henry Wynter. His argument was: first Australia was unlikely to be threatened by Japan unless Britain was otherwise occupied by a war in Europe; then Britain would be unwilling or unable to send a fleet to prevent invasion; therefore the Australian army and air force should have the capability to destroy an invasion force as it was being landed.

The Singapore Naval Base was opened in 1938. Strategists, working out their threat scenarios, at first said Fortress Singapore had to survive an attack and siege while the main battle fleet steamed to the rescue for 42 days. This was increased to 70 days, and then 180 days. This may have reflected the reality of the Royal Navy's capacity but represented an amazing stretch of the imagination concerning the worldwide capabilities of the army and the air force. The conservative Lyons government believed in Britain and the Royal Navy; John Curtin, elected opposition leader in 1935, did not. In a 1936 debate on defence allocations, with the government proposing concentration on naval spending, there was this exchange. Curtin, who had read Wynter's case, said Australia's dependence 'upon the competence, let along the readiness, of British statesmen to send forces to our aid is too dangerous a hazard upon which to found Australia's defence policy'. Uproar in the House. Government MP: 'Great Britain has never failed us yet.' Curtin: 'History has had no experience of the situation I am visualising.' He went on to say that Singapore was really designed by Britain for the protection of India and was as useless for the defence of Australia as Gibraltar was for the defence of New York.

Churchill believed, as historian Alan Warren has pointed out, that 'the Japanese would never attempt a siege of Singapore with a hostile, superior American fleet in the Pacific'. Warren says: 'The belief that the United States could and would contain Japan became the basic assumption behind the British Empire's defence policy in the Far East. Given the Royal Navy's inability to deploy force east of the Suez Canal, there was little alternative to that kind of wishful thinking.' Nobody expected Pearl Harbor.

AS THE FORCES of destruction built, the British imperial sun continued to shine on the tuans. However, there were those visitors who noticed something wrong. Somerset Maugham in his short stories peopled the jungles and the bars with characters comic, tragic-comic, tragic or just plain pathetic. In 'The Outstation', the British Resident, the snobbish but decent Warburton, changed for solitary dinner into white dinner jacket, boiled shirt with high collar, silk socks and patent leather shoes. He read his newspapers from home in chronological order. Every Monday morning he read *The Times* of six weeks back. During the Great War he would read of the start of a push then put up with agonies of suspense about the outcome until it was unveiled by the newspaper in proper sequence. Warburton's new assistant, the ill-mannered Cooper, insensitive to the feelings of the Malays, died with a kris through his heart. Maugham, like George Orwell in *Burmese Days*, has a cautionary tale of the perils of lonely white men taking up with native women and fathering children by them.

'I think perhaps I could have stood it,' the English wife says, 'if there's only been one child, but three; and the boys are quite big boys. For ten years you lived with her.' And now comes the racist crux of the matter: 'It's a physical thing, I can't help it, it's stronger than I am. I think of those thin black arms of hers around you and it fills me with physical nausea. I think of you holding those little black babies in your arms. Oh, it's loathsome.'

Later Maugham published *The Gentleman in the Parlour*, the story of his journey from Rangoon to Haiphong, in Vietnam. He writes that a historian of the decline and fall of the British Empire, coming across the book, would have hard things to say: Why hadn't Maugham noticed with what a nerveless hand the British held the power that their fathers had conquered? Why was there no mention of the spectacle of a horde of officials who held their positions only by force of the guns behind them trying to persuade the races they ruled that they were there only on sufferance? As if a man in whose house you have forcibly quartered yourself will welcome you any the more because you tell him you can run it better than he can!

THE HISTORY OF the British in Burma was one of conquest and gunboats and Japan took advantage of Burmese nationalism. Aung San, father of Burmese independence and of Aung San Suu Kyi, after Nelson Mandela the world's favourite political prisoner, was given shelter and training by the Japanese after escaping arrest in 1940.

Meanwhile in velvet-glove Singapore, the adolescent Lee Kuan Yew still knew his place. The upper echelons of the British community knew theirs too, playing, watching or drinking at the Singapore Cricket Club and the Swimming

Club, shopping at Robinson's, dining and dancing at Raffles, escaping the worst of the heat at Fraser's Hill on the mainland. Young women who shared the torments of Japanese prison camps with Australian nurses after fleeing the fall of Singapore would look back on a lost world and strict rituals. Newcomers left visiting cards. You reciprocated and, if everything was in order, issued an invitation for cocktails or dinner. Mothers attempted to choreograph matings. For the privileged, there could be an invitation to an At Home given by the Sultan of Johore, the friend and confidant of Australia's General Bennett, at his Green Palace across the strait.

Lee Kuan Yew had been asleep in the E block of Raffles College at four o'clock in the early morning of December 8, 1941 when he was awakened by the dull thud of exploding bombs. The war with Japan had begun but there was little doubt that the tuans would triumph. At about 8 am on January 31, 1942 Lee was sitting on the parapet of the administrative block of the college with a friend on stand-by ambulance duty. There was, he remembers, an earth-shaking explosion. To the north, part of the causeway linking Singapore with mainland Malaya had been destroyed behind the retreating Allied troops. Lee was stunned. He turned to his friend and said: 'That's the end of the British Empire.' The college principal, Professor Dyer, who was walking past on the way to his office, heard Lee, looked away and walked on.

With the fall of Malaya and Singapore, the tuans fell totally from grace in Lee's eyes. There is deep bitterness and a strange sense of outraged betrayal in his account of the patronisers and the patronised, and of the old order and the destruction of it. He writes of a small number of Asiatics, which is what Asians were called then, being allowed to mix socially with the white bosses, some appointed unofficial members of the governor's Executive Council or the Legislative Council, of photographs of them and their wives, appearing in the papers, attending garden parties and sometimes dinners at Government House, bowing and curtseying before the governor and his lady, the women duly wearing white gloves, and all on their best behaviour. They accepted their inferior status with aplomb, for they considered themselves superior to their fellow Asiatics. Conversely, any British, European or American who misbehaved or looked like a tramp was immediately packed off because he would demean the whole white race, whose superiority must never be thrown into doubt.

'This was the Malaya and Singapore that 60,000 attacking Japanese soldiers captured,' he says, 'together with more than 130,000 British, Indian and Australian troops.'

> In 70 days of surprises, upsets and stupidities, British colonial society was shattered, and with it all the assumptions of the Englishman's superiority. The Asiatics were supposed to panic when the firing started, yet they were the stoic ones who took the casualties and died without hysteria. It was the civilian bosses who ducked under tables when the bombs and shells fell. It was the white civilians and government officers in Penang who, on 16 December 1941, in the quiet of the night, fled the island for the 'safety' of Singapore, abandoning the Asiatics to their fate . . . The Asiatics had looked to them for leadership, and they had failed them.

Lee, a hard man, was given to hard judgments. Amid the chaos, panic and cowardice, there had been acts of selflessness and bravery. There was also some desperate laughter in the face of grim fate. This is the story of the last day together of the Russell-Roberts. Ruth was a beautiful former Hartnell mannequin; Denis was a captain with the 5/11th Sikhs of the

22nd Indian Brigade. As Denis fought and retreated towards Singapore, Ruth had given their year-old daughter to the care of a friend on one of the evacuation ships. The 22nd Brigade had been savaged and Denis, who was hiding in a rubber plantation in Johore, crossed the strait in a small boat and at the naval base got a 48-hour leave pass. The Russell-Robertses used it well. They cashed a cheque at Robinson's and bought new clothes and from a Chinese silk merchant got material for two pairs of pyjamas to be whipped up by an Indian tailor. They lunched at the Singapore Cricket Club, swam at the Tanglin Club and danced that night at Raffles to Dan Hopkins and his Band.

And this is the story of the engagement of Molly Ismail. Daughter of a barrister, Molly lived in Johore Bahru, capital of Johore state. She had beauty and she had status. As the Japanese drew closer she and her mother were evacuated to Singapore. There one of her suitors, an English planter, a officer in the Malay Volunteers preparing for the last stand, proposed. Molly accepted and they drove off to buy the engagement ring. On the way, Japanese bombers attacked the city, and the couple had to take cover in a monsoon drain. They continued on their mission and that night celebrated with smoked salmon and champagne at the Café Wein. On Molly's third finger was a hooped diamond ring.

The two couples disappeared into the fog of war, the Russell-Robertses and Molly Ismail as captives of the Japanese, and presumably Molly's fiancé too.

LEE KUAN YEW stayed in Singapore, renamed Syonan by the Japanese, meaning 'Light of the South'. He survived. He worked for the Japanese. The time of the tuan was over. Yet often during the Japanese occupation Lee Kuan Yew wished the British were still in charge. The driving out of the British had nothing to do with Singapore's liberation, he realised. 'It was about the master race coming down to govern us, and had they won we would have been kept down for the next thousand years.'

CHAPTER 7

Officers and gentlemen

*There is no limit to the good a man can do provided he
does not care who gets the credit.*

Commandant Coles Osborne,
Quetta Command and Staff College

While John Wyett takes his bath, Davad Khan, his Pathan bearer, lean and hawk-nosed, has laid out his clothes: underwear, shirt, No. 1 uniform. Khan helps button the shirt and fasten the trousers, then kneels down to put on the socks and the shoes he has worked to a high gloss. Now the tie and the jacket. Khan steps back with critical eye. Captain John Wyett, 8th Division, Australian Imperial Force, is ready to enter the mess at the Quetta Command and Staff College. It dazzles. It is the Raj at dinner. Most of his fellow officers are from the Indian army, their regimental colours splashed on puggaree and cummerbunds. White-clad servants wearing shining breastplates glide silently. They don't seem to touch the floor.

It is August 1941 at one of the world's most prestigious military colleges. Quetta is capital of Baluchistan, part of India, a dab of green in a barren landscape that halts abruptly against the ramparts of even more barren mountains. Distances are vast and empty; sight travels further here. Wyett has come to Quetta from Malaya, tropical, heavy of air, with tree-tangled mountains, its grids of rubber plantations, and, of course, its jungle.

To the newcomer, the jungle is fearsome, frightening. Its deathly silence is broken by the soft drip-drip from the hanging foliage, or by the crack of the twig as some strange animal sneaks about in search of prey . . . Now and then a heavy tropical rainstorm darkens the already dark twilight, and streams of water pour down the tree trunks, making the ground more marshy than ever and the deep leafy mould which covers it soggy and steamy, filling the air with a pungent odour of decay . . . Throughout the marshes are millions of bloodsucking leeches and mosquitoes, both malarial and otherwise. Here and there enormous snakes hang on the undergrowth or slither along the ground. Cobras, pythons, hamadryads and the dangerously poisonous krait show themselves. Mangy, smelly tigers, heavy, dangerous sladangs who will charge blindly into any human in their vicinity – all these give a horror to the jungle.

That is the description by General Henry Gordon Bennett, Wyett's commanding officer, leader of the 8th Division. Bennett sees beauty in the jungle too: rare orchids in the tree-tops gathered by tame, trained monkeys at the end of long ropes, birds of every hue, butterflies 12 inches across from wingtip to wingtip, glorious stately trees, the fragrance of beautiful, tropical flowers.

It is fitting that Bennett had an eye for opposites. He himself was hero and villain, adored and reviled, praised and damned.

The man who desperately wanted to lead the whole Australian army in World War II was found by a Royal Commission at the beginning of peace to have, without justification, relinquished command of the 8th Division and escaped from Singapore as it fell to the Japanese in February 1942. For some he would always be the wronged victim of lesser men; for others, 'to do a Gordon Bennett' was currency for behaving very badly, dishonourably even.

Wyett loved the Quetta experience. It was an induction into, or at least an introduction to, the elite levels of command. His final field exercise was a defence of the Kohat Pass, a passageway to and from Afghanistan studded with ruined watchtowers and haunted by ghostly armies. It was a long way from the jungle, but Quetta was about the unchanging art of leading men. Early on, the commandant of the college, Major General Coles Osborne, had unrolled a large scroll. 'There is no limit to the good a man can do,' it said, 'provided he does not care who gets the credit.' Ah! *Esprit de corps*, a team working towards victory; selflessness. The trouble was Wyett knew it wasn't like that at 8th Division headquarters even before the Japanese invaded Malaya. Nor would it be like that in the whole command structure, as chains of disasters built towards the climactic disaster of total surrender. When there was small credit, it was scrabbled over and then held high; there was blame aplenty to be ducked and to be pointed elsewhere. Scapegoats grazed in the generals' jungle. Battles went on within the senior Australian officer ranks in Malaya; a long, bitter, personal battle continued between Bennett and his winning rival for Australian army leadership, General Thomas Blamey. There was antagonism between Bennett and his British commander, General Arthur Percival; there was antagonism between Percival and his rival, General Sir Lewis Heath, commander of the III Indian Corps and victor over the Italians in Abyssinia. There was antagonism between the civilian and military leaderships. How convenient all this was for the Japanese commander, General Tomoyuki Yamashita.

What does it take to be a general, in particular, a winning general? Ego, certainly. But should he have imagination? Or lack of imagination? Should he see on the contour maps and the grid references the dying agonies and smashed bodies of men? Should he wonder when a fighting last stand becomes a futile gesture? According to the experts, it is a distinct disadvantage to be 'one of nature's gentlemen', which is how one subordinate described General Percival. There was never any danger that Gordon Bennett would be so slighted. Showmanship apparently helps. General Archibald Wavell, commander of the region, wished for a general with a 'streak of the impresario'. And ruthlessness, it seems, is essential. Britain's official historian, Major General S. Woodburn Kirby, said in review that what had been needed in Malaya was 'a ruthless, brilliant, no-nonsense, hard-driving, operational general'. Percival's biographer, Major General Clifford Kinvig, said: 'The quality which Percival lacked as a commander was ruthlessness and the one he had in excess was loyalty.' There was never any danger that many of Bennett's peers would describe him as loyal. Kinvig, a former Director of Army Education, wrote a book called *Scapegoat: General Percival of Singapore*, a sustained argument that Percival shouldn't be seen as one. Kinvig, and others, found a different beast for that burden: Henry Gordon Bennett.

JOHN WYETT WAS born in Beaconsfield, a small mining town in Tasmania, in 1908. He trained as a pharmacist and graduated with a science degree. He had a military pedigree which should have qualified him as an ally of Bennett. One of those who saw the shadow of war, he was a naval cadet. He later joined the militia, a volunteer force of citizen soldiers. Australia then did not have a large, standing professional army but a small, trained Staff Corps which administered the militia. This division could and did spawn jealousy, spite and unhelpful rivalry. Bennett was also an amateur, a citizen soldier. Blamey was a professional.

When war came, Wyett, to his annoyance, found himself listed as being in a reserved occupation. He was a chocolate-maker for Cadburys. He could see the administrators' point. Chocolate was an important component in the soldier's emergency iron rations and in lifeboat rations, but he wanted to fight and he persisted until he was allowed to enlist. Wyett's war was as eventful as that of anyone who survived. He went to the officers' heaven in Quetta; he went to the prisoners' hell in Outram Road jail. He was a participant in the retreat of the final unit from the Malayan mainland across the causeway to Singapore. It was his signature on the 8th Division order which sent the soldiers into captivity. He was tried by the Japanese and sentenced to death by beheading and as a reminder of how close he came, lived on with several crushed vertebrae in his neck from a blow from the flat of a *kempeitei* officer's samurai sword. He worked closely with Bennett and gave evidence at the Royal Commission into Bennett's behaviour. It was damaging.

Their relationship did not start auspiciously. Wyett recorded the first meeting in his memoir, *Staff Wallah at the Fall of Singapore*: 'He fixed me with his pale blue eyes and said "Wyett, are you lucky?" I looked at him with a mixture of amazement and despair. The classic question Napoleon had always asked! I found out later he was naturally superstitious and had the strange habit of consulting the stars before making a decision.' Wyett quickly identified a cluster of flaws: fiery temper, aggressive, controversial nature, overweening ambition and an unwavering belief in his own superiority. To these Wyett added paranoia, in all but name. He tells of once receiving, before the war began, at 11 pm a report that two officers had strayed across the Thai border and been arrested. Bennett was at a party, so Wyett decided to tell him in the morning. 'So you're another of them,' Bennett reacted. 'You're all against me. Hiding things from me, going behind my back . . . it's all part of a plot.'

Bennett was quite right to worry about enemies in the Allied ranks. They were led by his brother officers and superiors, General Percival and General Blamey. In March 1943 Percival was a prisoner of war in Formosa. He wrote a letter to the Military Board in Australia and gave it to Brigadier Cecil Callaghan, the man to whom Bennett had handed command and whom Percival had appointed in Bennett's place, promoting him to major general. Percival began: 'I have to report that Major-General H. Gordon Bennett, GOC, AIF, Malaya, voluntarily and without permission relinquished command of the AIF on 15 Feb. 1942 – the date on which the capitulation of the British Forces in Malaya took place.' Callaghan delivered the letter in 1945, on his release from captivity. Blamey, in a letter to the Minister for the Army, Frank Forde, supporting Callaghan's promotion, said: 'When General Bennett deserted his troops in Singapore and failed to support the surrender agreed upon with the Japanese troops . . .'

Kinvig, in a defence of Percival, described him as a man 'condemned by photography'. The most unflattering photograph of them all is reproduced on the dust jacket of Kinvig's book. Trimmed to an oval, on a dark background, it shows Percival wearing a topee, an unfortunate moustache, protruding teeth and not much of a chin. The effect is either a parody of a general or a fairly realistic portrait of a rabbit popping out of a hole. The Chief of the Imperial General Staff, General John Dill, whose protégé Percival was, was always concerned that people would judge him on first impressions. Another photograph seems to say a lot about the relationship between Bennett and Percival. Both are wearing the long, baggy shorts which were good for ventilation but did nothing to flatter the figure. Percival, tall, thin and slightly stooped, is looking at the camera, with a slight smile. Bennett, shorter and more compact, is standing to Percival's left and a little to the rear. He is unsmiling. He is looking in Percival's direction. It is not a look of warmth and respect. It is cool and sceptically appraising.

Bennett, before baldness set in, had red hair. He was one of those people who gave strength to the myth that red hair signalled a short and fiery temper. Yet whatever their physical differences, both men were similarly and unquestionably brave. Both officers, in soldiering terms, had an outstanding World War I.

Bennett was born in Balwyn, Melbourne, in 1887, at a time when the leafy, green suburb was a village on the city's outskirts. His father was a schoolteacher, a man of Victorian values. Bennett's biographer, Frank Legg, reports that when the Boer War broke out, George Bennett had a map on the classroom wall on which he tracked for his pupils the progress of operations in the Transvaal. He gave the school a half-holiday when Mafeking was relieved and Gordon Bennett led a tin-can band around neighbourhood streets. The boy declared that he was going to be a bishop or a general, but Legg does not draw a picture of a rock-solid soldier-to-be: Bennett had never done well at examinations because he tried too hard and worked himself into a state of nervous exhaustion; he was not particularly good at sport, his temperament being too volatile to enable him to concentrate sufficiently to master the skill of hitting a ball properly; handy with his fists, impetuous and with a sense of justice, he had many schoolyard fights. It's a character outline which allows for easy, hindsight analysis: young Bennett could make an outstanding leader of men under fire when daring action is required; he may not have the coolness and analytical skill required to plan strategy for and command large-group formations; he could be his own worst enemy.

As soon as he turned 21, Bennett joined the Militia. His day job was actuarial clerk but the army was his life. He joined the AIF in August 1914 when war was declared and was second in command of the 6th Battalion, led by Lieutenant Colonel Walter McNicoll. Naturally Bennett considered that job should have been his.

On April 24, 1915 the 6th Battalion was on the transport *Galeka*, sailing into the Bay of Purnea. McNicoll called an officers' meeting. They were told that the operation was to start at first light on the next day. The landing was to be on a beach just north of Gaba Tepe, a promontory on the western coast of the Gallipoli Peninsula. The beach would have been cleared by artillery fire. The battalion would move inland over the first ridge and into the gully beyond it, where packs would be dumped. And then? Well, as Bennett put it, with understatement, instructions were vague, though they knew they had to 'get forward'. Orders would be given to the battalion as the situation developed.

Early the next morning, the troops were wakened, or at least those who managed to sleep. Major Bennett moved among them, and spoke for a while with one he knew very well, his 20-year-old brother, Sergeant Godfrey Bennett. It was April 25, 1915. Henry Gordon Bennett and Godfrey Bennett were about to help create the Anzac myth.

The first contingent of the 6th scrambled into boats towed by naval pinnaces. In one of them was the body of a 9th

Battalion soldier killed in the landing of the covering force. They landed to machine-gun and rifle fire and chaos. Bennett, who had honed his map-reading skills in his Militia days could recognise no landmarks. Something had gone wrong. But by four o'clock that afternoon, Bennett had established a firing line well forward, dangerously well forward, on Pine Ridge, to the right front of Lone Pine, with other small groups on his flanks, a position not reached again by the Australians for the rest of the campaign.

Among the men he led was Private Staniforth Ricketson, a straggler from a company of the 5th Battalion, formed from Melbourne ex-public schoolboys, which had taken heavy casualities in its advance. Ricketson, one of the few survivors of Pine Ridge, and afterwards a company commander in France, later wrote of that incredible day.

From in front, through the shrapnel fire, a number of wounded men suddenly appeared, struggling down the slope towards us and calling out that the Turks were on the other side of the hill 'coming up in thousands'. Lying on the ground I overheard a discussion between two men lying beside me. One was a major from a New South Wales battalion, the other a sergeant. Both agreed that retirement was the only thing possible. They rose to a crouching position and began to make off. All of a sudden I became conscious of a slim, red-headed major standing just behind me. I recognised him immediately as the second-in-command of the 6th Battalion . . . Thrusting his revolver against the other major's chest, he said 'One more word about retirement and I'll shoot you out of hand'. This effectively silenced this major and the sergeant, whereupon Major Bennett ran along the line – there must have been some thirty of us there then – calling out at the top of his voice 'We'll never go back, men. We'll die here' . . .

. . . somebody yelled out 'Here they come!' We all leapt up to our feet, and I must confess I wondered whether we were going forward or backward. But at once Major Bennett dashed out in front, calling 'Come on, men', and in one wild rush we were running up the hill ahead, yelling like Dervishes. Our bayonets were fixed. As we reached the top of the slope we could see a party of Turks advancing towards us. I think our appearance and wild cries convinced the Turks they would be wiser to retire, which they promptly did at the double, with us chasing after them. I might add the Turks outstripped us!

About four o'clock in the afternoon a large group of Turks appeared on the ridgeline opposite Bennett's position. He stood up to direct fire, opened a map and was hit in the wrist and shoulder by one of the bullets in the first fusillade. He was knocked to the ground and with one arm useless, crawled to his junior officer and handed over command. He made his way under fire to the regimental aid post. On the way he caught up with a young man, wounded in the leg, trying to descend Snipers' Ridge. It was Staniforth Ricketson. With Bennett helping Ricketson with his good arm, the two eventually reached the beach. From brave landing place early in the morning, it had been turned into a casualty station. Bennett saw the wounded scattered everywhere and shrapnel lashing down to hit them where they lay. Many were crying for water. Processions of stretcher-bearers were bringing more in.

With his wounds field-dressed, Bennett was sent to a hospital ship. There the good news was the bullet had hit his left shoulder just above the collar bone, passed out through the pectoral muscle and hit him again in the wrist. Centimetres count. The senior medical officer told Bennett that as senior officer on board the hospital ship he must take over as officer commanding for the voyage back to the Mudros base.

What happened next raises questions about the blackening of Bennett in his next war as deserter. There are heroes in battles, and cowards. That seems a simple enough division, but if you could freeze the moment, bullet suspended in front of barrel, bomb in mid-explosion, mouth open in scream or exultant shout, if you could clear the smog and look into the minds of men, what emotions and motives would you find driving them forward, or back? In a grey area of blame, behind the lines wander stragglers, who may have lost many of their mates, lost their units, lost their officers but who can be led to fight again. Staniforth Ricketson was one. Then there are deserters, their individual sin compounded by the fact that they could contaminate the others, especially if the cause is dubious, the leadership flawed and the odds poor. For many armies the reflex was to shoot deserters *pour encourager les autres*. In *Gallipoli*, Les Carlyon records how 18-year-old Lieutenant Dallas Moor won the Victoria Cross during one of the battles for Krithia for stemming the retreat of British troops by shooting several of them, a strange type of action by which to win the highest award for valour.

Bennett refused the medical officer's request. He later lowered himself one-handed down a rope to a lighter loaded with rations of cheese and bacon alongside the hospital ship. That night it was towed to shore, its cargo, now bullet-pocked by Turkish fire from the heights, sheltering Bennett and several other wounded men rejoining their units. Bennett stumbled up Shrapnel Gully and eventually found 6th Battalion headquarters a little behind Bolton's Ridge. He searched for one face, asked for news. Pine Ridge, further forward, had been lost. So had Godfrey Bennett. In 1919, Charles Bean, war correspondent, chronicler of Gallipoli and custodian of the Anzac legend, found groups of skeletons along Pine Ridge, identified by their battalion colour patches.

Godfrey Bennett was presumably buried on Pine Ridge with his mates. Gordon Bennett fought on and, in military terms, prospered. By June he had been promoted to lieutenant colonel at age 28 and now, with McNicoll wounded, commanded the 6th Battalion. He was keeping a diary, writing, according to Legg, with perfect frankness. Diaries can be a worry. Surely most are written in the expectation that other people, and posterity, will peek into them at some time. In this instance, however, Bennett is not doing spadework for defence of his military decision-making; he is examining what happened to him personally in one of the terrible Krithia struggles.

Now I found that my dreadful experience there had shattered my complacent approach to the problem of facing dangers squarely in battle. I realised that I could not possibly allow this new weakness to rule me. If I could not fight down the dread and the fear I could not go on commanding men in battle. At the time I was like a whipped cur . . . To impose the strong self-discipline and self-control necessary to force myself to face another Krithia, with coolness and without flinching, was a most difficult psychological task. In the end I resolved very firmly that I would grip myself tightly and check every sign of weakening. I decided, too, that I would go forward into the front line daily, picking the noisiest and more dangerous period.

He commanded his men at the slaughter of German Officers' Trench, and wrote after that:

I could not help wondering why troops have been hurled into such disasters these last two days. Many more gallant men have been killed than the results seem to justify. It is clear that someone has blundered. All efforts to go forward seem to lead only to the grave. For myself, I have become a fatalist.

Bennett sailed away from Gallipoli's magnificent failure with a CMG (Companion of the Order of St Michael and St George), fought at Pozières and in November 1916 became a brigadier. He was 29, and at the time one of the youngest brigadiers in any of the British armies. In peacetime, Bennett was successful as a businessman, cultivated friends in high places, notably Prime Minister Billy Hughes, and alienated the professionals of the Staff Corps and Military Board. In 1937 he wrote a series of newspaper articles on defence preparedness. In one, he said: 'Experience has proved that citizen officers can handle our citizen army more efficiently than permanent officers. Our permanent officers are trained as staff officers and not as active soldiers.' This is arguable. In a second, he said: 'Our defences are worse now than at any time during the past twenty-five years . . . Our army has been equipped with promises – and little else.' This was undoubtedly correct and in the pattern of politicians in peace who speak loudly and provide the services with small sticks. The Military Board, though, had had enough. It stepped in and blocked the publication of further articles.

Like Bennett, Percival volunteered for service as soon as war broke out in 1914. Like Bennett, at war's end he was a decorated commander, winning the Military Cross, the Croix de Guerre and the DSO. He was born into a prominent Northamptonshire family in 1887, nine months after Bennett, and like Bennett, was brought up by a father with strong

Victorian values. He went to the elite Rugby School, developed as a cross-country runner and, unlike Bennett, as a batsman. He was junior colour sergeant in Rugby's Rifle Corps, leaving in 1906 for a pedestrian job in the City of London, where he worked until World War I broke out. While Bennett was fighting in the hills and gullies of Gallipoli, Percival and his company of the Bedfords were learning about life in trenches, at that time a mixture of danger and tedium. Impatient for action, he wrote in his diary: 'The only bag I have made is one rat which I slew with my stick in fine style.' Then came the Somme.

On July 1, 1916, the beginning of the bloody grind, the Bedfords, fortified a little by the rum issue, went over the top. The two assaulting companies and the support company lost all their officers killed or wounded within an hour. Percival's reserve company, advancing through artillery and machine-gun fire, lost two officers before they had crossed their own wire. By the end of the day, what remained of Percival's men had reached the objective, Maple Trench, and Percival had won the Military Cross. 'During the advance,' the citation said, 'he showed fine leadership and determination under heavy shell and machine-gun fire. He worked unceasingly, with absolute disregard of danger, in completing every detail in the consolidation of the captured position.' Some months later Percival was wounded, hit by four pieces of shrapnel. While he was recuperating, confirmation came through of his transfer to the Regular Army. He became a professional soldier and in 1919, instead of rejoining the men in the bowler hats in the City, he was fighting in northern Russia. Winston Churchill, not chastened by Gallipoli and watching civilisation 'being completely extinguished over gigantic areas' had a grand scheme to crush the Bolsheviks who 'hop and caper like troops of ferocious baboons amid the ruins of cities and the corpses of their victims'. All that was required was 'twenty or thirty thousand resolute, comprehending Europeans' who could 'without serious difficulty or loss, have made their way very swiftly along any of the great railroads which converged on Moscow'. The scheme was stillborn because of political opposition and a relief force was sent to cover the withdrawal of British troops already in northern Russia. Once more Percival showed initiative and leadership, emerging with a bar to his DSO.

Next came a very different sort of conflict, the nasty little guerilla war waged by the Irish Republican Army, a spell as student/teacher at the Staff College, Camberley, and four years serving the Empire in Nigeria. This was not a hardship posting. While Percival did revise the colony's defence system, he also managed to shock the civilians by winning the cup in the best-garden competition.

But what stands out in the *curriculum vitae* of the man who would surrender Singapore is his stint there as a senior officer in Malaya Command with a responsibility for defence planning in 1936 and 1937. In London he received a briefing note that resounded with warning bells. The author, an officer who had developed artillery defences, reported lack of cooperation by the RAF, a civilian–military divide and the vulnerability of Johore. He also used a phrase which clearly stuck in Percival's mind: 'the defence of the back door needs addressing'. At a time when there was complacent awe at the 15-inch guns pointing south and the Malayan jungle was regarded as a formidable barrier to an enemy, the officer saw the danger of a thrust from the north by land.

Percival spent 20 months on the ground which his army would lose in a few years' time. Kinvig makes a compelling case for Percival's prescience. In an echo of the briefing note, he warned a volunteer unit on the mainland that the Japanese might try to 'burgle Malaya by the back door'. Percival's commanding officer, Major General Dobbie, was concerned with the presumption that the weather, in the form of the north-west monsoon, would also be on the defenders' side. Percival set up an exercise that demonstrated that the monsoon would assist invaders. This must not have come to the attention of Air Chief Marshal Sir Robert Brooke-Popham, Commander-in-Chief of Far East Command at the time of the Japanese invasion. Percival was concerned about the strategy of scattering airfields and hoping small garrisons could defend them. In an end-of-tour appreciation, he warned of the vulnerability of the airfields and questioned the basic premise of the defence of Singapore, that the British fleet could steam to a timely rescue. This appreciation was distributed in Singapore and Percival, on return to London, gave a copy to the War Office, which found the usual space in a filing cabinet. When his mentor General Dill, Chief of the Imperial General Staff, asked whether Singapore was impregnable, Percival responded that 'far from being impregnable it would be in imminent danger if war broke out in the Far East unless there was an early realisation in high places of the complete change in the problem of its defence which was then taking place'.

After several home postings and a spell as Assistant Chief of the Imperial General Staff, Percival arrived back in Malaya in May 1941 to command the army. He was to find that he had been a prophet without honour or clout when it came to defence preparedness. There were other problems. In his book, *The War in Malaya* (which he had started mulling over while in captivity), he complains:

As chief of the general staff of Malaya Command, I had expected to be a person of some consequence until I realised that defence was of very little interest to the great majority of the people of Malaya in those days. Malaya was a rich commercial country whose people lived mainly on the production of rubber and tin. Before the arrival of the British more than a hundred years before, its people had been of a warlike disposition, but under British rule they had gradually learnt ways of peace and for many years they had been left alone to develop their industries and enjoy the benefits of civilisation.

This puts a fine gloss on the exploitative nature of the colonial process. The Japanese were just as bad when they proclaimed themselves liberators of the exploited. They wanted the rubber and tin. One of the reasons Percival found it difficult to turn the attention of civilian leaders to the looming military crisis was the insistence by Britain on the outbreak of war that keeping the exports flowing was of the first importance.

The Governor of Singapore, Sir Shenton Thomas, was a figure out of Somerset Maugham, a Colonial Service officer who came to the Far East after having charge of some African backwaters. What was the British Government thinking to pluck him from Nyasaland (later to descend into poverty-stricken dictatorship as Malawi) and place him in a posting of such economic and geopolitical significance? At a luncheon he hosted in Government House in 1935, the year after his arrival, he demonstrated the depth of his strategic thinking and set the tone for the relationship between the military and the civilian hierarchy. He boomed to a visiting army staff officer: 'I wish you bloody soldiers would go away; your presence here and your attempts to build up defences will only bring war to this country. We should be much better off without you.' While there was dissension in the ranks of the military leadership, there was an uncivil war among the civilians. Churchill sent a Cabinet Minister, Duff Cooper, to Singapore as Resident

Minister to see how the two arms could work together. Cooper arrived only three months before the Japanese invasion, accompanied by his socialite and actress wife, Lady Diana. She was observant, and, it would be nice to think, caustically observant. Here is her description of the welcome: 'Commander-in-Chief Brooke-Popham on the jetty and the whole set up entirely to my liking – liveries of ostentatious gold and white and scarlet on Malay and Indian servants, ADCs, movie-men, gaping coolies . . . God's acres being mown by the fingers and thumbs of natives advancing on all fours in a serried row and plucking the growing blades of grass.' Cooper, a fool, said of Thomas, another fool: 'The Governor, Sir Shenton Thomas, is one of those people who find it quite impossible to adjust their minds to war conditions. He is also the mouthpiece of the last person he speaks to.' Thomas said of Cooper: 'A rotten judge of men, arrogant, obstinate, vain; how he could have crept into office is beyond me.'

With friends and allies like these, the last thing Percival needed was an enemy like General Tomoyuki Yamashita. He was the son of a country doctor, as was Takashi Nagase, the interpreter for the *kempeitai* torturers, but the two were opposites. Nagase was small, frail, Christian, not Shinto, and attracted to mysticism. Yamashita, bulky, tall for a Japanese, and in later years shaven-headed, was born out of his time. He was a samurai warrior, a student of Zen Buddhism, a calligrapher with the *nom de plume Daisen,* 'Giant Cedar'. After postings in Europe, he was less insular than most Japanese and he moved in the highest echelons. In Berlin in June 1941 he had talks with Hitler, carrying back the Fuhrer's request that Japan attack Siberia if Germany declared war on the Soviet Union.

Though he was hanged as a war criminal, he was guided in some of his actions by the true spirit of *bushido*. A veteran of the China wars, he wanted no repetition of the Rape of Nanking, insisting on strict military discipline and punishing offenders and executing looters. He showed care for his soldiers, holding memorial services for the fallen and had a small statue of the God of Mercy made to whom he offered daily prayers. And in a war in which Japan's reputation was forever stained by the brutality of the treatment of prisoners of war, he was actually criticised by Japan's General Staff and the War Ministry because of his humane behaviour towards the defeated. He rejected demands to use them as slave labour. However *sook ching*, the purge of Chinese in surrendered Singapore in which tens of thousands died, took place on his watch and followed his orders for a military mopping-up operation. After receiving a report that within about a week between 4000 and 5000 Chinese had been executed or detained for execution, he instructed that the operation continue.

Yamashita was tough, fiery and driven by a desire to win back the Emperor's favour following his disgrace in the 1936 officers' revolt. In all of his headquarters, Yamashita positioned his desk facing in the direction of the Imperial Palace in Tokyo. He did not need an ego transplant. After the triumph of his Malayan blitzkrieg, he was widely hailed as the 'Tiger of Malaya'. He was not much for the term. Professor Emeritus Akashi Yoji, who has studied the Japanese occupation of Malaya, records an exchange between Yamashita and a German military attaché. The attaché congratulates Yamashita on the fall of Singapore, addressing him as 'General Tiger'. Yamashita responds, *'Nein, ich bin nicht der Tiger'*, explaining 'the tiger attacks its prey in stealth but I attack the enemy in a fair play'.

As is endemic in armies, Yamashita had bitter rivals among his peers: Hideki Tojo, general, war minister and prime minister; Takumo Nishimura, commander of the Imperial Guards Division. But as commander of the 25th Army, he was loved and respected down the ranks. That at least is how Masanobu Tsuji, his operations officer, presents the situation in his self-serving Japanese version of the Malayan campaign. Yamashita was 'of dignified physique and commanding mien' (he actually had a pot belly that preceded him by a fair margin). He had tolerance and a keen insight into human nature. 'Tears shone in the eyes of the generous-hearted general' when he heard how Tsuji had narrowly escaped injury or death when his car ran over a landmine. There is only one muted criticism, and it demonstrates the different mind-sets of the veteran general and the young militarists. Tsuji notes that Yamashita 'appeared still to prefer the tactic of large-scale out-flanking movements from the west coast'. Yamashita caused havoc in the defenders' lines by moving forces to their rear; younger officers, believing that the spirit of Japanese soldiers would beat numerical odds and exulting in a dash for glory, were prone to leading frontal assaults. Yamashita's response to these officers? 'They are all stupid.'

Certainly defenders outnumbered attackers in the Malayan campaign. Tsuji puts the Japanese strength, including support troops, at 60,000, claiming a two to one ratio in favour of the Allies; Warren puts the best estimate of Allied troops on December 1, 1941 at 91,209. After reinforcements, a defeated army of around 120,000 became prisoners of war. However, Japan did have an overwhelming advantage in the air, with 534 modern aircraft facing 158 obsolete or second-rate Allied aircraft.

IN THE WONDERFUL, closed world of Quetta's Command and Staff College, John Wyett received a most satisfying report but he also received news that events were moving rapidly in Malaya. The Japanese had landed in force. They had command of the sea and the air. He made his way back to Gordon Bennett at 8th Division headquarters and the reality of a war gone disastrously wrong.

CHAPTER 8

A toast to you, dear pals

Curtains of rain from the monsoon were falling over the beaches of Kota Bharu on the north-east coast of Malaya. The 21-year-old Spud Spurgeon had a pilot's eye view of burning transports, landing craft ploughing through heavy seas, troops pushing past bodies in the water's edge and running towards barbed wire which also held a harvest of the dead. Spurgeon took his Hudson bomber lower, swept towards a landing craft, squeezed the trigger of his front-mounted Browning machine guns and fired his first shots in action. It was 7.15 on the morning of December 8, 1941. About six hours earlier the Japanese had launched their assault on this nondescript piece of the British Empire to begin the Pacific War. They literally jumped the gun on their comrades half an ocean away who were still an hour's flying time from the giant United States naval base at Pearl Harbor with its flock of heavily armoured sitting ducks. 'Tora, Tora, Tora', and eight battleships would be sunk or damaged at Pearl Harbor, two destroyers so badly damaged that they had to be completely rebuilt and 13 other vessels hit. One hundred and twenty planes would be destroyed and 2403 service people killed.

On the eve of 'a date that will live in infamy', the twentieth century version of 9/11, with negotiations with Japan clearly

approaching breakdown point, President Roosevelt, in a concil-
iatory gesture to the Emperor of Japan, said that he and the
Emperor had 'a sacred duty to restore traditional amity and
prevent further death and destruction in the world'. But the
Japanese had made their plans. At a November conference in
Tokyo, the civilian foreign and finance ministers had argued
against war with the United States but the army and navy were
in favour. The military was always going to win. The terms for
peace that Japan sent to America were never going to be
accepted by President Roosevelt: no more aid to China, no
increase in British and American forces in the Far East, no
interference in Indo-China and American cooperation with
Japan in obtaining raw materials. The date for attacks on Pearl
Harbor, Malaya and Hong Kong was set at an Imperial conference on December 1 after General Tojo advised that war was
necessary to preserve the Japanese empire. The orders went out.
The assault troops jumped from the landing barges at Kota
Bharu, the aircraft lined up for their runs at Pearl Harbor and
Japan began unleashing death and destruction. Japan's final
victim would be itself. It had overreached. Winston Churchill,
in his first letter to Roosevelt after becoming Prime Minister,
had said: 'I am looking to you to keep that Japanese dog quiet
in the Pacific . . .' The Japanese dog attacked America; Roosevelt unleashed the American dogs of war. The Prime Minister
got what he wanted, United States involvement.

Churchill went to bed after Roosevelt declared war and
slept 'the sleep of the saved and thankful'. He wrote later in
The Grand Alliance: 'All the rest was merely the proper application of overwhelming force. The British Empire, the Soviet
Union, and now the United States, bound together with every
scrap of their life and strength, were, according to my lights,
twice or even thrice the force of their antagonists . . . I
expected terrible forfeits in the East; but all this would be

merely a passing phase . . . there was no more doubt about the end.' In the East, Australia was about to enter its period of greatest national danger and the terrible forfeits came, as expected: the suffering and the torture and the death. The mere passing phase for prisoners of war dragged on and on and on. There would be no sleep of the saved for almost four years for those struggling to survive.

OVER THE BEACHES of Kota Bharu in 1941, Spud Spurgeon was coming close to death. This battle wasn't supposed to be happening, according to the British Imperial hierarchy. A conference in Singapore in September had been attended by, among others, Air Chief Marshal Sir Robert Brooke-Popham, then Commander-in-Chief of the Far East Command; the naval Commander-in-Chief, China Station, Vice-Admiral Layton; the Governor of the Straits Settlements, Sir Shenton Thomas; and Australia's Sir Earle Page. It was decided that Japan would be concentrating on Russia and would be aware of the danger of confronting the United States, the British Commonwealth and the Netherlands East Indies. Moreover, Brooke-Popham insisted that the Japanese were most unlikely to attempt an invasion of Malaya during the north-east monsoon. Page would have more good news to take back to Australia after meeting in the Philippines with General Douglas MacArthur, Commander of the United States Army Forces in the Far East. MacArthur, not a man to understate his opinions, told Page that Japan, after a draining five years' war with China, was overextended and needed a long period of recuperation before she could undertake another major struggle. She had gone to the limit of her southward expansion if she wished to avoid war; under present conditions, further expansion could be successfully resisted.

So there was Spurgeon, of No. 8 Squadron RAAF, squinting and swearing at the north-east monsoon. Up till dawn No. 1 Squadron had carried out 15 sorties, losing two aircraft. 'If you see anything, shoot it,' had been Spurgeon's briefing, and there were these barges heading into a rain squall. On one of the strafing runs, Spurgeon's plane took a hit through the starboard wing. He decided to attack a larger ship that appeared to be on the beach. The Hudson carried four 250-pound bombs, two with instantaneous fuses, two with delayed action fuses. He let them all go. Not a good idea. The Hudson was rocked in the blast and sliced by shrapnel, hydraulics gone, instruments useless. As he describes it, Spurgeon headed for the Kota Bharu strip a mile and a half away and flung his heap of wreckage down on its guts at one end and finished up in the ditch at the other.

The main defending force on the beaches was the 8th Indian Brigade, established in concrete pillboxes behind barbed wire. Masanobu Tsuji later compiled an account of the landing from officers and observers. The naval escort bombarded the coastline and the pillboxes reacted with such heavy fire that the Japanese troops lying on the beach, half in and half out of the water, could not raise their heads. They burrowed forward like moles to the wire entanglements and threw grenades at the pillbox slits while wire-cutters worked their way through. The Indian line was broken in hand-to-hand fighting.

During the day the airfield was strafed by Japanese fighters. Late that afternoon, it was abandoned and soon after the army withdrew from the area. For the Japanese, it was one of the bloodiest actions of the campaign. Tsuji put losses from a total force of 5300 (this included field hospital and sanitation units) at 320 men killed and 538 wounded. Then he listed the spoils of victory: 27 field guns, 73 heavy and light machine guns, seven aircraft, 157 motor cars and trucks and 33 railway

goods wagons. But the Japanese gained much more than
matériel and a foothold on Malaya on the day. As the assault
craft were pushing onto the beaches, Lee Kuan Yew and the
rest of Singapore were being wakened by the sound of
Japanese bombs and were awakening to the shocked feeling of
vulnerability. Within two days of the landing at Kota Bharu,
the Allies had lost the equivalent of three bomber squadrons
and one fighter squadron in the air or on the ground.

False assumptions and false confidence are part of the
equipment of war. False confidence: the commander of the 2nd
Argyll and Sutherland Highlanders, Ian Stewart, reportedly
said to Brooke-Popham during the waiting time: 'I do hope,
sir, we are not getting too strong in Malaya because if so the
Japanese may never attempt a landing.' Stewart and his
battered battalion were the last to flee from the Malayan
mainland before the causeway was blown. Sir Shenton
Thomas, when informed of the landing at Kota Bharu,
allegedly said to the military man: 'Well, I suppose you'll shove
the little men off.' False assumptions: among the many, that
the British held air superiority. Brooke-Popham, he who did
not realise that a monsoon could be a screen for an invasion
task force, proceeded with the RAF scheme to expand the
network of aerodromes across Malaya. This would mean a
scattering of army resources northward up the peninsula from
Singapore to guard air facilities. Kota Bharu was the beginning
of the swift end of that strategy. And another deadly assumption: Admiral Tom Phillips, commander of Force Z, built
around two British navy capital ships, the battleship *Prince of
Wales*, newest of the fleet, though for Atlantic service, and the
ageing battle cruiser *Repulse*, did not think that properly
armed and well-fought ships had anything to fear from air
power, an assumption shared by Winston Churchill. Phillips
compounded this miscalculation with a second: that Force Z,

in a foray off the Malayan coast on December 10, was out of range of Japanese torpedo bombers, aircraft which did cause him some concern.

Poor Churchill. Two nights earlier he had gone sweetly to sleep after hearing the news of Pearl Harbor but early on the morning of the tenth he was given a message from Singapore, across the time zones. He had been in bed, opening his dispatch boxes before facing another day of crises. 'In all the war,' he later wrote in *The Grand Alliance*, 'I never received a more direct shock . . . As I turned and twisted in bed, the full horror of the news sunk in on me. There was no British or American capital ships in the Indian Ocean or the Pacific except the American survivors of Pearl Harbour . . . Over all this vast expanse of waters Japan was supreme, and we every-where were weak and naked.' Force Z had been destroyed, the *Prince of Wales* and the *Repulse* sunk by conventional and torpedo bombers.

The fate of Force Z provides rich opportunities for landborne admirals and armchair strategists. It was under pressure from Churchill that the ships had been sent 'to those waters [the Far East] to exercise that kind of vague menace which capital ships of the highest quality whose whereabouts is unknown can impose upon all hostile naval calculations'. The knowledge that they were steaming into Singapore certainly boosted morale there and lifted spirits in Australia where it was front-page news. On December 3, the *Argus* hailed the first reinforcements for the Royal Navy as ships which had become world famous for their exploits in other theatres of war. They were watched 'moving majestically' and greeted with the 'greatest jubilation'. Yet the new Singapore-based fleet was hardly formidable. They joined three small and outdated cruisers, four small and obsolete destroyers and a motley collection of small craft. To give Churchill his due, which is often not easy in the light of his war record when it concerns Australia, he had also managed to persuade the Admiralty, focused on the Atlantic and the Mediterranean, to send the aircraft carrier *Indomitable* east. However, the *Indomitable* ran aground in a training exercise.

Tom Phillips was a well-lit, sitting target for jealousy and backstabbing. The fact he had been promoted out of turn and jumped two steps in rank naturally annoyed his peers. Then he was small, inviting comments of 'small-man syndrome', 5 feet 2 inches. He had been in staff postings, rather than at sea. The Commander-in-Chief of the Mediterranean, Vice-Admiral Sir Andrew Cunningham, said: 'What on earth is Phillips going to the Far Eastern squadron for? He hardly knows one end of a ship from the other.' Vice-Admiral Sir James Somerville, Commander of H Force in Gibraltar, chimed in: 'I shudder to think of the Pocket Napoleon and his party . . . All the tricks to learn and no solid experience to fall back on. They ought to have someone who knows the stuff and can train the party properly on the way out.'

There were claims that Phillips may not have been quite up to date with the latest armaments and tactics. Churchill's chief of staff, General Hastings Ismay, 'Pug' to his friends, records in his memoirs an exchange between Phillips and Air Marshal Arthur 'Bomber' Harris: 'Bert Harris exploded, "One day, Tom, you will be standing on a box [small man] on your bridge, and your ship will be smashed to pieces by bombers and torpedo-aircraft. As she sinks, your last words will be 'That was a fucking great mine'."' On December 10, Phillips was last seen alive on the horizontal side of the bridge as the *Prince of Wales* rolled over. There is no doubt that by then he knew all about the vulnerability of capital ships to air power and had revised his opinion of the range of torpedo bombers.

Churchill said his idea of the role of Force Z had been that it would, after showing the flag in Singapore, 'disappear into the immense archipelago'. This, apparently, would constitute the 'vague menace' he had described earlier. It seems highly unlikely that the Japanese high command would have torn up, or even modified their plans because Force Z was somewhere out there. However, historian Alan Warren, while acknowledging that wherever Force Z had been deployed it might have been quickly sunk, suggests that events might have taken a different course if Phillips had taken a different course.

Phillips had flown from Singapore to Manila on December 4 for a conference with Admiral Thomas Hart, the Commander-in-Chief of the United States Asiatic Fleet. The conference quickly ended with the news that a large Japanese convoy was on its way from Camranh Bay, in Vietnam, towards the Gulf of Siam. Phillips flew back to a Force Z that was less than menacing. The *Prince of Wales* was undergoing running repairs in Singapore and because of Admiralty concerns about its exposed position at the base, the *Repulse* was slowly sailing towards Darwin on December 5. Force Z was still in the Singapore naval base on the morning of December 8 when Japanese landing craft were putting the invasion force on the beaches of Kota Bharu. Warren says that had Phillips been able to take Force Z to sea and sail north, its approach might have compelled the Japanese to divert the landing at Kota Bharu to Singora, in Thailand, where General Yamashita and the main Japanese force were landing. Perhaps Force Z could have intercepted the Kota Bharu fleet or engaged the convoys headed for Thailand. Yes, the pride of Force Z may still have finished on the ocean bottom, but, cold comfort though it would have been, as hunters and fighters rather than hunted and targets.

Phillips ordered Force Z to sail late on December 8. That morning the commander of the *Prince of Wales*, Captain Leach, was at the naval base swimming pool. He said to his son: 'I am going to do a couple of lengths now – you never know when it mightn't come in handy.' Premonition? British drollery? Leach went down with his ship.

For several reasons, including the limited range of the Buffaloes, the main strike fighters, RAF priorities and Phillips's insistence on maintaining radio silence at sea as far as possible, Force Z did not have the advantage of aerial reconnaissance or fighter protection. Force Z did not find the Japanese, but a Japanese submarine found it and Japanese aircraft out of Indo-China were above it on the morning of December 10.

Masanobu Tsuji describes the scene and the action:

Below them was a majestic sight – the superlative battleship *Prince of Wales* with the *Repulse* following and three destroyers forming a triangle around them, all steaming ahead in a single protective formation. At forty-five minutes past twelve the order 'attack' was given. As the bombers came down to a lower altitude, all the enemy warships opened up anti-aircraft fire. Each plane in succession dropped its heavy bombs, one of which beautifully hit the *Repulse* amidships, causing an eruption of brown fire. While the bombers were circling for a second attack the torpedo flight flew in, half going to port of the *Repulse* and the other half to starboard of the *Prince of Wales*. They came in low over the water and launched their torpedoes. Several colossal columns of water rose beside both battleships, showing that we were hitting the mark.

During the attack and for an hour after, an unexplained radio silence was maintained. Eleven Buffaloes were scrambled but when they arrived over the scene it was to see the *Prince of Wales* sink and hundreds of survivors struggling in the oil-covered water and being picked up by the destroyers. The comments of the officer commanding the Buffaloes, Flight Lieutenant T. A. Vigors, were recorded in an official dispatch: 'I have seen a show of spirit in this war over Dunkirk during the "Battle of Britain", and in the London night raids, but never before have I seen anything comparable with what I saw yesterday . . . After an hour, lack of petrol forced me to leave, but during that hour I had seen many men in dire danger waving, cheering, and joking as if they were holiday-makers at Brighton waving at a low-flying craft. It shook me, for there was something above human nature.' But Warren says more cynical commentators have suggested that the men in the water were waving their fists in fury at the late-arriving RAF fighters.

Tsuji, ever anxious to turn attention away from the dark side, claims that the next day a bomber unit flew over the scene of the battle. The waves undulated tranquilly and 'a large bouquet of flowers was dropped on the spot where . . . British seamen who had fought so bravely were now sleeping quietly'.

SPUD SPURGEON HAD a lifetime love affair with some aircraft. At career's end he was in charge of the front-line F-111. He trained in Demons, the sexiest aircraft he'd ever flown. He despised others, in particular the Brewster Buffalo, 'a blunt-nosed, dismissed Fleet Air Arm aeroplane from the States, useless, bloody useless'. He was simply bewildered by the Vildebeeste, a biplane from a bygone age. But the Hudson? 'Beautiful. It's an airliner, for Pete's sake. It had all the nice things about it. It was clean and tidy inside. In Singapore we even had carpet on the floor. But it was a beautiful aeroplane to fly. It had tons of power though it could do some peculiar things if you weren't careful. It has a nasty spin, apparently.'

The Hudson's spin would not be Spurgeon's problem. He and his fellow pilots flying reconnaissance off Malaya had a feeling that the Japanese might have something special out there. Brooke-Popham didn't. Japanese aircraft were not highly efficient, Brooke-Popham thought, not as good as the Buffalo, and the Japanese weren't 'airminded'.

As it happens, the Japanese had good tutors in the development of air power. In 1920 the Imperial Japanese Navy asked Britain for help. It was a prospect to delight arms dealers, who saw millions of yen, and diplomats, who saw it as a chance to build influence. As the British Military Attaché General Woodruffe said: 'The power who commands the aerial future of Japan opens for herself an undreamed-of vista of strategic possibilities in the Pacific Ocean and in Eastern Asia.' But couldn't there be dangers in helping build Japan as an air power? Here the British superiority complex kicked in. Japan would not be able to progress without help; the Japanese, with poor reflexes and sense of balance and its 'national psychology, a temperament that gets easily "rattled" in the face of an emergency, would most likely not become excellent pilots'. Still, there were wise heads in the Admiralty, and the British Government agreed only to an 'unofficial' mission. This was more than enough for the Japanese: 19 officers and nine warrant officers, led by Colonel William Forbes-Sempill, the Master of Sempill, one of the most influential figures in British aviation. The Japanese were instructed in basic flying, advanced deck-landing, photography, drawing and design, engine maintenance, armament and medical techniques and the development of an airbase. The mission carried gifts, as listed by John Ferris, strategic analyst and Professor of History at the University of Calgary: an almost complete inventory of the equipment of British aviation. British firms could tender their most modern equipment, so long as they did not refer to

RAF specifications. Japanese firms procured patent rights to produce much of the kit in Japan.

As the unofficial mission was leaving, a grateful Imperial Japanese Navy Air Force hosted a dinner. The commander, Rear Admiral Tajiri, proposed the toast: 'You departing members, to whose competent efforts we are so much indebted for this great development, and you dear pals, whose kindness has so richly earned our sincere friendly love and esteem, we are sorry to say good-bye to you.'

ON JANUARY 24, 1942 Spurgeon was in the air again and flying out of Singapore on a reconnaissance mission with another Hudson. They were searching for an invasion fleet they suspected to be heading for a landing halfway down the Malayan coast. They ran into Japanese fighter cover. One came out of the cloud. It was a deep royal blue colour, but Spurgeon didn't see much of it. It would attack from behind, break off and attack again. Spurgeon's plane was skimming on top of overnight mist, too shallow to dive into for cover. The co-pilot had been hit badly by the opening burst and the gunner was killed on the third or fourth pass. The wireless operator was dead too. The starboard engine was on fire. The other Hudson had headed south to try to outrun the fighters. 'His rear gunner saw me on fire. The dear old fella turned back to look for me. He got clobbered too.' The Hudsons had run into that something special: Zeroes.

Spurgeon put the crippled Hudson down on the sea. There was only a slight swell running. He and the wounded co-pilot got clear and wearing Mae Wests drifted through the day. During the night the co-pilot died. As the dawn light strength-ened, Spurgeon saw two small islands and swam to the closest. His bare feet were slashed by coral as he waded ashore. He spent two nights alone on the north coast and during the second one, heard Japanese ships go past. The next day he walked across the island and found a small village of Chinese charcoal-makers who gave him food and shelter and bandaged his feet. He was taken to the mainland in a *prau* and began walking south along the coastline. Crossing a road he was caught. 'Bloody Japs on bicycles, didn't hear them.' The first Japanese Spurgeon spoke with had a cultured American accent. He was a graduate of Columbia who had been visiting his parents in Japan and to his dismay found himself one of the troops of God. Spurgeon was taken to Kluang, on the west coast to be interrogated by a general. What did he know about Darwin? Nothing, nothing about bloody Darwin at all. He got clobbered on the ear. What did he know about America's Clark air base in the Philippines? Never been there. Another clobber. After the interrogation he was taken to Pudu prison in Kuala Lumpur. There was no room in the small car. He was put on the running board, handcuffed around the door post. So, precariously, he began his passing phase.

CHAPTER 9

Triumph of the two-pounders

There were small jungle sounds. Drops of old rain worked their way down the canopy. Here the Trunk Road passed through a cutting, 4 metres high and 36 metres long. Here Lieutenant Harry Head's 12 Platoon had hidden itself. Two Bren-gunners and three men with a pile of hand grenades were in the main position. The two other platoons of B Company of Australia's 2/30th Battalion were in invisible formation behind. Their silence was broken only by whispers. This was a classic ambush site. An enemy, growing in confidence every kilometre and every day, was moving down Malaya towards Fortress Singapore. For nearly 50 kilometres, since the town of Tampin, they had met no resistance. This was not unusual but this time the withdrawal of Allied forces was planned and synchronised. The nicely flat road here ran west–east. There was a small wooden bridge over the Gemencheh River. It had been mined. The road then curved gently to the left. There was no indication that tall jungle was about to crowd along the road, which then ran straight for a while.

Shortly before 4 pm, B Company commander Captain Desmond Duffy got word from an observer that a party of eight Japanese soldiers on bicycles had rounded the bend and were approaching the bridge. Following them was a solid column of cyclists, five or six abreast. They could have been on a Sunday ride, laughing and chattering, steel helmets slung on their backs, rifles strapped to the cycles. They were pedalling to their deaths.

It was January 14, 1942 and 'the moment,' Gordon Bennett wrote in his diary, 'for which the AIF in Malaya has been waiting. Will we stop the Japanese?' The Australians were going into action on the ground.

Since December 8, the day when Spud Spurgeon had strafed the Japanese invaders off Malaya's Kota Bharu beach and when the Japanese had also landed at Thailand's Singora and Patani, the Japanese advance down the Malayan peninsula had been relentless. Despite some instances of brave defence, the pattern had been one of defeat, retreat and then another defeat and then another retreat. Though sometimes there was retreat for its own sake. Perhaps there had been the chance to prevent the momentum building, right at the start, to halt the charging bull with Operation Matador.

The western third of Malaya was the most developed, with the main north–south road and rail communications with Thailand. Tempting roads giving access to this network ran from the Thai coastal towns on the Kra Isthmus, Patani and Singora. Both had airfields and Singora had a handy harbour. Percival, during his earlier tour in Singapore had warned of the danger of an attack on Singapore through the back door and it shouldn't take a general very long to run his finger down a map from the Thai ports, down to Butterworth air base, down through the Malayan capital, Kuala Lumpur, down and down the main roads to the causeway and Singapore and then look very worried. Major General Lionel Bond, a predecessor of Percival as General Office Commanding Malaya, and Air Chief Marshal Sir Robert Brooke-Popham, one of the passing parade of Commanders-in-Chief Far East, both did. The plan they put to the Chiefs of Staff was that, as soon as it was clear that Japan was going to begin its thrust on Malaya, there should be a pre-emptive strike by the British forces into Thailand to meet and repel the invasion. Both sides were aware of the potential of Singora: British and Japanese officers in plain clothes on reconnoitring expeditions had crossed paths there. The main Japanese force headed towards Singora and Patani for a planned landing on December 8. Had Operation Matador been put into action and had the RAF managed to deliver on its promised figure of damaging 40 per cent of the attacking force (not terribly likely), then history might well have been different. General Yamashita, determined to set an example, had his command ship *Ryujo Maru* positioned in the fleet at Singora so he could share the fate of the front-line troops.

Matador would be a matter of timing. At first the Chiefs of Staff said that Brooke-Popham would have to get authority from London before launching Matador. Then, on December 5, he was told he could give the signal himself if '(a) you have good information that a Japanese expedition is advancing with the apparent intention of landing on the Kra Isthmus or (b) the Japanese violated any other part of Thailand'. Brooke-Popham's Chief of Staff observed: 'They've now made you responsible for declaring war.' This was a heavy burden for a man who, reportedly, had a habit of falling asleep in conferences and of whom the acerbic Duff Cooper said he 'sometimes seems on the verge of nervous collapse'. So Brooke-Popham was bound to be in two minds, not the best of positions for a commander-in-chief. Life was also difficult for the leaders and soldiers of Major General Murray-Lyon's 11th Indian Division, part of the III Indian Corps commanded by Percival's rival, General Heath. If Matador went ahead, they would have to dash across the Thai border and fight on the beaches; if not, they had to set up a defensive line at the Malay town of Jitra, on the main road close to the Thai border, to stop a Japanese thrust from Singora, and, as well, send a detachment to an objective known as the Ledge, about 50 kilometres into Thailand, to block the road from Patani.

When the Japanese fleet was spotted 110 kilometres from Singora, it was not flying flags saying 'Singora or bust'. Brooke-Popham, worried that the devious Japanese might be trying to trick him into moving first, dithered. Matador ran out of time. The plan to stop a Japanese advance at the Ledge looked reasonable on paper too. There the road was carved for 10 kilometres along a hillside above the Patani River. Explosives could make it impassable to vehicles (though how effective this would be is doubtful: the Allies were yet to find out about the efficiency of the Japanese engineers or the use of bicycles by foot soldiers). But defence at the Ledge also remained marks on a map. Because of a delay in the transmission of orders, something which became routine in the Malaya campaign, the 3/16th Punjabis arrived within 10 kilometres of the Ledge on December 10. The Japanese had occupied the Ledge the day before, and the Punjabis had only advanced 600 metres closer when they were attacked by Japanese soldiers supported by tanks.

Things went wrong on the road from Singora too. After the first clash, the Japanese found a blood-smeared map in a wrecked armoured car. According to Masanobu Tsuji, the Japanese did not have one accurate map of the area. Now they did, and marked in pencil on this one were the details of the 11th Indian Division's defensive positions at Jitra. Heath wrote of the Japanese commander's 'almost uncanny sense of directing his attacks against the most profitable targets' there.

But if Tsuji is to be believed (and his versions should sometimes be taken with a sip of saki) the main factor in the rout at

Jitra was the misjudgment of young Second Lieutenant Oto, 'a handsome youth of rather feminine appearance'. Three brigades of the 11th Indian Division were deployed at the Jitra line; probing towards them was a detachment of a mere two battalions and 10 tanks, led by Lieutenant Colonel Saeki and accompanied by Tsuji, driving in a captured black car. The detachment dashed south, brushing aside opposition. At one stage, Tsuji related, they came upon the 'mystery' of 10 guns, their muzzles pointing north, but without crews. 'Probably between two and three thousand enemy troops had taken shelter from the rain under the rubber trees on both sides of the road, and through this slight negligence they suffered a crushing defeat which by degrees they seemed to understand.' Onward the Japanese pushed, the officers in the black car beating off attackers with revolver fire and stopping at bridges to sever with their swords wires to demolition charges.

Eventually they stopped at a demolished bridge where Oto reported the results of his patrol into enemy lines. His coat was bloodstained. He had killed a sentry. The line of advance was not difficult, he said. There were gaps in the wire entanglement and the enemy troops were not in position. A night attack would be possible. It was decided that Oto would lead it. However, the resistance was tougher than anticipated and after a time Tsuji saw coming towards him an officer smeared with mud and blood, wounded in the shoulder and weeping. It was Oto. 'Staff officer, sir,' he said, 'it is inexcusable. Oto has made a mistake in his estimate of the enemy's strength.' Tsuji consoled him, gave him a piece of chocolate and told him the battle could be won. Oto died later of gangrene in a hospital in Saigon, but the battle was indeed won and the defenders retreated.

On December 8, the day the Japanese had landed, Brooke-Popham had issued a pre-prepared Order of the Day, saying:

'We are ready. We have had plenty of warning and our preparations are made and tested . . . Our defences are strong and our weapons efficient . . . We see before us a Japan drained for years by the exhausting claims of her wanton onslaught on China.' In a few days he had been proven comprehensively wrong on all claims.

This was Tsuji's analysis of the battle of Jitra:

If we had judged this well-fortified position correctly, launched a full-scale attack with the whole strength of the division, and become locked in the struggle, it would have taken more than ten days to break through, and we would have had to be prepared for over a thousand casualties. [The Japanese suffered 110.] The much bragged about Jitra line, which was to have been defended by a division for three months, was penetrated in about 15 hours by barely five hundred men. If the handsome, pitiful Second Lieutenant Oto had not reported wrongly, even the courageous commander of the Saeki Detachment would not have been expected to make such a reckless attack.

This was Kinvig's observation:

In this anti-climactic manner, without a major action or his troops being driven from their lines by the Japanese main force, Percival lost what was perhaps the crucial land battle of the Malayan campaign. The three brigades of 11th Indian Division had been defeated by what was little more than an impetuous probing attack by the Japanese advance guard . . . The first, decisive moral victory had gone to the Japanese . . . The true, if undramatic explanation for the disaster of Jitra was that the troops did not have the training, the weapons or the time to put up a respectable defence, nor was it a good position at which to try to mount one.

Tsuji, in calmer mode, reflected that the Jitra advance would not even be considered commonsense; actual conditions on the battlefield determined hazardous issues; the Japanese success was due to the intangible belief in victory resulting from scores of insubstantial factors. However, what Tsuji referred to as a 'glorious exploit', was in fact a tactic decided upon by General Yamashita: *kirimoni sakusen*, or driving charge. Faced with opposing forces with an estimated two-to-one numerical advantage, Yamashita wanted the campaign over with stunning speed. Ordering *kirimoni sakusen*, this is what one battalion commander said: 'Do not stop but charge forward no matter what happens and do not respond to fire from behind.'

The Japanese surged and pedalled down the peninsula, outflanking the defenders by land and water. The island of Penang, also hollowly described as a fortress, was abandoned without a fight, the Europeans evacuated while the Asians were left to the mercies of the Japanese. On January 7 at Slim River, about halfway down the peninsula, another *kirimomi sakusen*: a night attack led by tanks crushed and crashed through line after line of defence. It was six hours of chaos and confusion, death and disaster. The Japanese received a bonanza of captured equipment and supplies. Tsuji would later say 1200 had surrendered and he erroneously reported the death in battle of Gordon Bennett, who was safe well to the south. According to Tsuji, Slim River had been no planned operation, but the result of daring by young tank commanders, in particular Second Lieutenant Sadanobu Watanabe. Watanabe leapt from his tank 'while enemy bullets fall around him like rain' to cut a demolition wire with his sabre; wounded, at the next bridge he fired with a machine gun to prevent demolition. With his usual understatement, Tsuji says Watanabe carried out his duties like a war god.

After the war, Brigadier Ian Stewart of the Argylls, commander of the 12th Indian Brigade, pondered what went wrong. Stewart had believed the threat of tank attack was exaggerated, an attitude which was strangely infectious among the Allied leaders. In his own dispatches Stewart wrote: 'The moral effect of meeting tanks for the first time was too much for the anti-tank gunners and some infantry.' He said in a letter to the British official historian: 'I am rightly criticised for the location of Brigade Headquarters, and for not using the Field Artillery in an anti-tank role . . . It is no excuse, but I had never taken part in an exercise embodying a coordinated anti-tank defence or this type of attack. The use of tanks on a road at night [was] a surprise.'

But then most things about the Japanese – their skill as pilots, the quality of their aircraft, the abilities of the foot soldiers – had come as an unwelcome surprise. On December 23, 15 days after the landings, Percival made this reassessment:

It is now clear that we were faced by an enemy who had made a special study of bush warfare on a grand scale and whose troops had been specially trained in those tactics. He relied in the main on outflanking movements and on infiltration by small parties into and behind our lines. For support of his forward troops he relied on the mortar and the infantry gun rather than on longer range weapons. His snipers operated from trees. He exploited the use of fireworks. For mobility he made a wise use of civilian bicycles seized in the country. His tanks he had up to date operated mainly on the roads. His infantry had displayed an ability to cross obstacles – rivers, swamps, jungles, etc – more rapidly than had previously been thought possible. Finally, speed was obviously of vital importance to him and he was prepared to press his attacks without elaborate preparations.

This knowledge was not strength. On January 10, the rich prize of Kuala Lumpur was in Japanese reach. Australian war correspondent Ian Morrison reported the panicked exodus.

All Saturday and Sunday, all day and all night, the great withdrawal continued. An interminable convoy, composed of all manner of vehicles, began to roll south; large lorries filled with British troops so dog-tired they slept in spite of bumps and jolts; civilian motor cars commandeered by the military and hastily camouflaged by being spattered with mud; lorries bearing the names of half the rubber estates in Malaya; dispatch riders darting in and out of the traffic on their motor-bicycles; eleven steam rollers . . . which had steamed all the way down from Kedah and Perak; two fire engines also making their way south; enormous tin-dredges towed by diesel tractors . . .; low trollies towing sticks of heavy aerial bombs saved from the northern airfields for further use; private motor cars from Austins to Rolls Royces, carrying Local Defence Volunteers, ARP wardens, police officials; camouflaged staff cars through whose windows one caught a glimpse of red tabs and hatbands . . .

In the villages and towns along the route Malays and Chinese and Indians stood in silent little groups . . . Neither pleasure nor malice nor sympathy were to be seen in their impassive countenances . . . War was a phenomenon completely strange to these pacific, indolent, happy people. And now they saw the white tuans, who had always been in Malaya since they could first remember, heading south . . .

Gordon Bennett was about to get what he wished for, a starring role, a chance to show what proper leadership and Australian diggers could do. The line was to be held in the southernmost mainland state, Johore. Bennett had under his command, besides the 8th Division of the AIF, the British forces in north-west Johore, designated Westforce. Bennett had full confidence in himself, which was never a problem. He was also confident that he had trained the Australians for the tropics and for the jungle. They had been touted by the press on their arrival as 'a huge force of matchless Australians, the peerless Anzacs', 'the finest shock troops in the world'. Apart from ensuring that troops did go out in the midday sun on exercises, Bennett tried imaginative and unconventional training methods. Through forest wardens, the Australians were put in touch with the Sakai, a Malayan aboriginal tribe who lived deep in the forest. Bennett arranged for small parties to spend short periods with the Sakai, learning what they could about the jungle.

On January 11, John Curtin cabled Winston Churchill:

It is naturally disturbing to learn that the Japanese have been able to overrun the whole of Malaya except Johore . . . It is observed that the 8th Australian Division is to be given the task of fighting the decisive battle . . . I urge you that nothing be left undone to reinforce Malaya to the greatest degree possible in accordance with my earlier representations and your intentions. I am particularly concerned in regard to air strength.

Churchill, in unrepentant mode, waved his hand at the loss of Malaya. 'I do not see,' he said in reply, 'how anyone could expect Malaya to be defended once the Japanese obtained the command of the sea and while we are fighting for our lives against Germany and Italy.' He said his anxiety had been that the fighting of rearguard actions down the peninsula had dissipated the force required for a prolonged defence of Singapore. 'Some [for "some" read Churchill] may think it would have been better to come back quicker with less loss.'

The troops could have done that, of course, and withdrawn to the island. The Japanese would then have cut off the water supply, which comes from Johore, and, with their command of the air, at leisure softened up the troops and what pathetic defences there were before invading.

Fortunately, the men who were to strike the first blow in this 'decisive' battle were unaware of these depressing, hindsight assessments. The men along the road to Gemas, the 2/30th Battalion, had faith in Bennett. They had even more faith in their commander, Lieutenant Colonel Frederick ('Black Jack') Galleghan, a ferocious disciplinarian. The battalion history has one man saying at the ambush site: 'Black Jack may be an old –, but I wouldn't swap him now for the Duke of Wellington.'

Kevin Ward was in the battalion's A Company. At headquarters, the company commanders drew lots to be the ambush detachment. B Company won. 'Lucky buggers,' Ward thought. B Company went forward to the site, about 5 kilometres along the road. D Company took position on the left of the road and C Company on the right. A Company was in the centre, artillery pieces among them.

If you could hover in the hush above the ambush site, you would find causes for concern. For one thing, B Company seems dangerously isolated. They could easily be outflanked and surrounded by alerted Japanese, with relief kilometres away. And then there is that glint along the roadside: the signal wires to the artillery command post and to battalion headquarters are exposed. Nor would you be comfortable if you could overhear a conversation between Galleghan and two Australian anti-tank gun commanders, Sergeant Ken Harrison and Sergeant Charlie Parsons. Galleghan tells them he does not believe tanks will be used against his men and that he regards the anti-tank detachment as little more than an encumbrance and hindrance to his plans. Permission is grudgingly given for them to take up their gun positions, Harrison will later record, but when a third anti-tank gun arrives, it is sent back as not required. This 12 days after the Japanese tanks had caused such deadly havoc at Slim River. News travels slowly in Malaya.

KEVIN WARD CAN'T recall hearing the sounds of the ambush. He doesn't know why this is so. Distance from the cutting? Thinking back all those decades? Captain Duffy had let one column of cyclists pass through towards the rear of the ambush. Another 40 or 50 cyclists were on the bridge. He gave the signal to the engineer who blew the super charge of gelignite and started the carnage: bodies and bicycles in the air and from the jungle a scythe of rifle and machine-gun bullets, a shower of grenades. When the crescendo died to occasional exchanges of rifle fire and a grenade blast now and then, Duffy saw from his observation post a grim sight, the entire 275 metres of road thickly covered with dead and dying men. It could have been worse for the Japanese. Men and motor transports had banked up behind the blown bridge, and Australian artillery fire was to have been brought down on them. The first group of Japanese who had been allowed to cross the bridge and ride down the cutting had spotted and cut both the artillery and headquarters signal wires.

Galleghan, Ward and the rest could only wait and worry.

The elements of B Company began to fall back, meeting isolated Japanese parties. Now there was no firing from the cover of jungle and no element of surprise. Harry Head and several men fought bayonet to bayonet with Japanese soldiers, parrying and stabbing. It was the warfare of the ancients. Private Silvester was badly wounded in a grenade blast. Head and Private Ray Brown, temporarily cut off round a bend, found two Japanese officers and three soldiers setting up a 4-inch mortar on the road. Brown was battered and stabbed to the ground by the three soldiers; Head was confronted by one officer with a sword, shot him with his last bullet, was wounded by the other officer and then hit in the leg by a grenade fragment. Other members of 11 Platoon rounded the bend and killed the surviving attackers. Along jungle tracks, sometimes hacking paths, carrying their wounded, fighting occasionally, they made their way through the night to the battalion formation.

THE JAPANESE ENGINEERS rebuilt the Gemencheh bridge in six hours and battalion patrols were involved in forward clashes through that night as the Japanese moved up in strength. Though Galleghan did not know it at the time, between 2000 and 2500 more Japanese troops were massing in the vicinity of the bridge. He had 800 men. He also had, against his desires and judgment, two two-pounder guns from the 2/4th Anti-Tank Regiment. Which was just as well.

On the morning of January 15 there was a rumble from a cutting ahead of the battalion position and a 12-ton tank came slowly round the bend, stopping short of a roadblock. Was Black Jack Galleghan just a touch embarrassed and apologetic? The gun crews were using their two-pounders, small pieces but with fierce muzzle velocity, for the first time. Harrison described his mate and himself as amateurs. They were facing the 5th Japanese Division, which had been on bitter active service in China from 1937 to 1941. Both crews fired at the reconnaissance tank without effect. Just before nine o'clock, a light tank came round the bend and a medium tank ranged up beside it. 'This time there was no mistake,' Harrison wrote. 'Charlie stopped the medium tank with his first shot and our second shell struck the light tank. It was stirring to watch the sheet of flame, and the turret top fly open as the crew attempted to escape from their blazing metal coffin.' Despite taking casualties, the gun crews destroyed six tanks and at the end of the day had four shells left.

B Company and its wounded returned successful; the tanks had been defeated. The battalion was now under dive bomber attack. No trenches had been dug so as not to give notice of the battalion's presence and the ambush. Men lay flat on the ground, protected by hope. The battalion sent out fighting patrols which battled with men and tanks in the rubber. Then D Company advanced. Sergeant Stan Arneil, who had led a party through the darkness the night before in an attempt to find out what had happened to B Company, and who had fought a scrambling fight to the light of muzzle flashes, described this set piece.

> At fifteen minutes to one o'clock a great cry went up from the platoon on my left, and there on the flank was Don Company advancing in open formation across the clearing. It was magnificent to see them, each man in place, with his rifle held high across his body, walking as if on a training exercise . . . We had prepared for this for two years, and as we others watched we yelled and roared with excitement to see Don Company doing its job so well.

'Doing its job so well . . .' Young men stepping out to a silent drumbeat. What were they thinking as they went with bayonets gleaming? They were marching together towards the possibility of that most solitary of human actions, dying. The Japanese cyclists the day before were surprised by death. D Company knew it was waiting. They crested young rubber trees and began the messy business of war. The commanding officer, Captain Melville, was wounded. On the left flank 16 and 17 platoons were now in thick lalang grass and several men fell to machine-gun fire. On the right there was strong opposition to 18 Platoon. 'When the right section was kept down by heavy fire,' the battalion history records, 'Private Beatty made a gallant effort to reach the enemy light machine gun, which was about sixty yards in front, holding them up, but in running across the open alone, he was killed about 20 yards from the enemy gun.' The platoon fell back after coming under fire from six or eight tanks among the rubber.

D Company pushed about three hundred yards into enemy lines and when it withdrew it left Japanese casualties estimated to be at least 100. Its own casualties were 'comparatively light': five known killed, six missing and 17 wounded. There was not much to show for the action. The battalion history, however, sums up the whole operation with perhaps too much restraint: 'Thus ended the first action against the Japanese, who in this area were now, temporarily at least, halted in their triumphant and incautious southwards march.'

Bravery was demonstrated and pride built at a bloody price. Decades later Kevin Ward, who endured the Thai–Burma railway and Hellfire Pass, described those two January days as 'our glory' and Tsuji who customarily praises only the Japanese, wrote: 'The 8th Australian Division, which had newly arrived on the battlefield, relying on the advantage of its position, fought with a bravery we had not previously seen.'

IN SINGAPORE THERE was elation. Mafeking had been relieved; or at least there was reason to believe that the tide of battle had turned with, an excited commentator said on radio, 'the AIF as our seawall against the vicious flood'. However, a disastrous wave was building at Muar, on the coast at the western end of Westforce's defensive line. While Gemas was an important intersection of the Trunk Road and railways, the coastal road from Malacca had links to the Trunk Road to the south of Gemas.

Throughout his career, 'Ginger' Bennett came under fire for his temperament, his arrogance, his ambition and his inability often to have a good, working relationship with superiors, peers or subordinates. But now, with the Muar battle, it was his generalship that was to be judged and found wanting. There are two basic issues: first, his assessment of the threat to the left flank; second, his tactics to meet it. Percival, in his postwar explanation of why he had nothing to apologise for, said: 'I have the impression that Gordon Bennett's attention was concentrated on what he considered his main front and that he looked upon the Muar section rather as a flank from which no real danger was likely to develop.' Defence academic A. B. Lodge, author of *The Fall of General Gordon Bennett*, is the most savage and succinct: 'He had misread enemy intentions, made an elementary error in disposing of the 45th Brigade, and was slow to recognise the full impact of the crossing of the river. Admittedly his task was made much harder by incomplete and sometimes faulty intelligence, poor troops, and the absence of an adequate reserve, but it was his inadequacies as a commander which most directly led to the defeat.'

On January 14, the day the Australian 2/30th had ambushed elements of the 5th Japanese Division on the Trunk Road, detachments of the elite Japanese Imperial Guards had walked unchallenged into the coastal centre, Malacca. From Malacca it was a short, easy passage to Muar, where Bennett had positioned the 45th Indian Brigade. Of this brigade, Percival later wrote: 'The troops were very young, unseasoned and undertrained, and straight off the ship after their first experience of the sea. Such training as the brigade had done had been for warfare in the open spaces of the Middle East, which had been its intended destination until war with Japan broke out. Only a short time before it left for Malaya its divisional commander had expressed his opinion that it was unfit for service overseas.' Colonel James Thyer, Bennett's assistant, visited the brigade in its defence lines at Muar. He watched aghast as an officer coached a soldier in the correct handling of a rifle in firing position.

Did Bennett know just how unsuited the 45th Brigade was for combat? Probably, though this is not certain, given the parlous state of communications. Did he know which enemy force they would face, and its quality? No. Percival himself only found out from the so-called intelligence services two days after the event that it was the Imperial Guards Division that had overrun Muar. Did Bennett have to use the 45th? Answer that with another question: what option did he have? Most other units had been through the mincer and he had been pressing unsuccessfully for the transfer of the 22nd Australian Brigade from the east coast. Should he have used them the way he did? This is where the critics attack. For a start, he ordered two companies from each forward battalion to be positioned on the north bank of the Muar River. Wigmore, the official historian, said this no doubt reflected Bennett's policy of 'aggressive defence' and his enthusiasm for ambushing the enemy, but it was done at the expense of the forward line south of the river. The commander of Australia's 2/19th Battalion, Charles Anderson, Victoria Cross-winning hero of the

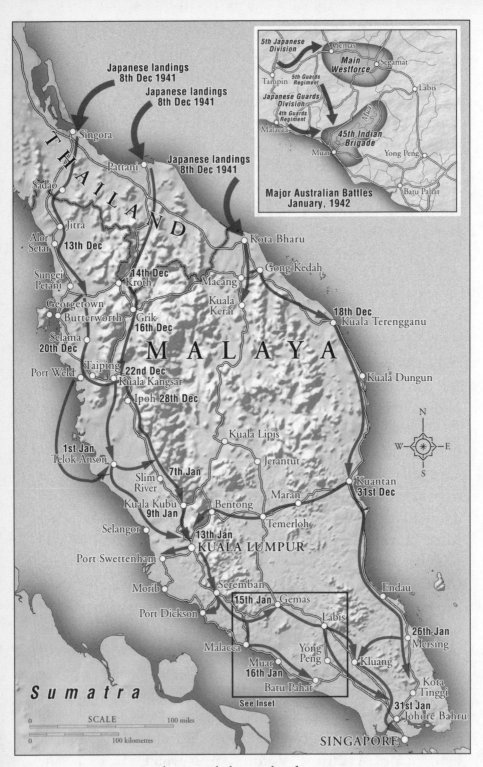

**Japanese landings
8th Dec 1941**

**Japanese landings
8th Dec 1941**

**Japanese landings
8th Dec 1941**

THAILAND

Singora

Pattani

Sadao

Jitra
Alor
Setar **13th Dec**

Sungei **14th Dec**
Petani Kroth

Georgetown
Butterworth Grik
Selama **16th Dec**
20th Dec
Port Weld Taiping **22nd Dec**
Kuala Kangsar
Ipoh **28th Dec**

Macang

Gong Kedah

Kota Bharu

Kuala
Kerai

MALAYA

18th Dec
Kuala Terengganu

Kuala Dungun

Kuala Lipis

Jerantut

1st Jan
Telok Anson

Slim **7th Jan**
River

Kuala Kubu
9th Jan

Bentong

Maran

Kuantan
31st Dec

N
W E
S

Selangor

Port Swettenham

Morib

13th Jan
KUALA LUMPUR

Temerloh

Seremban

15th Jan Gemas

Endau

Port Dickson

Malacca

Muar
16th Jan
Batu Pahat

Labis

Yong
Peng

Kluang

26th Jan
Mersing

Kota
Tinggi

31st Jan
Johore Bahru

See Inset

Sumatra

SCALE
0   100 miles
0   100 kilometres

SINGAPORE

**Major Australian Battles
January, 1942** (inset)

*5th Japanese
Division*   Gemas
              Main
              Westforce   Segamat
Tampin *5th Guards
        Regiment*   Labis
*Japanese Guards
Division*
        *4th Guards
        Regiment*
Malacca   45th Indian
                     Brigade
        Muar   Yong Peng

                              Batu Pahat

Malaya and the path of conquest

fighting withdrawal, who took over the 45th Brigade on the injury of its commander, said: 'The use of the 45th Brigade was a crime. Anyone who had seen the troops must have realised they were totally untrained for the task and then Gordon Bennett's disposition of them compounded the offence. The only possibility of a faint chance of effectiveness was to keep them in tight formation or in entrenchments.' Lodge argues that by allotting the Muar area to the inexperienced 45th Brigade and then disposing it as he did, Bennett had sown the seeds for defeat in Johore.

Bennett ordered that there be no withdrawal from Muar, another example of a general's bravery from a safe distance. It was one thing for Don Company of the 2/30th to advance to the cheers of their mates; it was something else to be the forward battalions of the 45th, isolated and unsure of themselves, waiting for the Japanese with a river at their backs and no bridge in the vicinity to retreat over, the main crossing being by ferry. At least their agony did not last long. They were overwhelmed, and the river, supposedly a barrier to the Japanese, wasn't. The Japanese took small boats from rice fields on the northern side and crossed to the large boats moored on the southern bank. They had the transport they needed. From Muar, a road ran through Bakri, headquarters of the 45th Brigade, to Yong Peng on the Trunk Road. The Imperial Guards commander, General Nishimura, must have expected that his forces, full of momentum, would make a quick thrust along this route. However, Anderson's men, though caught in a pincer, made a determined stand near Bakri and then a fighting withdrawal. Tsuji described the prolonged action as a desperate fight and a war of extermination.

Playing a central role once more were the crews of the 4th Anti-Tank Regiment. And once more the infantry's commanding officer showed ignorance of Japanese tactics. Lieutenant

Bill McCure, in charge of the four anti-tank guns, asked Lieutenant Colonel John Robertson, of the 2/29th, where the guns should be placed in the convoy. Robertson responded: 'For all I care, Mr McCure, you can take them back to base.' This exchange was recorded by Ken Harrison, veteran of the battle of Gemas. Harrison would remain puzzled by Robertson's attitude, as he had been by Galleghan's. There had been long-running antipathy between Robertson and McCure. But hadn't Robertson heard about the tanks at Slim River? Or at Gemas?

Early on the morning of January 18, Japanese tanks moved down the road towards Bakri. Two of the two-pounders were waiting at each end of a cutting; eight tanks were destroyed. Later a motorcycle rider took Robertson on pillion for a conference at brigade headquarters. On the way back they were ambushed. The badly wounded rider got back to the lines and soldiers in a Bren-gun carrier went out and brought back the wounded Robertson. As he lay dying Robertson said to McCure: 'Bill, I was wrong, terribly wrong. But for you and the guns not one of my boys would be alive now.'

That night the Japanese were at close quarters. Jim Tangie was guarding one of the two-pounder guns when a figure loomed in the darkness. Tangie challenged. 'Halt. Who's there?' The reply was 'Yimmy'. Tangie fired immediately and killed the Japanese private who had been near enough earlier, Harrison reasoned, to hear the gun crew call Tangie 'Jimmy'. Later, in the uneasy hush, a harsh voice shouted from the jungle: 'Yoh die, yoh die tomorroh.' And from the Australian ranks came a response: 'Get stuffed, you yellow bastard.' Many did die in the days that followed, Japanese, Australians and Indians. On January 19, two companies from Anderson's jungle-skilled 2/19th pincered an attacking Japanese force on a ridge. In a bayonet charge and hand-to-hand fighting, the Japanese were routed. The body count of the enemy was 140; 10 Australians died. It was as brutal and ruthless as battle gets. Charles (Chick) Warden, then a 17-year-old infantryman with the 2/19th, later recorded: 'There were some nasty little incidents involving some of B Company coming up behind us doing a body count and gathering up automatic weapons. Some of the assumed to be dead that we had passed suddenly came to life and started throwing grenades around and the enemy wounded wanted to make their last fanatical shot.' Warden's company then took up a defensive position in a rubber plantation. 'While in this position we were told that as we were on the defensive we were not in a situation to take any prisoners and due to past recent experience we were to leave no wounded. Approach to any assumed dead or wounded enemy was to be done with a degree of caution and the bayonet was to be used. In brief the order was: take no prisoners, leave no wounded.' Warden's belief was the orders had come from Anderson. He also believed that this Australian tactic played a role in the coming massacre at Parit Sulong.

The next day Anderson ordered a withdrawal along the road towards Yong Peng. They battered and bayoneted their way through roadblocks. At one, where a quick breakthrough was essential, Anderson instructed Lieutenant Frank Beverley, commander of the 2/19th's A Company, on what he wanted for a spirited assault. So the company charged, singing

> Once a jolly swagman camped by a billabong
> Under the shade of a coolibah tree . . .

Anderson's own contribution was to silence two machine-gun posts with grenades and kill two Japanese with his pistol.

HARRISON'S RECORD OF the battle of Muar and the withdrawal is part of the book he later wrote. He called it *The*

Brave Japanese. This is how he explained the title. Most Japanese, he said, were barbaric or sadistic; there were others who were kind at a time when kindness and gentleness were the rarest of gems. However, good or bad, kind or sadistic, they had a courage that he envied. It is a book that can be wry and raucous but which captures the poignancy of individuals as they die.

Harrison was with a group of men running for cover from two Japanese machine-gun nests. A few feet from him was Major Sydney Olliff, acting commander of the 2/29th in place of Robertson. Olliff was almost safe when a bullet took off four fingers of his left hand. He stopped, looked at his hand in astonishment and said: 'O God.' As he spoke a burst of fire ripped through his back.

Harrison was with a group sheltering at night in the Bakri swamps. The Japanese were lighting the area with flares and spraying it with machine-gun fire. There were wounded among the Australians, including a young infantryman who had been gravely injured by friendly artillery fire. He kept calling to his friend, 'Shoot me, Jim, kill me.' Eventually his friend did shoot him but, in the dark, the shot was not fatal. Before the boy died he cried loudly in a shocked and bewildered voice, 'Oh, Jim, what did you do that for?' Then silence fell again over the dark swamp.

AS ANDERSON'S COLUMN struggled on, the number of wounded multiplied. They never reached Yong Peng and safety. In a flanking movement, the Japanese had taken control of the village of Parit Sulong and its vital bridge. Pressed by ground troops and strafed from the air, without the strength to take the bridge, the column stalled. A request to the Japanese to let two ambulances carrying the dying pass was rejected and the Japanese commander ordered them to remain on the bridge approach as a roadblock. Two of the wounded managed to release the brakes and let them roll away during the night.

The next day Anderson faced a bitter decision. He ordered those who were fit enough to make their way through swamp and jungle round the Japanese force. He had to leave the badly wounded to their fate. Their fate was torture and massacre.

Only 900 out of an Allied total of 4500 involved in the Battle of Muar and the withdrawal made it back to Allied lines and joined the retreat from the mainland to Singapore. Some were lost in that last push past Parit Sulong. Harrison and some anti-tank crew mates tried to reach the coast, hoping to escape to Sumatra. They sheltered for a time with Chinese communist guerillas and Bill McCure stayed with them and saw out the war in the jungle. Harrison and the others continued on to eventual capture. On April 25, 1943 Harrison was one of the group of Australian prisoners of war building their camp in the Thai jungle. He would work, sweat and suffer with Kevin Ward in Hellfire Pass.

CHAPTER 10

Fall of the fortress

Of course, the reason was that the people we sent out were an inferior troop of military and naval men.

Winston Churchill

This was a strange scene. On the northern end of the causeway that joins the Malayan mainland with the fabled island fortress of Singapore, an Australian major was pointing his revolver at a British sapper. It was January 31, 1942 and a fitting conclusion to this phase of the Allied campaign against the rampaging Japanese: confusion, chaos and tragedy melting into farce. The Allied troops were making their tormented way across Johore, along road and rail corridors, through swamp and jungle, across rubber plantations, on foot and in trucks, to the capital, Johore Bahru. They would funnel across the causeway for the end game in Singapore. Then as large a hole as possible would be blown in this only link. Trouble was, the sapper had his timetable, and that timetable did not take into account the fact that some troops were still hours away on the Malay side. Sapper: 'Orders is orders, and I am going to carry them out. I won't take orders from an Australian.' The major, John Wyett, drawing his revolver: 'If you will not take orders from me, perhaps you will take orders from this. If you make any attempt to blow that bridge before I say so, I am going to blow your bloody head off.'

The remnants of the 2nd Argyll and Sutherland High-landers, who had formed the inner bridgehead, were the last to cross. On the walls of the Argyll's regimental mess in Stirling Castle is a painting of the troops gathering at the end of the causeway. Wyett has a copy of it on a Christmas card sent by an old military friend. It captures the scene, except for one detail: Wyett himself is missing. He stood beside the commander, Lieutenant Colonel Ian Stewart, in the rosy dawn as the men formed ranks. Stewart positioned his two surviving pipers in front and to the skirl of bagpipes playing 'Heilan Laddie', the Argylls marched off. Behind them there was a booming explosion as the sapper blew the causeway. This was the sound that carried to the young Harry Lee on the other side of the island. Water swirled through a 20 metre gap. When the battalion reached the Singapore shore, Wyett nodded towards the pipers and asked Stewart: 'Now, sir, tell me why you did that?'

'You know, Wyett,' Stewart said, 'the trouble with you Australians is that you have no sense of history. When the story of the Argylls is written you will find that they go down in history as the last unit to cross the causeway and were piped across by their pipers.' It was a brave front: 250 Argylls followed the pipers; left behind were many more killed or taken prisoner.

Major General Henry Gordon Bennett had left the mainland the day before. He made a melancholy entry in his diary:

I toured slowly through Johore Bahru, past derelict cars and destroyed houses and the bomb holes that were

149

everywhere. There was a deathly silence. There was not the usual crowd of chattering Malays and busy Chinese. The streets were deserted. It was a funeral march. I have never felt so sad and upset . . . I always thought we would hold Johore. Its loss was never contemplated.

Two days before, Bennett had visited the Sultan of Johore in his palace, and, Australia's official historian said, 'was entertained by him at length and presented with gifts'. A whiff of reproach here? Quite likely, and deservedly. This was, after all, an intense and busy time, with troops in jeopardy and the retreat over the causeway a very risky business. However, Bennett makes it quite clear in his diary that he is flattered to be in the company of Sultan Sir Ibrahim, one of Malaya's hereditary traditional rulers. The sultans were rich, powerful and highly conscious of their positions and the obeisances due to them. Bennett would carry away from visits gifts such as the sultan's special cigars and the rare, aged whisky bottled for him in Scotland. On this farewell visit, despite having had lunch at his headquarters, he sat down to another with the sultan. As usual, Bennett was presented with gifts, but this time he had a special request.

Bennett's diary note is full of bathos.

Tears rolled down his rugged cheeks as this rough but big-hearted ruler of Johore discussed the capture of his country by the Japanese. He realises that he will be a poor man in Malaya and even considers it possible that the Japanese might treat him roughly. He has invested much of his wealth in England, the United States of America and Australia. He said: 'I suppose I can live on rice and fish, like the rest of my people.'

As it turns out, there was no cause for the general to worry about the sultan's treatment by the Japanese, or his diet. Malaya's people may have suffered severely because of the economic disruption caused by the invasion and many may have died through disease or starvation on the Thai–Burma railway, but the Japanese regarded the sultans as useful props, soon restored their perks and privileges and even enhanced their religious authority. Sultan Ibrahim, who inherited his position in 1895, held it for 64 years until his death in 1959. The sultan survived the war better than Bennett did. The seeds of Bennett's professional destruction were in the scheme he put to the sultan over that long lunch: he wanted to avoid becoming a prisoner of war. Would the sultan help him obtain a boat to escape in? The next evening, he told one of his officers the Allied troops would be 'caught like rats in a trap' on Singapore. 'But they won't get me.' The Japanese didn't; his enemies at home did.

THE ALLIED TROOPS were now concentrated on Churchill's small, 'naked' island. Having failed to see the flaws in the Singapore strategy and having failed to provide the men and matériel needed, Churchill, when preparing his (in part) self-serving memoirs, said of the disaster: 'Of course, the reason was that the people we sent out were an inferior troop of military and naval men.' This was an outrageous, sweeping condemnation. These were troops often ill-served by their political and military leaders. There were troops who had never seen the jungle and never seen a tank. Some had barely seen a rifle. There was a multitude of troops who had no anti-tank guns. The Argylls, proud and professional, had trained in the jungle but even they had no answer to a Japanese attack led by eight tanks. As we have seen, the 45th Indian Brigade was abysmally ill prepared. The freshest British reinforcements basically went straight into action after a long sea voyage. An Australian officer said of the Norfolks: 'They were a fine body of men but almost dazed by the position they were in. Their training had been for open warfare, and not the very close warfare of the Malayan countryside.' Detachments of the British 18th Division arrived on February 5. They carried a burden of expectations but little else. Most of their equipment was on the transport *Empress of Asia,* which had been bombed and was burning off the coast.

Perhaps when Churchill wrote '[of the inferior] people we sent out', he was taking some blame. And some blame must be accepted by the Australian Government and military leadership for sending reinforcements who stood little chance against battle-hardened Japanese. The detachment that arrived on January 24 was largely untrained. Some had been in the army only weeks. Kevin Ward, of the 2/30th, then a 19-year-old veteran, remained angry at the memory. 'This young fellow comes up to me and says, "What happens when you fire a rifle?" And I say, "It goes BANG!" It wasn't funny. It was terrible.'

GENERAL YAMASHITA WAS now in the place where Bennett had spent so many pleasant hours puffing cigars and sipping single-malt Scotch. He had made the Istana Hijau, the Sultan of Johore's Green Palace, his headquarters. Tsuji, who referred to it as the Imperial Palace, was much taken by its 'beauty and majestic appearance'; Yamashita was attracted by the view from the five-storey tower across the Johore Strait to Singapore, his waiting prize. The top floor was a glassed-in observation room. From there he sent a telegram to his supremely confident officers: 'I, this whole day, pushing forward the command post to the heights of the Johore Imperial Palace, will observe directly the strenuous efforts of every divisional commander.' Australian and British officers, including Bennett, knew observers were using the tower but Bennett would not have expected Yamashita to have been in such an exposed position. One well-placed round would have been at least a great psychological blow, but Bennett refused to allow the artillery to open fire. He said the post would just move on and that unnecessary shelling of Johore Bahru should be avoided. Thank you for the whisky and cigars?

Meanwhile, Percival was floundering. His reputation had suffered during the battle for the mainland. Reviewing the Battle of Muar, Warren says: 'Percival's inability to concentrate his forces at a point of crisis, even with the locality of crisis clearly identified, was one of the enduring themes of the Malayan campaign.' It was on display again as he planned the final defence of Singapore. According to Wigmore, the official Australian historian, Percival had under his command as fighting troops 70,000 men, but this total included second-line combat units, and battalions varying widely in quality, training and equipment. 'The general effect,' Wigmore says, with understatement, 'was bad'. The 'rifle strength' of the Japanese was less than 25,000. However, Percival was relying on greatly exaggerated estimates.

Singapore Island is 42 kilometres from east to west and 22 kilometres north to south, with 113 kilometres of coastline. The strait separating it from Johore is at its widest, 4600 metres, to the east of the causeway (though Pulau Ubin is a large island stepping stone). To the west it narrows from 1800 metres to 550 metres. Percival had been critical of Bennett's disposition of forces at Muar. Now he had to work out where the Japanese would make their main-force landing and put his freshest, fittest troops, the British 18th Division, in their way.

This is what the newly appointed Allied commander-in-chief, General Wavell, had suggested, saying that in his view the north-west of the island was the most likely to be attacked and the 18th Division should be posted there.

In the Green Palace, Tsuji, the operations officer, had been drawing up what he called 'the plan for the final reduction of Singapore'. He took into account factors such as the impact of the refugees and non-combatants on military strategy (the troops would not fight to the last man), the rise and fall of the tide and the strength of the current (the Japanese would be able to use collapsible motor boats), and the morale of the defenders (exhausted and demoralised). He worked through the night and on February 1 at 10 am in the shelter of a rubber plantation, Yamashita read the orders to about 40 divisional commanders and senior officers. All then received in their canteen lids a gift from the Emperor, a sip of *kikumasumune*, a wine for deeply solemn occasions. They drank a toast: 'It is a good place to die. Certainly we shall conquer.'

The Japanese would launch their main attack to the west of the causeway; Percival would prepare his main defence on the east. He positioned the Australians on the west and the larger British forces, the 18th Division, along with the best of the Indian forces, on the east. Kinvig, Percival's biographer, says that the strongest evidence that Percival in fact thought the attack would come from the north-west came on January 29 when he nominated the actual focus of the Japanese attack and pointed it out on a map during a meeting with Admiral Layton, Commander of the Eastern Fleet, and senior army officers. But he did not act on this. Legg, Bennett's biographer, surmises Percival could have made a faulty appreciation, one that would be easy to rationalise in retrospect. And it seems some rationalisation did go on. In December 1945 Percival wrote: 'In point of fact I had put the Australians in the north

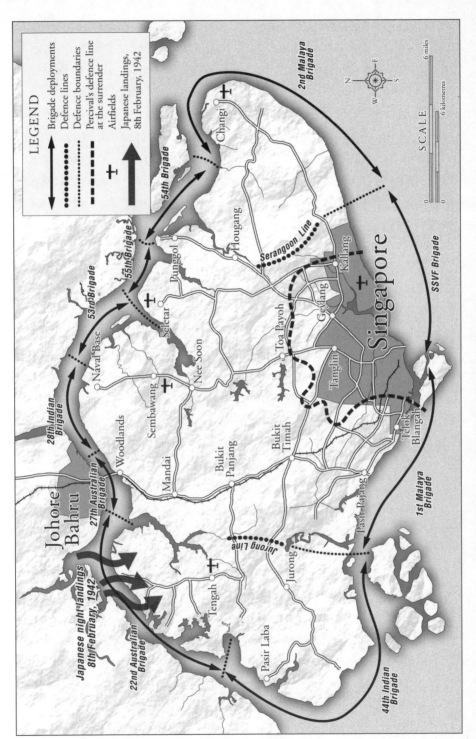

The defence of Singapore, 1942

LEGEND

- Brigade deployments
- Defence lines
- Defence boundaries
- Percival's defence line at the surrender
- Airfields
- Japanese landings, 8th February, 1942

SCALE

0 — 6 miles
0 — 6 kilometres

N E S W

54th Brigade
2nd Malaya Brigade
55th Brigade
53rd Brigade
28th Indian Brigade
27th Australian Brigade
22nd Australian Brigade
44th Indian Brigade
1st Malaya Brigade
SSVF Brigade

Japanese night landings 8th February, 1942

Serangoon Line
Jurong Line

Johore Bahru
Singapore

Changi
Hougang
Punggol
Seletar
Naval Base
Nee Soon
Sembawang
Woodlands
Mandai
Bukit Panjang
Bukit Timah
Tengah
Pasir Laba
Jurong
Pasir Panjang
Telok Blangah
Tanglin
Geylang
Toa Payoh
Kallang

west chiefly because I thought it was the most vulnerable area and that as the Australians had had experience of fighting on the mainland and training in bush warfare, it would be better to put them there than the newly arrived 18th Division.' In 1953, he wrote to the official British historian: 'I was probably wrong when I said in my despatch that I expected the attack to develop from the west and . . . I probably had little preference between the two lines of advance i.e. from the west or down the river from Kota Tinggi [towards the north-east coast of Singapore].'

EVEN A LARGE-SCALE, flat, black-and-white map of dispositions of the 22nd Australian Brigade and part of the 27th Brigade gives the impression of very difficult terrain to defend. There is the broad estuary of the Kranji River with a network of its tributaries snaking behind company positions. There are at least half a dozen other minor creeks and estuaries. In real life there is brown swirling water, thick black mud and dense green foliage with few fields of fire. Lieutenant Colonel Roland Oakes of the 2/19th gloomily surveyed the area allotted to his unit:

. . . a scraggy waste of stunted rubber and tangled under-growth, apparently miles from anywhere, our vision limited to the next rise in the undulating ground and our means of movement confined to a few native foot-tracks winding through the wilderness . . . Maps showed that we were a mile and a half from the west coast with . . . the 2/18th away to the north in a similar desola-tion of waste and confusion . . . A mile of single-file track led through the belukar [secondary jungle] eight feet high, where the visibility was no more than a stone's throw, to Tom Vincent's headquarters where D Company looked out on the beauties of a mangrove swamp which was under water at high tide.

It was not so much a thin, khaki line of Australians, and their neighbours, the 44th Indian Brigade, but isolated clumps. Bennett and Percival went on a tour of the area on February 5. They stood together on one of Singapore's rare high hills, looking down on one company of a Punjab regiment and across a mangrove swamp to another company. The gap was more than 2 kilometres. Bennett's diary note said: 'General Percival again expressed his serious concern at the thinness of the defence and asked how we could defend the place. He agreed with my reply which was "only with more troops". I wired Australia advising of the gravity of the situation.'

The Australian Government already had before it the gloomy view of its representative in Singapore and member of the War Council there, V. G. Bowden, who emerged from a council meeting on January 26 doubting whether there was a firm intention of holding the island and regarding a rapid collapse as probable. He cabled Australia's Minister for External Affairs the comment he had made to the council: 'My deduction . . . is that Singapore will not be held, for with the naval base and all natural resources of Malaya gone, Singapore will have nothing more than sentimental value.'

For several days as the Japanese prepared for the assault they fed the fiction that they would descend from the north-east. The Imperial Guards set up dummy camps there and on February 7 made a decoy landing on Pulau Ubin. On the night of February 8, at 11 o'clock, the 25th Army's massed artillery, 480 guns, opened fire on the Australian positions; the field guns fired 200 rounds each that night and the heavy guns 100 rounds each. As the landing craft approached things went much as you would expect in the Allies' ill-starred campaign.

Through blunder, beach lights were not switched on; communication lines to artillery command had been destroyed by shellfire so there was little support for the defenders. There was some stiff, even heroic resistance and much Japanese blood in the water, but a sieve is a sieve. The Japanese were inside the fortress in strength. Their passage was made easier the next night by the actions of Brigadier Duncan Maxwell, commander of the 27th Australian Brigade which was to hold the area west of the causeway to the Kranji River. This they did for a time, at cost to the Japanese, but Maxwell ordered a withdrawal which had a ripple effect down the flanks of defenders to the brigade's rear. Hours before the attack, Maxwell had gone to the Western area headquarters. He told Lieutenant Colonel Thyer he was a doctor in civil life and his function was to save life. He considered that what was going on on Singapore Island after the Japanese landings was senseless slaughter. He was going back to Percival to urge him to surrender.

These were the words of a man unfit to lead. But Maxwell's attitude raises again the old, familiar question: in a hopeless position, how long to fight, and to what point? Churchill vacillated. On January 20, he cabled Wavell that 'no question of surrender [was] to be entertained until after protracted fighting among the ruins of Singapore City'. The next day a meeting of the Defence Committee in London considered a note from Churchill in response to Wavell's doubts that Singapore could hold for more than a few weeks. Churchill questioned whether 'we should not at once blow the docks and batteries and workshops to pieces and concentrate everything on the defence of Burma and keeping open the Burma road . . . if it is only for a few weeks, it is certainly not worth losing all our reinforcements and aircraft.' (It was this discussion which led to Australia's cable warning that evacuation of Singapore would be regarded as an 'inexcusable betrayal'.)

On February 10, Churchill cabled Wavell:

> . . . the defenders must greatly outnumber Japanese forces who have crossed the strait, and in a well-contested battle they should destroy them. There must be at this stage no thought of saving the troops or sparing the population. The battle must be fought to the bitter end at all costs. The 18th Division has a chance to make its name in history. Commanders and senior officers should die with their troops. The honour of the British Empire and the British Army is at stake. With the Russians fighting as they are and the Americans so stubborn at Luzon, the whole reputation of our country and our race is involved.

Wavell looked at this cable, added a few flourishes and issued it as an order of the day: 'no weakness must be shown in any shape or form'; 'I look forward to you and your men to fight to the end to prove that the fighting spirit that won our Empire still exists to enable us to defend it.' Then Percival sent it out to the various headquarters with a covering note and his own touches: '. . . In some units the troops have not shown the fighting spirit expected of men of the British Empire. It will be a lasting disgrace if we are defeated by an army of clever gangsters many times inferior in numbers to our own men.' John Wyett remembers Lieutenant Colonel Wilfred Kent Hughes, Bennett's principal administrative officer, reading the order, saying to the messenger, 'Wait here', turning to the wastepaper basket and holding the paper delicately between fingers and thumbs, tearing it up, dropping it in and saying, 'Now go back and tell your boss that is what I think'. Which was better than it deserved. It was as bad a combination of ignorance, elitism, hollow rhetoric, racism and courage from a distance as ever bubbles to the surface of the morass of war.

The population which Churchill ordered his commander to

have no thought of sparing lived under the flag of the Empire, helped create its wealth and in moments of romantic flight was regarded as its children. They were suffering enough already. In a diary entry, Bennett described returning to his headquarters from a conference where commanders had decided unanimously that further resistance was futile. He said it was also realised that it was the civilian population which were the main sufferers. They were unable to escape through the enemy cordon, innocent victims being killed and maimed.

I could smell the blast of aerial bombs in the air. There was devastation everywhere. There were holes in the road, churned-up rubble lying in great clods all around, tangled masses of telephone, telegraph and electric cables strewn across the street, here and there smashed cars, trucks, electric trams and buses . . . Bombs were falling in a nearby street. On reaching the spot, one saw that the side of a building had fallen on an air raid shelter, the bomb penetrating deep into the ground. A group of Chinese, Malays, Europeans and Australian soldiers were already at work shovelling and dragging the debris away . . . The rescuers dug furiously among the fallen masonry, one little Chinese man doing twice as much as the others, the sweat streaming down his body. At last the top of the shelter was uncovered. Beneath was a crushed mass of old men, women, young and old, and young children, some still living . . . The little Oriental never stopped with his work, his sallow face showing the strain of his anguish. His wife and four children were there. Gradually he unearthed them – dead.

There is, in the Australian War Memorial, one of those iconic photographs, a moment of grief frozen and captured for all time. Two women, surely mother and grandmother, sit among the rubble and the background of rickshaws with buckled wheels and wail at the body of a child.

CERTAINLY THERE WERE soldiers who had lost the will to fight. For some who had done their duty on the mainland, this costly and failed defence of the island, with its false fortress and only the ghost of the naval base, killed their spirit. Pedalling home one morning from duty as a medical auxiliary service volunteer, Lee Kuan Yew passed a parked line of military vehicles and, standing beside them, Australian soldiers who looked frightened and demoralised. Lee stopped and asked them where the front was. One soldier said, 'It's over, here, take this', and offered Lee his rifle. These were most likely not front-line soldiers, but reinforcements or rear-echelon troops. They would probably have become part of the small army of stragglers and deserters who rampaged, looted and, some of them, forced their way onto boats fleeing the island.

The day Percival sent out the Churchill/Wavell exhortation, the Japanese had captured the island's high ground, Bukit Timah hill. It was February 11, and the great national day, *Kigensetsu*, the festival marking the coronation of the first emperor, Jimmu, the source of Imperial divinity. There had been hopes that the Japanese could have proclaimed victory this day, but Bukit Timah was a great consolation prize. Yamashita could, with confidence, take up his pen, assume his *bushido* mien, and write a capitulation request to be dropped behind British lines. The Japanese aircraft, of course, met no opposition. That day Percival was driving along Bukit Timah Road, the major artery, to check troop positions. He recorded later: 'It was a strange sensation. This great road, usually so full of traffic, was almost deserted. Japanese aircraft were floating about, unopposed except for our anti-aircraft fire, looking for targets. One felt horribly naked driving up that wide road in a lone motor. Why, I asked myself, does Britain, our improvident Britain, with all her great resources, allow her sons to fight without any air support?'

Yamashita took advantage of his ownership of the skies to send aircraft carrying 29 wooden boxes over the defenders. The boxes fell, trailing red and white streamers, one into the Australian lines. The letter addressed to the High Command of the British Army, Singapore, said:

Your Excellency,

I, the High Command of the Nippon Army based on the spirit of Japanese chivalry, have the honour of presenting this note to Your Excellency advising you to surrender the whole force in Malaya.

My sincere respect is due to your army which true to the traditional spirit of Great Britain, is bravely defending Singapore which now stands isolated and unaided. Many fierce and gallant fights have been fought by you gallant men and officers, to the honour of British warriorship. But the developments of the general war situation has already sealed the fate of Singapore, and the continuation of resistance would only serve to inflict direct harm and injuries to thousands of non-combatants living in the city, throwing them into further miseries and horrors of war, but also would not add anything to the honour of your army.

I expect that Your Excellency accepting my advice, will give up this meaningless and desperate resistance . . . If, on the contrary, Your Excellency should neglect my advice and the present resistance be continued, I shall be obliged, though reluctantly from humanitarian considerations to order my army to make annihilating attacks on Singapore.

In closing this note of advice, I pay again my respects to Your Excellency.

(signed) Tomoyuki Yamashita.

The final instruction was that the British delegation should proceed along Bukit Timah Road, bearing a large white flag and a Union Jack. Percival did not respond. Some units, including Australian, kept fighting and dying gamely. Some, including Australian, had disintegrated. Civilians continued not to be spared. Bodies lay unburied in the streets and Singapore ceased to be a place of civilisation. Bombs fell in its heart: 'We pulled up near a building which had collapsed onto the road,' an officer wrote, '– it looked like a caved-in slaughter house. Blood splashed what was left of the lower rooms; chunks of human beings – men, women and children – littered the place. Everywhere bits of steaming flesh, smouldering rags, clouds of dust – and the shriek and groan of those who still survived.'

Two days later, on February 13, Percival reported to Wavell on the failing food and water supplies and the exhaustion of troops. Even the gesture of an offensive was not possible, he said, as there were no troops who could carry out an attack. 'There must come a stage when in the interests of troops and civil population further bloodshed will serve no useful purpose. Your instructions of February 10 are being carried out, but in above circumstances would you consider giving me wider discretionary powers?'

Wavell's response the next day was: 'You must continue to

inflict maximum damage on enemy for as long as possible by house-to-house fighting if necessary. Your action in tying down enemy and inflicting casualties may have vital influence in other theatres. Fully appreciate your situation, but continued action essential.'

Vital influence? Where? That very day, Japan invaded Sumatra and British forces in Burma's south-east fell back from the defensive line at the Salween River to the Bilin River. Japanese invasion units had landed on Rabaul on January 23 and on Ambon on January 31.

Churchill, in *The Hinge of Fate*, is absolutely unapologetic about the appalling instructions given to Percival. 'It is always right,' he says, 'that whatever may be the doubts at the summit of war direction, the general on the spot should have no knowledge of them and should receive instructions which are simple and plain. But now when it was certain that all was lost at Singapore I was sure it would be wrong to enforce needless slaughter, and without hope of victory to inflict the horrors of street fighting on the vast city, with its teeming, helpless and now panic-stricken population.'

On February 15, after some days of needless slaughter, Wavell cabled Percival: 'So long as you are in a position to inflict losses and damage to enemy and your troops are physically capable of doing so, you must fight on. Time gained and damage to enemy are of vital importance at this crisis. When you are fully satisfied that this is no longer possible I give you discretion to cease resistance.' Percival called a meeting of his senior commanders. Astonishingly, Percival spoke of continued resistance, pointing to Wavell's instructions to fight on. Bennett opposed this. So did Heath, who told Percival he should have surrendered two days before, when he and Bennett had urged it. He was referring to a command conference on February 13, when Percival responded: 'I have my honour to consider and there is also the question of what posterity will think of us if we surrender this large army and valuable fortress.' Heath's devastating reply was: 'You need not bother about your honour. You lost that a long time ago up in the North.'

In the ruined city, with the smell of defeat as strong as the stench of death, Percival was clearly not in proper touch with reality. Perhaps he never would be again. In the foreword to his book on the war in Malaya, he would write: 'I do not believe in apologies when there is no need for them.' Someone owed an apology to those civilians who died while Percival was considering his honour.

On February 15, Percival sent his last cable to his commander-in-chief: 'Owing to the losses from enemy action, water, petrol, food, and ammunition practically finished. Unable therefore to continue to fight any longer. All ranks have done their best and are grateful for your help.'

CHAPTER 11

The great escape

There is honour in the shadow of their shame:
They did not flinch when fate proclaimed the hour
Of their defeat. All in their humble pow'r
Was done – they felt no cold disgracing shame
About their efforts, they hung no head
Before their fallen comrades . . .
. . . Without pause
They marched to their internment head upraised.

George Harding, 2/19th Battalion

Perhaps there is a good time to sail away to war: when it is young and the cause thought just, when everyone chooses to believe it will be all over by Christmas, when somehow the race memory has been lost of just how terrible the last war was, when bands play and people cheer. Lieutenant Fred (Smudger) Ransome Smith and the 5th Suffolks did not sail to Malaya at a good time. There had been blitzes on England, defeats and disasters in the European and Middle East theatres, the loss of the great ships, the *Repulse* and the *Prince of Wales* in the South China Sea, and the relentless drive of the Japanese down the Malayan peninsula.

The Suffolks took a long cruise to war. They docked in Nova Scotia, visited the Amazon estuary and luckily dodged U-boats. In Cape Town, Ransome Smith, who had played cricket for the army, borrowed a set of stumps from the professionals and organised a game. They sailed to India. Having been trained first of all for the desert, they spent a few weeks on the upland plains around Poona where the platoons had to march 90 metres apart so they could see through the dust.

Most of the men had gone into uniform having never been outside their Suffolk villages. Ransome Smith, an artist, had at least read Somerset Maugham. He tried to prepare his men for the jungle. He gave lectures as the ship steamed towards Singapore and he painted from his imagination scenes of bamboo, coconut palms, snakes and scorpions. The Suffolks' convoy was bombed as it left the Indian Ocean and passed through the Sunda Strait to berth in Singapore. Evacuees were pushing up the gangway as they went down.

The Suffolks did not see much of the jungle Ransome Smith had drawn for them, except coconut palms. In the brief attempt to defend the island from invasion, the Suffolks were based in an area of Chinese fish ponds and duck farms, but when they fell back they were tormented by Japanese snipers who strapped themselves up coconut palms among the fronds.

February 15, around noon: the Suffolks were at the intersection of Bukit Timah Road and Adam Road, a strategic point in the city. They had erected barbed-wire barricades. Ransome Smith looked south along Bukit Timah Road and saw a car approaching with a white flag out the window. He thought perhaps someone was sending them medical supplies. The car stopped and a group emerged and walked towards the roadblock. A Union Jack was now being carried beside the white flag. From behind Ransome Smith came a shout of anger and the company's second-in-command, Captain Bill Oliver, rushed forward, held his revolver at the chest of an officer and demanded: 'What the hell are you doing?'

'How dare you?' the officer said. 'I'm Brigadier Newbigging.'

Newbigging was on that most distasteful mission for a soldier; he was going to the headquarters of the Japanese 25th Army to arrange a capitulation. Captain Oliver returned to the Suffolks ranks and spoke to the company commander, his brother Jack. Jack Oliver came over and sat on the edge of Ransome Smith's trench and cried. When Newbigging returned from Japanese headquarters, he was carrying a large Japanese flag to be flown from the top of the Cathay Pacific building to signal that Percival the conquered would meet Yamashita the conqueror at 4 pm.

In his account of the war, Percival says he feels sure his readers would not wish him to recount in any detail the painful events which took place during the remainder of that day. This was a failed attempt to draw a veil across the shame. Percival would once more be condemned by photograph. The still camera captured him on that short, endless walk from the car to meet Yamashita, a gangly figure, out of step with his British officer companions, eyes downcast. He knew he was in no position to bargain. He could make suggestions on the cease-fire time and request the keeping of 1000 British troops under arms against disorder overnight. Perhaps his thoughts strayed to his honour and whether he could find any specks of dignity in the dust. He didn't. He knew his future. The British public would be shocked by the fall of Singapore and there would be the usual hunt for scapegoats. Press and public would charge the military commanders and civil administration of Malaya with gross incompetence. Such has always been the British custom, he thought.

IN THE AUSTRALIAN War Memorial, through the ante-chamber filled with the rich tones of Robert Gordon Menzies telling the nation it is at war, past the display of the Syrian campaign, the model of a prisoner-of-war's hut in Germany and an accusatory presentation about the massacre at Tol plantation in New Britain, there is a room in which a large, no-frills table is fixed to the wall. On its surface from an overhead camera play, in endless silent loop, filmed scenes from the Malayan campaign with jumpy black-and-white action sequences and Japanese soldiers in Singapore throwing their arms in the air as they shout *banzai*. The centrepiece is the confrontation between Yamashita and Percival, which took place across this table in the Ford factory at Bukit Timah. The quality is poor, but Yamashita projects bulky presence. In the Japanese Defence Agency translated transcript of the meeting, Percival raises the question of the safety of non-combatants. Yamashita (having a memory lapse about Nanking) says: 'Non-combatants will be protected by the spirit of *bushido*. So everything will be all right.' Yamashita warns Percival twice that a night attack will go ahead if agreement on terms is not reached and twice Percival asks that it be postponed.

Then Yamashita demands: 'Does the British Army intend to surrender or not?'

Percival: (a pause) 'I wish to have a cease-fire.'

Yamashita: 'The time for a night attack is drawing near. Is the British Army going to surrender or not?'

In English, he says: 'Answer "yes" or "no".'

This scene flickers across the table top. Yamashita bangs his fist down. Surely the table shook in 1942. Percival's head moves sharply from side to side. His eyes dart. He looks, I'm afraid, like a trapped rabbit.

Percival: 'Yes. But I would like the retention of 1000 armed men sanctioned.'

The surrender document is signed.

After Percival and his entourage had been escorted from the factory, the Japanese returned to the 25th Army headquarters. Maps and documents had been removed from the table in the operations room. On a white cloth were spread the Emperor's gifts: dried cuttlefish, chestnuts and wine. The officers filled their cups, turned to face north-east towards the Imperial Palace in Tokyo and drank a silent toast.

That night Yamashita was sleepless. He wept often and several times walked the grounds of his headquarters. He bowed deeply towards the palace. This was his atonement. The next morning, he received an Imperial Rescript:

> Throughout the campaign in Malaya the Army and the Navy, in close and appropriate association, have carried out difficult and dangerous sea convoys, transport duties, and military landing operations. Officers and men, risking malaria, and enduring intense heat, have struck violently at the enemy, engaged in unremitting pursuit at lightning speed, destroyed his powerful army and captured Singapore. As a consequence, Britain's base of operations in the Far East is overthrown and annihilated.
>
> I deeply approve of this.

RANSOME SMITH AND the Suffolks were in shock as they watched Percival's entourage return. They were told the cease-fire had been set for 8.30 pm and that they should rejoin their battalion at its headquarters in central Singapore. Sporadic fighting was continuing and an occasional wounded soldier struggled to the lines. Ransome Smith felt shame, confusion, anger. 'We were finally told to move off Bukit Timah Road, in as orderly manner as we could. You just assumed that if you got back to Singapore you'd get back on the boats and leave or something. We were mortared and shelled all the way in. It was shocking. You imagine a retreat of thousands in a horrible crocodile and there were some real bad casualties. In Singapore there was chaos, looting and burning. Christ, it was in a shocking state. Groups had disintegrated, milling, all mixed up. Another subaltern and I had the address of headquarters in a girls' school so we pinched this car from Raffles, a dirty, great old German job. We were lucky to get there, otherwise we would have been part of that dreadful mob in Singapore.'

That dreadful mob included many Australians. 'Stragglers' became part of the chaotic Singapore landscape soon after the invasion. Bennett admitted the problem got out of hand. There were the untrained reinforcements, and he said, the 'bad hats', the black sheep of the family, criminal classes who joined the army to avoid the police or were pushed that way by magistrates. Most of these morally weak men avoided the danger zones.

There were, however, men who emerged from the danger zone convinced that for defenders the war was over. They wanted to escape. So did Major General Henry Gordon Bennett but he had not made his decision staggering out of the haze of battle. Wyett, reviewing the period after Bennett's January 28 meeting with the Sultan of Johore and the way Bennett fought the dying phase of the campaign on the island, came to the simple conclusion: his mind was elsewhere. He had become even more abrasive and intolerant. Once Wyett looked at a map on which Bennett had marked a forming-up area and said it was in enemy hands. He had just been to observe it. 'You're a coward, Wyett,' Bennett said. 'You're all cowards.'

On the morning of February 15, in the dispatch from Wavell to Percival telling him that he could use his discretion to cease resistance, Wavell added: 'Also just before final cessation of fighting, opportunity should be given to any determined bodies of men or individuals to try and effect escape by any means possible. They must be armed. Inform me of intentions.' Percival did not inform Bennett of Wavell's green light to escapes. And Bennett did not tell his military superiors, Wavell and Percival, of his escape plan. He did not tell his Australian political masters. He mentioned it once to Wyett, but did not follow up. There are different versions concerning Bennett's Chief of Staff and dedicated critic, Colonel Thyer. One has Thyer being offered a place in the group, but declining. Another has Thyer aware of the plan, in a general way, suspecting that Bennett would have liked to include him but feeling the matter was not broached because Bennett knew he would disapprove.

Following Percival's decision to capitulate, Bennett arranged for the troops to be issued with boots and two days' rations. He also ordered the preparation of a complete nominal roll to be handed to the Japanese with the request that the names be communicated to Australia as soon as possible to alleviate the worries of relatives. This was a touching consideration for the men he was about to abandon. He then made a final tour of the Australian lines, admitting a twofold purpose: first, to inspect his troops for the last time, 'a sad business', he says in his diary; second, to reconnoitre his escape route. Bennett really was a strange man. He felt the need to record that he found the headquarters of the 2/20th Battalion 'in a beautifully furnished house where I had afternoon tea from unusually high quality dishes'.

Early that evening, Bennett sent for his administrative officer, Wilfred Kent Hughes. Bennett asked him whether he should try to escape. Why he did this is unclear. In his personal recordings, Bennett shows an unwavering determination not to

fall into Japanese hands. Perhaps he wanted eleventh-hour bol-
stering. Kent Hughes replied that it was a choice only Bennett
could make, pointing out the commanding officer's dual
responsibilities: to his troops and to the Australian Government. Bennett said that after the surrender he would not be
able to do any more for his men than could Brigadier
Callaghan (the 8th Division's artillery commander), who
would take over from him. Bennett said his responsibility to
his government required him to get back to Australia. This is
how he put it in words designed for posterity and for his
critics: '. . . I must at all costs return to Australia to tell our
people the story of our conflict with the Japanese, to warn
them of the danger to Australia, and to advise them of the best
means of defeating the Japanese tactics.'

Some time after 10 pm Bennett and two companions, his
aide-de-camp, Lieutenant Gordon Walker, and Major Charles
Moses, drove through the wreckage of Singapore to the
seafront. Walker stripped off and swam to a moored sampan
and brought it back to a jetty. And so by sampan, then by a
larger boat owned by a reluctant, opium-smoking Chinese,
then by launch, Bennett made his way to Sumatra. On
February 27, he flew into Broome. He air-hopped across the
outback and down to Sydney, bathing in warmth and con-
gratulations. On March 2, he reached Victoria Barracks, Melbourne, the heart of the army. The heart was cold. He went to
the office of the Chief of the General Staff, General Sturdee.
He left in a daze. Sturdee had said to him – what was it? –
something like, 'Your escape was ill-advised', then turned back
to his work, leaving Bennett standing there like a schoolboy.

Others had left Singapore in the days before capitulation
and in the confusion of the night: Australian deserters who
forced their way onto the *Empire Star*; nurses, reluctant
evacuees, headed, some of them, for death at sea, on a beach,

in prison camps; soldiers who did not want to fight; soldiers who wanted to fight on; service personnel whose special skills warranted a berth on a boat; and Colonel Stewart, the Argyll's commander with a sense of history, who had been sent from Singapore by Percival, at the request of Wavell, to provide expertise on fighting the Japanese.

Two men go on a mission. One is self-appointed. Certainly there was much to learn about the Japanese from the Malayan campaign, but Bennett, it seems, had more in mind than producing a handbook on tactics. Biographer Frank Legg raises the question: 'Was this belief of Gordon Bennett's that he was to inherit the mantle of Sir John Monash the cause of his downfall? He had mentioned his belief to very few even of his friends, but he had mentioned it.' Given Bennett's arrogance, ambition and selfless serving of his own cause, it is a difficult question to say no to. Surely he hoped, as he clambered onto the sampan that he was on his way to leadership of the whole Australian army, to being hailed, in time, as Australia's greatest general. As it turned out, his reputation would have to rest on the Malayan campaign and his escape from Singapore. That reputation would be put to the test, and the sword, after the war.

Of the men he left behind, Bennett wrote, under the date February 15 (though it was written much later):

Their war was over. Their hopes and ambitions were shattered. They were to become prisoners of the despised Japanese. They were to submit to the ignominious position of spending the rest of the war behind barbed wire – at the mercy of the Japanese, who had a very bad reputation for the way in which they treated their prisoners. Their wives and children, their friends, their homes in Australia were suddenly cut off. None knew when they would see them again.

Could their leader have helped them in their captivity? Not over the years, because in August, 1942 Percival and the other senior officers were shipped to Formosa. It was a tactic designed to separate possibly inspirational leaders from their men. Bennett would not have lasted long in Singapore. But in those first numbing days and weeks, with morale mostly destroyed, a general might have come in handy.

ARMIES LOVE PAPERWORK. There was some to do after the surrender. John Wyett stood beside Wilfred Kent Hughes at a desk. He was staring at the order that would finish the war for the 8th Division, sending them to captivity. Kent Hughes was tearful. He said: 'John, I can't. I simply can't. This is the saddest moment of my life. I simply cannot put my signature on that document ordering all our men into a prison camp.' Wyett signed the order himself. During his captivity, Kent Hughes, at considerable risk, wrote a long, narrative poem, *Slaves of the Samurai*. It ranged over issues such as the lack of military preparedness that led to the Singapore disaster; it recorded his personal reaction to captivity as he was marched towards a prison camp on Formosa:

> *The route was lined with citizens, who stared*
> *Impassively, as if they too had shared*
> *The sordid shame and stings of slavery,*
> *And sympathised with those no longer free.*
> *School-children stood in rows, well-drilled and neat,*
> *Upon the kerb of each succeeding street,*
> *As steadily as if they'd taken root*
> *Incurious, disinterested, mute.*

Sadness, anger, shame, relief, resignation: there would have been a kaleidoscope of emotions in Singapore. Kevin Ward laid his rifle down but kept going back to it. It was not he, Kevin Ward, surrendering. Someone had done it for him, an administrative thing. It wasn't right. Ward and a few fellow bushies wondered if they could somehow get back to the mainland and fight as guerillas. Bill Dunn felt dismay. The anti-tank men had gathered in Tanglin barracks. It was close to cease-fire time. 'This infantryman came in and there was blood on his bayonet. He had just dropped the Jap population by one. He was dirty, tired, unshaven and he didn't want to surrender.' Snowy Marsh, attached to the 2/10th Artillery, was at the Botanical Gardens. They had been backing for days down the road, firing at Japanese on bicycles. He was buggered, just buggered, after three nights without sleep. Colin Finkemeyer, with his shoulder wound, left hospital and walked to find his regiment, passing women who were weeping and searching through rubble, passing Japanese. They didn't look at one another. He was happy for a moment when he rejoined his mates and they were happy to see him, but then they shared depression, uncertainty and a little fear about what could be coming.

Tsuji claimed the British soldiers looked like men who had finished their work by contract at a suitable salary and were taking a rest from the anxiety of the battlefield. They even bowed courteously to the Japanese, whom they hated, he said. Of course, he could not read their minds. The young Lee Kuan Yew stood by the roadside as the captives made their way to Changi. He was impressed by Highlanders and Gurkhas, marching 'erect, unbroken and doughty in defeat . . . the Australians were dispirited, not marching in step'. This sounds like Colonel Stewart with his sense of history again. Lee must have missed seeing Finkemeyer's 4th Australian Anti-Tank Regiment. Among its recruits had been most of the members of the Mildura Pipe Band. One of them, Colin MacDonald, had successfully resisted Japanese demands to add his bagpipes to the pile of weapons at the Tanglin marshalling point. The anti-tankers marched tall into Changi.

In Singapore and Malaya, the ranks of prisoners were swollen: at least 120,000 British Commonwealth troops including 15,000 Australians going into captivity. On Rabaul, Ambon, Timor, Sumatra and Java, the Japanese gathered in thousands more Australians: soldiers, airmen, sailors from the *Perth* and nurses who survived drownings and massacres.

CHAPTER 12

Birds in a cage

*It's not the first time a few thousand men have been
thrown away and it won't be the last.*

Major General Sidney Rowell, Deputy Chief of the
Australian General Staff, after the fall of Rabaul

On August 23, 1942 Iris Flight took up her pen, reached
for a sheet of foolscap paper and began writing a letter, a
love letter. It was a spur-of-the-moment thing. She was in
Western Australia, on her evening shift as a member of the air-
raid precautions team. She used just that single sheet and
signed it 'still your fiancée, Iris'. She then addressed it to 'TX
3395, Driver Dawson N. T., H. Q Coy, 2/40th Battalion, AIF,
last heard of Timor'. The army limited communications to
next of kin so she posted it in hope. Two years later Neil
Dawson received the letter in a prisoner-of-war camp along the
Thai–Burma railway, the sole letter to reach him from anyone
during three and a half years in captivity. Iris would have had
difficulty recognising him, emaciated, half his pre-war weight.

When I say it was a love letter, I don't mean that it was
passionate. It was decorous, as was Miss Iris Flight herself, but
it had warmth and it had, so importantly, steadfastness. Iris

Flight was still bemused at being engaged to Neil Dawson. They had met in the pretty village of Forth on the north-west coast of Tasmania. Dawson's sister and her husband had a shop there and when his brother-in-law became ill, he went to help out. Iris was minding the children. They went out a couple of times, and Iris thought probably nothing would come of it. They didn't know each other very well. She went to Western Australia in 1939 for a short holiday and when war broke out she was marooned there because of travel restrictions. Dawson enlisted in the 2/40th Battalion, Tasmania's own. He wrote to her from training camp, surprising her with a proposal of marriage. On Christmas Eve, she received another letter. Enclosed was an engagement ring. They would not be together as an engaged couple until October 17, 1945.

Neil and Iris won't mind sharing the love letter with you. After all, it was read by everyone in the prisoner-of-war camp. That's what they did, these men cut off from the world: shared food, shared suffering, shared letters and the precious affection they carried, particularly with those who received no word from home.

My dearest Neil,
This is my first attempt at a letter to a prisoner of war, and am following directions closely, hoping it will get through to you. First of all, my dear, let me tell you how thankful I was to hear from your mother that you were safe, after all the months of waiting and no news and while it could have been better, still the main thing to us is that you are alive and safe. Hope you are well, and trying to keep your chin up, as I know you will, though I suppose it's easy enough for me to tell you to do these things. When, or if, it is possible for you to write to me, let me know if there is anything at all I am allowed to

send you, dear, and if you can't write to me, just put a little message in your mother's letter, and that will have to do. As you will see Neil, I'm still in the West, though at a different address, and hoping to go home for good some time this year and will be there waiting for you when you come back. What a day that will be for all of us. Anyhow, till then think of me now and again, won't you. Neil, I shall be waiting and praying for you till we meet again. Keep smiling, darling. All my love. Still your fiancée, Iris Flight.

Neil Dawson had been one of the few Australians to have any contact with the Japanese before the war. When he was six or seven years old, living in Hobart, the Japanese fleet visited. Japanese sailors walked past the Dawson home and his parents invited them in. They played the pianola, had a feed, had a good time, sang songs. 'They didn't reciprocate when I was on the railway,' Dawson says.

A MAP OF the hemisphere, like the one used by Billy Hughes at the Paris Peace Conference in 1919, shows Australia sheltering under an umbrella, a chain of big and small islands from the Solomons in the east through New Guinea to the Indonesian archipelago in the west. In October 1940 staff officers from India, Australia, New Zealand and Burma met in Singapore to discuss Japan's likely strategy if it entered the war. They had before them the considered opinion of the Chiefs of Staff in London that if American intervention were a strong possibility, attempts by Japan to invade Australia and New Zealand could be ruled out altogether. But look at that map: the islands seem to form a comforting buffer. Now imagine the enemy there, with nothing between them and the Australian homeland but empty tropical seas. The buffer is now a base for raids. It is also a line of stepping stones towards the heart of Indonesia.

A perennial strategic debate in Australia has been forward defences versus fortress Australia. The official war historian records that the Australian Chiefs of Staff were anxious to establish air forces in the islands as far north as possible but the Chief of the Air Staff was unwilling to do this unless there were army garrisons to protect the airfields. The General Officer Commanding, Lieutenant General Vernon Sturdee, agreed to send a battalion group to Rabaul and to hold two others ready to go to Ambon and Timor for airfield defence. 'With reluctance', the historian says. And certainly General Sturdee should have been reluctant: the battalions would be going to their doom.

Lark Force went to Rabaul. Gull Force went to Ambon. Sparrow Force went to Timor. Perhaps there was something subconsciously symbolic in those chosen names: not Hawk and Eagle and Falcon, not birds of prey. The three forces, undermanned and relatively poorly armed, were never going to be able to withstand the scale of attack the Japanese could throw at them. General Wavell, the regional commander, knew it, the Chiefs of Staff in Australia knew it and the commanders on the islands knew it. Perhaps the troops knew or sensed they would be preyed upon. So why place them in harm's way? The rationale of the Chiefs of Staff, knowing that Lark Force in Rabaul would be overwhelmed, was that the enemy should be made to fight for the islands.

Rabaul is, or was, on the north-east coast of New Britain, a long, narrow island between mainland New Guinea and the Solomons group. It was an attractive town on a superb natural harbour. Flying in and out was interesting, involving a sharp bank through the fumes of active volcanoes. In 1994, Tarurvur and Vulcan erupted, destroying the town and surrounding villages. Rabaul was within easy reach of Japan's bases on islands in its mandated territory to the north.

Lark Force, basically the 2/22nd Battalion of the 23rd Brigade, had a strength, or weakness, of 1400. Its aerial defences were two outdated 3-inch anti-aircraft guns. On New Year's Day 1942 the area commander, Colonel John Scanlan, sent a message to his troops, ordering them to fight to the last. The final words, as they appeared, were: THERE SHALL BE NO WITHDRAWAL. On January 4, 22 Japanese bombers made a high-level attack on the airport. On January 20, 120 aircraft converged on Rabaul. Heavy bombers pounded the area and Zeroes made strafing runs. On January 22, 45 fighters and dive-bombers attacked. Early on January 23, the invasion by Japan's South Seas Force, about 5300-strong, began from a convoy of at least 20 vessels including destroyers, cruisers, transports and an aircraft carrier. The defenders knew the odds were heavily against them. Before taking off, Wing Commander John Lerew, leader of the small RAAF squadron, outnumbered and outgunned, signalled Air Force Headquarters in Melbourne: 'Those who are about to die salute you.' Lerew survived, but the Japanese landing could not be stopped.

This is how Sergeant Ken Hale later reported it:

We could see dimly the shapes of the boats, and men getting out. As they landed the Japanese were laughing, talking and striking matches . . . one of them even shone a torch . . . We allowed most of them to get out of the boats and then fired everything we had. In my section we had one Lewis gun, one Tommy gun, eight rifles. The Vickers gun also opened up with us. We gave the mortars' the position . . . and in a matter of minutes they were sending their bombs over.

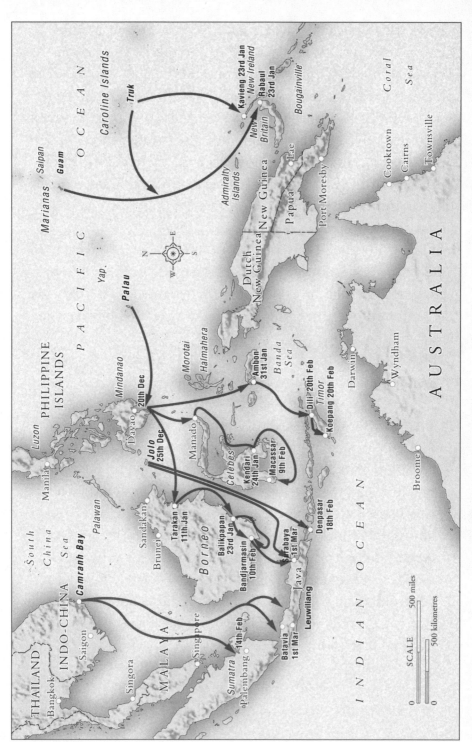

The Japanese advance to Rabaul, Ambon, Timor and Indonesia

The battle for Rabaul was basically over by the evening of January 23. Twenty-six Australians were killed in action. At Tol plantation on February 4, about 160 were massacred. The plantation was on the south-east coast of the Gazelle peninsula. Some of the men who had been pushing south in small groups had given up their flight and were waiting to surrender; others were captured. Wigmore records the story of Private Bill Cook of the 2/10th Field Ambulance. Cook and his mates unsuccessfully protested to the Japanese that they were Red Cross. Their brassards were torn off. Soldiers took the Australians away in groups of two or three. Cook's group was asked in sign language whether they would prefer to be bayoneted or shot. The men indicated they wanted to be shot. At the bottom of the track, three Japanese with fixed bayonets fell in behind them.

'They then stabbed us in the back with their bayonets,' Cook said later.

> The first blow knocked the three of us to the ground . . . They stood above us and stabbed us several times more. I received five stabs. I pretended death and held my breath. The Japanese then walked away. The soldier who was lying next to me groaned. One Japanese came back and stabbed him again. I could not hold my breath any longer and when I breathed he heard it and stabbed me another six times. The last thrust caused the blood to gush out of my mouth. He then placed coconut fronds and vines over the three of us. I lay there and heard the last two men shot.

Gunner Max Hazelgrove and five mates reached the plantation soon after the first massacre, unaware the Japanese were there. Bound and stripped of possessions, they were taken through kunai grass. The Japanese suddenly opened fire and Hazel-grove was hit in the back. He lay very still. Later he freed himself. His mates were dead and he struggled to the beach. He was found by a group led by Lieutenant David Selby, the officer who had been in charge of Lark Force's antiquated anti-aircraft guns.

At the time of the slaughter, other Australians were playing a perilous game of hide-and-seek with the Japanese, in the jungle and on the sea. One group had reached neighbouring New Ireland, across St George's Channel. We are talking frying pan and fire here. New Ireland had also been invaded on January 23. In his diary, Jack Ballantyne refers to that day simply as 'the debacle'. He records three weeks on the run from Rabaul, crossing flooded rivers, climbing mountains and taking refuge in missions and in plantation homesteads

> January 27, 1942: An air alarm as we were about to move on again. A recce seaplane came over about 100 ft up and dropped pamphlets (urging to surrender) Moved on then towards Massaura . . . on the hillside overlooking the bay we were greeted with the pleasant sight of 5 Jap transports escorted by 3 destroyers and 11 landing craft streaking for the beach and our objective. We turned back, rejoined the others at Laku. High, cold and wet.

The story of the group is a mini-odyssey, not of heroism, but determination and the small skills that mean survival. Ballantyne was an academic who helped produce a classic book, *Land Utilisation in Australia*, and then turned farmer. He had a way with engines, including the intuitive ability to kick a faltering one just at the right time to keep it going. They crossed from New Britain to New Ireland on February 16, leaving in a plantation owner's boat, the *Lotte Don*, just ahead of Japanese patrols. Three cylinders working and clutch slipping, the *Lotte Don* carried them across the strait and along the New Ireland coast.

> February 18: Another good night. I was getting very tired as there was no-one else to attend to the engine. This time we were running down the coast within sight of land all the time. We anchored in the beautiful Lambon anchorage at 7.00 a.m. This was the fateful spot where the infamous Marquis de Reis attempted to establish his fantastic colony, calling it La Nouvelle France, in the 1870s.

It was not a place of good omens. Many of the men, women and children the marquis sent to found his tropical utopia died awaiting rescue. They were buried in a cemetery near the beach.

Another of the Rabaul party, Jack Moyle, also kept a diary. He records a meeting with a patrol officer, Bill Kyle, a coast-watcher guided to them by a native. Kyle had a radio and they sent a message to Port Moresby asking for a Catalina to pick them up. They waited, and waited and waited. No plane, but the Japanese found Kyle's hut, led by a renegade native, and burnt it down. The party escaped detection. (So did Kyle, though he was later captured by the Japanese and executed in September 1942.) Malaria increased and the *Lotte Don* was wrecked by Japanese or natives. There were close encounters. The group sheltered in a plantation homestead, and were eating a pig they cooked and resting when a native rushed up. 'Boat belong Japan-e stop,' he said. They escaped, Moyle running through the jungle carrying the pig's head.

With no medicine and food nearly gone, Ballantyne and Moyle caught two plantation horses to ride out looking for help. There was only one saddle, and they improvised bridles from parachute harness and fencing wire.

> March 19th, 1942: Wednesday we pushed off for the village of Boski over mountains rising to 2-3000 feet. The ponies were too soft and the going too steep. The worst journey I have ever made. We covered about 20 miles, but only one horse reached Boski; the other collapsed half a mile away on the steepest hill I have ever had a horse on. She died there later, poor thing. I reached the village with a roaring temperature and another bout of fever. Jack Moyle was also weak after fever.

Eventually they became the proud owners of the *Quong Wha*, bought from a Chinese trader with the promise of payment after the war. They were about to set off across hundreds of kilometres of open ocean for New Guinea when the German priest from the nearby mission appeared on the beach. He was carrying a hurricane lantern and leading 20 or more native children. They lined up and sang 'Silent Night'. Then, as the ship pulled away, they sang 'God Save the King'. It was a touching gesture by a man nominally the enemy, and the *Quong Wha* could do with good wishes and godspeeds. It was leaky and idiosyncratic, the engine started by heating two metal balls fixed to the cylinders with a blow lamp until red hot when men on each side with a rope would swing the flywheel backwards and forwards to get compression.

> May 2: Engine stopped at 00.15 hours. Jib Hoisted. Decarbonised. Engine started at 4.00 a.m. and we ran due south. Sea still choppy. Engine stopped at 1.00 p.m (9 hours). Sailed SW. Engine started at 4.00 p.m. after trouble with clutch and water pump. Engine stopped at

9.00 p.m. We left her and slept while McInnes and someone else took off the head. We sailed SW sea fair.

And so the good ship *Quong Wha* brought the group to the
safety of the New Guinea mainland on May 4.

After officer training in Australia, Jack Ballantyne returned
to New Guinea as a platoon commander. Jack Moyle was
trained as an instructor in jungle warfare. Twist of fate: he
arrived at Cowra, where his recruit battalion was based, the
morning after the breakout of Japanese prisoners of war.

We were ordered to round up the escapees and found a
few hiding in a nearby gully – most of them wounded.
They had traveled about six miles during the night. On
being found all they could say was 'shoot shoot' and they
pointed to themselves as they wanted to die. They knew
it would be a disgrace to ever return to Japan now that
they had been taken prisoner. One of our chaps was
going to oblige them, but a nearby officer put a stop to
that.

For most of Lark Force capture was inevitable, despite some
ingenious efforts. Private Norris Kennedy managed to reach
the Australian nurses' quarters at Kokopo where they disguised him as a native by covering him with boot black. What
happened to Kennedy, more than 1000 of his Lark Force
comrades and the men of the civil administration would
remain a mystery until October 1945.

AMBON, A SMALL island on the outer eastern edge of the
Indonesia archipelago, and Timor had been pawns over the
centuries in the European powers' game of empire-building. In

1941, the Dutch held Ambon and West Timor. The Portuguese held East Timor. Gull Force (core, the 2/21st Battalion) and Sparrow Force (core, the 2/40th Battalion) were ordered on December 5 to take up their airport garrison duties. The commander of the 23rd Brigade, Brigadier Edmund Lind, and the battalion commanders had reconnoitred the islands. They did not have the comfort of false illusions. Lind told his superiors the forces were inadequately armed for their tasks.

Colonel Leonard Roach of Gull Force sent rapid-fire messages to army headquarters in Melbourne, pleading for more men and equipment. On December 13, he asked for anti-tank guns and field guns, mortars, anti-aircraft guns, automatic weapons and two additional infantry companies. On December 17, as Gull Force was landing on Ambon, he repeated his plea, and again on December 23. He got no reply so the next day he sent this blunt assessment: 'Present combined army forces inadequate to hold vital localities more than a day or two against determined attack from more than one direction simultaneously.' Again he asked for equipment but warned 'owing enemy strategy now employed indications are this position will be precarious even with above additional if adequate support other services NOT provided. Would appreciate indication proposed policy.' The response from headquarters was that Roach's task was, in cooperation with local Dutch forces, to put up the best defence possible with the resources he had at his disposal.

Reading this, Roach knew Gull Force was regarded as expendable. On December 29, he tried a different approach: 'Additional requested would make immeasurable difference to this strategically important centre as feel confident enemy will waver before Australian fire and bayonets. All most eager to administer salutary punishment.' But he revealed his true feelings in a message to Major William Scott, Gull Force's representative at Melbourne headquarters: 'I find it difficult to overcome a feeling of disgust,' he said, 'and more than a little concern at the way in which we have seemingly been "dumped" at this outpost position . . . without any instructions whatsover.'

Overnight on January 6, Japanese seaplanes bombed Ambon and Roach sent a signal saying 'prospects are gloomy'. Others shared his pessimism. From the area combined headquarters went this message to Melbourne on the need for fighter and dive-bomber reinforcements: 'Only token resistance possible with present unsuitable aircraft all of which will certainly be destroyed in one day's action against carrier-borne forces.'

Roach, now desperate, sent what would be his last message to Melbourne: '. . . in view of overwhelming enemy combined forces successfully operating Menado area and indications early attack on similar scale here we could NOT hold out for more that ONE day.' He recommended immediate evacuation.

The generals reviewed Roach's dispatches and sprang into action. They shot the messenger. On January 14 Roach was replaced by Scott, who had recommended his recall and volunteered to take command. Applauding this move was General Wavell who, when briefed on it by Australian GOC Sturdee, responded: 'So far as I can judge position at Ambon not critical and in any case I am opposed to handing out important objectives to enemy without making them fight for it. Quite appreciate feelings of lonely garrison but am sure Australians will put up stout fight whatever happens. No doubt it is wise to change commander. If circumstances allow hope to fly there for short visit soon.'

Circumstances and the Japanese did not allow. On January 24, 35 aircraft flying off the carriers *Soryu* and *Huryu*, in action for the first time since taking part in the attack on Pearl

Harbor, bombed Ambon. The invasion began on the night of January 30. The Japanese sent in 5300 men, including an infantry regiment, a light tank unit, a mountain artillery battalion and part of a howitzer battery. By now the Australian contingent at Laha airfield, that forward base desired by the Chiefs of Staff, was defending an empty piece of real estate. The surviving Allied aircraft had fled. Japanese troops attacked on February 2. Genichi Yamamoto of the Naval Press Corps, who had the advantage of not being there, said the 'human bullet battle' was 'a record of blasting through forbidding mountains, thickly woven jungles, and impassable roads, or literally going over the bodies of dead comrades, and hacking with blood and death in the midst of the enemy . . . a battle during which took place such heroism as to make the Gods weep'. It was like fighting in a blast furnace, Yamamoto said.

In Japanese eyes, Laha was a famous victory and the naval landing party was later awarded a citation. It was also, like Tol plantation on New Britain, an infamous massacre. Wigmore can only record that Gull Force lost 309 officers and men there, killed in action or in later massacres, though a Japanese prisoner of war later said 150 Australians, two or three Dutchmen and a few natives had remained after Laha had been overrun. After Ambon, it was Timor's turn, and Sparrow Force's.

NEIL DAWSON WAS on the perimeter of Penfui airfield near the south-west tip of Timor. He looked at his World War I vintage .303. He was not impressed. The 2/40th had no modern quick-fire weapons for close combat. He looked at the surrounding countryside and felt vulnerable. There was no support, no air force, no navy, or anything else. 'We're on our own,' he thought.

Sparrow Force, 70 officers and 1330 men, had landed on December 12, 1941. The year had begun well with street parades in Victoria by the 23rd Brigade. Soldiers ten feet tall marched past a dense crowd, clapping, cheering and throwing confetti. Then they were trucked to Albury, close to their training camp. The *Border Morning Mail* reported that the people of Albury 'formed a living, emotional avenue for the march. Flags fluttered, hands waved and streamers soared across the marching columns as the men went down the street.' At Dean Street, 'anomalously what had been a tremendous outburst died away as the people were awed into silence'. But the *Border Morning Mail* was trumpeting to a crescendo: march tunes throbbing on the air, tin hats glinting dully in the sun, boots thudding rhythmically against the bitumen and bayonets flashing in formation of a veritable forest of steel.

And after this for the 2/40th there was the routine of training, the flatness of the country round the remote camps, the frustration of seeing other units go to war in the Middle East and of losing 10 per cent of its strength as reinforcements overseas. When the embarkation orders did come, the battalion had a new commander. Lieutenant Colonel William Leggatt had replaced Colonel Geoffrey Youll. It is a familiar syndrome: commander goes to island, sees the difficulties of terrain, assesses the strength of his force and their equipment, balances all this against the likely strength of the Japanese and, quite properly, reports his conclusions to his superiors. Perhaps he was a tad blunt. According to Peter Henning, who wrote *Doomed Battalion*, the history of the 2/40th, Youll described the decision to deploy to Timor as 'purely suicidal'. As with Roach and Ambon, the generals took aim and fired. However, Leggatt, in his turn, soon saw the reality of Sparrow Force's mission. He wrote to his commander, Brigadier Lind, on January 4:

We are looking at four-and-a-half miles of beach and there is still about six miles of beach on our right flank which we should cover, but all I can do is to put a mobile reserve well out on that flank to deal with anything that tries to come through there. The Dutch have about seven miles of beach to cover from the eastern end of the town to Tenau and about 180 men at present with which to do it . . . No ship has called here yet from Australia and we have no news about our [Bren-gun] carriers and extra MT, our leave personnel or our reinforcements – all of course badly needed and awaited eagerly.

On February 19, Sparrow Force received bad news. Two convoys were approaching and Darwin had been bombed so there would be no aircraft flying to their aid from that direction. As on Ambon, the 2/40th was defending an empty airfield.

NOW NEIL DAWSON is sitting on a couch with Iris in their Hobart home. He points out the window. 'They dropped 600 paratroopers up there,' he says. He points the other way: 'They landed about 10,000 on the beach back there. We were the meat in the sandwich. We saw off the paratroopers but got caught up with this mob behind us. Hopeless from the start. It ends when we are in a convoy heading north towards Portuguese Timor. That's where the bombers catch up with us and the main Japanese force catch up with us. It was surrender or be slaughtered.'

Hopeless from the start. The official historian agrees. The 2/40th was tied down to a defensive role with little chance of doing more than delaying its eventual defeat by mobile forces possessing the initiative and complete control of the sea and the air. But they did it bravely, moving and fighting for four days, taking heavy toll of the enemy. At the end, they had little food, water or ammunition. They had lost 84 officers and men killed and at the rear of the convoy, they carried 132 wounded or seriously ill. (The heaviest losses suffered by an Australian battalion in Crete were 53 killed and 126 wounded of the 2/11th.)

The surrender itself was a surreal moment. An enemy convoy led by light tanks towing field guns moved up to the rear of the Australian convoy. The leading tank was flying a flag thought at first to be a white flag, but later seen to be a furled Japanese flag. Henning relates the story:

Major Campbell was attracted to the scene by a shout from the men. He approached the lead tank and a Japanese 'popped his head out and said "Good morning".' Campbell was so surprised he said 'Good morning' back. He then went and reported to the commanding officer, Bill Leggatt, who called Fred East, the batallion's intelligence officer, who spoke a smattering of Japanese. Leggatt told East to go and ask the Japanese what he wanted. East walked towards an estimated 2000 Japanese troops lining the road and was met by Captain Kosaki. In Japanese, he referred to the white flags and the question of the Japanese surrender. But Kosaki said: 'We thought you might like to put down.' East replied: 'You put down.' 'Yes,' Kosaki said, 'but you put down first.' East went back to Leggatt and said, 'They want to surrender, sir.'

Picture Leggatt looking bemusedly at the well-armed Japanese, who outnumbered his men. He told East to go back and get confirmation from the Japanese. East went and spoke again to Kosaki. He came back to Leggatt. 'I'm sorry sir,' he said. 'They want us to surrender.'

ABOUT 60 MEMBERS of the 2/40th managed to evade the Japanese and join up with the 2/2nd Independent Company operating in Portuguese Timor. Most of these returned to Australia when the 2/2nd was evacuated in December 1942. Others tried to escape but failed. Clyde McKay was with 15 Platoon on forward patrol when word came that the battalion had surrendered. They made their way to the south coast, looking for a lifeboat they had heard was beached. McKay was confident he would make it to Australia. He prided himself with being the only seaman in the 2/40th. He sailed Bass Strait in ketches and schooners. When he tried to join the navy, he was told he was doing a good job where he was, so he worked ashore for a while and then joined the army. The platoon's hopes were dashed; the boat had been wrecked by natives. With food running out and malaria increasing, McKay answered a call for volunteers to go to a village for help. A mistake, he says. Never volunteer. 'As we walked along, more and more natives joined us. By gee, they were wild looking. When we got to the village, they made a big fuss. They cooked a chook and gave us a feed and then they jumped us. After the fight, they took our boots and socks and about two in the afternoon marched us off, hands tied behind our backs.'

That afternoon, that night and until midday the next day, the four were pushed along. Then McKay sat down. 'I wasn't going to move another inch without my boots. They bashed me and kicked me and one of my mates cracked it and said "Oh, they'll kill us". I said "You only bloody die once and if it's going to be here and now, it can be." I got my boots back.' McKay's first experience of the Japanese was a misleading prelude. 'A Nip orderly cut the blisters off our feet and sprinkled them with powder. That night we were in this bit of a hut and this crowd of Nips came up and they brought a mouth organ with them. One of our blokes played it. We had a real party. They even gave us a bottle of plonk. They were the best Nips we struck. It was going to be different. About 400 of us went into prison camps in Java and only eight died there. About 400 of us were sent to different places. I went to the railway.'

McKay carried two things with him through the jungles. One was an Australian 5-shilling piece, minted in 1937, kept in a small pocket of his tattered shorts. In the hungry times, he could have exchanged it for food, and a mate urged him to. 'Once it's gone, it's gone,' McKay said. 'This way I'll always have a bit of Australia with me.' The other was a memory. All the McKays were sailors and fishermen. They lived in a cottage beside the D'Entrecasteaux Channel and every night Granny McKay put a light in the window to guide them past the reef near the pier. Lying in his bamboo and atap hut, Clyde McKay would think of Granny McKay's light. In October 1945 McKay reached Sydney. He picked up a newspaper a couple of days old, Tasmania's *Mercury*. He glanced at the death notices. Granny McKay had died, but she had helped guide him home.

Two hundred and seventy-two of the 2/40th Battalion did not return. Eighty of them died at sea; no light in the window for them when the American submarine *Tang* attacked and sank the Japanese freighter *Tamahoko Maru* which was transporting them to Japan. Most of Lark Force who were captured on New Britain died when the *Montevideo Maru* was torpedoed. And only a third of Gull Force captured on Ambon survived.

ON FEBRUARY 15, 1942, the day Singapore fell, General Sturdee presented a paper to the War Cabinet urging immediate reconsideration of the future employment of the AIF. It was too late for Lark Force and Gull Force, of course. Those birds were caged. Sparrow Force would be overwhelmed in a few days. But the advance elements of the Australian Corps, including Desmond Jackson's 2/3rd Machine Gun Battalion, which had returned from the Middle East, could still have been saved from disaster in Java. Sturdee, the reluctant general, remember, on the deployments to Rabaul, Ambon and Timor, said:

> So far in this war against Japan we have violated the principle of concentration of forces in our efforts to hold numerous small localities with totally inadequate forces which are progressively overwhelmed by vastly superior numbers. These small garrisons alone without adequate reinforcement or support never appeared to have any prospect of withstanding even a moderate scale of attack. In my opinion, the present policy of trying to hold isolated islands with inadequate resources needs review. Our object at the present time should be to ensure the holding of some continental area from which we can eventually launch an offensive in the Pacific when American aid can be fully developed.

As he stood on the deck of the *Orcades* in the port of Batavia, then centre of a crumbling remnant of the Dutch empire and now Indonesia's capital, Jakarta, Desmond Jackson felt disbelief that the battalion would be landed. He had heard, shocked, over the ship's loudspeakers, the BBC broadcast of the fall of Singapore. There was chaos in the harbour and a motley armada of vessels that had fled Singapore. What purpose would the battalion serve? Long after the war, when the machinations of generals and politicians were revealed, Jackson's disbelief would turn to anger and bitterness. He learned of Sturdee's urging that all Australian troops be returned to Australia and that Wavell himself on February 16 had cabled Churchill that the loss of Java, though a severe blow from every point of view, would not be fatal and 'efforts should not therefore be made to reinforce Java which might compromise defence of Burma or Australia'. Wavell said he considered the risk of landing the Australian Corps on Java 'unjustifiable from a tactical and strategic point of view'. However, when the corps commander, General John Lavarack, argued with Wavell that the contingent on the *Orcades* should not be disembarked, Wavell disagreed. According to Lavarack's cable to Curtin, Wavell was 'anxious to avoid appearance pre-cipitately changed plans which might compromise relations Dutch and prestige generally'.

So, as Jackson suspected, the 2/3rd Machine Gun Battalion had been conscripted to the ranks of sacrificial lambs. On February 19 they disembarked. Along with the 2/2nd Pioneers and other Australian units, they were placed under the overall command of Dutch General H. ter Poorten and deployed at Leuwiliang in central western Java to face a Japanese thrust from the north-west coast. The area was mainly flat, with an occasional small knoll, a patchwork of villages, large paddy fields ankle-deep in water, coconut and rubber plantations, a scattering of native houses and patches of thick jungle.

On March 3, at 11.50 am, Arthur Blackburn, the Australian commander, now promoted to brigadier, relayed a Dutch intel-ligence report from his headquarters to the Pioneers. 'No Japanese landings on Java,' it said. Five minutes later five Japanese light tanks arrived at the Leuwiliang bridge.

The next day the Japanese attacked in force. Afterwards Jackson thought C Company, firing their first shots since Syria, but without their Vickers, had done pretty well. Ninety of them were on two hillocks in a paddy field. The Japanese were about 100 metres away in a coconut grove. Three times the Japanese rushed and three times they were beaten off, with heavy casualties, an estimated 200. Seven of C Company were killed and 28 wounded. Three officers had been captured the previous night and another wounded. The only remaining officer, Tim Brettingham-Moore, 21 years old, took command. He won the Military Cross that day. Decades later Jackson could remember him as ice-cold. Once he went from one hillock to check on the small platoon holding out on the other about 70 metres away. Jackson's platoon opened up in covering fire. Brettingham-Moore walked calmly, bullets splashing round him. Ten minutes later Jackson heard the Japanese start firing again and Brettingham-Moore made his steady way back, in a pattern of bullet splashes. 'Is everything all right, corporal?' he asked Jackson.

After 12 hours, with the Japanese operating a pincer movement, C Company withdrew. They had to leave six of their dead behind. In 1985, Jackson returned, with two companions, Charlie Chapple and Alan Whelan. A village had been built around the hillocks. While Jackson looked at the old battlefield, the village headman took Chapple and Whelan to a house. 'I suppose you have come to find out what happened to your six friends,' he said through an interpreter. 'They are buried here, under this house. I helped bury them.' Why had he built a house over the graves? the Australians asked. 'Because we knew that this way the dead would rest more easily,' the headman said. It was a moment of consolation.

THE AUSTRALIANS RETREATED through Java, hoping to reach the coast and navy ships to take them home. They travelled about 200 kilometres. On the night of March 8 the Japanese were not far behind. The next day, from a mountain road, there was the tantalising sight of the Indian Ocean. The Australians were intact as a fighting force. Perhaps this was the place to make a stand while an evacuation could be organised, Jackson thought. However, on March 8 General ter Poorten broadcast that resistance had ceased and all were to lay down their arms. Arthur Blackburn, with the monsoon starting, no shelter and an inadequate supply of drugs and medicine, reluctantly decided to follow ter Poorten's orders on March 9.

Jackson remembered it as a numbing moment. He knew of the barbarism of the Japanese in Nanking. He expected to be captured and executed. He was angry too. The relationship with the Dutch had not been a happy one. It started with the so-called intelligence report. Then on the retreat from Leuwiliang, a battalion team was sent into Bandung, a major town, to contact Dutch army headquarters. Oil storages on the outskirts had been set alight by Japanese bombers. Bandung was blacked out and the battalion team went to a big hotel for directions. They found Dutch officers in dress uniforms dancing with women in evening dress. An English-speaking officer did not believe that the Japanese had landed or that Australian troops had been in action.

After the Japanese invasion of Malaya, as the Netherlands East Indies mobilised for defence of the colony, General ter Poorten made a famous rallying broadcast. It was better, he said, 'to die standing rather than live on our knees'. His army numbered 25,000. Australia's General Sturdee had warned that it 'should be regarded more as well-equipped Home Guards than an army capable of undertaking active operations in the field'. This was, as it turns out, an insult to Home Guards. However, only one in 40 of the Dutch army was European and there were many Indonesians who felt that they were living on their knees under Dutch rule.

The night the 2/3rd Battalion team found the pride of the Dutch officer corps waltzing the night away, Allied officers met General ter Poorten at Bandung. The general told them that guerilla warfare would be impossible because of the great hostility of the Indonesians towards the Dutch. He also gave them the puzzling information that he had instructed his troops to disregard any order he might later give to cease fighting.

His order for the capitulation of the troops under his command came swiftly. General Wavell had avoided compromising relations with the Dutch and losing prestige at a heavy cost.

The day after the surrender was Desmond Jackson's twenty-second birthday. He spent it lying on a groundsheet on a dirt track near the pile of the Australians' disabled rifles. He was shivering uncontrollably with a severe attack of dengue fever. Lieutenant Lance Gibson asked him where his blanket was. It had been lost at Leuwiliang. Gibson went away then returned to lay a grey blanket, one of his two, over the sick man. It was the most important birthday present Jackson ever received. He kept it until the end of the war. It was a thin and tattered thing by then, but Jackson was convinced it had saved his life. Along the railway, an ounce of comfort and protection could make the difference between living and dying. For decades Gibson and Jackson talked to each other on Jackson's birthday. They called it Blanket Day.

RABAUL, AMBON, TIMOR and Java too, clearly were the material for object lessons. Frank Forde, the Minister for the Army, was interested in an inquiry into the roles of the 23rd Brigade forces, their equipment, their leadership and 'whether proper measures were taken to rescue the garrisons'. Sensible questions these, but come a parliamentary debate after the war, Forde had changed his mind. 'We did not have trained and equipped forces to withstand the attack of a well-prepared enemy like the Japanese,' he said. 'Therefore, we cannot set up commissions of inquiry to find out why this island or that was overrun. Strategy was in the hands of the operational command, and the government's military advisers planned the sending of a certain number of troops to Ambon, Timor and elsewhere because they did not have enough men and equipment to send divisions.'

Henning says, succinctly, the strategy was fundamentally defective. So why weren't moves and motives examined? Lark Force, Gull Force and Sparrow Force were left exposed and fatally vulnerable; the contingent from the *Orcades* was sent on a futile mission; generals and politicians were shielded.

IN AUGUST 1942, Iris Flight wrote her letter of love to Neil Dawson, Sparrow Force soldier, prisoner of the Japanese. In December 1995, David Selby of Lark Force, then 89, wrote to his comrade David Bloomfield, a member of his ack-ack company in Rabaul. It was a letter written in anger and bitter with betrayal.

Dear David,

Many thanks for the article about Robbins. It was interesting reading.

Did you know that it has been revealed that the whole Rabaul force had been officially written off by what I regard as one of the most disgraceful episodes in Australian history. This is the official War Cabinet memo. 'They must be regarded as hostages to fortune. They must not be reinforced, withdrawn or re-equipped.'

Lovely! None of us are supposed to be alive today.

All the best.

David S.

CHAPTER 13

Sea-dog and ship's cat

Eternal Father, strong to save
Whose arm doth bind the restless wave,
Who bidd'st the mighty ocean deep
Its own appointed limits keep;
O hear us when we cry to Thee
For those in peril on the sea.

Mariners' Hymn

Bob Collins is on a wrecked raft, reaching out desperately with an oar. A moment before he had Redlead in his arms, but he couldn't hold her as he pushed the raft from the stricken ship. He calls, 'Get on here, you stupid cat, get on the paddle.' She swims frantically the wrong way. This is the dying time, for ships and men and for a ship's cat. As Redlead is grasped by the current, a light burden, Chilla Goodchap is being tumbled under water by the ship's propellers. The turbines are still working in one engine room, despite the four torpedo blows, and the ship is slowly moving forward. It's a most peculiar feeling, a feeling of bliss really. He knows he's going to die. The propellers don't touch him. They twist and turn him. Pleasant. Then he is thrust to the surface, through a thick coating of oil. It's a night of the full moon but the gentle light is lost in the blazes on the Australian cruiser *Perth* and glare of searchlights and flash of guns as the Japanese warships deliver the *coup de grace* to the American cruiser *Houston*, burning, fighting still. The living struggle among the floating dead. The Battle of Sunda Strait is over.

Perth's captain, Hec Waller, is last seen on the bridge, looking down at the silent guns; Captain Rooks of the *Houston* will stay with his ship too. Traditions attach themselves to navies like barnacles. So does superstition. Perhaps it is partly atavism. The oceans are full of mysteries and monsters. There are doldrums and perfect storms. Early sailors could plunge off the end of the earth, longitude was long a puzzle and ancient navigators were magicians reading wind, wave and stars. Little wonder that, as ships touch the water for the first time at launchings, sailors, in expectation of peril, sing the naval hymn asking for God's help.

Ships are living things. They creak and moan and mutter to themselves. They can be dogged in the face of giant waves and howling winds. But not all win the hearts of the crew. Some are not quite right, not quite trustworthy. *Perth* was loved. But there are unlucky ships, and the *Perth* was one, the survivors say. The signs were there from the start. A Modified Leander-class cruiser, the *Perth* was launched in England in 1934 as HMS *Amphion*. The closest *Amphion* came to action was when it was ordered to proceed with utmost dispatch to Tenerife in the Canary Islands. The military governor, General Franco, was plotting to overthrow the Spanish Government but everything was quiet when the *Amphion* arrived. It contented itself with firing a 21-gun salute.

The Australian Government bought the *Amphion* and its two sister ships, *Phaeton* and *Apollo*. The *Phaeton* became the *Sydney* and the *Apollo* the *Hobart*. On July 10, 1939 the

204

Duchess of Kent pulled a silken bell rope near a gun turret, revealing coat of arms and name, and said: 'I name this ship *Perth* and may God bless all who sail in her. A safe voyage and the best of luck.' But sailors are superstitious about changing of names. The *Perth* and the *Sydney* were both lost; the *Hobart* was torpedoed in 1943, taking heavy casualties, and was out of action for almost two years. Waller did his best to fend off ill-fortune. Once in Fremantle he delayed sailing until 0300 on a Saturday so *Perth* would not have to leave port on Friday the Thirteenth. Yet days before it sank, worrying things happened. During the Battle of the Java Sea, the portrait of Lord Nelson which was hanging in *Perth*'s wardroom had dropped from the bulkhead. It had been left lying face downward and not restored to its proper place. Then there were the two padres. 'Sin bosuns', Goodchap called them. 'A ship never has two sin bosuns. It's a bad omen.' The *Perth* carried a padre to Tanjong Priok, the port of Batavia (now Jakarta, Indonesia's capital) for transfer to the *Hobart*, but this was aborted because of an air raid. And then there was Redlead.

In January 1942, the *Perth* was being farewelled in Sydney for the tour of duty that would take it to Java and to the sea bottom. Among the crowd on the wharf at Man o' War steps was the family of Bob Collins's mate, Ray Firminger. Firminger's two-year-old daughter Pat suddenly thrust a small grey-and-white kitten at Collins. He stuffed it, wriggling, inside his jacket, and smuggled it on board past the First Lieu-tenant, Charlie (Pricky) Reid, who had a rule against animals on the ship. Collins hid the kitten below deck and made a little hammock for her. He realised the only way to get her accepted as part of the ship's company would be if Captain Waller took to her. One day Collins carried her to the bridge inside his jacket. Waller was sitting in his chair. Collins put the kitten down. It went to Waller, rubbed against his leg, and meowed. 'What have we here, Collins?' said Waller.

'It looks like a cat, sir,' said Collins.

'Well don't just stand there,' Waller said. 'Get something I can give it to play with.' And so Captain Hector Waller DSO came to be seen on the bridge by First Lieutenant Pricky Reid playing with a kitten chasing a piece of paper on a string. The ship had a mascot, and the mascot had a name after tipping a tin of red-lead paint over herself.

However, if a mascot tries to leave ship that, according to Chilla Goodchap, is the worst possible omen. Redlead did it three times in Tanjong Priok before the *Perth* sailed for the Sunda Strait. This was recorded in an official report after the war: 'Redlead the ship's kitten endeavoured to desert, but was brought back on board.'

Redlead died on March 1, 1942 and so did Ray Firminger and 351 other sailors. Goodchap wondered at his luck. For Australia, the loss of the *Perth* was a bitter blow. Rabaul, Ambon, Timor, Singapore and Sumatra had fallen. Java was about to. Darwin had been bombed. On the seas the British capital ships the *Prince of Wales* and the *Repulse* had been sunk and now, this twin Australian calamity: first the *Sydney*, now the sister ship. Goodchap, who had left the Light Horse because horses didn't like him, and joined the navy, had been drafted to the *Sydney*. He had expected to pick it up on the east coast, but was travelling by train to join it in Fremantle. At Adelaide he was ordered back to Melbourne. The *Sydney* had disappeared.

No word was ever received from the *Sydney* itself about its fate. All the sea gave up was one small, shell-torn float. The story of *Sydney*'s end came from the survivors of the ship that fought with it to the death, the German raider *Kormoran*. Outwardly the *Kormoran* looked like a conventional merchant ship. Under its captain, Lieutenant Commander Anton Detmers, and in peaceful disguise, the *Kormoran* was an efficient killer as it roamed the Atlantic. On January 6, 1941 it sank its first victim, the Greek steamer *Antonis*. Next, on January 18, was the tanker *British Union*. January 29 was a very good day for raiding: the *Kormoran* sank the British ships *Afric Star* and *Eurylochus*. During March and April, it sank three more ships and took another as a prize. In May the *Kormoran* found a new hunting ground, rounding the Cape of Good Hope and entering the Indian Ocean. It was now disguised as the Japanese *Sakito Maru*. Pickings were slim until June 26, when in the early morning it sank the Yugoslav steamer *Velebit* and in the afternoon captured the Australian steamer *Mareeba*. But with tension between Japan and the Allies increasing rapidly, the *Kormoran* slipped into a new disguise. To the unwary eye, it was the Dutch merchant ship *Straat Malakka*.

ON DECEMBER 19, 1941 *The Times* of London published a letter from Admiral Sir Ragnar Colvin who had come from England to Australia to serve as Chief of the Naval Staff. It was a fulsome tribute to Captain Joseph Burnett, commander of the *Sydney*. '. . . his capacity to grasp a situation rapidly and to formulate decisions was quite remarkable,' Admiral Colvin wrote. 'His thoroughness, his appetite for hard work and his powers of organisation were invaluable, and he had a special faculty for getting at the heart of a problem and of stripping it of unessentials which are given to few.' Clearly Burnett was an excellent staff officer; it seems he was a failure as a commander at sea. Colvin's testimony has to be put beside the assessment of G. Hermon Gill in the official Royal Australian Navy history: '. . . he lacked that experience which, gained in a recognised war zone, sharpens suspicion and counsels caution on all chance meetings'.

Under Burnett, the *Sydney* had been on routine escort duty, taking the troop transport *Zealandia* to the Sunda Strait. In its last message to the world, the *Sydney* signalled that it would arrive back in port in Fremantle on Thursday, November 20. But it would have a rendezvous with the *Kormoran* and fate about 200 kilometres off the West Australian coast on November 19. On paper the ships were mismatched. The *Kormoran* had a top speed of about 15 knots. It was heavily armed as a raider, with six 5.9-inch and four 3.7-inch guns, five anti-aircraft machine guns and six torpedo tubes. But the *Sydney* had a top speed of 32.5 knots and was armed with eight 6-inch guns and four 4-inch guns as well as Vickers and Lewis machine guns. It had eight torpedo tubes.

The *Kormoran*'s lookout reported a sighting just before 4 pm and it was quickly identified as a warship. This was not Detmers's prey of choice. He ordered action stations but altered course at full speed into the sun. With the faster *Sydney* steadily overhauling it, the *Kormoran* flew Dutch colours and hoisted the identification signal for the *Straat Malakka*. It pretended innocence by broadcasting a message that it had sighted a suspicious ship. The *Sydney* was now under a mile from the *Kormoran*, sailing parallel. It was at action stations, but its guard was down, perilously. The *Sydney* signalled: 'Show your secret sign.' In seconds Detmers had instead shown his true colours, replacing Dutch with German, and opened deadly fire at short range. For Burnett, the man with the capacity to grasp a situation rapidly, it must have been pure horror. The *Sydney* struck back and the *Kormoran* was also mortally wounded. After about half an hour, the *Sydney* slowly disappeared into the dusk and was lost forever, with all 645 hands.

On November 24, as a sea and air search continued, the British tanker *Trocus* found the answer when it picked up a raft carrying 25 German sailors. That same day the *Perth* was carrying out a full-power trial after a refit in Sydney. Like foot soldiers such as Desmond Jackson, the *Perth* had returned from the Middle East and distant foes to fight the Japanese in Australia's region. Its last action in the Middle East had been a bombardment of Vichy French batteries in the Syrian campaign. The Mediterranean had been a blooding for the *Perth*. It took part in the Battle of Matapan between British and Italian naval forces off southern Greece on March 28–29, 1941, which was the high point of a grim year. So did the Australian destroyer the *Stuart*, commanded by Hec Waller. The *Stuart* had a particularly good night, firing salvos and torpedoes, claiming many hits.

Hotspur's First Lieutenant Hugh Hodgkinson was inspired to lyricism when he described the destroyers in action: 'As the executive signal was made, the great arc of the destroyer screen faded and became shapeless as each destroyer foamed up to 30 knots and, turning and twisting like snipe, they fell into single lines astern of their leaders.' And the Admiral of the Fleet, Viscount Cunningham, on the battleship *Warsprite*, was moved to pity: 'Our searchlights shone out with the first salvo and provided illumination for what was a ghastly sight. Full in the beam I saw our six great projectiles flying through the air. Five out of the six hit a few feet above the level of the cruiser's upper deck with splashes of orange flame. The Italians were quite unprepared. Their guns were trained fore and aft. They were helplessly shattered before they could put up any resistance.'

Lyricism comes easily and pity is affordable in victory. The Italian battle fleet lost three cruisers, the *Zara*, the *Pola* and the *Fiume*, two destroyers, the *Alfieri* and the *Carducci*, and about 2400 officers and men. It also lost the will to fight.

There was nothing heady about the next task for the *Perth* and the *Stuart*. In April they helped gather the flotsam from a military wreck, the ill-fated Greece campaign. Thousands of troops were evacuated by warships; thousands were left ashore, bound for captivity. Then, in May the *Perth* was off Crete for a full-dress rehearsal for the debacle to Australia's north. There were lessons about vulnerability when the enemy had superiority in the air. The *Perth* was lucky. There were two near-misses. Then a *Perth* diarist watched an attack on the British destroyer *Juno*: 'They are leaving us alone this time. Now I see why, they are going after the *Juno*. She's hit and is now a great pillar of flame and smoke. She's sunk. It only took one minute and forty-five seconds for the gallant little ship to plunge to her grave.' Again the navy managed to evacuate thousands of trapped soldiers, but again many were left behind. Cunningham looked at his losses: three cruisers and six destroyers and several ships out of action for months, including the aircraft carrier *Formidable*. The gloss had gone off Matapan. Cunningham wrote, gloomily, prosaically: 'We had been fighting against the strength of the Luftwaffe, and once again it had been borne in upon us that the Navy and the Army could not make up for the lack of air forces.'

THROUGHOUT ITS HISTORY, Japan has been a great importer, synthesiser and improver of ideas and technologies. Just as at the start of World War II it could give thanks to the British for assistance in developing its air power, it had reason to be grateful to the Royal Navy for its strength at sea. The Japanese navy's firepower was formidable; in particular it outmatched the combined fleets of the Allies in the new superweapons, aircraft carriers, with 10 compared to America's three in the Pacific. But the spirit of the men in the machines can determine battles, and that can be shaped by a sense of tradition. When the navy was being created, Japan's leaders naturally enough looked to the Royal Navy as a model. Britannia ruled the waves and the Royal Navy was the essential builder and defender of the Empire. The Japanese navy was disciplined and cohesive. It also had its own touch of the militarists' version of *bushido*. Soldiers were taught it was better to die than to surrender; sailors went into battle on ships that did not carry lifebelts.

The *Perth*, under the command of a Royal Navy officer Sir Philip Bowyer-Smith, had fought in the Mediterranean as part of British fleets. Now commanded by Hec Waller, it sailed into a sea of confusion. In January 1942 it became part of the American, British, Dutch and Australian Command, known as ABDA, in an attempt to defend Java. General Wavell, in a report to Churchill, bleakly summarised the situation in the pure terms of naval resources: 'Maximum of three to four cruisers and about ten destroyers as striking force. If this is divided between the two threatened ends of the island it is too weak for either. If kept concentrated, it is difficult, owing to distance involved to reach vital point in time. Wherever it is, it is liable to heavy air attack.'

Then there was the matter of the men in the machines. On January 1, American Admiral T. C. Hart, commander of the US Asiatic Fleet, arrived by submarine from the Philippines to head ABDA naval forces, Abdafloat. At this desperate time, it was a poor appointment. Hart was a reluctant recruit, 64 years old. He arrived in Java tired and ill, and he told Admiral Geoffrey Layton, commander of the British Eastern Fleet, that the appointment was 'not of his seeking and little to his liking. What he needed was a rest.' Not one to put on a brave face, Hart told both the Governor-General of the Netherlands East

Indies and the Dutch commander, Admiral C. E. L. Helfrick, that he felt too old for the job. Hart's and Helfrick's photographs are side by side in the official Australian history. Hart has the look of an aesthete, of a man who perhaps thinks too much; Helfrick is an old sea-dog, a well-fed one. Hart took command of Abdafloat on January 15 and asked to be relieved of his duties on February 9. Helfrick took over. Abdafloat had not been a happy ship but, in the circumstances, the miscellany of vessels was never going to be moulded into a potent striking force. There was no time for training and exercising together; the ships did not even speak the same language. In the dash, dart and surge of a sea battle, with salvos falling and torpedoes arrowing, seconds are precious at the helm. Hodgkinson could write of destroyers twisting and turning like snipe but reaction time is stretched by poor communications. On February 25, Dutch Admiral K. W. F. M. Doorman, in his flagship, the cruiser *De Ruyter*, led a striking force out to face the Japanese invasion force. Doorman's signals had to be translated by the American liaison officer on the *De Ruyter* to the American cruiser *Houston* which passed them on by voice or lamp.

The Battle of the Java Sea began on February 27. Adding to the Japanese advantage were the use of aerial spotting and more and better torpedoes. It was sitting-duck time. The British cruiser *Exeter* was hit and would later be lost. The Dutch destroyer *Kortenaer* blew up, capsized and dived under in seconds. The British destroyer *Electra* was next, and its senior surviving officer, Gunner T. J. Cain, wrote a touching farewell to the ship and its captain. *Electra*, Cain said, 'sighed, listed heavily to port and down by the bows'. Commander C. W. May came to the starboard side of the bridge and waved to the men in the water who 'cheered lustily'. *Electra* 'settled more sleepily', then sank.

Doorman went down with flagship *De Ruyter* and Waller of *Perth* was now in command. He said in his report: 'I now had under my orders one undamaged six-inch cruiser (*Perth*), one 8-inch cruiser (*Houston*) with very little ammunition and no guns aft. I had no destroyers. The force was subjected throughout the day and night operations to the most superbly organised air reconnaissance. I was opposed by six cruisers, one of them possibly sunk, and twelve destroyers . . . I had therefore no hesitation in withdrawing what remained of the striking force.'

Admiral Helfrick was not pleased. From his vantage point on Java, the old sea-dog barked. 'Strictly speaking,' he wrote, 'the return of the *Perth* and the *Houston* was against my order 2055/26 – "You must continue attacks until enemy is destroyed." This signal was intended to make it clear that I wanted the Combined Striking Force to continue action whatever the cost, and to the bitter end.' Old sea-dogs and those generals given to fighting from afar to the last man could do with some of the wisdom of good poker players, who know when to hold 'em, know when to fold 'em, know when to walk away and know when to run. Helfrick was confirmed in his opinion of Waller's decision to withdraw by the fact that *Perth* and *Houston* did meet their bitter end 24 hours later. However, when the two cruisers made their last voyage, they were not deliberately sailing towards enemy guns, but endeavouring to escape and fight another day.

At 7 pm on February 28, the *Perth* and the *Houston* left Tanjong Priok. The port had been a shambles. 'A state of despair', Chilla Goodchap said, sunken craft in the water and ·on the wharves Dutch soldiers and civilians trying to crowd their families on any boat that was sailing out. With only about 20 rounds of ammunition each for the 6-inch guns and fuel tanks half-full, the *Perth* sailed but Waller had ordered the loading of 24 rafts he had spotted on the wharves. Sailors called them pilgrim rafts. They would save lives. 'We were to go with the *Houston* full speed through the Sunda Strait which divides Sumatra from Java,' Goodchap said. 'That's where the China Sea meets the Indian Ocean, the fastest flowing waters in the world. We were going to evacuate troops from somewhere near Krakatoa. The Old Man spoke to us soon after we left port.'

Waller said: 'This is the captain speaking. We are sailing for Sunda Strait for Tjilatjap and will shortly close up to the first degree of readiness, relaxed. Dutch air reconnaissance reports that Sunda Strait is free of enemy shipping. But I have a report that a large enemy convoy is about fifty miles north-east of Batavia moving east. I do not expect, however, to meet enemy forces.'

Dutch reconnaissance was wrong. The *Perth* hoped to clear Sunda Strait by dawn, but it was being shadowed by a Japanese destroyer. Lieutenant William Gay recorded later: 'The hope ended at 2306 when the yeoman of the watch sighted a destroyer fine on the starboard bow.' Captain Waller, who had woken up shortly before and was feeling fresh and alert, ordered 'make the challenge'. The enemy destroyer answered with a series of meaningless green flashes and turned away at full speed, making smoke. *Perth* altered course and went after the Japanese destroyer, making a signal to *Houston*: 'Follow me.' They were sailing into the middle of a Japanese invasion fleet.

WALLER PUTS THE *Perth* into a mad, zig-and-zag circle, firing and being fired at, launching and dodging torpedoes. At one stage there are four enemy ships to starboard and five to port. Goodchap is in B turret working the hydraulic hoist, bringing up ammunition from the magazine deep below. He looks at a shell as it emerges. He realises the battle's over. It's a practice shell! They're firing practice shells! They're out of ammunition. Deep down in the *Perth*, below the waterline, his mate Ern Toovey is at his action station in the cordite-handling room supplying Y gun house. The temperature is over 110 degrees in the confined space, and the deck slippery with oil fuel that has leaked through the bulkheads. Waller hurls the ship to port and they crash to starboard; Waller hurls the ship to starboard and they crash to port. The ammunition is gone. Toovey has reported 'all finished Y room' when the third torpedo hits. On the bridge Waller says: 'Christ! That's torn it . . . Abandon ship.' Ship's bugler Allan Gee has been on the bridge near Waller during the action. He pipes the dreaded Abandon Ship order with his bugle over the loudspeakers.

The message reaches Toovey in the bowels of the *Perth*. He scrambles his way up through the half-light in the dying ship and, carefully stepping over or around dead shipmates, past the 6-inch guns, silent but still smoking, reaches his abandon-ship station. The small skiff has been smashed. He helps throw a couple of garden-type benches and some heavy timber over the starboard waist and somehow finds himself besides Y turret, when the *Perth* is lifted out of the water. The fourth torpedo has struck. Shrapnel is flying. He feels a sharp pain in his right thigh. The water looks safer. He jumps.

Goodchap and the B turret crew, 21 of them, have opened the scupper and emerged on B deck. More gather. He thinks it might be a target and goes to the upper deck. He is right; a shell explodes in the crowd, killing all but two who are blown into the water with shrapnel wounds. They survive until Burma. Goodchap cuts some men out of their heavy anti-flash gear, then decides its time to say goodbye. He goes to the port rail, looks over, and thinks, 'Christ, that's a long way.' He jumps.

Allan Gee, a boy from a farm near the small settlement of Silver Creek, in Victoria, helps cut off some Carley floats. Next to him is a very close friend, born and bred in Melbourne's tough inner city. His name is George Catmull, but he is always called Moggy, of course. People have started to go over the side, so Gee grabs a life jacket and he and Moggy go to the port side. They hold hands, and as they jump, Moggy shouts to Gee, 'I'll see you in Young and Jackson's.' It's a favourite Melbourne meeting place, a pub that is the home of the iconic and nude portrait of Chloe. Moggy can't swim. Gee never sees him again.

David Manning has been on the 4-inch gun deck, firing anti-aircraft guns at the Japanese destroyers. When the Abandon Ship order comes, he goes first to the quarterdeck and helps throw anything that will serve as a float overboard. He goes to the port side, climbing over the guard rail at Y turret and is willing himself to jump. His mind is made up for him. The torpedo hits and he finds himself corkscrewing into the water.

Toovey lands nearby, injuring his knee, swims away from the *Perth*, then turns back to watch the end. It rights itself, as if reluctant to go, fighting to stay on the surface, then disappears in a swirl of foaming water, ensign still flying. Not far away, the *Houston* is being torn apart and soon it is gone too. Now there is only the sound of the Japanese ships, and the cries of men. He has lost his Mae West and looks for something to cling to. There's a 44-gallon drum, with a plank attached, some sort of raft that has been smashed. Soon Toovey and about a dozen others have congregated around it. They are from different parts of the ship. They exchange names and ask about shipmates. Once Toovey finds himself in argument, not heated, but the sort you would have over a beer. Keith is all right, but he's from the south. Toovey is from Queensland. Imagine anyone thinking that there is a better wicket-keeper in the world than Don Tallon.

In the water there are two enemies: clogging, blinding oil and the current. Goodchap watches, helpless, as Commander William Martin, straddling a spar, is swept past, as quickly and easily as Redlead, towards the open Indian Ocean. Many men drown. Some swim for shore, but even close in there are treacherous cross-currents. Toovey, who has drifted away from the drum, first of all supports himself on a small wooden cask. As the hot dawn breaks, he drifts, and once he sees a beach and palm trees. He swims, but is tugged backwards. Through the day, the oil on his face starts to sizzle, then, about three o'clock, he guesses by the sun, a small boat approaches. Strange. It is manned by mostly naked sailors. A Japanese destroyer has ordered them to pick up survivors, but they have to strip themselves of oil-fouled clothes before going on board. Manning is picked up too. Toovey's mate Chilla Goodchap is one of the oarsmen. As they pull alongside the destroyer, the captain sends a message in English that he has to leave the area because of an aircraft alert, but that he will return. He doesn't.

They bury Neville McWilliam at sea. He was Fleet Air Arm and he had been in the water when the port torpedo hit. The concussion left a terrible wound. On the rescue boat is one of the sin bosuns, Padre Keith Mathieson, who had been supposed to transfer to the *Hobart*. It is a simple ceremony but they take comfort that it has been properly done. That night they weather a squall, pick up two men from the *Houston* and in the morning rig a sail and steer for the Java coast. The boat disintegrates on the rocks as it touches shore. They have reached land, but not safety.

LONELY OR IN groups, the men of the *Perth* and the *Houston* struggled to survive. Sangiang Island is in the middle of Sunda Strait. In the aftermath of the battle, a cat and a commodore and the living and the dead were swept past it. Some escaped the current in a lifeboat. There was one landing spot, a beach between two cliffs, with a surf running. Petty Officer Horace Abbott rigged an oar as a sweep and the lifeboat rode the waves in Bondi style. Others managed to swim in. A third group arrived by raft from Toppers Island, a small, rocky outcrop with a manned lighthouse about 10 kilometres north of Sangiang. They had created their raft over several days out of spars, hatches from Japanese merchant ships and buoyant material. They carved 12 paddles from wreckage. It took them four and a half hours to break the current's grip and land on the larger island.

Sangiang, home to a small number of Sundanese subsistence farmers, was shelter for about 50 *Perth* survivors. As Japanese destroyers patrolled the strait and, in the distance, the business of invasion went on, they nursed the wounded, chased scrawny chickens and planned escape. Briefly their lives and fortunes brushed against those of another group: a tough British sailor, a shipwrecked Australian stoker, two young English children, Mary and Robin, and their Singhalese nanny who had sailed through the Sunda Strait in a small skiff on the night of the battle. The children and their mother had been trying to flee Singapore; their father, a judge, had stayed behind. The sailor had plucked them from the sea after Japanese bombers had struck their ship and they had become separated from their mother. The sailor, the stoker, Mary, Robin and the nanny sailed out of their lives again, hoping to reach Australia.

Some of the *Perth* survivors set that course too, but failed. Fifteen days after the *Perth* sank they entered the southern Javanese port of Tjilatjap, short of food and water, assuming that this vital facility at least would be held against the Japanese onslaught. The devastation of bombing was an ominous sign, but, physically weak, they were being carried by a flood tide and an onshore wind towards the Japanese and captivity. Lieutenant Thode, a New Zealander whose background was Merchant Service, had commanded the lifeboat. He was taken with four others to Japanese headquarters. The commanding officer stood at the top of the steps while the group was interrogated. Then something happened that chilled Thode. The officer came down until he was a few steps above him. 'He then pointed to my left,' Thode recorded, 'and spoke in Japanese, then deliberately swung his arm slowly to the right of my face. This was not a slap, but it was an unpleasant contact and possibly some sort of insult.' Survivors of battle and sea faced a new peril.

Oh Trinity of love and power,
Our brethren shield in danger's hour
From rock and tempest, fire and foe,
Protect them wheresoe'er they go;
Thus evermore shall rise to Thee
Glad hymns of praise from land and sea.
                                   Mariners' Hymn

THE FIGHTING UNIT that was the crew of the *Perth* began to lose shape as men were killed or wounded and the guns went out of action. In the water they helped one another survive for as long as possible. Hundreds had been lost in the peril of battle on the sea; some of those who survived this sinking would, in some years' time, face peril on the sea again as American submarines attacked Japanese ships carrying prisoners of war to Japan. But now there was peril on land, a foe who could be determinedly callously and casually brutal: no brother enemy here; no freemasonry of warriors.

In boats, on rafts and clinging to wreckage, survivors washed up on Java and the offshore islands. Some swam. It took Bob Collins two days and perhaps 15 kilometres to beat the currents and reach a beach. On shore, many of them were modern men at their most vulnerable: naked, though Padre Mathieson had insisted on keeping his shirt on. Some who hadn't been ordered by Japanese to strip off did so to rid themselves of dragging, oil-soaked clothes. And so they set off through the countryside, hoping for help, not even protected by modesty. Walking with a companion, David Manning was wearing only a money belt until an old Indonesian woman gave him a small piece of cloth which he draped strategically. After the third village, he saw an Indonesian pushing a bicycle with a stack of blue sarongs on the handlebars. He took his total wealth, a soggy Australian 10-shilling note, and started to bargain for two sarongs. Then a third Australian appeared, waving his arms, everything flapping in the wind, and shouting 'make it three'. Turned out it was Gordon Black, one of the lieutenants, though he wasn't wearing badges of rank at the time. Manning returned to the bargaining and soon three sailors, in fetching blue, were walking along the road to the main town, Labuhan. There they saw a crowd of men from the *Perth* and the *Houston* also in blue sarongs. The man with the bicycle had been sent out to distribute them.

Manning and three others, one a big Polish American called Golloski, walked on through the hills. One day a horse-drawn cart went by, carrying a Japanese flag. 'Oh, God,' said Manning.

'Oh boy,' said Golloski. 'Am I glad to see that.'

'What do you mean?' Manning asked.

'Well, look at the flag,' Golloski said. 'It must be some local form of the Red Cross.' Shortly after they were herded by natives into an abandoned theatre in Serang. About 500 would have watched flickering films there; now 1500 or so prisoners were crowded in. Manning still had not seen a Japanese. He slept, exhausted, then was woken by a little man. 'He was wearing glasses and screaming at me in a language I didn't understand but he was getting his message across with the point of a bayonet. The first thing that went through my mind when I woke up and looked at him was "He is not yellow, he is brown". That was the start of it all.'

Packed in among the reluctant audience under a machine gun mounted on the gallery was Rohan Rivett, jotting in a secret diary.

> We've had no food all day until four o'clock this afternoon when we got exactly eleven spoonfuls of boiled rice . . .
>
> The *Perth* boys are grand with their six or seven wounded mates who have to be carried to and from the wretched latrine day and night. If we stay here much longer on this ration, which is less than one eats for a sweet for one meal at home, there won't be a man here who can carry anybody but himself. Still no bandages, antiseptics or treatment for these boys, although it is now thirteen days since *Perth* was sunk . . .
>
> Our friend the frog-faced officer came in today and again started threatening some of the officers with his revolver. On his last visit he asked one of the English naval officers if he would commit hara-kiri then and there if he lent him his gun . . .

Manning and Rivett met when groups were moved from the theatre to the Serang jail. More than 30 were pushed into each eight-prisoner cell. Manning had been in the cell for a few hours when he decided to get some exercise, which meant a slow walk, stepping round and over people to the wall about 4 metres away and back. On the third journey he noticed an oval drawn on the whitewashed wall, with four pegs at each end. 'Who's the Aussie Rules fan?' he asked. A figure curled up in the corner said: 'Me, why?' It was Rivett. The cell contained Americans from the *Houston* and Australians, but none from Victoria, the heartland of Australian Rules football. Rivett had been attempting to explain to them the rules of this peculiar and peculiarly Australian game. Aussie Rules then was tribal and suburban; barring cataclysm or betrayal, teams were followed for life. Disputes could split families and end friend-ships. It never quite came to that with Manning and Rivett, though there was the day late in the war when they were both in hospital in Thanbyuzayat base camp in Burma. Manning suffered blackouts, the aftermath of being blown off the *Perth* by the torpedo. Rivett's body was covered with sores. American Liberators had begun bombing the railway and installations and during raids the prisoners were evacuated to the jungle. One day, as the giants circled above, Manning and Rivett were by themselves as the rain poured on to them and bombs fell nearby. Talk turned into heated argument. A line had been crossed. Rivett had claimed that Fitzroy's Haydn Bunton was a better player than Essendon's Dick Reynolds.

THIRTY HOURS AFTER the sinking of the *Perth*, Chilla Goodchap, Ern Toovey and the others from the wrecked lifeboat had a council of war. They decided to leave the 'heavy' sick with volunteers, and to go for help, striking inland over the hills, fording small streams, crossing paddy fields, walking through tall timber, ferns and orchid-draped trees, Goodchap sometimes pulling, sometimes pushing, sometimes carrying the injured Toovey. Groups joined together then split again. Somehow Toovey lost touch with Goodchap who with about 10 others went looking for Dutch troops. But they were found and surrounded by Sundanese hillsmen who bound them with jungle vines and slashed three of them with machetes. Indonesian policemen intervened and the party was delivered to the jail in the small town of Pandelang. Here Goodchap met his first Japanese. From the larrikin stream of Australian life, Goodchap was always going to attract more than a fair share of beltings and bruises. There would be, over the years, mutual antagonism and incomprehension. For a start, he expected tiny, short-sighted fellas. But he looked through the jail fence and saw big men, around 6 feet tall in the old measure. These were the elite Imperial Guards. Then they didn't come through the gate, but threw coir rope ladders over the fence, climbed up like bloody monkeys and down inside the jail. The Japanese officer, neat, wearing a samurai sword, looked at the group of men, some in sarongs, some in loincloths, some naked, all oil-stained men, and asked, 'Where is your leader?' The men pushed forward Frank Gillen, an engineer, an older man, quiet, gentle, not used to command. 'What do you want to do?' the officer asked Gillen who just stood, silent, mouth open. 'What do you want to do?' the officer asked again. From the ranks came a voice, and *Perth* folklore is that it was Goodchap. Someone said, 'Tell the bludger we want to go home.'

'We want to go home,' Gillen said. The officer stared for a moment, shouted something in Japanese, then drew his sword and hit Gillen with the flat of it.

Goodchap was to remain naked for two and a half months until a batch of prisoners were taken to what was called the Bicycle Camp in Batavia, formerly barracks for Indonesian troops in the Dutch army. Already there were Australian soldiers captured when the Japanese intercepted craft from the motley armada trying to escape Singapore. Some were 8th Division transport drivers, 'old and bolds', men in their forties. One of them looked closely at Goodchap as he walked off the truck, skinny, naked, oil-covered. The old and bold had flaming red hair and red cheeks and he had not yet lost his enormous beer belly. 'You poor bastard,' he said to Goodchap. 'What are you? A Gurkha, a Punjabi, or what are you?'

'No. I'm an Australian sailor.'

'What ship?'

'*Perth*.'

'Where are you from?'

'Brisbane.'

'What's your name?'

'Goodchap.'

'Know George Goodchap?'

'He's my father.'

The old and bold took Goodchap to a hut, cut his matted hair off with clippers and gave him soap to wash the surface oil off under the camp's warm bore water. Then he fossicked and found a length of material. From this Goodchap fashioned a G-string. He was clothed; and this was how he would be clothed, in Burma and Thailand during the building of the railway, except for one famous day which he will tell about later.

Goodchap, Toovey and other *Perth* survivors were reunited at the Bicycle Camp. One day the senior officer, Lieutenant Commander Ralph Lowe, called them together. They counted their dead. By process of elimination, they reckoned they'd lost 350. 'For what?' someone asked. It is the oldest question in warfare. Admiral Helfrick would have preferred the *Perth* and the *Houston* to have gone down with guns blazing in the Battle of the Java Sea rather than 24 hours later in the Battle of Sunda Strait. His reasoning? 'Probably on the night of the 27–28 February they would have sold their lives at greater cost to the enemy.' That is not necessarily so. In the Java Sea, warships fought warships; in the Sunda Strait, the Japanese invasion convoy was anchored in Bantam Bay, close to the action. One minute the aide to General Hitoshi Imamura, the Japanese commander-in-chief, was sitting in his cabin on the headquarters transport *Ryujo Maru*, disappointed that he had travelled a long distance without hearing a shot fired in anger, the next he was stunned by 'the tremendous sound of the guns'. 'About 16 kilometres NNE of our anchorage there were two battleships continuously firing their large guns. To our left I could clearly see what appeared to be a destroyer which was actively carrying on the fight.' Not long after, the aide, having got what he wished for, was in the water with General Imamura, clinging to a piece of wood. One transport had been sunk and several, including the *Ryujo Maru*, had been hit. Imamura and the aide were picked up 20 minutes later. It is difficult to give credit or blame for the damage of the enemy ships, for in the fury the Japanese themselves fired 2650 shells and launched 35 torpedoes.

The answer to the question 'for what?' is damage to the transports, discomfort to the commander-in-chief and a 24-hour delay in the Japanese landing. All this adds up to nothing in the overall sweep of conflict, or in the Java campaign itself. But perhaps for individuals, for civilians as well as soldiers, a day did make a difference for good or ill in the lottery of existence. Perhaps some escaped death, or found it. The men of the *Perth* took what consolation they could from the possibility that the Battle of the Sunda Strait had mattered. Then Lieutenant Commander Lowe looked to the future. He said he hoped the men would keep together as a unit, watch out for one another, help one another. It was invaluable advice. They were entering a nether world where survival would depend as much on the care and kindness of mates as it did on the will and strength of the individual. They would be lost from sight and succour.

In March 1942 the navy released the news of *Perth*'s sinking and published the list of the missing. The headmaster of Brisbane's Church of England Grammar School, W. P. Morris, wrote in his authoritative hand to George Goodchap. 'It is perhaps out of place to try to soften a parent's grief for the loss of his son,' he said. 'Yet this loss is accompanied by so much honour as those brave boys died so gallantly for their country that it is not as if the death were through sickness or an accident in peacetime. Your boy has brought honour to the school and to his country. Please accept our sympathy and thanks.' Soon after, George Goodchap opened an impressive envelope. The small, single sheet of paper carried the Royal coat of arms, under it the words 'Buckingham Palace' and this message: 'The Queen and I offer you our heartfelt sympathy in your great sorrow. We pray that your country's gratitude for a life so nobly given in its service may bring you some measure of consolation.' It was signed 'George R.I.'.

At this time Chilla Goodchap was one of 44 packed into a cell for 14 in Serang jail, naked, oil-smeared, but determined to survive. He had left death behind him when he broke the surface of Sunda Strait. His new life was a learning, a slow descent towards hell, with skills and toughness to develop and sickness to encounter and levels of brutality to endure.

The party reached the Bicycle Camp on May 13, 1942. For a start, the problem was boredom. Imagine that. Work parties were voluntary and opportunities for scrounging. While stripping a house for the Japanese, Goodchap smuggled back to camp a light shade. He plugged the hole with bamboo and now he had a rice dixie. He also had a close relationship with Dutch Queen Wilhelmina. 'The Japs were mad to get metal and round the city were the statues of Wilhelmina. We had sledgehammers to break them up. Queen Wilhelmina would be most upset to know that I know the exact size of her bust and her backside and everything else to do with it.' The cars of the tuans were collected too, the Rolls Royces and Cadillacs that had ferried them around their colonial cocoon. They were parked in row after row on the golf course. As they were dismantled, prisoners filched pieces of mudguard for frying pans. Goodchap himself had a sideline in eight-day clocks he levered out of the dashboard with a pick. He sold a couple to Japanese guards.

They nicked aeroplane fuel too. With deteriorating diet and the bite of the tropical climate, the men developed weeping tinea on toes, ears, nose, mouth, scrotum and anus; a fungus-like growth that itched and pained, especially round the testicles. They made little bags out of gauze to hold and protect them. The blokes working in warehouses pinched whitewash brushes and put them into a pool. Everything valuable like that went into a pool. The doctors and the medical orderlies would fill a half 44-gallon drum with aeroplane fuel and the men would parade past and pull their G-string back and bend over and the orderly would go through their legs with this big whitewash brush. That would be terrific and they'd put their G-string back and walk about four paces and someone would say, 'How did it go?' and with that it would hit them and you'd never see fellas do a standing leap like it in all your life. And they'd be standing there fanning away with their slouch hats with all their might. And there would be laughter in the camp. Dysentery, beri-beri, malaria, tropical ulcers and cholera lay ahead.

There was an apprenticeship in mistreatment too. Ern Toovey met a guard, the 'Brown Bomber', whom he displeased. Toovey was tall; the Brown Bomber was short. The Brown Bomber climbed on a box to deliver his 'boxing presento'.

Lieutenant Colonel John Williams met the *kempeitai* who were in search of military information. For five days he was given no food and then some was put on the table in front of him. If he talked, it was his. Later he was tied to a chair and hauled and tumbled round the room. The rope was tightened, his legs twisted. They tried to make him drink water to fill up his lungs, but fortunately he did not get the whole of it. They burnt his feet with cigarette butts. They took him outside, blindfolded him and told him if he did not answer questions they would shoot him. They promised him a house in Batavia with a servant.

They let him go.

The whole camp met the new commandant, Lieutenant Sonai, who strutted around, the point of his samurai sword scabbard dragging in the dust beside his highly polished boots. The Korean guards became even more vicious. On work parties, as prisoners marched past the guardhouse, the leader had to cry *kashira migi* (eyes right) and *nakai* (front) or on the way in *kashira hadare* and if the guards were not happy with the way the command was given, each prisoner was slapped. Sonai devised a new punishment. If two men were caught breaking a camp rule, smoking in the wrong area, perhaps, they had to stand opposite and slap one another. It started with a soft hit, but somehow, if they were not careful, even if they were mates, they ended up really hurting one another.

The men hoped the change meant the war was not going well for the Japanese.

IN SEPTEMBER THERE were rumours of a move. The men were inoculated and told they were going to a land of nectar where life would be better and they would earn extra money. In October, a party of about 1200 was taken by train to Tanjong Priok. From here the *Perth* had sailed on its last voyage to Sunda Strait. In the early light they saw against the

wharf a rusting hulk of a ship, the *Kinkon Maru*. More prisoners arrived and 1500 looked doubtfully at the ship. How could
the Japanese possibly fit them on? With rifle butts and hob-
nailed boots. Six hundred to seven hundred were crammed
into a hold. Lying down was impossible, sitting up barely. For
four days the ship lay berthed while the sun scorched steel.
Some of the men developed diarrhoea which turned into
dysentery. The weak could not climb to the latrines, two boxes
lashed to the starboard side of the ship, and stench filled the
holds.

On October 8, the *Kinkon Maru*, rust-bucket that it was,
stirred and came alive. The survivors of the HMAS *Perth* were
at sea again, but not as fighting sailors. They were cargo being
carried as slave labour towards the Thai–Burma railway.

CHAPTER 14

Getting to know you

Lieutenant Okasaka arranged a tableau on Changi beach. He spaced four men in a line with their backs to the sea. In front of them he placed a squad of Sikhs, renegades who had gone over to the Japanese, lured by talk of the liberation of India. To one side were a group of officers, British and Australian, and two chaplains. Rod Breavington, Vic Gale, two Australians, and two British privates, Waters and Fletcher, would soon die. It was an execution to punish the four and to send a message to 15,400 of their comrades crowded in nearby Selarang Barracks Square: escape was forbidden; to attempt it meant death.

After the surrender of Singapore, the mass of prisoners had been broken into work parties. There were roads to repair, ships to load and, on the heights of Bukit Timah, ground to be levelled for a Japanese memorial to their fallen during the Malayan campaign, a task particularly galling to the prisoners of war. Breavington and Gale escaped from Bukit Timah on May 12, 1942, crept their way to the coast and rowed in a small boat a marathon 320 kilometres to Colomba Island. There they were slowly starving when they were recaptured. Back in Singapore, Breavington was treated in hospital for malaria and beri-beri. The Japanese took him from his hospital bed to the beach.

Breavington, a corporal, was 38 years old. He had been a policeman before enlisting. Gale, only 23, had been a fitter and turner. Breavington made a last bid to save Gale, claiming to Okasaka that Gale had been obeying orders. He should be shot; Gale should be spared. Okasaka rejected the plea. The firing squad knelt, preparing to fire. The four men and the officers, including the senior Australian, Lieutenant Colonel Frederick Galleghan, stood to attention and saluted crisply one another. Breavington shook hands with his companions and waved aside the handkerchief Okasaka offered as a blindfold. So did the others. To Galleghan he called out goodbye and good luck. Fletcher remarked to the Church of England chaplain, John Bryan: 'I hope they are good shots, sir.' They were not. Bryan had closed his eyes in prayer. He heard shot after shot and Breavington's shout: 'For God's sake shoot me through the heart.'

The men died on September 2, 1942. In November 1945 Gale's father and Breavington's wife received letters from Galleghan. He had written them after the executions and buried them along with official records in Changi for recovery at liberation. A leader of men in battle, Galleghan had been deeply moved by the behaviour of his men as prisoners. In the letter to Gale's father he said that both men 'displayed such calmness and bravery in the face of death that they excited the admiration of the commanders of the British troops'. In the letter to Mrs Breavington, he said 'your husband's bravery was an inspiration to those who saw it and will remain an inspiration to us all . . . He was the bravest man I have ever seen.'

GALLEGHAN RETURNED FROM the beach to the crisis on Selarang Barracks Square. Two days before, the Japanese had demanded that all prisoners sign this statement: 'I, the undersigned, hereby solemnly swear on my honour that I will not, under any circumstances, attempt escape.'

It was the duty of prisoners of war to attempt to escape. The men refused to sign. The Japanese then ordered all prisoners in the area to Selarang Barracks Square. Some Australians remembered this place from those days when the Japanese threat seemed far away and overconfidence in their capacity to resist it was high. This was the Far Eastern home of the Gordon Highlanders and in a ceremonial competition they would have whipped the Japanese: white spats, kilts swinging, meticulous marching to the drums. Now 15,400, including the ill brought from hospital, were crowded into space for 1200. There was only one water tap and on the first day, no food was provided. They dug latrines through the asphalt. That night Galleghan ordered a concert and at the end instructed: 'Play the *King*.' The thousands sang 'God Save the King' with spirit. On the third day, Galleghan stood on a flat-topped trailer and outlined the situation: men suffering from dysentery, men dying, very little pressure in the water tap. He said they should discuss it among themselves 'but my word to you is that we can sign this document and save further loss of life because it would be signed under duress and it would not be binding'.

Just to be sure, Cyril Gilbert and his mate signed each other's declaration. Gilbert, who had run ammunition supplies by truck up to the Muar battle front and then been part of a rifle company in the defence of the island, had not even seen a Japanese until the day after the surrender. Like all the prisoners, he had been on a steep learning curve. To the shock of humiliating defeat was added the shock of the foreign: language, food (Rice! Rice was pudding), bowing (you had to bow to every one of these men), brutal, unpredictable discipline. Most of all, you had to learn that you had no rights.

You were the prisoner of an army that had been commanded to die rather than face the disgrace of capture.

Japan signed but did not ratify the 1929 Geneva Convention on the treatment of prisoners of war. It is a detailed document, with 143 articles designed to create an environment in which prisoners would be treated humanely: there would be no torture, there would be adequate medical attention, there would be a limit on the duration of punishment, there would be evacuation from danger zones. For privates who were physically fit there would be work, but it would not be excessive or dangerous and it would not be related to the enemy's war effort. Officers could not be compelled to work. The Japanese would probably have been in breach of every one of the 143 articles had they ratified the convention. They did make an empty promise to 'correspondingly apply' the provisions of the convention; that is, to act as if they had ratified it. Of course, there is something ironic, or worse, about decrying the failure to implement this convention to protect prisoners when in this war hundreds of thousands of civilian men, women and children were deliberately or indiscriminately targeted. But that's another matter.

The Japanese set up bureaucracies in Tokyo which, on paper, were to cope with the astounding flood of prisoners of war, but which, in reality, had responsibility without power. That resided in the hands of the individual commands in the field and, indeed, in microcosm, in the hands of the individual guards. The army directive on prisoners and work was based on instructions issued by General Tojo: 'In keeping with the current situation in our own country, where nobody can be permitted to live a life of idleness, and in order to help preserve the health of the prisoners, it is a central requirement that all prisoners, regardless of rank, should be encouraged to willingly perform labour commensurate with their bodily strength and capabilities.' Beneath the weasel words, this translated into a program of slave labour. The army's intentions were made absolutely clear in another directive which was distributed down the ranks to the camp guards and said: 'Prisoners of war are a form of military power, and should be used as such to the maximum advantage.'

For the prisoners there was no international legal fairy godmother. Survival in the labour camps would depend on will, luck, mates, humour, cunning, the quality of leaders, discipline and self-discipline, the miracles worked by medical men, the whims of guards and the nature and/or idiosyncrasies of Japanese officers. It was a lottery, a grand dice game. There could be, on rare occasions, strange meetings. In July 1942, Captain Leslie Greener was being interrogated by Lieutenant Yamaguchi about the war and his reasons for fighting. It developed into sophisticated word play.

Yamaguchi: Is it wise, do you think, to appoint a man with only one eye [Wavell] to watch over all India?

Greener: India can be fixed firmly with the glass eye. With the other he will watch the Japanese. (*Japanese laughter*)

Yamaguchi: Are the Australians not worried that there are so many Americans in Australia, making advances to their women while they are away at the war?

Greener: They do not seem to worry. You see, we have great confidence in our women. (*Laughter*)

Yamaguchi: It is said that they are marrying many of your girls. There will perhaps be none left when you get back. Is that not bad?

Greener: Oh no. Those Americans will stay in Australia and we wish to increase our population.

Yamaguchi: And who will your young men marry?

Greener: We will send for some girls from America. It is only fair. (*Laughter*)

Yamaguchi: We are told the Americans in India have better conditions than the British and they are stuck up.

Greener: People are often stuck up when they have more money.

Yamaguchi: But will not jealousy impair your war effort?

Greener: In the last war there was much jealousy. American and British troops used to fight in the esta-minets in France. Yet we won the war together.

Yamaguchi: I cannot believe there is affinity of spirit between the Allied nations sufficient to win the war.

Greener: Do you believe that there is much affinity of spirit between the Germans and the Italians? (*Loud and prolonged mirth*)

Some exceedingly dangerous games were played. The highest duty and highest honour for a Japanese soldier was to die for the Emperor. During the battle on Singapore, Tom Dowling of the 4th Anti-Tank Regiment watched with awe and, yes, some admiration, as Japanese troops attacked over barbed-wire fortifications. A wave charged forward, screaming *banzai, banzai, banzai*, throwing themselves on the wire as machine guns cut them down. Another wave, and more headway was made across the bodies. And others, with shouts of *banzai, banzai*, until the barbed-wire coils were flattened by a mat of the dead in an attack that failed. 'All this in the name of their emperor,' Dowling later wrote, and then told the story of the Emperor's Birthday.

For the Japanese, raised in emperor worship, the Emperor's Birthday, April 29, was the most important day of the year. The Anti-Tankers were in Changi for the first of the four

Emperor's Birthdays they endured. They were called on parade and asked to bring their drinking mugs. A Japanese officer, gold braid and campaign ribbons on his uniform, sword at side, stood on a raised dais and said: 'Today it is the Emperor of Japan's Birthday and we are to celebrate.' Guards moved along the ranks, half-filling the mugs with saki.

'Now we drink to the Emperor,' the officer said.

No-one moved.

'You *will* drink to the Emperor.'

Tension. Then Vern Rae, 15th Battalion Intelligence Officer and rugged Tasmanian footballer, stepped forward and boomed: 'Boys, we will drink to the Emperor. FaaaaARK the Emperor!'

A great roar went up. 'The Emperor – faaaaARK the Emperor!'

Apocryphal? I asked Colin Finkemeyer. 'No,' said Finkemeyer. 'Dowling and Rae are dead so you can't check with them. But I was there. I toasted and drank my saki. Enjoyed it.'

There is another story that became part of 8th Division folklore. It is about scrounging (stealing, if you like), developed by some of the Australians as an art form. Scrounging, in the worst of the bad days on the Thai–Burma railway, could be a life-or-death matter, providing essential food. It was also a satisfying, hidden act of defiance by powerless men.

In the early days of captivity, the wharves of Singapore were full of rich pickings. Here skills were honed under the suspicious eyes of the Japanese guards. One, nicknamed as was common the Brown Bomber, had a smattering of English and a high opinion of himself. The Brown Bomber one morning stopped drivers and crews in a shed. He warned them that he knew their thieving ways and that they faced a bashing and a handover to the *kempeitai*. He then gave a one-man show, going silently to a truck loaded with cartons, looking smartly right and left, easing open one, grabbing a tin of condensed milk, putting it on the road and quickly dropping his cap over it. He walked to the front of the truck to check there were no guards, and then to the back. He turned to the men: 'No Nippon . . . *joto*,' he said. The coast was clear. Then, looking smug, he lifted up his cap. The can of condensed milk was gone. A digger had removed it during the charade. The popular version of this story has the Brown Bomber using a slouch hat to cover the tin and telling the men before his demonstration: 'Now you Australian soldier you think we know fuck nothing that's going on here. You are wrong. We know fuck all!'

There are several versions of the famous petrol-milking incident. In one, Colonel Tamura, Singapore commandant, arrives with his interpreter, Hank the Yank, to complain about the theft of petrol by prisoners. They are driving in a little red MG, a prize of war. Hank is one of many foreign-resident Japanese who had been visiting their homeland at the outbreak of war and were swept into the army. He is sympathetic to the prisoners. He knows punishment is inevitable so he manipulates the confessions. He does not want too many culprits; he does not want claims of petty theft that the Japanese will not believe; he does not want admissions of major siphoning, which will anger the Japanese. Hank asks the men engaged in the racket to step forward. Stops them at 10. 'Don't get too keen,' he says. He manipulates the confessions of the amount stolen. Two gallons: small-timer; make that 10. Two hundred and fifty: big-time racketeer; let's say 30. The men are taken away for punishment. The colonel and Hank hop into the MG and drive out of the camp. They only get as far as the sentry when the car splutters to a stop. Its tank had been milked.

In another, Galleghan is short of petrol for his cigarette

lighter. A Japanese officer comes to his headquarters to complain about petrol thefts. When he leaves, he only makes it half a mile down the road. Galleghan had detailed Captains Peach and Macauley to milk the car. They had been too successful.

So there could be small wins, but the reality of the relationship between captors and captives was literally demonstrated at a blow. Cyril Gilbert was on a party building a road to a Shinto shrine on Bukit Timah. Each man was given a quota of earth to shift, perhaps a metre and a half a day. 'You could hop into it,' Gilbert said, 'and finish it by noon. But if you finished so early, your quota the next day would be doubled, and so on. You made it stretch out and when you weren't working you'd rely on your mates to warn you, pass the red light along. Red light coming; Jap coming. This day someone missed on passing the red light. This big, tall fellow, he was about six foot, came over the top of the hill and let out a scream, *kura!* He lined five of us up. I was the first one. He started with his hand almost down to the ground and went WHACK. I had a scar on my jaw a month later. Then they made us stand there arms outstretched, not dropping our hands. You try to do that, even for a couple of minutes, and there is a Jap there with a rattan and he beats under your arms, then along the top and over your head and down again.'

Retaliation was perilous. Sergeant Stan Arneil had fought at Gemas with Lieutenant Colonel Galleghan's 2/30th Battalion. On the day after the surrender Galleghan had spoken to his men, according to Arneil, like a father to his sons, urging them to hold together, as never before, as a fighting unit. That was a Galleghan refrain throughout the years of captivity: 'You are soldiers.' He promised a grand parade through city streets when they returned to Australia, and that wouldn't be long, he said. Rescue was on the way. Months later there was no sign of the cavalry and Japanese attitudes were worsening. Arneil was a magnet for animosity. He was 6 foot 6 inches, towering above the Japanese guards. One day he was in charge of a party of prisoners loading bags of salt from a small warehouse onto trucks. The bags of wet salt weighed about 135 kilograms each. Four men would lift a bag onto the shoulders of a fifth who tried to run 140 metres in a rhythmic jog to the truck where another four men would lift it from his shoulders and load. The senior guard, a corporal, stood beside Arneil at the lifting spot, calling the carriers to run faster. He hit three of them with a thick piece of wood as they passed him. Arneil chased the corporal out of the shed, pushed him to the ground, then tripped and sprawled himself. Arneil resumed supervising; the corporal stood nearby, testing the blade of his sword and swishing it.

At the end of the lunchbreak, Arneil was bashed, kicked and belted by the three guards. Knocked to the ground, he would get up again and stand to attention. When the corporal demanded he stand to attention in the Japanese fashion, fingers straight down his sides, Arneil stood with fists clenched, Australian-style. He says in his journal: '. . . I thought that as I wasn't in the Japanese army anyway, I was not going to act like a Jap.' They smashed at his finger joints with billets of wood. After work had finished for the day, they bashed him again. While he was in hospital recovering, Arneil received a message from Galleghan thanking him for the example he had set.

THE 8TH DIVISION had lost a general and, while some units had won battles, it had lost a campaign. How can a defeated army remain an army still? An army has discipline and a chain of command. Australian egalitarianism, while it has been stronger in myth than in reality, nevertheless means the officer corps has to work hard for respect. After February 15, the task became harder still.

The official historian quotes this poem written in Changi and circulated among the prisoners in 1942.

It's the fashion now to laugh
When one talks about the Staff
In a cynical and deprecating way.
But now that they're not manning
The defences at Fort Canning,
I think it's time we let them have their say.

'What really made us sore,'
Says Command, 'Is that Third Corps
Simply never would see eye to eye with us'
And 'Q' believes that 'G'
Were as stupid as can be
And as for 'I' they always missed the bus.

Third Corps do not confess
That they got us in the mess
But blames the whole disaster on Command;
While the men that did the fighting
Are now all busy writing,
And 'sack the bloody lot' is their demand.

The high command, the staff officers, the people at a safe distance who plan strategy, issue orders and, at times, make mistakes, are inviting targets, but within months of the surrender the senior echelons were gone from the lives of the men they had led. They were taken to camps deep inside Japanese-controlled territory. The Japanese wanted to destroy the military structure of the defeated army. Had this happened immediately after the surrender, Bennett would have been better able to defend his reputation.

Those middle-ranked officers who took command had a remarkable opportunity in Changi to structure the camp and mould the men. The area, which was the prisoner-of-war head-quarters, was one of the more pleasant parts of the island, with barracks, bungalows and parade grounds surrounded by treed lawns. The very best thing about Changi was that the Japanese seldom ventured there. Administration and internal discipline were left to the prisoner-of-war officers. Frederick Galleghan, in charge of the Australians and second in command of the whole camp, took opportunity by the throat.

It had to be said, at the start, that no-one ever murmured polite, colourless observations about Galleghan. Within 40 or so words, Russell Braddon, prisoner of war and author of *The Naked Island*, managed to describe him as sincere, conceited, vain, hysterical, egomaniacal, brave, conscientious and destruc-tive. To Clyde McKay of the 2/40th, he was 'that bloody mongrel'; to Arneil, of Galleghan's own 2/30th, he was 'our beloved Black Jack'. That nickname needs explaining. Galleghan was a strict disciplinarian. He believed in drill and he believed in saluting. 'A big martinet of a man', Warren's description, seems a neat fit. He believed that a good commander had to be an egotist. He believed that England's wealthy and aristocratic classes were born to rule. He was so strict that Arneil, in his biography of Galleghan, actually ponders the question of why his trained soldiers did not mutiny or seek transfer to another unit. He points out that they once and only once refused to obey an order, a serious occurrence, surely, though he does not say what the order was. Arneil's answer to this loyalty is that Gal-leghan was as hard on himself as on others and that he did not use discipline for its own sake. He wanted fighting soldiers.

Galleghan introduced himself to his 2/30th Battalion in

Tamworth by telling them they would train on Saturdays and Sundays and would start by learning to stand to attention. He said the battalion would be no place for malingerers and that he had instructed the medical officer to send any soldier who reported sick to another unit. Then, as an encore, he ordered them that hot afternoon on a 10-mile route march through the hills.

There was something else about the man, apart from his parade-ground ferocity, something physical. He was dark-complexioned or, Arneil puts it, of mixed descent. He became Black Jack that day. Galleghan's great-grandparents were West Indians. This has been suggested as the reason why he was not given a commission in World War I. White Australia ruled then. It perhaps also explains his abrasiveness and aggressiveness and his determination to enforce regulations.

Perhaps for some of the beaten men in a beaten army, Galleghan was a necessary martinet. But tougher, more resilient men appreciated him too. Cyril Gilbert: 'The Japs respected only one thing and that was strength and he was a strong man. I can remember one day he actually inspected the Japanese guard and ticked one off for having a button loose. He got one of our chaps to sew it on. He demanded his due in respect. He'd say to us, "You stand up for those bastards, so you'll stand up for me." He said to them, "If you want my men punished, hand them over to me." That's what happened to a group of us. We had a jail within the jail and we were marched there. The next day we went before Black Jack, told him what had happened and he said: "As far as those yellow bastards are concerned, you have been severely punished; as far as the AIF is concerned, go back to your lines".'

IN THE FILES of the AIF in Changi is a memo re NX 69235 Sergeant Griffin C. D. It concerns the man who would later be

Sir David Griffin, Lord Mayor of Sydney. Griffin had sent it to Leslie Greener, the man who had discussed General Wavell and glass eyes with Lieutenant Yamaguchi. Greener was education officer in the camp. It said:

1. It is requested that permission be granted to the above soldier to grow a beard.
2. The request is made for the purpose of his participation in the forthcoming production of 'Macbeth' under the direction of Maj. Bradshaw RA.

Greener passed the typewritten request on with his recommendation and it was returned with the handwritten notation of Webster, Lt Col, of 'approval for temporary growth during the named performance'. It is difficult to think of Macbeth, the Scot, without a beard. It is impossible to think of one of Black Jack's soldiers with beard or stubble, not when he had decreed all must be clean-shaven and ordered table knives and military jackknives ground to razor sharpness.

Into this world of order and strict discipline Galleghan had created came, on a January day in 1943 . . . came what? It's hard to think of the proper collective noun: some of these men were in rags, many were shoeless, all were unshaven, many stank of sweat and shit, all were malnourished. They took to calling themselves, with a combination of anger and pride, 'Java rabble', which, they were convinced, was how Galleghan had described them. They had sailed to Singapore, crammed into the fetid holds of a small tramp steamer, sharing the space with rats and cockroaches. Their leader was a tall man, a presence. Like Desmond Jackson, machine-gunner turned foot soldier, his war had started in the Middle East. He had been one of the Rats of Tobruk, under siege in one of the epic events in Australian military history. Like

Jackson, he had sailed to Java on the *Orcades* towards captivity. He was an expert on war: the smash and shatter of bullets, the tearing of shrapnel, the terrible things blasts could do to bodies, organs pulverised, limbs torn off. He was, however, a non-combatant, not in Galleghan's eyes the man who should lead men who had been in combat. When Jackson and his mates were fighting with inferior weapons against the Japanese at Leuwiliang, he was behind the lines using scalpel and sutures, operating hour after hour, watching ambulances and lorries roll in with macerated bodies until he had a feeling of 'unreality about wounded men'. Once he moved towards an ambulance where a man lay, leg blown off at the thigh. The morphia he was about to administer was rejected. 'Don't worry about me, sir,' the soldier said, 'I'm done for'. He was a healer of terrible wounds and battle trauma. Soon he would be fighting diseases rarely seen in the developed world: beri-beri, avitaminosis, amoebic dysentery, malaria, pellagra, flesh-eating tropical ulcers, cholera, the diseases of prisoners of war.

Ernest Edward Dunlop was born on July 12, 1907 to a farming family in rural Victoria, a patriotic child of those times. His great grandfather Henry Walpole was a warrior of the Raj, serving in the British army in Burma and fighting the Sikhs who were driving for independence back in 1848. 'How passionately British we were,' Dunlop wrote, looking back on the declaration of the Great War. War was glory, adventure, high honour. 'It was in the very air in my boyhood . . . we kids pined impotently [at] the lack of opportunity to go and die in "some corner of a foreign field".'

Unlike Colin Finkemeyer, who loved the western sweep of the Wimmera, Dunlop wanted escape from north-eastern Victoria and its horizons. 'In my boyhood in the Victorian countryside, I never saw anything admirable at all. I was only half in love with

[it],' he wrote. 'I saw all the shabby confinement of our lives, even in our best clothes.' For an unforgettable vision of 24-year-old Dunlop, in the big city now, a medical student at Melbourne University's Ormond College, go to Ebury's biography. There, in a photograph, riding on the hood of a truck in the university's Commen Day procession, wearing a tutu, pink undoubtedly, and carrying a wand, is a giant fairy. His nickname had been inscribed in the Students' Club Book of Doom. Undergraduates can be clever: Dunlop = tires = Weary. Dunlop was a considerable athlete, a boxer and a rugby player. Tom Uren saw Weary Dunlop for the first time in 1934, a charging colossus scattering New Zealand All Blacks as the Wallabies won the Test 25–11. He saw him for the first time face to face in Konyu prisoner-of-war camp on the Thai–Burma railway in 1943. (Konyu was referred to as Kanyu by some prisoners of war.)

Like Cyril Gilbert, Dunlop after surrender had to discover the unwritten rules of survival in a strange new world. It was not just a matter of getting to know the Japanese as well as possible. That was essential. Their culture was alien and their behaviour often unpredictable. To misread could mean a brutal beating, even the possibility of death. But there were also important things to learn about fellow prisoners, about who could be trusted to be responsible and strong, about who could be trusted to be unselfish. Some Australian officers were a bitter disappointment.

Dunlop did not tread lightly around the Japanese from the start. That was not something he was capable of. He drove through the chaos of Bandung, on Java, the day after the surrender, a pistol in each pocket of his bush jacket. He was going to a Dutch house to escort two nurses out of reach of the Japanese. They came to the door with the suitcases. Dunlop turned to a soldier who reached less than halfway up his chest, and shouted, 'I *shoko* [officer]. You carry suitcases!' The soldier declined. Dunlop carried the suitcases himself, but brought the nurses to at least temporary safety.

In his diaries, Dunlop chronicled the Japanese assertion of power, first on the ritual of the salute. In any army, saluting is no trivial matter. The Geneva Convention even regulates saluting by an army in captivity: prisoners of war, with the exception of officers, must salute and show all officers of the detaining power marks of respect provided by the regulations applying in their own forces. Saluting is a method of reinforcing the chain of command. Inferior salutes superior on sight. It emphasises the importance of the badge of rank, not the individual wearing it. A salute is a sign of willingness to obey. For the Japanese army, spawned by a society that is authoritarian and group-focused, in which bows are calibrated to show proper respect and in which having a cup of tea can be an elaborate ceremony, saluting is not negotiable and is demanded by an Emperor's decree. Headgear must always be worn out of doors as to salute without it is an insult; it is an insult to wear headgear inside, and the salute becomes a bow.

Within the Australian army, saluting can be a grudging practice; there were always going to be problems. Dunlop was no stickler, but he had become enough of an army man to be annoyed with his men's laissez faire approach. In Bandung, he acknowledged to his diary that Warrant Officer Hoshina was justified in his disgust at the 'slovenly, half-hearted way' in which Australians saluted at him. '(True – same when they salute anybody!)' Failure to salute, or to salute in a perceived incorrect manner was a constant source of beatings and bashings for the prisoners of war.

Dunlop records the descent from harshness to brutality. Life was lived at times on a bayonet edge.

April 17: Captain Nakazawa, who had ordered the break-up of the Allied General Hospital and the dispatch of most of the patients to prison, insisted it happen immediately. Dunlop took him to a ward of the severely injured to show that this was impossible. There were two paraplegics, a blinded boy and Billy Griffiths. A British aircraftsman, Griffiths suffered horrifically in a mine explosion; blinded, face shattered, both hands blown off, a leg broken, his whole body peppered with fragments. Griffiths had wanted to die. Dunlop had kept him alive. Nakazawa looked at Griffiths, turned to his guards and motioned towards their bayonets. Dunlop moved between bayonets and patient, saying, 'If you are going to do that, you must go through me first' and staring down Nakazawa. On August 7, Dunlop reported, 'Bill Griffiths, the sightless and armless boy, now moves about cheerfully'. (Griffiths survived the war, thrived and attended Dunlop's state funeral in 1993.)

Food became a preoccupation, malnutrition a serious concern. Dunlop reported 'the revolting spectacle' of diggers salvaging the food scraps of the better-off Dutch. What sickened Dunlop more than the plight of his men was the attitude of some of the officers. Only by supplementing Japanese provisions could a health disaster be averted. The Japanese decision to pay officers promised a steady source of funds. Dunlop supported a proposal that officers donate all but a small proportion of their pay to buy extra foodstuffs. This was vigorously opposed by some officers at a meeting which concluded with Dunlop stating that he would write to each officer personally requesting donations at the recommended level. 'I left this melancholy affair', was that day's diary entry, 'in almost the lowest frame of mind imaginable and disgusted at the light in which Australian officers had been shown. Imagine, after a clear statement of the miserable health of the troops and low finances, to hear a discussion by officers as to whether they would give the help required. Where is that principle "my horse, my men, myself"?'

ALL THINGS ARE relative. Laurens van der Post, a British soldier who led a guerilla group in the jungles of Java, has described three months he spent in Bandung prison, with Dunlop as overall commander, as 'a kind of golden prison age in the totality of our prison memories'. Yet on the first morning he had joined a parade of officers there the men had booed. The atmosphere had been sour and fragmented; the contempt for the abnormally large numbers of unemployed officers profoundly shocking. Van der Post and another combat officer, Wing Commander Nichols, urged Dunlop to lead the Commonwealth and English-speaking prisoners.

> We . . . argued that, as our short prison experience had already showed, we were going to be engaged in a new war, a war for physical and moral survival, a war against disease, malnutrition and most probably a protracted process of starvation as well as against disintegration from within by the apparent helplessness and futility of life in the prisons of an impervious, archaic and ruthless enemy. It would be a war for sanity of mind and body, and who, we asked Weary, could be more fitted to conduct such a war than a doctor and healer?

Van der Post's golden-age prison was a place where every man had half a duck's egg a day to give him the minimum needed protein, where an English officer from a fashionable Hussar regiment taught the illiterate to read and write, where a classics don from Cambridge lectured on the Greek and Roman past and the myths of the *Iliad* and the *Odyssey* to prisoners in tropical exile.

Dunlop as Odysseus. 'I think a great deal of Helen these days. Poor darling I don't know how she can stand these long dreary years of waiting at home. If she packs up and marries an American or something I suppose it would be best for her, but I don't know what I would do with my life then. She is the only stable thing left in my life – the only thing which enables me to see anything to look forward to in peace.'

There were more dreary years ahead, and Dunlop voyaged further away from Helen. For months he had been receiving news from X, his description in his diary of his secret radio. To be caught with it would be death. Throughout 1943, he recorded both the minutiae of camp life and news from the parallel universe of the war fronts: a very dignified chaplain took mass and the Japanese fleet suffered heavily in the Coral Sea; Lt Chadwick, who had a recurrence of malaria, had a fit and fell heavily; slovenly morning and more heavy Japanese losses at Wake and Midway; on October 5, COs parade – troops looking pretty rotten and more collapses going on; troops collapsing as their health declined and in New Guinea diggers pushed Japanese back over the Owen Stanleys.

This good news for the Allied war effort was terrible news for prisoners of the Japanese. The Battle of the Coral Sea was a draw, but it stopped Japanese momentum. The Battle of Midway broke Japanese sea power. Churchill was driven to paroxysms of praise for the Americans: 'As the Japanese Fleet withdrew to their far-off home ports their commanders knew not only that their aircraft-carrier strength was irretrievably broken, but that they were confronted with a will-power and passion in the foe they had challenged equal to the highest traditions of their Samurai ancestors, and backed with a development of power, numbers and science to which no limit could be set.' With its sea-transport capacity desperately overstretched, Japan had already been examining a land-link to Burma, the western flank of its new empire. In mid-1942, the vast slave army was being formed to be sent to Burma and Thailand. Many inevitably would have been worked to death in building the railway, but Tokyo reacted to loss of superiority on the sea and in the air by demanding the project be speeded up. Work-rate, brutality and dying all increased greatly.

THE JAVA RABBLE arrived in Changi on January 7, 1943. Changi made a similar impression on leader and men. Dunlop said: '. . . to my astonishment, neatly-dressed officers came up carrying canes, blowing out puffy little moustaches and talking in an "old chappy way." . . . The commander of AIF details on the island is Lt-Col Galleghan DSO (Black Jack). He insists on a proper dress and smart turn out and has lashed verbally all Australian troops into smartness and saluting – a praiseworthy achievement! Much 5 and 28 days in detention barracks!"'

Clyde McKay: 'The Japs had taken our colonel, Bill Leggatt, off us some time before we left Timor and lo and behold, there he was in Singapore and he and an officer called Gordon came marching down to us. You ought to have seen them, dressed up like pox doctors' clerks, fair dinkum, even had little red and white tabs in their socks, like boy scouts. I can see them now. And that officer, Gordon, he was Flash Gordon from then on. That Changi mob gave us nothing and they tried to take Weary away.'

Dunlop and Black Jack were never likely to be best friends but the relationship got off to a bad start. A party with red armbands, clearly officers, visited the area the Java contingent had been allotted. As the Japanese had decreed that no badges of rank be worn, Dunlop was not aware that Galleghan was a member. 'Unfortunately,' Dunlop wrote ruefully, 'the troops did not pay compliments as the party entered.' The next day Dunlop was shocked to receive a short note from Galleghan suggesting the command of the Java party be handed over to the senior combatant officer. Dunlop sent a polite response, welcoming the suggestion, but visited his friend Brigadier Arthur Blackburn, who had been AIF commander in Java, and who outranked Galleghan. He tucked a note from Blackburn in his pocket and went to dinner at AIF headquarters, a 'formal and swagger affair'. In the buzz of conversation, Dunlop heard the words 'Java rabble'. He rose quickly. He was angry, saying the troops referred to as Java rabble had fought in the Battle for Britain, the Atlantic, the Mediterranean, the Western Desert, Greece, Crete and Syria and then Java. He was cutting and sarcastic: 'And now we, the Java rabble, salute you, the 8th Division, who have fought so gallantly here in Malaya.' Later that evening Dunlop trumped Galleghan with Blackburn's note saying he desired Dunlop to retain command.

DUNLOP AND GALLEGHAN parted on bad terms. The last diary reference to the Changi commander, after a dispute over help with finance, was 'more blustering nonsense'. Dunlop also made a bitter, official complaint over lack of response to a request for footwear for the rabble. He had written to Galleghan saying, 'Position: no boots, 178, and situation deteriorating rapidly. Unserviceable boots, 204; urgently needing repair 304.'

On January 20, 1943, Dunlop and the Java rabble left Singapore to join the other elements of the slave army that had been gathered from Changi and other prison camps in the region. Many of those who survived the horror would look back on Changi as Clyde McKay did, with scorn, almost, as a 'ten-star hotel', or as a sanctuary.

CHAPTER 15

Across the Three Pagodas Pass

How would we get into that jungle and how was it
possible to survive in it? ... It was a monstrosity.

Yoshihiko Futamatsu, Japanese engineer

In 1942, U Kok, a 19-year-old Mon villager in eastern Burma, and Bum Tham, a 21-year-old Thai farmer in the River Kwai valley, lived their separate existences about 250 kilometres apart. They shared some facts of life: the rhythm of the rice-growing seasons and the waterfalls of rain pouring down during the monsoon. Jungle was part of their world too. Burma and Thailand have been nicely described as the Siamese twins of South-East Asia, joined at a mountain spine, but looking in opposite directions to the outside world through their port cities, Rangoon and Bangkok. Not that they ignored one another entirely. U Kok's and Bum Tham's villages lay close to the ancient invasion and trading route between the two countries, which crosses the border at Three Pagodas Pass, a low saddle on the range. For centuries in the region kingdoms rose and fell, borders expanded and contracted. In the sixteenth century there were invasions and counter-invasions between Burma and Thailand. In the eighteenth century, Burmese king

252

Hsinbyushin sent three armies into Thailand, one across the Three Pagodas Pass, to besiege the capital, Ayutthaya. They took away 10,000 captives and left behind nothing but ashes and buddhas stripped of their gold leaf. However, in the nineteenth century Burma faced what was at that time the irresistible force of British expansionism. After three wars, the last particularly ruthless, Burma was swallowed into the British Empire. Burmese nationalism lived on, however, as had Mon nationalism down the centuries.

The Mon had established a kingdom in the south-east of Burma in the sixth century and were a channel for the introduction of Theravada Buddhism into South-East Asia. Increasingly, they came under pressure from the more powerful Burmans, and in the eleventh century Anawartha, his kingdom based at Pagan on the northern Irrawaddy River, conquered the Mon and took to his capital not just their Buddhist treasures but their leaders and, indeed, the Mon culture. The river plain on the east bank of the Irrawaddy is now one of the archeological wonders of the world. At sunset, from the roof of the Bagan Archeological Museum oche and gold spires of stupas shine above the green foliage. The museum has a superlative collection of buddhas and inscription stones. Anawartha was followed to the throne by King Kyansittha (1084–1113) and his stone reads: 'Graceful and solar king of the three worlds . . . there were no thieves and enemies during Kyansittha's reign. There were no dangers in his country called Arimaddhana which was pleasant with plenty of mushrooms, bamboo shoots, fruits and so on.' There were, however, slaves to be given in parcels of hundreds to temples to demonstrate piety.

Golden ages never last long. Burma, independent or conquered, has been and remains one of the least homogeneous of Asian nations as the minorities, including the Mon, struggle for some autonomy from central control. Thailand managed a

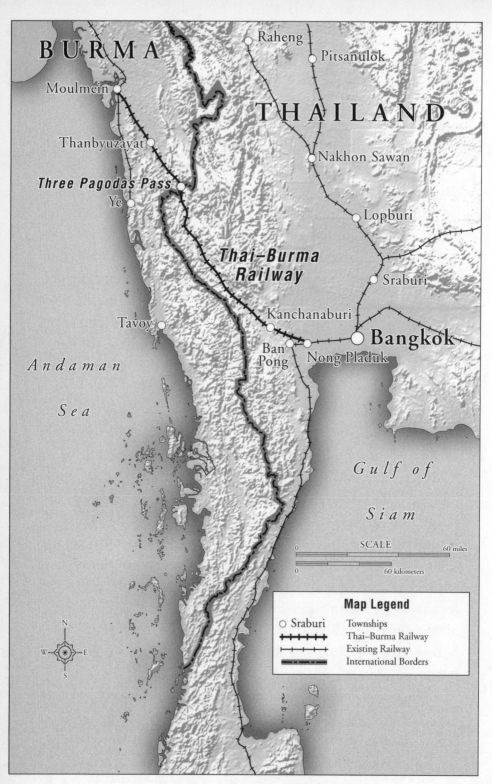

BURMA

Moulmein

Thanbyuzayat

Three Pagodas Pass
Ye

THAILAND

Raheng

Pitsanulok

Nakhon Sawan

Lopburi

*Thai–Burma
Railway*

Sraburi

A n d a m a n

S e a

Tavoy

Kanchanaburi

Ban
Pong Nong Pladuk

Bangkok

G u l f   o f

S i a m

SCALE

0 ———————————————— 60 miles

0 ———————————————— 60 kilometers

Map Legend

○ Sraburi   Townships
+++++++++   Thai–Burma Railway
+++++++++   Existing Railway
▬▬▬▬▬   International Borders

Thailand and Burma

tenuous independence, doing deals and playing off European imperial powers against one another. For Thai nationalists, as for other nationalists in the region, Japan's promise to drive out the colonisers was potent. On December 9, 1941 the Thai Foreign Minister informed Britain that his government had, under duress, signed an agreement with Japan allowing the passage of Japanese troops across Thailand to attack Malaya or Burma. The day before, however, the Thai Prime Minister, Luang Phibun, had considered a message from Winston Churchill urging resistance against the Japanese. Phibun took a gamble on the likely outcome. Japan, he thought, would win. In a broadcast to the Thai people, he said: 'I would like you to know that Japan is our greatest friend in life and death and we have to walk together, shoulder to shoulder, to fight our common enemy. All of you should remember that Britain took a large piece of our land in the south for which Japan is now fighting. I hope our army will be proud to be in the same front with the Japanese army. Presently we will ally ourselves with Japan.' On December 11, Phibun signed a mutual-defence treaty with Japan. On January 25, 1942, with Singapore almost in Japan's grasp, Thailand declared war on the United States. This was a bizarre diplomatic event. The Thai ambassador in Washington, Seni Pramoj, refused to deliver the declaration, saying it was not the will of the people, so the United States did not declare war on Thailand. Pramoj founded *Seri Thai*, the underground movement trained by the United Office of Strategic Studies, ancestor of the Central Intelligence Agency. Phibun's government acquiesced to Japanese use of Thai territory for the invasion of Burma and the building of the Thai–Burma railway.

BURMA, IN THE 1930s a rice bowl in a distant corner of the British Empire, had become strategically important. Over its western border was British India with its immense pool of human resources. To the north was the world's other giant, China, which for years had absorbed Japan's military blows. Burma provided a land lifeline to the Chiang Kai-shek regime. Japan demanded the lifeline, the Burma Road, be cut and in 1940 Britain bowed, in the humiliating sense of the word, to its wishes. For three months, though admittedly during the monsoon season, the road was closed to the passage of arms, ammunition and other war matériel. With an eye to the favour of America, Churchill had it reopened. In January 1942 he told his military leaders: 'As a strategic object, I regard keeping the Burma Road open as more important than the retention of Singapore.' On February 16, the day after the fall of Singapore, Wavell cabled Churchill that 'Burma and Australia are absolutely vital for war against Japan. Loss of Java, though a severe blow from every point of view, would not be fatal. Efforts should not therefore be made to reinforce Java, which might compromise defence of Burma or Australia'. In a note to General Ismay on February 17, Churchill said he was sure it would be impossible to act contrary to Wavell's main opinion. Personally he agreed with him.

The campaign to hold Burma was a disastrous sequel to the campaign to hold the Malayan mainland and Singapore. The Japanese push began on January 16; Rangoon was in Japanese hands on March 8.

In their isolated communities, U Kok and Bum Tham were for a time untouched by the world war and unaware of the grand plan Japan had for them. The Total War Institute, declaring that 'the Japanese empire is a manifestation of morality and its special characteristic is the propagation of the Imperial Way', promised the Asian nations that the yoke of America and Britain would be shaken off and an independence established in which 'the peoples of the sphere shall obtain their proper positions, the unity of the people's mind shall be effected and the unification of the sphere shall be realised with the empire as its centre'. The young men's first glimpse of their liberators was not of soldiers with rifles and bayonets but of engineers with survey equipment. Several times since the late nineteenth century, colonial powers had considered then discarded the idea of a rail link between Thailand and Burma. The construction difficulties were too great and the probable returns too small. But in 1942, with sea lanes under threat, sea transport in crisis and an army in Burma to supply, a railway became an imperative for Japan. Crossing plains and rivers, carving through jungle and hard rock, it would be a link with the existing systems in Thailand and Burma.

On June 5, Yoshihiko Futamatsu stood beside the railway line at Nong Pladuk in Thailand. Futamatsu was a *gunzoku*, a civilian engineer attached to the 9th Railway Regiment. He was as much a soldier of the Emperor as his military colleagues. He wrote of his emotions on the day of Pearl Harbor: 'One renews his decision to give selfless patriotic service and even if one became a victim there's nothing he can do about it but resign himself to the thought that in the end he returns as a hero to the Yasukuni shrine.' At Nong Pladuk the main railway which runs west from Bangkok curves south towards the Malayan peninsula and Singapore. Here, as Thai farmers drove water buffaloes through the surrounding paddy fields, Futamatsu watched soldiers, stripped to the waist, hammer a squared timber post into the ground. On it was written in *sumi*, Japanese ink, the figure 0.

More than 400 kilometres away, the 5th Railway Regiment was preparing to send a detachment south-east from Thanbyuzayat in Burma. It was an easy path for a start and only 8 kilometres along at the Mon village of Wagale there was an auspicious find, a hot springs which later would be turned, amid the coconut palms, into traditional Japanese baths. They still survive, though the railway and its path have disappeared completely. Soon the country wrinkles and the jungle begins. U Kok's village is much as it was then. Tall timber and betel-nut trees grow over the site of the prisoner-of-war hospital. The Australians came. Some of them died. He points through the jungle sameness: they were buried over there. The Japanese came and went. He worked for them, did odd jobs. He rode the railway to Kanchanaburi and was frightened of the iron bridge. It was very dangerous because of the bombing. He feels nothing for the Japanese, though one of the munitions they left behind blew off his left hand. It wasn't his war and the peace between the Japanese and the British wasn't his peace. Before the Mon had fought the Burmese, afterwards the Mon fought the Burmese. They still do. Along the road running past the village towards Three Pagodas Pass are flags which mark the drop-off and pick-up points for Burmese army patrols searching for Mon National Liberation Front units.

Forty years after the war Yoshihiko Futamatsu wrote his memoir, *Across the Three Pagodas Pass: The Story of the Thai-Burma Railway*, a rare account from the Japanese perspective. It was translated and annotated by Ewart Escritt and is now part of the Escritt Collection in the Imperial War Museum. Futamatsu addressed it to the younger generation of Japanese. In the preface he asks: 'How can the present generation who have no experience understand what war is? By the same token, how can they bear malice, how criticise, how amend the real truth?' It is also a response to David Lean's classic film, *The Bridge on the River Kwai*, a thoroughly distorted account that angered Japanese and prisoners of war alike. Yet while Futamatsu writes of 'the real truth', he displays the moral ambiguity towards the war endemic among many of the generation who were part of it. It is summed up in one sentence: 'Moreover, because so many were sacrificed, the slur "Death Railway", was slammed on it.' Out in Futamatsu's jungle there are heroes to be praised who love the Emperor, who pause in their work to bow to the Imperial tomb. 'The youthful survey unit commander squared his chest and looked out across the jungle-forest. As leading soldier on the construction of the railway, the heavy responsibility he shouldered floated uppermost in his heart, whether he had his eyes fixed on the sky over the Three Pagodas Pass or perhaps the sky above his beloved homeland.'

FROM THE THAI terminus, the projected railway ran close to the Mae Klong, Thailand's second largest river. For 50 kilometres to Kanchanaburi there was no challenge for the Japanese engineers. Then the troubles began. Futamatsu's first viewing of the terrain from Kanchanaburi towards the Three Pagodas Pass left him uneasy, with premonitions of a terrible life. And that was only in photographs. He looked at a mosaic of topographical photographs 10 metres long. He saw, in the middle, a river (the Kwai, a tributary of the Mae Klong) 'spread out like a white cloth curving about as it flowed', now narrow, now wide. He saw what looked like impenetrable jungle. The reality was worse. In August 1942 Futamatsu set off by boat in a reconnaissance party led by the commanding officer of the 9th Railway Regiment, Colonel Imai. The monsoon season was ending and the Mae Klong was still running high, muddy, a slimy grey, and spilling over its banks. A major task would be the bridging of the Mae Klong. The Kwai branched to the left and soon, at Chungkai, Futamatsu saw the first, daunting land obstacle, 'a rocky crag sticking out like a bone' down to the water's edge. A tunnel was the obvious answer, but the railway regiment had neither the necessary equipment nor the expertise. Futamatsu marked it for a cutting, by blasting and by hand. He knew it would be a life-sapping task. The party chugged on. Jungle crowded in, a barrier of tall trees and towering clumps of bamboo. At dusk there were clouds of mosquitoes, at dawn chill mists over the water and the boatmen warmed their engines with blow-lamps. Noon the second day they met the forward survey led by Second Lieutenant Mori. The jungle, he told them, was ferociously sultry. To be deep in it was like shutting the door on a small room. You got a headache, walking was difficult and your head and your arms kept getting caught by twisted branches. You could find peahen and pheasants' eggs and catch big embroidered snakes and iguanas to eat. There were crocodiles in the river, snakes, centipedes and scorpions on land.

The third day out they came to a cliff on the north bank, 50 metres high and 200 metres long. Futamatsu did a quick calculation. Again, tunnelling would be impossible. It would have to be a plank viaduct. (The impressive structure still stands, and trains edge along today on the section of the railway that still operates, carrying locals and tourists, many of them Japanese. Paying ten times the normal price, tourists can travel in a special carriage and receive a 'certificate of pride', which welcomes them as 'a lucky visitor who has set foot on these famous places of the Second World War: the Death Railway and the Bridge on the River Kwai'.)

Futamatsu's party worked its way up rapids, watched waterfalls lace down a cliff and then passed Bum Tham's village on the north bank. Here Futamatsu marked that the railway trace would climb up and along the flank of a ridge. This was hard country. There would have to be a series of cuttings, bridges (two of them ambitious) and embankments. The first cutting the prisoners knew for a time simply as

Konyu 3; then a name comes to it. No-one knows who looked at it in bitterness and called it Hellfire Pass.

To Bum Tham and his people the Japanese were not good, not bad, but in the middle. They paid the Thai half a baht a day (then twopence). But they were cruel to the prisoners, who did the terrible work, Bum Tham says. He watched them, so tall, so thin, go into the jungle. Most were barefoot. Some had arrived in rags. Others sold their clothes for food. The railway was not for the Thai people; it was for the Japanese war in Burma. Bum Tham was pleased when the Japanese went. He saw the railway and the bridges up the flank of his valley disintegrate and was pleased when he heard that there was no longer an iron path across the Three Pagodas Pass. Burma could have used that for war against Thailand, he said.

On the fifth day, Futamatsu's party passed crocodiles sleeping on sandbanks. Peacocks flew overhead. Rain upstream lifted the river level 6 metres in hours. They reached Takanun, 200 kilometres along the Kwai. It had the air of the last outpost, a miserable place with a dozen or so inhabitants working a tungsten mine, loading the heavy ore on elephant-back. The people were subject to recurring attacks of malaria; the children were pot-bellied from hypertrophy of the liver. Sixty kilometres upstream was Nieke and another 40 kilometres on was the source of the Kwai near Three Pagodas Pass. At Nieke the track being pushed south-east from Burma and the track being pushed north-west through Thailand, would meet. In this area, the monsoon had crushing force. From April to August 490 inches of the annual 620 inches of rain fell, 127 of them in August. Futamatsu would have looked east from Takanun towards high, saw-toothed mountains. He would have looked forward, along the phantom path of his railway, over jungle valleys and ridges basically unexplored, literally and figuratively tiger country.

The party turned around and were raced by the current back to Kanchanaburi in two days. Futamatsu was doing his sums. The railway and its construction can be measured in different ways. Futamatsu records basic statistics: gauge, 1 metre; gradient, maximum 25/1000; line curvature minimum 200 metres radius; planned transport volume 3000 tonnes a day each way. Futamatsu, the Japanese engineer, was proud of the railway. What he called the 'real truth' was that, in his opinion, the Japanese had created a record of considerable enterprise; 'Today, as far as the Burma-Thai Railway is concerned, Japan has left behind her a civilised heritage in Thailand'; the construction should be measured alongside the opening of the Panama Canal as a world record in engineering; and (hear the *banzais*) 'even today in my memory the Thai-Burma railway construction goes on playing an *allegro*, an attack-note of loyalty to the Throne'. But there were a multitude of requiems. Futamatsu said in his preface it was meaningless to go on dwelling on the deaths and destructions one-sidedly. It was clearly a struggle for him to acknowledge that there were nightmares and evil along the railway. 'One ought not to forget,' he says later, 'the large numbers of prisoners of war and coolies with whose help it was done and whose bones lie buried in the jungle, respect is due to them. We offer our sincere condolences.' He defends Japanese troops, rehearsing the indoctrination about surrender: 'Troops taught that in battle you must not be captured but die had nothing but contempt for men whose disgraceful cowardice allowed them to obey an order to become captives and still live.' He defends his fellow engineers (and himself?): 'Our men were not really conscious of having ill-treated prisoners of war, but in my opinion there were in fact from time to time rough practices which amounted to many cases of ill-treatment. It is regrettable that men were made responsible, in the one-sided

War Crimes trials after the war in Singapore, for cruel acts committed unintentionally.'

At Chungkai, the first challenge, Futamatsu planned a cutting 100 metres long, with a maximum depth of 40 metres. About 10,000 cubic metres of rock had to be excavated. When he writes of it, Futamatsu again acknowledges ill-treatment but denies guilt: 'The job involved blasting the face of the crag and was very dangerous and there was no lack of victims, even sick men being forced to come out to work. In the cemetery at Chungkai they left behind hundreds of crosses. At the Singapore War Crimes trials after the war Captain Jugi Tarumoto, the unit CO responsible for the labourers at the time, was unfortunately condemned to life imprisonment for ill-treatment of British, Australian and Dutch prisoners of war, an unexpected hardship to endure.'

It is impossible to feel pity for Tarumoto in his prison cell. He drove men to their deaths brutally and at times sadistically, according to one source. Along the railway prisoners endured terrible hardship or died. Seventy per cent of the terrain was malarial jungle, and this is what was accomplished in ten months: four million cubic metres of earthworks were built, three million cubic metres of rock was shifted, 14 kilometres of bridgework was constructed. This was the prisoner-of-war slave-labour force: 30,000 British prisoners of war; 18,000 Dutch; 13,000 Australians; and 700 Americans. Many of these men were malnourished already; many had had their first attacks of debilitating disease. Suffering along with them would be an estimated 250,000 Asians.

THE *MAYEBASSI MARU* had been wallowing for days north-west along the Malay coast, carrying a cargo of 1799 prisoners from Singapore to Burma. It pushed through the sluggish sea and the heavy air accompanied by its own miasma. In one of the two holds, a pit 23 metres by 14 metres in the bowels of the ship, 650 men were crammed. Half the floor space was covered with Japanese gear. For 54 hours after loading, the *Mayebassi Maru* stayed at anchor in Keppel Harbour. In sweat and stiffling heat, men had to sleep on top of one another. The slow movement brought little relief. The first cases of dysentery appeared. The latrines were small boxes on the starboard side of the ship and as the days passed few of the weakened men could make the trip. There were flurries of violence, the kicks and the blows of rifle butts.

One evening, as miserable as any other evening, Jim Hamilton, from Hampton, Melbourne, walked slowly across the deck from his hold and perched on the ladder above the one which held the 650 men. He started to sing, in a rich baritone:

> *Over the desert where the red sun gleams,*
> *Staggering blindly along,*
> *Here comes the regiment of legionnaires,*
> *Singing their dare-devil song.*

The guards listened. The prisoners stirred. Peter Dawson, the Australian baritone had made this a favourite of military men. Then at the end of the verse, the men in the hold joined in the chorus:

> *The legion of the lost they call us,*
> *The legion of the lost are we,*
> *Legionnaires and outcasts,*
> *Un beau geste, and then fini.*
> *Marching on to hell with flags swaying,*
> *Marching on to hell with drums playing.*

Listen to the drum, what's the drum saying?
Scum, Scum, every tap of the drum says
Scum of the earth, scum of the earth,
Still we come to fight and die for La Belle France.

Hamilton sang of prodigals, criminals from who knows where, though 'not a coward in the lot'. Again the men joined in the chorus, *Scum of the earth, scum of the earth.*

He sang other songs too, one of them, fittingly, Rudyard Kipling's, about the old Moulmein pagoda on the road to Mandalay. He received an ovation from prisoners and Japanese.

Transhipped at Rangoon, the men were landed at Moulmein, on the Salween River and marched to the prison. Towering above it is Kyaikthanlan Paya, the pagoda with a tall, elegant golden stupa. In a Moulmein prison cell Rohan Rivett thought bitterly of the voyage. He would write: '... many men were murdered as surely as if a knife had been thrust into their vitals.' Many more would die. They were on their way to join A Force working on the Thai–Burma railway. Kipling, the Imperial balladeer, had also written about a legion of the lost in his poem 'Gentlemen-Rankers'. There were words that applied to these prisoners of war. They certainly had learnt the worst too young. And 'damned from here to eternity': for many in the diaspora of prison camps and those along the railway, it would come to seem like that. The mature, like Weary Dunlop, felt the weight of the wasted years.

Chilla Goodchap, *Perth* survivor, was a passenger on the *Mayebassi Maru*. When he got to his first camp along the Burma end of the railway, the 35-kilo (kilometre) camp, he made a hammock out of two rice bags sewn together to sling between two bamboo poles. It was a memory of ships and the sea, but also very sensible in this jungle land of scorpions, centipedes and snakes. He made one for a mate, Alf Davies. 'He had the best body on a young bloke I'd even seen. He was one of those Greek god blokes. I was 19 then and he was 23, a good style of a bloke. And he said to me the first night: "You know, I'm not going to go through this." And I said: "What do you mean, Alf?" And he said: "No," he said, "we're going to be here for the rest of our lives. We don't know where we are anyway. We know we're in Burma some-where, but we'll never go home." "Oh," I said to Alf, "don't cop that. We've all got to have an aim. We've got to get home." It was a bit of a shock for a 19-year-old to hear a bloke say that. "What are you going to do, Alf?" I asked. He said: "I'm going to bloody die." I told him he was too bloody fit to die, in bloody good condition compared to where he was. By Christ, in three days we buried him.' Chilla Goodchap cried.

ON MAY 15, 1942 A Force had sailed from Singapore for Burma, 3000 Australians, mainly from the 22nd Brigade. They were packed into two 'small, very dirty steamers', the *Celebes Maru* and the *Tohohasi Maru*, sister hell ships of the *Mayebassi Maru*, and landed 12 bad days later at Tavoy, which had been an important port town for centuries. They were under the command of Brigadier Arthur Varley who had led the 2/18th Battalion and then the 22nd Brigade in the battle for Singapore. He was a World War I veteran, an infantry man, who was inclined to prefer the brave old boys of the 1st AIF: more disciplined, despite exaggerated claims to the contrary, and no army achieved success without strict disci-pline. It was Japanese discipline that appeared lax in the early days, temptingly so, dangerously so, and the Burmese seemed friendly. There was one stipulation, however. Officers, including Lieutenant Ken Dumbrell, of the 4th Anti-Tank Regiment, were taken outside the hangar which housed the prisoners and addressed by the Japanese commander through an interpreter. He pointed over the fence to a line of telegraph poles. 'Anybody out there get shot. That is it.'

The next night Mattie Quittendon a 37-year-old anti-tanker sergeant, came to Dumbrell and said: 'Look, we're going through.'

Dumbrell was angry: 'Look, I've got a compass hidden at the bottom of my water bottle, but I'm telling you now that there's no way anyone should try to escape. The Nips have said they'll shoot anyone outside and the natives will get the equivalent of a year's pay by reporting us. We've just arrived. We don't know what's what.'

Quittendon: 'But we're closer to India.'

Dumbrell: 'Jesus! Closer to India.' He looked north-west. India was 1300 kilometres away.

Quittendon: 'Well, we can't stand this bloody bullshit here. We're going to piss off.'

Dumbrell: 'If I could bloody well order you, which I can't, I'd bloody well order you to stop. For God's sake think about it some more. If you go, I'll try to cover for you as much as I can.'

Quittendon and seven others escaped. Ray Wheeler had intended to go too, but he had a bout of malaria. Instead he was a member of the burial party. They were free for four days before being betrayed. Dumbrell watched them driven past, roped together in the back of a truck. The next day they were tied to posts behind shallow graves. Brigadier Varley, who had tried to stop the executions, was a witness. He wrote in his diary: 'The spirit of these eight Australians was wonderful. They all spoke cheerio and good luck messages to one another and never showed any sign of fear. A truly courageous end.' Decades later, Ken Dumbrell described it a little differently: 'They said they didn't want blindfolds and told the Nips to go to buggery.' He was still saddened by it. 'Well, the buggers went, and I say buggers because they bloody well shouldn't have. They were in a no-win situation. They might have all died along the line, but the chances are maybe more than half of them would have got back. A bloody waste.'

CHAPTER 16

The race that stops a nation

*Work cheerfully, and from henceforth you shall be
guided by my motto.*
Lieutenant Colonel Yoshitada Nagatomo, war criminal

The Battle of El Alamein was over, 11 days of hell in the
North African desert. At last a great victory over the great
Rommel. The British generals were pleased. Of the Australian
9th Division, Montgomery said, 'magnificent, beyond all
praise'. General Leese found a fine one-word hymn: Homeric.
Churchill was delighted. This was the turning point. There had
not been a victory before, he said (the pain of Singapore);
there would not be a defeat after. He ordered the ringing
of church bells throughout England. The battle had begun
on October 23, 1942; the British tanks broke through on
November 2. Artillery had been crucial. The 2/8th Australian
Field Regiment with their 25-pounders had fallen back
overnight 30 kilometres behind the line and breakfast had
been brought to them, a hot meal, a stew of bully-beef and
biscuits. They deserved it.

At about the same time, at Tavoy in Burma, Australian prisoners of war were listening with increasing anger to Lieutenant

Colonel Yoshitada Nagatomo. 'You are only a few remaining
skeletons after the invasion of East Asia for the past few
centuries and are pititful victims,' he told them through an
interpreter. But he quickly offered reassurances: His Majesty
the Emperor was deeply anxious about prisoners of war; the
Imperial thoughts were inestimable and the Imperial favours
were infinite and they should weep with gratitude at the greatness of them and should correct or mend misleading and
improper anti-Japanese ideas. At a time of shortness of materials
their lives would be preserved by the military and all of them
should reward the military with their labours. Nagatomo
warned them of countless difficulties and sufferings in the
historic building of the railway. 'But you shall have the honour
to join in this great work which was never done before.' Then
he told them to work cheerfully. *Perth* mates Ern Toovey and
Chilla Goodchap stood side by side. They looked up at
Nagatomo on his raised platform with disgust.

Toovey knew nothing of the victory at El Alamein or of the
Australians' role in it. Nor did he know his brother Syd had
been wounded at Derna, in Libya, and brother Peter more seriously at Tobruk. Isolation was one of the heavy burdens in the
prisoner-of-war camps. Because the penalty of having a radio
was almost inevitably death, information was shared guard-
edly, and the Japanese, with deliberate cruelty, often withheld
prisoners' mail. Did his parents even know Toovey, like
Goodchap posted missing, was alive?

IN THE NORTH AFRICAN desert, the men of the 2/8th Field
Regiment crowded around a radio. Jim Osborne watched his
mates, Dennis and Jim Robbie closely. The three of them loved
horses, not for the punt, the flutter with the bookies. They
loved horses as animals, as more than animals. The Robbies'

father had been studmaster at Shirley Park stud; after the war Osborne bred horses himself. Thoroughbreds are strength, fragility, beauty (though that can be in the eye of the beholder). They can inherit looks and ability. Genes may determine whether they are sprinters or stayers, whether they are ducks in the mud or need it firm. The matter of heart is something else. There are horses that just want to win. There are horses that simply surprise, ordinary lookers (ugly maybe), unimpressive in conformation, donkeys on the training track but champions on race day. Osborne and the Robbies were bred themselves under the spell of Phar Lap, the giant chestnut who lit up the Great Depression. There was romance in the story of the people's horse, bought for only 160 guineas, but racing into greatness, winning the 1930 Melbourne Cup with ease as odds-on favourite. There was tragedy in his death but the fitting finding that his heart was perhaps the biggest ever found in a thoroughbred. Jim Osborne and the Robbies chatted now and then about The Dream. Everyone who owns a horse, or wants to, has it. You dream you own the winner of the Melbourne Cup. After that eternal three minutes or so, you walk along the avenue of roses at Flemington racecourse and you lead in your horse, patting it, taking your share of its glory. Jim Robbie, the more gregarious brother, told Osborne about Colonus. Pity about Colonus. He was a small bay, a speedy squib, won three races as a two-year-old, but only one out of 15 as a three-year-old. The judgment was he was not quite up to metropolitan standards. The Robbies sold him before they enlisted: for next to nothing, as Jim Osborne remembers them telling him, perhaps 25 quid, or 50. So, on a November morning in 1942 in the desert and a wet afternoon across the time zones in Melbourne, the Cup field lined up. The track was heavy. Colonus, the speedy squib was there, drawn on the outside, barrier 24. At the jump, jockey Harry

McLeod, 17 years old, rode Colonus for speed, cleared the big field, took the lead and stayed and stayed and stayed for two miles. He won by seven lengths. Genes had run true. Colonus was descended from the European mudlark Sansovino. Jim Robbie said one word: 'Fuck!' Colonus's new owner, Lou Menck, had thought about the horse's headstrong habits and started him in the Herbert Power Handicap, a mile and a half race, and a good lead-up to the Cup. He instructed McLeod to let the horse run. Colonus did, and won. Menck backed him overnight before the Cup from 200 to 1 to 33 to 1.

At Tavoy, Burma, in October, thoughts had turned to the Cup too. Jimmy Sutherland, who had been and would be again, in that catch-all phrase, a racing identity, came up to Ron Wells, the former jockey, and said: 'Do you know it's the bloody Melbourne Cup in two weeks' time? Can't we do something about it?'

'What do you mean?' Wells said.

'Well, have a bit of a day, or something. Can't we tell the bloody Japs it's an important public holiday in Australia on Melbourne Cup day?'

Wells was keen. He had ridden the country circuit. He had won quite a few races on a little mare he loved, Carmeltine. He'd ridden city winners. And of course, he had dreamed the jockey's dream, riding the winner of the Melbourne Cup. He approached the officers and the officers approached the Japanese. At that time they were comparatively reasonable. Wells put the biggest and strongest men in training. He cast an experienced eye over the contenders. He picked Wilf Muir, who once played Australian Rules for Richmond, and named him Sweet Potato. Riding Sweet Potato would be Bluey Cooper, another ex-jockey. One of the prisoners crafted the cup, a half coconut stuck on the leg of an old chair.

On the day, the Governor, also known as Colonel George

Ramsey, the camp commanding officer, made a grand entrance, towed on the two-wheeled tanker used to cart water from the well. He descended and sat, surrounded by Japanese and Allied officers, in a makeshift stand. The men lined the circuit and felt closer to home. Wells was the starter. He dropped the flag to send the field away and then cut across the flat. He and Jimmy Sutherland were the judges. Sweet Potato, ridden by Bluey Cooper, came first. The Robbies had held the dream in their hands and let it go. Ron Wells held aloft the coconut cup. However, at Flemington Lou Menck did not have the traditional moment of golden triumph. The race had been renamed the Melbourne Austerity Cup, and while the prize-money was a considerable £5250, instead of a trophy he held in his hands a £200 Austerity Bond.

John Curtin, one-time champion of the socialist revolution and now wartime Prime Minister, had seized the day. In those dark times, he wanted to mould a new, better Australia. On August 19 he made a speech at the Brisbane Town Hall. 'I ask you to reconcile yourselves to a season of austerity,' he said to the people, 'to make your habits of life conform to those of the fighting forces. The civil population can learn to discipline itself. It can learn to go without . . . Every day you read about some man you knew dying fighting far distant from the places of entertainment, of even relaxation, fighting with all he knows for your defence.' Austerity, he told them, meant a new way of life, a new spirit of action to do the things the nation needed and not to do the things that weakened the nation. 'The strength of a nation is determined by the character of its people, and so in this hour of peril I call on each individual to examine himself honestly and, having done so, to go about his task guided by a new conscience and a new realization of his responsibility to his nation and to each individual member of it. By doing so we will be a nation which is morally and spiritually rearmed and be adequate not only to meet the tasks of war but also the tasks of peace.'

It is probably just as well the men and women in the prison camps were unaware of the nature of the sacrifices the government wanted the people to make in this season of austerity. Excessive drinking was to be ended by measures such as the reduction of trading hours, the exclusion of women from public bars and the banning of drinking in public places. They did not work. Meals in restaurants and pubs were limited to three courses. Clothing was simplified under the banner 'Fashions for Victory': no double-breasted suits for the men, or cuffs on sleeves and trousers, no waistcoats (the ban on waistcoats lasted only six months; the men of Australia were prepared to sacrifice only so much for victory); no evening wear, evening cloaks, evening wraps, bridge coats, dinner gowns or hostess gowns for women; no children's party frocks. Chilla Goodchap and tens of thousands of others wore G-string scraps of clothing and went dangerously barefooted; Australian nurses in their Sumatran prison camps made rough clothes out of any fabric scraps they could find; malnutrition readied people for death blows from diseases.

BRIGADIER VARLEY'S A Force was in better condition than most to face the hardships to come. At the end of June 1942, in Burma the Japanese began paying working prisoners of war and increased their rations. Those who didn't work got less. In some camps, the sick got nothing. In Japanese eyes, the sick were doubly despised. Colonel Sijuo Nakamura, taking command of the prisoner-of-war camps during the cholera epidemic, sent out a letter saying he was pleased to find in general the prisoners were keeping discipline and working diligently. Did he know of the iron fists of the guards and engineers? He then told the victims of mistreatment that their physical deterioration was due to their lack of firm belief, unlike the Japanese, that 'health follows will'. Nakamura issued 'instructions': 'Those who fail to reach objective in charge by lack of health or spirit is considered in Japanese Army as most shameful deed . . . You are expected to charge to the last of the work with good spirit and taking care of your own health.'

Even in the best of times the food provided by the Japanese was inadequate in calories, protein and vitamins. The wages were a pittance: 25 cents a day for warrant officers, 15 cents for non-commissioned officers and 10 cents for privates. Five cents was equivalent to an Australian penny, but there was enough to supplement the diet by buying from the Burmese. Varley tried to keep as many men working as possible and when possible sent medical officers to join them to get extra benefits. In helping his men, Varley was helping the Japanese war effort but providing a labour force for the Japanese was not optional. He wanted as many of A Force as possible to survive the war.

Ray Wheeler was lucky to survive Burma. Had he made the escape bid in May, he almost certainly would have lined up with the Quittendon eight for execution. Then in September he was a member of a party of 200 sent to build bridges and repair roads between Thanbyuzayat and Ye, a river port and the terminus of the existing railway running from the southern coast to Rangoon. Wheeler's first face-to-face meeting with a Japanese had been on an infiltration patrol in Johore Bahru in January. They were trying to make contact with members of the 2/29th Battalion withdrawing through the jungle from the battle at Bakri. The Japanese soldier came at Wheeler from behind a tree. Wheeler bayoneted him. 'What upset me was that you had to take everything off them for intelligence purposes. He had photographs of his family. He had three children. I took everything else but I put the photographs back in his pocket.' Wheeler had expected the worst from the guards in the camp near Ye. 'They were pretty good to us but they would belt the Dutchmen at the drop of a hat. We wondered why then we found out when they started talking to us that they were all members of the Imperial Guards Division and every one of the blokes there was on recuperation leave from being wounded, 90 per cent of them by Australians. I was talking one day to this bloke Termoza. He was an Olympic Games wrestler. He spoke reasonably good English. I said to him, "Why do you belt those Dutchmen? I come through a bit late going onto parade and you say "Hurry, hurry". A Dutchman comes through and he's right on the dot, not a second late and you go and slap him down. "Oh," he says, "they are not soldiers. They ran away." '

Every tenth day for the prisoners was *yasume*, a rest day. The prisoners were given an armband by the Imperial Guards that allowed them to leave the camp and go within a mile radius. Wheeler had become mates with Les Marlin, 'an old Mallee bloke. You sort of drifted to people you had something in common with. His people were from around Swan Hill way and his uncles had been World War I soldiers. He was the sort of bloke who would do anything for you.' Wheeler and Marvin pushed the boundaries of their precious freedom. 'We'd beg, borrow or steal food. The jungle had a lot of stuff that could feed you. Wild ginger used to grow there, and there was a yellow fungus that you'd reckon was poisonous but the natives showed us how to cook it. It was just like mushroom soup, very sustaining. You could get fish out of the streams and in the next valley we found an old salt mine. We got to know the people in that valley, all rice farmers. Their proudest possession was a copy of the *English Post* magazine, a

Riding high: Henry Gordon Bennett at the end of World War I. Aged 31, he was one of the youngest brigadier generals in the British armies. In World War II his dream was to lead the Australian army, to inherit John Monash's mantle as Australia's greatest general. That was shattered, and so was his reputation. (AWM E04462)

Brother enemies: Lieutenant General Arthur Percival, leader of the Allied Forces in the Malayan campaign, smiles at the camera; Bennett looks coolly at the man who would set in train his professional destruction. (AWM 134877)

Before the mast: son of a World War I Lighthorseman, David Manning as a 13-year-old naval cadet. He survived the sinking of the cruiser *Perth* in the Battle of Sunda Strait and Japanese prisoner of war camps.

Peril on the sea: Lance Gibson, farmer from north-central Victoria, was an officer in the 2/3rd Machine Gun Battalion. He survived the sinking of the *Tamahoko Maru* by the American submarine *Tang*. Thousands of prisoners of war, including sailors from the *Perth*, died in similar attacks while being transported to Japan. Irony: *Tang* later sank itself.

Bill Dunn steps out along a Melbourne street on the way to war. Hellfire Pass and an unhappy homecoming await him.

Takashi Nagase was educated to want to die for the Emperor and to be worshipped as a god at Yasukuni Shrine. An interpreter for the torturers of the *kempetei*, the Japanese military police, he became driven by remorse and convinced that the Emperor should take the blame for the disastrous war.

'The jungle is fearsome, frightening', Bennett wrote, listing leeches, malaria, cobras and tigers. Then there were the Japanese. Bennett insisted that his troops train in the jungle. (AWM 007179)

Hudsons of No. 1 Squadron RAAF, first to strike at Japanese invaders at Kota Bharu on December 8, 1942. Spud Spurgeon and No. 8 Squadron went into action six hours later. They had no chance against the Zeroes. (AWM 006647)

Allied commanders were slow to learn the striking power of Japanese tanks; Australian commanders were slow to learn the value of the 4th Anti-tank Regiment's two-pounders. (AWM 009288)

The proof: smouldering tanks near Bakri. (AWM 011307)

Singapore's naval base, the heart of the false fortress, burns, sending smoke over the doomed city. (AWM 012447)

'There must be at this stage no thought of saving the troops or sparing the population', Winston Churchill cabled his commander, General Archibald Wavell, on February 10, 1942. In this streetscape a small child lies dead and women wail their grief. (AWM 011529/22)

'The Tiger of Malaya', General Tomoyuki Yamashita, inspects the site of yet another victory. (AWM 127913)

The conqueror, General Yamashita (left), on February 15, 1942 dictates the terms of surrender to General Percival (front right). It was, in Churchill's description, Britain's greatest military humiliation. (AWM 127903)

Banzai: Japanese troops at Singapore harbour. (AWM 127905)

George (Moggy) Catmull. He jumped hand-in-hand with Allan Gee from the stricken *Perth*, shouting, 'I'll see you in Young and Jackson's.' He could not swim. He drowned. (AWM 006845)

'Without any inhibitions of any kind, I make it quite clear that Australia looks to America': Australia's wartime prime minister, John Curtin, with General Douglas Macarthur, representative of a new great and powerful friend. (AWM 139812)

Perth fights to the death in the Battle of Sunda Strait, February 28, 1942. (Dennis Adams; AWM ART27557)

Pat Gunther, nurse. She survived the long years in Japanese prison camps on Sumatra.

Gunther's best friend, Kath Neuss. She died in the massacre on the beach at Banka Island on February 16, 1942. (AWM P02783.033)

Gunther's silver spoon: the starvation diet did taste better.
(AWM REL28267)

Australians of A Force in October 1942 on their trek through the Burmese jungle to railway work sites. Many would die. (AWM P00406.006)

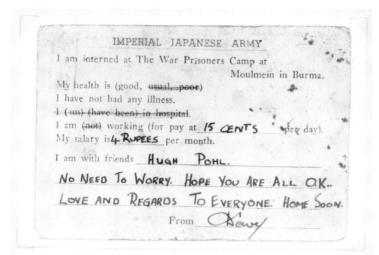

David Manning's card home. The Japanese allowed carefully censored details. Manning told consoling lies. He knew he would not be home soon.

IMPERIAL JAPANESE ARMY

I am interned at The War Prisoners Camp at
Moulmein in Burma.

My health is (good, ~~usual, poor~~)
I have not had any illness.
I ~~(am) (have been) in hospital.~~
I am (~~not~~) working (for pay at 15 CENTS per day).
My salary is 4 RUPEES per month.

I am with friends HUGH POHL.

NO NEED TO WORRY. HOPE YOU ARE ALL O.K..
LOVE AND REGARDS TO EVERYONE. HOME SOON.
From Dave

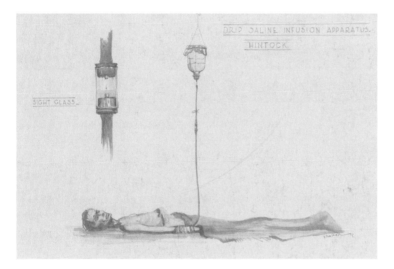

DRIP SALINE INFUSION APPARATUS.
HINTOCK

SIGHT GLASS

And this was the truth: slave labour and lack of food and medicine drove tens of thousands towards death. (Jack Chalker; AWM ART90927)

Ulcers ate flesh. In attempts to save limbs, devoted orderlies scraped them out. The pain was terrible. (Jack Chalker; AWM ART90839)

Living victims of the *Speedo* period, the monsoon months from mid-1943 when the Japanese relentlessly pushed the railway to completion. 'Nippon very sorry but many men must die', an officer said. (AWM P00761.011)

Mates: Jack Chalker called this sketch, ironically, 'Working men, Kanyu Camp, October 1942'. The sketch escaped the destruction of Chalker's collection when it was discovered by a Korean guard. Chalker himself was savagely beaten over two days. (AWM ART91811)

For its Japanese builders, the Thai–Burma railway was an engineering triumph to be ranked with the Panama Canal. They wrote of Japanese heroism and took stylised photographs of soldiers at work. Japanese histories are silent on the suffering and deaths of the massive slave army of prisoners of war and Asian labourers. (Courtesy of Rod Beattie)

Heroic medical officers stood between the men and death from disease, and shielded them when they could from Japanese brutality. Albert Coates (left) and Weary Dunlop were leaders, but in camps all along the railway other doctors performed their own miracles. (AWM 117362)

Prisoners starved. Japanese subsisted often on short rations. This fish, caught during the monsoon, would have been welcome a supplement. (Courtesy of Rod Beattie)

Senior engineer Renichi Sugano in proud pose on engine C5631. It transported generals to the joining ceremony at Koneitra and now stands, gleaming and lustrous, in the entrance hall of the militaristic Yushukan Museum in Tokyo.

(Courtesy of Rod Beattie)

Like soldiers, many Japanese nurses on the retreat through Burma in 1945 chose to die rather than surrender. An estimated 180,000 Japanese died in the disastrous Burma campaign. (Courtesy of Rod Beattie)

The lucky ones: oil-covered prisoners of war about to be rescued by the American submarine *Sealion*. Thousands died in submarine attacks. Survivors carried the news of Japanese brutality in prison camps and, in particular, along the railway. (AWM P02018.326)

The railway in operation. A supply train crosses one of six trestle bridges built on three kilometres of track in the rugged country north of Hellfire Pass. (AWM 122309)

Nagaski's mushroom-shaped cloud. Underneath it, among the devastation, Allan Chick was miraculously alive. (AWM P02018.406)

Nagasaki after the Fat Man: US President Harry Truman had kept his promise of a rain of ruin from the sky. He broke his word that atomic targets would be purely military ones. (AWM 044646/01)

In 1942, after the sinking of *Perth*, 19-year-old Chilla Goodchap's parents received a letter with an impressive crest and signed George R.I., expressing sympathy 'for a life so nobly given'. But Goodchap was a survivor. This photograph was taken towards war's end at Sendyru camp, 30 kilometres from Nagasaki.

Home: Owen Campbell, one of only six who survived Sandakan and the death marches by escaping, on the day he was welcomed home by son Alan and wife Evelyn. Campbell, the last of the six, died in 2003.

8th Division prisoners of war arrive on the hospital ship *Manunda* in Sydney Harbour. They were uncertain of their own welcome and they knew that their leader, Henry Gordon Bennett, had been in a legal battle for his reputation. They scrawled a message on a sheet showing whose side they were on. Military authorities removed it. (AWM 122156)

Allan Chick survived the atom bomb and returned to Australia. He went back to Japan in 1946 as a member of the occupation forces. When this picture was taken he had made up his mind to marry a Japanese woman, Haruko Kojima. He brought her home to tiny St Helens in Tasmania, and helped end the White Australia policy.

pictorial, printed in Burmese with English subtitles. The patriarch of the clan showed us this story on a Spitfire squadron.
The people in the valley were pro-British. They had contributed money towards supplying one Spitfire. One day the
patriarch told us his son was going to get married. He was
with the Burmese Rifles, fighting for the British near the Indian
border. It was arranged so we could be there. He walked
across the country. It was such a warming experience, these
people treating us like their own. It was much like Australia.
The men went down one end and the women the other.'

'HOW STRANGE IS the life we are leading compared with
that of three and a half years ago,' the young man wrote to his
sister Evelyn. 'Our surroundings are so different, the environment so peculiarly contrasted with that of pre-war days, with
the result we are different men with changed ideas altogether
... We who have been out here have become hardened and
will never be the same men again.' That was in November
1917, from the Western Front. Albert Coates was 22. In 1915
he had been at Gallipoli for the whimper that was the end of
that disaster. At 10 pm on December 19 he was medical
orderly with the second last group to leave, silently stealing
away wearing muffled boots, following a line of bleaching
powder to the beach and a waiting lighter. He had been at the
Somme and endured the shelling at Sausage Valley and the
Chalk Pits. He had walked in German trenches, empty except
for the dead, and walking over the blown-up decomposing
bodies was like treading on a floor of rubber pillows. Now, in
1942, having through enormous personal effort in peacetime
become a leader on the new frontier of neurosurgery, he was at
war again. Aged 47, he was facing another three and a half
years of a life strange beyond imaginings, one that would

change and scar those who survived it. He was a doctor, physician and surgeon to his fellow prisoners of war but in terms of drugs, equipment and facilities, he had returned to the medical dark ages.

Coates enlisted at the outbreak of World War II and at first was refused permission to leave his post at the Royal Melbourne Hospital. He was called up in 1941 and went to Malaya as senior surgeon of the 10th Australian General Hospital of the 8th Division. Just before the fall of Singapore he was instructed by General Bennett to return to Australia. He reached Sumatra, where he set up a casualty station. He could have continued on to safety. He stayed with his patients and awaited capture. Like Ray Wheeler, Coates in Burma puzzled over Japanese contradictions. He met reasonableness, rage and the perversity of the military mind. At a hospital camp in Tavoy, the guard was under the command of Corporal Kumada, an English-speaker and an economics graduate from Kobe University. In his biography, Coates calls him his friend and refers to him as 'the good Kumada', a man of kindness and humanity. He described the hospital as 'our little haven'. When Coates gave evidence at the war crimes hearings in Tokyo after the war he held Kumada up as an example of how the Japanese should have treated their prisoners. Yet in one of their conversations Kumada talked of discipline in the Japanese army and how he was bound to obey the orders of his superiors. He liked and respected Coates, he said, but if he was told to torture him, he would. Coates would be forced to eat his fill of rice then water would be poured down his throat. After the rice had swollen, the good Kumada would jump on Coates's stomach.

Coates and Dunlop and their fellow doctors were to become front-line defenders of the prisoners against the fanaticism of the Japanese.

CHAPTER 17

Hearts of darkness

The Thai–Burma railway as metaphor? Those building it certainly took a journey into the heart of darkness: country becoming more rugged, malaria more prevalent, no chance of trading for precious scraps of life-sustaining food in these uninhabited jungles. In the monsoon the supply lines were cut, rough tracks becoming morasses of mud. Men became weaker in this playground of diseases, and medicines to treat them were increasingly rare. From the starting points in Burma and in Thailand, the railway was pushed over plains and paddy fields towards the hard country. It moved through space as embankments were built, ballast laid, sleepers positioned and rails spiked, snaking, rising, descending, crossing ravines and rivers, towards the joining point. It moved through time, though time was relative for the prisoners of war. Time was an endless greyness, but time was compacted when the Japanese Imperial Headquarters decided the railway must be finished months ahead of schedule. As time shrank, the suffering increased enormously, horrendously.

On October 1, 1942 Australians started work 4.8 kilometres from Thanbyuzayat, on what the Japanese called the Burma-side. Four days later a group under the command of Charles Anderson started to clear a 15 metre wide strip

Map Legend

○ *Tonchan*	POW Camps (not all shown)
○ Ban Pong	Townships
+++++	Thai–Burma Railway
+++++	Existing Railway
———	Roads
▓▓▓▓	International Border

Length of POW railway:
Nong Pladuk to Three Pagodas Pass = 306km
Nong Pladuk to Thanbyuzayat = 415km

This map is not to scale, and is intended only to show
relative positions of camps and other features

BURMA

Moulmein

Thanbyuzayat
Khandaw
Thethaw
Retpu
Thanbaya
Meilo
105 Kilo
Three Pagodas Pass
Kami Songkurai
Shimo Songkurai
Thimongta
Konkoita
Tamajo
Takanun
Brangkassi
Hintok River
Kui Yae
Kinsaiyok
Hintok Road & Hintok Mountain
Konyu & Malayan Hamlet
Hellfire Pass
Tampii
Tonchan
Tonchan South
Tarsao/Nam Tok
Wampo North
Wampo
Wampo South & viaduct

Ye

River Mae Klong

Kwei Noi

River Kwai

THAILAND

Nakhon
Sawan

Lopburi

N
W ✦ E
S

Takilan
Arrow Hill
Ban Kao
Wan Tow Kien
Wan Lan
Chungkai
Tamarkan & steel bridge
Kanchanaburi (Kanburi)
Tamuang

Ban Pong
Nong Pladuk
Nakhon Pathom

Bangkok

Thonburi

Tavoy

*Andaman
Sea*

*Gulf of
Siam*

Ratburi

Thai–Burma Railway, 1942–1945

of jungle to build an embankment. Anderson had a Victoria Cross waiting for him after the war, earned at the battle of Muar, but that fighting withdrawal, with its bullets, bayonets, grenade and mortar blasts, its man-to-man, hand-to-hand fighting took place in a different world. In November the Japanese guards were replaced by Korean troops, 'purely amoral coolie vermin . . . brutal by nature as well as by orders', a medical officer noted. Already Varley was finding that 'it is so difficult and heart-breaking to fight for the lives of our men . . . and meet a brick wall on all occasions'.

Already the sick, denied medicine and any comforts, were sinking into death. Already dreaded cholera had broken out and Varley could not even get 44-gallon drums for the boiling of safe water. Already Varley had ordered the sale of the personal effects of the dead, the belongings that normally would be sent back, if possible, to fathers, mothers, children – small things to touch and remember by, watches, fountain pens. Sentimentally priceless, the little money they brought meant life-saving food. Only wallets and photographs would be retained, in the hope that somehow they would find their way home. Varley wrote in his diary: 'This sort of nightmare goes on.' There was much worse to come.

While Varley's A Force sailed to Burma on hell ships, the men sent from Changi to Thailand travelled in hellish trains. Waiting for them at Singapore station were steel boxcars used to transport rice. They had been told they were going to a better place. 'A land of milk and honey' was the vision implanted in Clyde McKay's mind. Desmond Jackson remembers the dawn over Singapore the day he left as serene and beautiful. At 11 am the sliding door of his boxcar was slammed shut. About 30 men and their gear had been packed into the 5.5 metre by 2.4 metre space. They organised themselves. Each man took the essentials from his kit and piled the kits in one corner, up to the roof. By lying down in ranks, legs bent so heels touched buttocks, head pillowed on the feet of the man behind, each got floor space to attempt sleep. Days were a swelter, nights uncomfortably cold. There was a toilet stop in the mornings and they were allowed to keep the sliding doors slightly open during the day. They took turns in snatching a little of the passing breeze and watching the change from Malayan jungle to Thai paddy fields. They also held their mates with dysentery out through the door. Most meals were handfuls of rice. Often there was no water. Dirty, hungry, thirsty, a knot of cramps, they made their slow way north to Ban Pong, a station a few kilometres from Nong Pladuk, Thai terminus of the planned railway. They left the boxcars and were crammed into open 3-ton trucks, which jolted towards the hills and mountains of western Thailand through dense green jungle. Dust from the track coated the men and then became mud with their sweat. Overnight they slept on the ground at a transit camp. In 30 hours their only food had been half a dozen small bananas and now Jackson had his first taste of the meal he came to detest: half a pint of steamed rice and a tiny portion of stinking dried fish. The next day they were trucked deeper into the jungle then marched into the middle of dense rainforest. It was a river flat. Nearby flowed the River Kwai. Here they would build the first of the jungle camps out of bamboo and atap, a thatching. They were welcomed by a Japanese camp commander, Lieutenant Osuki, who told them apologetically there was very little food and said the orders of the Nipponese must be obeyed implicitly. It was very important to work hard, he said.

Many of the prisoners would be worked to death.

THE RAILWAY JOINED the Japanese and the workers in an iron bond. There was no escape for either from the task. It was built, in the harshest of times, on brutality and hate but at least there was a purpose to the inhumanity. There were other hearts of darkness in the prison diaspora where brutality was practised for brutality's sake.

In July 1942 Australian members of Gull Force, prisoners on the island of Ambon watched as 34 Dutch prisoners, including two doctors and a padre, were lined up on a rise overlooking their camp. The men were accused of sending messages to their wives in a neighbouring camp. They were not of military importance. These are the words of the witnesses:

> Jack Panaotie: They had them stand out in the sun from early in the morning and then when we came back they were still there. That was a Sunday, I remember. Then out came two truckloads of drunken Japanese marines. They were armed with baseball bats and pick handles and all that sort of thing. The ones that didn't have them were getting star pickets.
>
> John Devenish: The commandant [Captain Ando] would blow a whistle, and he'd give his troops three-minute rounds, just like a heavyweight boxing championship, bashing the Dutchmen with these posts.
>
> John van Nooten: I was some one hundred yards away. It went on for two hours or more; at the time it seemed to go on all day. There were terrible screams of agony, and the Dutch eventually quietened down because a lot of them were unconscious.

Lieutenant Colonel Bill Scott, commander of Gull Force, said in an official report: 'Ando then rose, struck each unconscious man a blow on the head with a pick handle, entered his car and drove off. The sight on the hill was a ghastly one . . . and at the conclusion the whole rise was slippery with blood. Everyone was filled with horror and fear as it was our first experience of the Japanese way of enforcing discipline.'

The next day Captain Ando attended the funeral of the Dutch who died, placed a wreath on the coffins and bowed.

In October 1942, Scott was ordered to accompany a party including 263 Australians, all of whom had to be sick, on a voyage to a 'convalescent camp'. They were bound for Hainan, a desolate island off the Indo-China coast. Treatment of the Australians and other prisoners left behind on Ambon steadily deteriorated. The Japanese 'deliberately set out to kill off the prisoners by extra labour and short rations', an officer reported after the war. By June 1944 each man was receiving only 4 ounces of rice a day. Of the 528 left behind on Ambon, 405 died.

On Hainan, by August 1943 'a scandalous state of affairs existed and the situation was very alarming'. These are the words of the medical officer, Captain William Aitken, in an appendix to Scott's report.

Five men had died and many more were dying. The hospital was full of men with ataxia, paralysis and oedema – some able to stagger about and others could not. Every bed held a man with complete oedema of the whole body and gasping for breath. Others in the same condition were being nursed on the floor, propped up against the wall and boxes with kit bags etc; everywhere one looked in the camp one saw men with oedema of the legs and almost every man in the force had the disease to some extent. The Japanese were insisting on 120 men going to work and the work party consisted partly of ataxic and oedematous men scarcely able to stagger to work at which they were flogged and kicked . . . various

Japanese officers visited the camp during these months and men described above were subjected to roars of laughter.

Oedema (fluid retention) can be prevented simply by including vitamin B in the diet. But in 1945 the Japanese were reducing the diet. In June men were dying of starvation; in August the rice ration was stopped and replaced by dried sweet potato. One prisoner tried rat stew and pronounced it beautiful. When the prisoners were released later that month, 250 tons of rice were found in a nearby store.

Wherever prisoners were scattered across the Greater East Asia Co-Prosperity Sphere, life or death could depend on the quality and the compassion of the Japanese camp commander. There was a brief interlude on Hainan in September 1943 when rations improved and a fund was established for the purchase of drugs and clothing.

Tom Uren was sent to Saganoseki, on the eastern tip of Kyushu, one of the Japanese home islands. On Christmas Day 1944 he was belted across the back with an iron bar but, he says, there was little of the brutality that characterised the railway. However, at one camp on an island in Nagasaki Bay, working hours at a dockyard were long, slaps and punches were customary and so were beatings on the buttocks with full-bodied blows from baseball bats for offences considered more serious. At Fukuoka Camp No. 22, Sergeant Irio established a regime of individual beatings and mass punishments. All prisoners would be compelled to kneel for hours in the snow, sometimes with bamboo sticks under their knees. The men became wrecks physically and psychologically.

There were the blackest hearts: Outram Road jail in Singapore, the domain of the *kempeitai*, the military police, and Sandakan, in Borneo. We will visit them later.

CHILLA GOODCHAP AND Ern Toovey began their new life as railway builders on October 30, 1942 at Tanyin camp, 35 kilometres from Thanbyuzayat. A Force hacked into the Burma earth with picks and hoes and piled it in carriers of their own invention, rice bags slung between two bamboo poles like stretchers. They built embankments and bridges and were ant swarms chewing their way through cuttings. They didn't always follow the survey. The Japanese pirated the rails from existing railways in Burma and Malaya and what should have been a straight line became a sweeping curve.

A group of the *Perth* sailors became a mobile gang. As construction pushed on, they walked ahead of railway trucks on the completed line loaded with sleepers and rails. The sleepers were positioned on the embankment. A rail was lifted by 20 men and dropped on the sleepers. A spiking gang moved in, one man with an auger to drill the spike holes, another with a 25-pound bar to lever the rail into a set position and two with 14-pound hammers to fix the spikes. They were followed by a ballast party using heavy, square-nosed picks to ram the ballast under sleepers and rails and keep the correct height. As the railway lengthened, the men became thinner. They worked in rags or G-strings. Most went barefooted. Though for a month or so there was bliss for Toovey; a mate gave him a fashionable pair of leather shoes, shiny with pointed toes. They would have caught the eye on Brisbane streets. They were soon slashed to pieces by the ballast.

Mates are the currency of survival; mates and the marvellous medical men. When a mate is too crook to eat, you have his share. He'll scrounge for you. He may even pinch for you. When you are lying in the primitive hospital and need food, he'll come in with some of his. Rohan Rivett wrote in his diary on September 30, 1943:

Was talking to Johnnie when his cobber Bert came in with four eggs for him. Johnnie didn't want to take them, but finally gave in when Bert said he had four himself. Later, walking round the lines I struck Bert eating his rice. No sign of eggs. When questioned, he said: 'No, I only got two bucks for last month because I was down with fever most of the time. The b—— boong would only give me four eggs for that.' 'When did you last have an egg yourself?' I asked. Bert: 'Oh, a couple of months ago – that day we all had two.' I wonder if anybody at home could ever appreciate what it costs a man who's craving for food of any kind to give his all as Bert did tonight.

Without a mate, you're dead and when a mate dies or is shifted away you just have to find another one. Decades later you can't remember the names of some of them, just their presence. There was one who was taken away in a draft to Japan. You never did find out whether this man who for a short while was central to your life and you to his, survived the treacherous voyage.

Goodchap and Toovey were mates. Goodchap, having carried Toovey on his back in the jungles of Java, would help him in a different way in the jungles of Burma. In March Toovey's knee, injured when he jumped from the stricken *Perth*, gave way. He was sent to a 'light-duty' camp. Light duty meant two men carrying a half 44-gallon drum of water half a kilometre from a well from dawn to dusk. Toovey fell often, and a doctor managed to get him transferred back to work on the line. On May 16 Toovey went on sick parade again. He simply didn't want to work, not on this day. It was the rite of passage, his twenty-first birthday. He did not want the shame of spending this day working for the Japanese. The doctor was not sympathetic.

THE BIG WET started. Rice supplies diminished. Rarely the drovers came through the camps with the yaks, the small cattle that were the source of protein. Like the prisoners, the yaks were mostly skin and bone. Each day, perhaps several times, men on the work parties, some lifting rails, some in mid-hammer stroke heard the melancholy notes of the Last Post. They did not stop work. They could not, though to their surprise and anger the guards would stand to attention. It was not until they returned to camp in the dark that they would find out who had died. Sometimes a burial had to wait until the fitter men from the line could carry the body, wrapped in rags, to the grave. Soon they began clearing jungle to expand the areas allocated for the graveyard.

Toovey wrote in a memoir:

> It was in this camp that I reached a low in my life. Continual bouts of malaria, dengue fever and worst of all dysentery almost made me give up. This may sound weak but it became very easy not wanting to live. Although in a different hut and in a different working party, Chilla heard that I was crook. One day he came into the so-called hospital and gave me a serve, casting reflections on my ancestry, besides calling me a 'Catholic bludger etc . . .' It must have awakened the Irish in me, as others said I wanted to fight him. It must have helped as I was back on the line again in a week or two.

Ken Dumbrell, who as a officer was bashed many times by the Japanese for standing up for his men, practised tough love too, though none of the diggers would use that phrase. He had been in the 105-kilo camp, losing three days in a malaria attack. He knew when he came out of it he had been nursed by his mates Johnny Vance and Benny Cook. He went back to see one of his blokes. 'I've got a bloody ulcer,' the bloke said.

'Jesus, that's no good,' Dumbrell said.

'I've had this. I'm giving up,' the bloke said.

'Like bloody hell you are,' Dumbrell said and belted him over the face. 'That talk is a lot of crazy business.' The bloke stared at him hard, but at last smiled. Dumbrell said, 'I'll belt you up again tomorrow if you're not feeling any brighter.'

Then there were times for tenderness. Long after the war, Chilla Goodchap nursed his wife during a debilitating illness. She died in April 2003, on Chilla's eightieth birthday. He thought of her when he thought of his dead mates: 'In Burma we would link up in a group of say four or five of us and you'd work as a family of four or five. You'd know every mortal thing about them. They've told you every one of their stories of home and their upsets and their pleasures and Christ knows what. With those five fellows, no matter what you get, you'd share. So help me Christ if you got it, it would be five ways. It's self-protection really. And if one bloke is crook, you stand with a bloke in his dying moments, his bloody awful bloody death, and you're holding his bloody hand. Like I do with my wife up here now. It sounds bloody effeminate, but it isn't effeminate because you're affected by this poor bastard and you know the things he did for your Burma family.'

All along the railway, men helped their mates live and die. Allan Gee, partially blind, arrived at the Thai camp Tamarkan, after a gruelling six-day trip sitting on top of a freight car. Slim Hedrick was waiting for him.

He was rotten with dysentery and fever. Diarrhoea was running down his legs and he was blown up with beri beri. He was standing there with this big smile. He said: 'I've got your wardrobe here, your urn for boiling water and a bamboo container for washing. And I've got you a new pair of pants made out of a piece of canvas. But the best news is I've got you an egg' . . . Slim was my mate. I owe him my life. I loved Slim.

They had another mate, a *Perth* man too, Seamus O'Brien:

So many died I don't even like to think about it. This particular day I had buried quite a few people and I went over to see Seamus who was extremely ill. 'Seamus, is there anything I can do for you?' 'No,' he said. 'I am going to die tonight.' We didn't have a Catholic priest but a man called Mike Taylor looked after the Catholics. I asked Seamus if he would like me to get Mike to come over to see him, but he said, 'No, Elmo [Gee's nickname], I would like you to talk to me about all the happy times we had in the Navy, and the fun we had in Jamaica, and tonight I will die peacefully.' I buried him at about ten o'clock the next night and cried my eyes out.

It was only a small ulcer on Ern Toovey's left shin. The pain wasn't too bad and he felt guilty about going on sick parade. The Dutch doctor reached for a scalpel and made two quick cuts. It was as if a trapdoor had opened on rottenness. For a few days he was tranferred to light duties, but the Japanese engineers, who set the numbers they wanted to work on the line each day, asked for more men. Gaping leg roughly bandaged, Toovey worked in mud, ballast and pain until one day, without notice, he was sent back up the line to the 55-kilo ulcer camp. Next to the cholera camps, the isolation areas set up for the quick dying, men hated and feared most the 55-kilo camp. Suffering was a certainty; the loss of a leg a distinct possibility. A steel boxcar of patients was left more than half a mile from the camp. It took Toovey, ulcer on one leg, injured knee ballooned on the other, more than two hours to reach the perimeter of the long lines of bamboo huts. Some of the others had dysentery; some had dysentery and malaria. The worst were still crawling in, dragging their belongings, at nightfall.

The senior medical officer himself had arrived on a stretcher. Albert Coates, recovering from delirium and a high fever, had scrub typhus when Nagatomo and Varley asked him to take over the hospital. This so-called hospital was an abandoned working camp, the atap roofing of the huts in bad condition. None of the men was fit enough to fix them. In rain showers, the roofs leaked, in the monsoon water poured down on the sick. No matter. The men either wore no clothes or a scattering of rags and in their illnesses and suffering this was mere inconvenience. Coates and his small team were attempting to care for 1800 of the seriously ill from forward jungle camps, including 500 with ulcers. For two weeks orderlies carried him on rounds of the patients. An accidental cut or a graze, a rock thrown by a Japanese guard, which is how Kevin Ward's ulcer began, or a beating and the unsanitary jungle conditions will do the rest to malnourished men. Once the ulcer reached muscle, it spread rapidly. If its progress could not be stopped, there was only one, radical solution. Coates was grateful that in his student and post-student days, he had studied closely the work of two surgical pioneers, Ambroise Paré (1510–90) and John Hunter (1728–93). In Paré's era, surgery was a specialisation of certain barbers. He joined the French army as a barber-surgeon, devising artificial limbs and the technique of binding arteries after amputation instead of cauterising them with a red-hot iron. Hunter was one of Coates's heroes, regarded as the founder of scientific surgery. He was a staff-surgeon in the British army during the war with France. His legacy was a contribution to understanding the results likely to follow the removal of a diseased organ which might otherwise infect the whole body, causing death or chronic illness.

Paré and Hunter would have been appalled at the conditions Coates and his colleagues worked under. Surely medicine had advanced over the centuries? There were eight bamboo huts roofed with atap and one small isolation hut in which 100 dysentery patients were nursed. With difficulty, Coates got permission to build an operating room, a small bamboo hut 2.4 metres by 1.8 metres and about 1.8 metres high. The Japanese had thoughtfully constructed an elaborate mortuary. No beds or bedding were supplied or equipment of any kind. For the 500 ulcer patients, Coates received six bandages a fortnight and a few cakes of sulphur. For hundreds of dysentery patients, he received 1 pound of Epsom salts a fortnight. Sections of giant bamboo became water containers; knives, spoons and forks, and the saw used by the camp's butcher and carpenter, became surgical instruments. Sutures were made from the gut of yaks. At least there was some anaesthetic for major surgery, though some patients would find themselves missing a toe or two as Coates briskly made his rounds with a pair of scissors. An inventive chemist, Dutch Captain van Boxtel produced tiny doses of solutions of cocaine from tablets. They were injected into the spines of ulcer patients undergoing amputations. Van Boxtel also made a liquid to sterilise the skin from Burmese brandy and waste rice. He conjured up equipment to extract a vital medicine to treat amoebic dysentery, a disease the Japanese doctor refused to acknowledge as haunting the camp. A young army man, Sapper Dixon, ill himself, created surgical needles out of darning needles. (Dixon in a later camp made a 2-inch diameter circular saw and attached it to a treadle machine for a brain tumour operation.)

For the procedure for an amputation, Coates again turned to an old medical hero. He adopted the Listerian circular amputation: a cut round the leg, a coning out of the flesh and bone (not too much flesh on these patients, he would ruefully observe), large arteries ligated with yak-gut, the stump loosely stitched and a bit of sterilised rag, usually part of the patient's pants, inserted into the lower end of the wound for drainage.

Coates had a no-nonsense approach to what was needed for survival. Early on, he said: 'The route home is inscribed in the bottom of every man's dixie.' (This became the Coates dictum and passed along the railway.) 'Every time it is filled with rice, eat it. If you vomit it up again, eat some more; even if it comes up again some good will remain. If you get a bad egg, eat it no matter how bad it may appear. An egg is bad only when the stomach will not hold it.' At the 55-kilo camp he would say to the ulcer men that he could get them home with one leg or leave them dead in the jungle with two. Ern Toovey went cold. Cricket dominated his peacetime life. Coates performed many amputations a day, 114 of the 120 total carried out at 55-kilo camp. But Toovey kept his leg. Medical orderlies scraped the open, suppurating ulcer once or twice a day with a spoon that had been bent and sharpened. It was the worst pain he had ever endured. Hot rice poultices were applied. This went on for weeks but after the war Ern Toovey played Sheffield Shield cricket for 14 years and was chairman of Queensland selectors for 27 years.

Albert Coates would look back at the 55-kilo camp and say he believed that there the best work he had ever done in his life was accomplished. Each day he rose at daylight, walked among the men and supervised the work of four other medical officers. Each day he segregated the sick from the very sick, working particularly on the leg ulcer cases, inspecting legs likely to be amputated that day, curetting 70 or 80 ulcers during the morning and supervising the dressing by teams of volunteer orderlies, trying to cheer up the men and in the afternoon amputating nine or ten legs.

One day the Japanese invited Coates and a selected number of medical orderlies to a performance by a Japanese army band. 'Nice gesture,' he thought. The party entered the heat and the strange light of the jungle, sometimes dim, sometimes dappled, but it was a freedom from the hospital camp. The 14-kilometre trek was long for men who were using their last reserves to live and to work. They emerged into a camp clearing, sweaty and footsore, to find an immaculately uniformed band. Hours later Coates and his party re-entered the jungle. Coates walked with memories of Western music well-played. Once they came to another clearing. For Coates the music died. Here was a Japanese hospital, lavishly equipped and lavishly supplied with drugs. Angry and bitter, Coates returned to the stinking, down-at-heel 55-kilo camp. The anger at the contrast stayed alive. In November 1946, Coates gave evidence at the International Military Tribunal trying Japanese war criminals.

> Prosecuting Counsel: Will you describe the conditions in the camp?
> Coates: . . . We had a big element of malaria in the camp. It was practically universal. The quinine supplied was only sufficient for three hundred patients, but practically eighteen hundred had malaria. I protested to the medical authorities at Thanbyuzayat, that is the Japanese, and it was pointed out that the Japanese allowed a man to have only one disease; if he had malaria he couldn't have an ulcer of the leg, and if he had an ulcer of the leg he couldn't have dysentery. Unfortunately there were men who had three or more diseases. Quinine was the only

drug supplied in a quantity which was measurable. The rest of the drugs supplied were in infinitesimal quantities. Malaria was a great underlying cause of blood destruction, that is anemia, and consequently seriously afflicted men suffered from other diseases. Even more important was the lack of food.

Q: Is it your opinion as a medical officer that the deaths occurring at Kilo-55 could have been avoided?

A: I am quite sure they could.

Q: By what methods?

A: Adequate feeding, adequate drugs, particularly quinine in amounts sufficient not only to treat but to use as a preventive; the recognition by the Japanese of such diseases as we had, avitaminosis, dysentery, and the provision of simple specifics [for their treatment]. This together with adequate feeding, would have been quite possible, seeing, as we did, any number of cattle in the neighbourhood. Even in the absence of amenities such as beds, bedding, towels and soap, we could have saved most lives.

Q: What was the mortality in that camp?

A: We lost 330 out of some 1600 that were there.

Senior Japanese officers could not pretend ignorance of the desperation that was the 55-kilo camp. Coates wrote in a report to them: 'The spectacle of emaciated skeletons of men on the one hand, the oedematous, water-logged wrecks on the other, many with rotting, gangrenous ulcers of the leg emitting a nauseating stench, lying in their pain and misery, was such as I never wish to witness again. The daily procession to the graveyard of numbers of patients was a reminder to those still alive that the consolation of death would soon end their suffering. The memory of it is not easily obliterated.'

For Coates, the agony of frustration was increased by the knowledge of the way the tide of war had changed. Like Weary Dunlop, he had access to a secret radio, helped again by the invaluable van Boxtel. Using his preparation of ox-hoof jelly and ammonium chloride obtained from traders, van Boxtel made batteries for the radio which had been cobbled together by a patient from a motorcycle magneto, an emery wheel and valves, again bought from traders. At night the patient would make his careful way through the jungle to his hiding place in a hollow tree about a mile from the camp. Coates, after a day of amputations and watching the dead carried away, would be informed of the good news: the Allied have landed at Cape Merkus, New Britain. But he knew that help was far away from the railway. The dying would continue.

LATE IN 1943, Lieutenant Colonel Yoshitada Nagatomo, the man who had suggested that A Force weep with gratitude at the greatness of the Imperial thoughts and favours, and who had counselled them, as they set out to build a railway, to work cheerfully, visited the 55-kilo camp. Once more Ern Toovey, grateful to be standing on his own two legs, looked up in disgust at Nagatomo on a rostrum. Nagatomo was there for the dedication of the camp cemetery, hundreds of graves in neat rows cleared out of the jungle tangle. It was part of a perplexing pattern, this ceremonial respect of the Japanese for the prisoner-of-war dead, the people they reviled in life as cowards and non-persons: guards standing to attention at the distant sound of the Last Post, the laying of wreaths, the saying of prayers. Nagatomo was followed on the rostrum by Lieutenant Colonel Arie Gottschell, the senior Dutch officer at the 55-kilo camp. Perhaps Nagatomo expected politeness and circumlocution but Gottschell attacked on behalf of the living and partly living. Why were they being treated like this? Where were the Red Cross parcels they were entitled to? Where were the letters from loved ones, the links with their lost worlds? Gottschell stirred the men, lifted their spirits, helped them in their daily struggle. He helped them survive. He did not. After the railway was finished, Gottschell was among those prisoners evacuated to Tha Makham camp. There, in March 1944 he died from starvation and avitaminosis, died needlessly.

CHAPTER 18

A day in the life of Desmond Jackson

In Hintok Mountain camp, Desmond Jackson is wrenched from sleep. Darkness is deep in the camp, deeper in the jungle but Sergeant George Tate's brassy bugle and the hated notes of the Japanese reveille are ordering the day to start. In the Greater East Asia Co-Prosperity Sphere, the clocks are set to Tokyo time which means that in Thailand they have been turned back three hours. It is cold, not much over 12 degrees. Jackson pushes down his blanket, the birthday blanket Lance Gibson gave him so long ago on Java. It is precious to him. Some men shiver without cover and try to sleep on the rough bamboo platform. The mosquito net he now folds up is precious too. The net is not just a protection against mosquitoes and myriad biting insects, it is also a cocoon of privacy in this place where men are packed together in long bamboo and atap huts.

He puts on ragged shirt and ragged shorts, still wet from the previous day. He has a pair of wooden clogs to wear around the camp but they are useless to work in. He will go barefoot into the jungle. He slips and slides through misty rain to the latrines, open pits, stinking pits. He has to move quickly.

There is not much time between the bugle call and parade. He goes back to the hut, washes, collects his haversack with eating utensils and the cigarettes he rolled the night before.

The camp is built on a gently sloping hillside. There are two fenced compounds, one for the Korean guards, the other for the Japanese engineers. In between are the six huts for the prisoners. Down the valley side, near a small mountain stream, are administration, hospital and kitchen buildings and a small parade ground. In the kitchen the cooks are stirring steaming *kwalis*, large cooking pots. Breakfast is served: a very thin rice gruel. Today, as on most days, it is tasteless, unappetising, something to be eaten in accordance with Coates's dictum that the path home is an empty bowl. Sometimes it has the slightest flavour of salt. On the good days it will have a faint sprinkling of sugar. It makes Jackson urinate a lot, a nuisance. The gruel is washed down with the parody of coffee, brewed from burnt rice. Before and after eating, he dips his utensils into water boiling in another *kwali*. He collects his lunch, just plain rice. Jackson looks hopefully for an egg, or even a small piece of foul, dried fish. Nothing.

In the first light of dawn the Japanese engineers come from their compound, shouting '*Koorah! Speedo!* All soldja *tenko!*' *Tenko* is the counting of heads on the parade ground by the Korean guards. The engineers set the tasks for the day and the number of men required. Their commander is Lieutenant Eiji Hirota, young (they call him the Konyu Kid) and hated. He was recently the bearer of bad news: he came to the line to tell each working party that the railway was to be completed as soon as possible. Everything had to be done *speedo*. Rest days were abolished. Every hour of daylight had to be used. The Japanese medical NCO is Corporal Okada. He is hated too. His mission is not to oversee the treatment of the sick but to make the sick work. In April a Japanese general had come to inspect Hintok Mountain camp. Okada decided to disguise the fact that many of the prisoners, ill and malnourished, were in hospital. He marched about 50 of the hospital patients to a hiding place in the jungle, men with large tropical ulcers and protein oedema. Clearly they were incapable of work, but the engineers ordered them to roll 44-gallon drums of oil over a rough hillside track and down a steep slope, several miles of torture. Lose control of a drum, get beaten.

Jackson is part of one of the two groups of 100 men who will work this day chipping a deep cutting through a solid-rock spur. This is a brutally difficult section of the railway. The trace, the path chosen by the survey teams, climbs up from the River Kwai valley and ascends the flank of a high hill. There are winding ledges hacked into the precipitous slope and several cuttings. The first, known as Konyu 3, or K3, becomes infamous as Hellfire Pass. The second, where Jackson now works, is called Hammer and Tap cutting. There are long embankments and there are bridges spanning the deep paths of the monsoon run-off. One is known as Pack of Cards bridge, a name it earns. It is 367 metres long and 25 metres high, built of green timber fastened with wooden wedges, spikes, bamboo ties, rattan or cane rope and wooden dowels. Three times during construction it tumbled down. Thirty-one men fell to die on the rocks below and, Wigmore, the official historian, reports, 29 men were beaten to death there.

The light is still dim when Jackson and his group leave the camp. They are not marched out. There are no guards. Thoughts of escape are rare. Everyone knows of the executions of those who tried and failed. Everyone knows that, as white men in a brown world, a sometimes hostile world, they have no camouflage and that friendly troops are jungles and mountains away in one direction, an ocean away in the other. As

Jackson scrambles down over logs and rocks, despair keeps him company. It always does, but he usually manages to hold it at arm's length. He has to do that to keep his spirit from dying; his body, weakened though it is, fights on. To survive he has to obey orders. He has to go out and do the work and get back to camp. So simple. So hard. He has adopted what he calls the six-month method. He tells himself he can last six months. At the end of that eternity, he tells himself he can last another six months. He knows his mates have their own strategies, but they never talk about it.

AFTER THE WAR he will find out that there was a radio in the camp, but for security reasons Weary Dunlop and the senior officers keep the news to themselves. He nurses a conviction that the Allies are winning. He has protected it from doubt since he went to a lecture in a Java prison camp by the captured British guerilla leader Laurens van der Post in September 1942. Van der Post had access to a radio. 'I am quite satisfied,' he had said, 'that the Japanese have lost their attempt and from now on they will be pushed back and back and they will have no further advances. It will take a long time, but they will not win the war.'

Something else helps him, though he feels guilty about it. Throughout the diaspora there are prisoners who have no contact with home, not a single letter during the long years from a wife or a mother or father. Somehow Jackson receives five or six parcels of letters, 70 in all, from relatives and friends. From Jackson his family receives a few 25-word postcards, written to the formula the Japanese demand. They don't know if he has got their letters so from February 1943, Esmae Jackson writes each month to tell her son, gently and sadly, that his father Cyril has died.

IT TAKES ABOUT three-quarters of an hour, wary every step of the sharp rock or bamboo spike that could mean an ulcer, for Jackson to reach the cutting. He walks past the engineer in charge of the job, a sergeant the prisoners call Molly the Monk. It is always a nervous moment. One day without warning Molly had beaten him with a crowbar, 12 heavy blows on legs, buttocks and back. There had been no cause, no provocation. The bruises remained for a long time; the anger and sense of injustice never faded. Nor did the memory of the killing of Mickey Hallam.

ON JUNE 22, Hallam set out with Jackson's work gang. He should have been in the camp hospital, but the Japanese were insisting on a full complement. The least ill of the men filled the ranks first of all, and then men were forced from hospital beds to make up the numbers. Hallam, ill with fever, went because if he did not someone worse off would be taken from a hospital bed. Jackson was at the tail of the column when Hallam stumbled as he said: 'I just can't go. I can't go.' He struggled back to camp and was admitted to hospital with malaria and enteritis. The idea was that when the party returned that night Hallam would join it for *tenko* and the Japanese numbers would tally. But when the work party reached Hammer and Tap cutting there was a disaster: the Japanese could see they did not have enough men and held a *tenko*. One hundred men had set out. Only 85 had arrived. Fourteen had slipped off the path to spend the day in the jungle. Their action doomed Hallam, who was legitimately in hospital. That night the Japanese demanded that the men who had not reached the cutting give themselves up. Hallam left his hospital bed to stand with six other men who had come forward. They were taken to the engineers' compound and

Jackson and the rest of the work party were herded after them. Then the beating started. Molly the Monk, a sergeant the men called Billie the Pig and other engineers used open hands, then fists. One would hold the back of a prisoner's head while the other hit his face. They used bamboo staves, thrashed the men until they fell down, kicked them, forced them to stand up again, thrashed them again, kicked them again, forced them to stand up again. It lasted an interminable three hours. When it was over and the men were lying on the ground, the Japanese put lanterns in front of them and made the 85 walk past a foot or so away. Later the seven were brought to the parade ground to be counted in by the Korean guards, who ordered them to go to work the next day. Charlie Atterton called to Mickey Hallam: 'How are you going, Mickey?' Hallam called back: 'All right Charlie. These bastards can't kill me.' But they had. He returned to hospital, face swollen, neck and chest contused, abrasions to his legs, his temperature 103.4. Three times he dropped into deep unconsciousness. The third time he died. Weary Dunlop wrote as cause of death: 'Contusion to the heart causing cardiac arrest, a result of beating by a Nippon engineer sergeant whilst suffering from malaria on the night of 22 June, 1943.' Mickey Hallam was buried in grave No. 14 in the Hintok Mountain camp cemetery.

JACKSON LOOKS ALONG the cutting. Over the weeks, it has ground forward so slowly. It is basically divided into two sections. The previous afternoon, the 100-man team had cleared away from half the cutting rocks and debris blasted by dynamite charges. In the other half charges were exploded last thing at night to leave a fresh harvest for Jackson and the rock-clearers. The 50 two-man hammer-and-tap teams begin their work in the cleared section. Once Jackson had wangled his way to work on a hammer-and-tap team. Hammer-and-tap men finish work before the rock clearers. That was the attraction. But soon Jackson was manoeuvring to return to his old job. The hammer-and-tap men bored holes for the dynamite charges, though boring hardly describes the process. One sits on the solid rock holding a drill, the other swings an 8-pound hammer. The drill is turned one-third. The hammer is swung. The drill is turned another third, the hammer swung. Hammer, turn. Hammer, turn. Hammer, turn. Change places. Hammer, turn. Scrape the dust out with a small scoop. Pour a little water into the hole. Hammer, turn. Work a metre down into the hardness.

It would have killed me, Jackson thinks. He is in a chain of about 12 men, from the cutting to the edge of the hillside, passing rocks from hand to hand to send them crashing down through the jungle. Other men roll large, rounded rocks. An engineer shouts *koorah*. The prisoners dash from the cutting as the dynamite fuse is lit. Men have been badly injured as rocks hail and ricochet. The guards call a smoko. It's a five-minute escape. Jackson coughs his way through cigarettes filled with native tobacco that he has washed, turning the water jet-black, and dried. Thai traders sell it to the camp canteen and the Japanese get a squeeze of the proceeds. Most of the men are addicted, spending much of their meagre pay on it, going hungrier, if necessary. After the plain-rice lunch, the teams swap areas. Pass the rock. Hammer and turn. Pass the rock. Hammer and turn. The man next to Jackson says: 'I wonder what the doover is tonight.' Pass the rock. Hammer and turn. Jackson struggles back to camp in the numbness of exhaustion, uphill, in the dark. The evening meal is half a pint of rice and a very thin stew. No meat again. But there is a doover. The cooks, bless them, have pulped some of the rice, found a little chilli and onion and added a few eggs. Jackson holds his small doover in the palm of his hand. He is savouring the eating of something with taste.

Then another pleasure. The officers have built a weir across the mountain stream and thrust hollowed-out bamboo through the wall. Cool water spurts and gushes. Back in the hut, there is little talk: who was hurt this day, who was bashed, who had died. It's been much more than a year in captivity now, and they have said all they can bear to say about home and about hope. Jackson used to lie wondering whether there was a God. He doesn't any more. God does not exist. He rolls some cigarettes, climbs under his mosquito net, pulls up his blanket. Tomorrow the bugle will sound, and the day after, and the day after, for the next six months of survival.

CHAPTER 19

In the time of cholera

Kevin Ward fought, and predictably lost, his own small, personal war in Changi in May 1943. By now the railway's appetite for men and lives was voracious. The vast Asian-labourer army from Malaya and the 'sweat army' from Burma had been marched into the jungle. In April, the Japanese had dipped again into their reservoir of prisoners of war in Changi. On April 8, Malaya Command Headquarters had been ordered to have 7000 medically fit British and Australian troops organised in batches and ready to start departing in under a fortnight. They were designated F Force. A Force, 3000 men, had been shipped to Burma in May 1942. B Force, 1496 men, was sent to Borneo in July to build an airstrip. In November, C Force, 2200-strong, including 563 Australians, was sent to Japan to work in factories, ship-yards and mines. On June 18, the first British contingent was sent north from Singapore. Twenty thousand British and Dutch prisoners were in Thailand when Dunlop Force, a party of 900 Australians named after its commander, Weary Dunlop, left to join them in January 1943. In March D Force followed, 5000 men, including 2242 Australians, sent with the warning by the Japanese that all would need to be fit for heavy manual labour in malarial areas. At the end of March, a second contingent was sent to Borneo, E Force, 1000 men, including 600 Australians.

The Japanese did not say exactly where F Force was going, but there was no doubt it would be a rest camp in comparison with Changi, a Shangri-la compared with Singapore. There the food situation was deteriorating, the rations issued by the Imperial Japanese Army poor and shrinking. F Force would go, the Japanese said, to a place where food was plentiful and the climate better. There was no warning of malaria and heavy labour and clearly F Force would be particularly blessed. Include sufficient Army Medical Corps personnel to staff a 300-bed hospital, the Japanese said. Stocks of mosquito nets, blankets and clothing would be awaiting men who did not have them. Officers should take their trunks and valises and men whatever personal effects they could carry. Canteens would be set up in the camps. There would be a field electric lighting set. There would be no long marches. There would be transport for the heavy equipment and for unfit men. And there would be food for the soul too. A band would accompany each 1000 men, and gramophones would be issued after arrival. But do take a piano. The 27th Infantry Brigade concert party was included, and the British 18th Division concert party with four celebrity artists.

There was an immediate flaw in the grand Japanese plan: Malaya Command could not muster 7000 fit men in Changi. The Japanese refused to reduce the size of F Force but said that 30 per cent of the complement could be unfit men. The Australian command, suspicious of the enticing picture the Japanese had painted, decided that no more than 125 unfit Australians would go. Major Bruce Hunt, senior medical officer, told his group of F Force: 'We have been told we are going to a convalescent camp somewhere up north. The commanding officer (Lieutenant-Colonel S. W. Harris, of the British 18th Division) believes it but I don't. We will be going to a land where disease will be rife, so prepare yourselves for the worst. You will encounter diseases you have never heard of and I fear for the future.' Fatally, the British sent almost 1000 unfit men.

Kevin Ward shared the suspicions and was relieved when he was passed over for F Force. He was ill, malnourished and losing his sight. The detachment of F Force he would have travelled with left Changi on April 22, his twentieth birthday. He thought being left behind was a wonderful present. Two weeks after F Force's departure, the Japanese ordered up H Force, 3000 men, including 600 Australians. The day before, Ward had been to the camp's eye specialist. 'You'll never leave Changi,' the specialist said. 'Your vision is too depleted.' But the numbers had to be made up. The Japanese came for Ward. He fought and it took five of them to throw him like a bag of spuds onto the truck. 'I called out to an officer, but he was just powerless. He couldn't do anything. I realised I was gone.' Ward was right to go to the railway kicking and screaming.

ON APRIL 18 the first contingent of F Force left Singapore for the promised land. The first sign of betrayal was at the station: no carriages of even basic comfort, but rice wagons into which the men were crammed. They set off on a slow train, confined for long periods in what soon became a stinking swelter. Often there was no food for 24 hours and once, for 40 hours. On one train there was no water from midday one day until nightfall the next. After the crossing of the Malay–Thai border, military police refused permission for men to leave trains to exercise and defecate at the frequent halts. In places where permission was granted, there were either no latrines, or the pits quickly became foul and overflowing. All of this was fitting for a journey towards disease and death.

At Ban Pong, the men of F Force arrived in trainloads after five-day ordeals. They stumbled, filthy, hungry, thirsty, from their rice trucks: Wally Mulvena, father of eight and 45 years old; Black Jack Galleghan's disciple Stan Arneil, 24; Cyril Gilbert, 23, the tough Queenslander; Harry Weiss, from country New South Wales, who had turned 33 that month; and thousands of others, almost every second man doomed. A little over a year later, by May 1944, 2036 of the 3334 British troops were dead and 1060 of the 3666 Australians. The 18th Division concert party suffered particularly, losing the majority of its members. Three of the four celebrity artists died. The toll of H Force was lighter, but still atrocious: 885 of the 3000 died, including 179 Australians.

After the war, Lieutenant Colonel Charles Kappe and Captain Adrian Curlewis compiled *The Story of F Force*. During the misery some of the men kept secret diaries.

> Harry Weiss: Tuesday 27 April '43. Reached Ban Pong at 7 am, and detrained, a funny looking place it is. Japanese made us dump everything we couldn't carry – kitchen stuff and officers' gear etc., and say the trucks will bring it. We marched to Stinking Camp, hardly any water and are the Japanese cranky.

Asian-labourer parties had passed through the transit camp and the pit latrines were full of maggots and overflowing. The guards would not issue tools to dig new ones. The water supply was a filthy well which provided only enough for cooking and the filling of one water bottle each. Three hundred men crowded into each bamboo and atap hut. They looked around for the promised transport. There was none for men or equipment. The partly fit, the ill, the halt and the lame would have to 'spend the next few days marching', the

Japanese told them. The officers stacked and looked for the last time on their personal possessions. Precious tools were discarded, medical supplies had to be abandoned. And there, standing plaintively in the tropical sun, was the band's piano.

The men sold their extra clothing to Thai traders. This would leave them near naked months later on the railway, but at least they had full stomachs for the first few days. They marched at night to avoid the heat. The first contingent stepped out from Ban Pong at 10.30 pm. On a good road, with full stomachs and the passing illusion of freedom, they swung along for a while, singing the old marching songs. By 3 am, reality had nibbled away at high spirits. Boots, in poor condition for a start, were chaffing through thin socks and giving birth to blisters. Pathetic loads started to drag at limbs. The sun was blazing at nine o'clock when the vanguard reached the first stop, Tha Rua, 27 kilometres from Ban Pong. At least for the last few kilometres they had been able to hire some ox carts and tricycle-rickshaws to carry the medical boxes and some of the sick stragglers. They had 16 nights and more than 290 kilometres to go.

There was little rest at Tha Rua, a padang with just one roofed but unwalled building. Latrines had to be dug and the pattern of lengthy, confused check parades, deliberately inconvenient, designed for a meaningless exercise of authority, began. At 9.30 pm the march restarted, a 24-kilometre slog to Kanchanaburi. Here, among a few stunted bushes, was one, small open-sided shelter for the sick. Again Asian labourers had fouled the ground and flies swarmed.

Stan Arneil: 29 April. A frightful night march brought us to 'desert camp' at daybreak. We stop here for the night. The camp is a dry, stony, thorny half acre, as hot as a frying pan and the kindly Thai natives sell us filthy water at ten cents a bucket and are prepared to rob us, hand over fist, at every opportunity. Everybody is against us in this country.

The column left at nine o'clock the next evening. More men were sick; more were straggling, more had diarrhoea. Those who fell from illness and exhaustion were carried on stretchers. Fitter men like Cyril Gilbert carried their mates' gear. Sweat soaked them and intermittent rain drenched them. At Wampo, the next stop, the only shade came from a few trees. The next night they marched 25 kilometres. By now they were climbing into the hills along jungle tracks and into the force of the monsoon.

Cyril Gilbert: The mud was treacherous and the night was black. It was hell carrying the stretchers. Sometimes you had to hang on to one another's shoulders to stop going over the side into the ravine. Some men did. Ten minutes every hour you were supposed to be able to rest, but if you were at the back of the column, the head was taking off again so you wouldn't get your break. We marched into the dawn on Mother's Day. I'll never forget that.

The word passed down the column. It was Mother's Day. Exhausted men, sick men picked a vine with small, white jungle flowers and draped it on their packs. They spelled the following night and then struggled through another night to Tarsau, an established camp, the headquarters of D Force, which had a jungle hospital. Here Major Bruce Hunt, the senior medical officer of F Force, saw a chance to leave the sickest men for treatment. Hunt and a Japanese medical officer agreed that 37 men were unfit to travel. The Japanese officer put this in writing but the corporal of the guard insisted that only 10 men could remain. Hunt fell in the 37 men separately from the main parade and stood in front of them. With him was Major Cyril Wild, the officer who had carried the white flag in the Percival surrender party and now an interpreter. Wild attempted to placate the corporal who had approached them with a large bamboo staff in his hand. This is Hunt's report on what happened next:

> The corporal's only reply was to hit Major Wild in the face. Another guard followed suit and as Major Wild staggered back the corporal thrust at the major's genitals with his bamboo. I was left standing in front of the patients and was immediately set upon by the corporal and two other guards. One tripped me while two others pushed me to the ground. The three then set about me with bamboos, causing extensive bruising of skull, back, hands and arms, and a fractured 5th metacarpal bone. This episode took place in front of the whole parade of the troops. After I was disposed of the corporal then made the majority of the sick march with the rest of the troops.

At 7.30 that night, the men set out along a rough, slushy jungle track. The column soon straggled and some of the men at the rear were attacked by Thai bandits. Once a Japanese guard drove one off with a bayonet, but as the march progressed, the guards, frightened of tigers, took position in the middle of the column. The next camp, Konyu, marked the start of the worst of times for F Force. They were entering primal jungle, supply lines were stretched, poor rations became poorer, with no possibility of buying food from native vendors or at kampongs. They were, night by night, becoming weaker, their passing marked by the sick who had to be left behind. They were going into extreme danger.

> Harry Weiss: Thursday, 13 May. A twenty-five kilo march and a lot of climbing to reach this large unfinished camp. I call it 'Cholera Camp', but believe it's called Tamaranpat. 29 Bn. Lads are here doing roadwork and don't like the place. Although the river is large and clear, it is cholera infested. I was on boiling water fatigue. They won't even rely on chlorination now. Kitchen could only feed us two meals of rice and onion so we are glad to move on, especially as the Asiatics, who are roofing the huts, are particularly filthy – passing their excreta whenever the mood takes them. They are said to be (many of them) sick, and two were carried away this afternoon apparently dead. An Indian told us they came from Penang mainly and the Japanese told them this would be a good job just over the Thailand border.

CHOLERA WAS FIRST recorded in a medical report from India in 1573 and experts regard the Far East as its ancestral home. Since 1817, pandemics have swept across the world seven times. In 1849 there were 1000 deaths a day in England. The latest started in Indonesia in 1961 and by 1995 more than a million cases had been reported in the Americas. The real figure is much higher. This seventh pandemic has caused a conservative 400,000 deaths and still stalks areas where people and sanitation are poor. Infection is caused by a bacteria, *vibrio cholerae*, which is present in drinking water and contaminated food. The main source is the faeces of infected people. Cholera is a swift and brutal disease. The symptoms are acute, watery diarrhoea, vomiting, suppression of urine, rapid and severe dehydration, fall of blood pressure, cramps in legs and abdomen, subnormal temperature and complete collapse. Without proper treatment, death occurs within 24 hours. Vaccination is an incomplete and unreliable protection for a short duration. The World Health Organisation does not recommend it. In the region the Thai–Burma railway was pushed through, the many streams and rivers are quick and efficient distributors of cholera.

In November 1942 A Force commander Brigadier Varley recorded in his diary chilling news: 'Cholera broke out in Moulmein and Rangoon a couple of weeks ago and there has now been one death in the village a few hundred yards from our camp.' From then on fear was a constant, flowing down the waterways. The source of cholera was always going to be the coolies, the Asian labourers, most wretched of the wretched along the railway. These were the sons and daughters of the Greater East Asia Co-Prosperity Sphere, liberated by the Japanese from their colonial masters. Some of them brought their families with them to their deaths. They had none of the weapons needed to fight disease, and particularly cholera. They did not have that backbone of military organisation and discipline. They had little knowledge of the requirements of sanitation. And they did not have among them heroic medical officers.

AT TAMARONPAT THE Japanese ordered a group of 700 men under the command of Colonel Samuel Pond north to a camp called Konkoita where they were to be permanently based. They began work on road and bridge building while the other elements of F Force marched through towards the Burma border and camps at Lower Nieke and Shimo Songkurai. Disease waited for them wherever they went.

George Harding, bushman-poet, the 2/19th Battalion soldier who refused to feel that in forced surrender he had shamed his dead mates, faced a new battle. Harding had survived bayonet and bomb but in a jungle camp he contracted beri-beri, a crippling disease affecting muscles, heart, nerves and the digestive system. In Singhalese it translates as 'I can't, I can't'. His diet had been mainly polished rice, and little of that. The removal of rice husk robs the diet of thiamine, a vital vitamin, such a small thing, so deadly. Harding, so ill that even the Japanese could not force him to work, was sent down the River Kwai by barge to Kanchanaburi. You can find his gravestone in the war cemetery there. It shows he died on May 10, 1943, aged 34. There was no shame for George Harding in this death. The odds were simply too great.

But the worst of enemies was approaching. On May 15 Japanese medical officers told Pond that cholera had broken out among coolies at Konkoita. The evidence was clear enough: the camp was littered with the bodies of the Tamil and Burmese dead and dying. Pond's battalion moved further north to Upper Konkoita. On May 16 Private Arthur English and Private Harry Godbolt died of cholera at Lower Nieke and several cases were diagnosed among the Australians at Shimo Songkurai. Bruce Hunt called the officers to a meeting. 'Gentlemen, things are grim,' he said. 'I have diagnosed a disease of which I have had no experience. It does not occur in Australia. But I have read of it in text books and I am sure it is cholera. I have conferred with the Japanese command and have learnt that they are, with good reason, terrified of the disease. They understand that without vaccination their prisoners could all die and they would lose their workforce and much face . . . Fires will be kept alight at intervals in every hut. Before you use your eating utensils you will pass them through the flames and you will see that your men do the same. Water must be boiled for seven minutes. No water will be drunk direct from the creek. Tomorrow we will scrape the surface filth from the camp area and it will be burnt or sterilised in the fire we will light over it. If a fly alights on the rice you are about to eat, the grains it lands on must be spooned out and burnt, for, I assure you, if one contracts cholera, one dies in great distress.'

Stan Arneil: May 23. Four more cholera suspects this morning. Anyone visiting the latrines during the night said that the whole area was covered with men crawling to the latrines, some falling over and finding it impossible to get up again. The area this morning is dotted with vomit and excreta from the dysentery cases. I have not bothered to mention dysentery lately on account of the cholera taking precedence, but at least 25 per cent of the camp, including Doug, have dysentery . . . Yesterday the camp purchased ten miserable looking yaks as thin as skeletons, but they will eat alright in the next few days. Even Major Johnston was slapped this morning. Had a delicious dream of home last night. Most of us dream of home now and I awake from these dreams with a sigh of regret. Crumpets, hot and dripping with butter and honey! How does it sound to you? The war will finish this year. I must live. Keep your chin up, sister, I will be home yet.

That day Hunt had, as usual, visited the hospital and, as usual, paused to put his hand on the forehead of the desperately ill, saying 'Poor old boy'. That day Wally Mulvena died. Gwen, his eighth child, the one he would never see, was one year, nine months and 17 days old.

MULVENA WAS ONE of five early cholera victims at Shimo Songkurai. Until May 24 the epidemic had been relatively well contained, but a second wave of infection, developed since arrival at the camp, began. Deaths on succeeding days were four, four, ten, eleven, ten, four and eight.

It was the testing time all along the railway, this time of disease and near-starvation. Some men did steal. Many lost heart. Some officers failed as leaders and as men. So did some chaplains. But, the report on F Force by Kappe and Curlewis records, 'it was at this stage that Major Bruce Hunt made an impassioned and dramatic appeal to the men which finally dispelled the lethargy that had been so apparent and imbued the men with a new spirit of determination to fight the crisis out. It was one of many such addresses that Major Hunt gave at this and other camps, all of which had an enormous effect on the morale of the force.' He did not rely on words alone. There is a cryptic reference by his personal orderly, Lieutenant Norm Couch, who says Hunt regarded maintenance of morale as an instrument of survival: 'When thieving threatened discipline, Major Hunt restored control with one application of corporal punishment. In retrospect the uninformed may deplore this courageous and desperate action. The perilous conditions demanded drastic action.' Major Johnston, who commanded the prisoners from the 2/30th Battalion, said: 'Such crises produce the best and worst in men, but it is always the best that will be remembered when the cholera epidemic at (Shimo) Songkurai comes to mind.'

The epidemic overwhelmed the medical staff. In one 24-hour period, 35 men were struck down. When the work parties returned to camp at night, soaked to the skin by monsoon rain, exhausted by 12 hours of hard labour in the mud, Hunt told them what had happened. He told them of the risks involved in contact with cholera patients, that cholera carried a 50 per cent mortality and asked for volunteers to help immediately with the nursing of highly infectious men. He gave up taking names when he had 75 on the list. There were several dozen more waiting to offer their services.

In June cholera had been beaten in Shimo Songkurai but it made its relentless way south down the River Kwai. Across the border in Burma it contaminated rivers flowing west. Ray Wheeler's section of A Force was based at the 105-kilo camp in the Aungkannaung district, with English, Dutch and a few American prisoners, a total of about 3000. Just across the boundary was a native camp of about 3000 where cholera bred.

Wheeler: 'It took about three weeks to run its course, the cholera. We lost some blokes. Of the 3000 natives, there were only 28 left, though some of them would have taken to the jungle and tried to make their way home. A mate, Les Marvin and I, were put on burying them. The Japs wouldn't touch them. At the start we dug a grave four feet deep or something and then she got a bit rocky and the graves were only about two and a half feet deep. We would lift their heads or legs, whichever way you were going to tow them and put a lasso around them. Well, we started off putting a cross at the head of their graves, even though it was against their religion, and when we tied the cross in the centre we would put there some item of clothing or anything that might identify them but after about three days of that you got so callous that when you dragged them to the edge of the grave you were betting a cigarette on whether they fell on their face or on their back. That is how low you were sinking.'

'Was it part of your defence mechanism?' I asked.

'Could have been. One old bloke, he survived the cholera. We were going out to work again and we found him along a jungle trail. He was skin and bone. We used to take some of our rice out to him every morning and he was starting to get better again. This morning we go out and we find what's left of him after a tiger had got him. You weigh the position: Should you have eaten the rice yourself? Was it worth it?'

'At this stage, do you believe there is a God?' I asked.

'I still do.'

AT HINTOK MOUNTAIN camp, 145 kilometres south of Shimo Songkurai, Weary Dunlop had been waiting for this enemy since February 1943. 'Ns [Nippons] now say there is a cholera outbreak up the river and we must not swim in river or clean teeth etc with the water though we can bathe and wash our clothes. Cholera would be the final touch!' he recorded. Then on May 22: 'Further rumours of cholera by two fleeing coolies from up the line.' On June 19 Dunlop was conducting evening sick parade at 9.30. Private Harris was carried in on a stretcher. He had become sick early in the afternoon and now was severely dehydrated with no perceptible pulse. He had shrunken 'washerwoman's' fingers. He could not speak, but indicated severe pains in his stomach and cramps in the back of his legs. He died at 1.20 am.

Soon Kevin Ward was in the cholera isolation hut at the nearby Konyu No. 2 camp. F Force had been sent to the most isolated sections of the railway; H Force was spread along the middle section where the work had fallen behind schedule. At least Ward had only to march four nights and the deep blackness of the jungle tracks meant his failing eyesight was no additional handicap. He first worked on the railway in the 24-hour-a-day light of Hellfire Pass. He hated the night shift most. Even exhausted he found it difficult to sleep in the daytime stillness and airlessness of the jungle. He hated the brutality, the inhumanity. It put him in conflict with his Catholic religion and decades later he would be trying to work through it.

When cholera came down these reaches of the Kwai, Ward became ill. His mates looked at him with fear and pity. He lay among the cholera victims. Many of them died. He didn't. He was a cholera carrier; he had the symptoms, but the disease did not develop. What threatened Ward's life was a casual act of violence by a Japanese engineer. He was working in Hellfire Pass and the Japanese were on the rim, shouting orders and '*speedo*'. One threw a rock at Ward. It grazed down his shin, opening it up. Soon an ulcer was eating away at the leg. He was lucky. He had a billycan and could boil water and he tore strips off his shirt to bathe it. Still it grew, and he had no shirt left. It destroyed sinews.

He worked on but was eventually evacuated downriver to Chungkai and its jungle hospital. Men with smaller ulcers were having legs amputated, and dying. Maggots ate at the rotten flesh. The man lying next to Ward watched them crawl along the slatted bamboo bed surface. 'Why don't you keep your maggots to yourself?' he said, and laughed. The orderlies scraped Ward's ulcer and cared for him. His leg was saved.

The Japanese who threw the rock had managed to diminish the labour force by one. He probably thought the supply was inexhaustible. Ray Parkin at Hintok Road camp listened to the reading-out of a Japanese order which heralded the *speedo* period and the start of 150 days without a break. Nippon was pleased with their willing and cheerful working. The railway was of great importance to the Japanese and must be completed. They should make a great and glorious effort so that the Emperor would be justly proud of them. It would mean much hard work but it must be completed at all costs. 'Nippon very sorry but many men must die.'

In the camps the medical officers had two battles to fight, one against diseases, the other against the Japanese engineers and doctors determined to meet Tokyo's deadline. Like Albert

Coates in Burma, amputating limbs with the carpenter's saw, they had little equipment and few drugs. At Takanun, Captain Roy Mills made saline solution for the essential rehydration of cholera victims from monsoon rain caught off tent tops and kitchen salt. It was boiled, filtered through charcoal. The solution was funnelled through an old tin can, Mills's stethoscope rubber and then into veins through bamboo scorched in the flame and used as a coarse needle. Once Mills remarked to field ambulanceman George Beecham, an aide, 'George, if only we had some sulphur'. The next day Beecham came up to him and said: 'Sulphur ointment, sir.' Three 8th Division signallers had gone up the line, a distance from the camp, climbed a telegraph pole, and smashed the insulators. The Japanese had used molten sulphur over the bridge spike holding the insulator on the crossbar. Had the signallers been found out, they would almost certainly have been executed for sabotage.

Doctors trying to prevent men slipping deeper into disease or nursing them back to health could lose them to the Japanese. The Chief Medical Officer of the Japanese 9th Railway Regiment, Major Tagami, describing the railway as 'the great epoch-making construction' of the century, said it had been constructed in a time they scarcely considered possible. But it was only possible because men were driven to death. At Takanun on July 15, 1943, the camp population was 564. Of these 464 were sick. The Japanese engineers demanded 160 for work. At Shimo Songkurai on July 19, the camp population was 1850, 1350 were sick and the Japanese demanded 1343 workers. Each camp needed medical men, orderlies, cooks, administrators, people to patch up the dilapidated atap and bamboo huts, people to clean the latrines, do the general dirty work of keeping the camp as clean as possible, and to carry out malaria prevention. So some of the sick were forced from their rough hospitals.

Many of the Japanese medical staff discarded the principles and even the pretence of proper practice. Robert Hardie, a British doctor at Takanun, recorded in his diary Lieutenant Hisashi Nobusawa ('the so-called doctor') ordering a parade of all the sick in camp who could walk at all. Refusing all information, he selected a dozen men whom he said must work. Dunlop, in his diary, reported a Japanese doctor parading all the sick men who could walk and evicting 45 men from the hospital without examining them, simply by having some go to the left and others go to the right.

Protection of the sick was a battle of wits and wills. Hardie carefully falsified figures to have a group of men, pretty much recovered, still listed as sick. These could be substituted for men who were still sick when the Japanese raided the hospital. Dunlop played what he called the log-sitting game. In the monsoon men developed acute dermatitis of the feet which became red-raw with tinea, injury and secondary infection. Grossly swollen and weeping, the feet soon lost their skin. Men took hours to walk three or four kilometres to the line and worked there in mud or water or on rocks. Beside the parade ground was a large teak log, the wailing log, the men called it. Those with crippling feet rested on it. One morning Dunlop instructed 26 of them to ignore the shout of *kura*, the order to stand up to attention, from the engineers' NCO, Billie the Pig. A man who could stand was a man who could go to work. Eventually the Japanese allowed 13 of them to be carried to hospital. The rest went to the line, but with the concession they could go slowly and would not be bashed for arriving late. The next day men again sat through the shouts of *kura*, crawled or were carried to the front of the parade. Seven were carried to hospital; the others struggled to work, arriving back at 11 pm or later. One crawled most of the way through blackness and rain.

Parkin watched one morning when Billie the Pig shouted *kura* at a man on the log. Dunlop, emaciated, sinew and bone, but still strong, smiled at the engineer, picked up the man in his arms and walked over to him. 'This man can't walk, Nippon,' he said. The Japanese medical orderly, Corporal Okada, soon accepted log-sitting. The men did not have to go to the line. They would do light work and the hospital numbers were kept down, important to Okada, whose superiors would be angered by a high sick list.

Okada was a power in the camp. So far as the prisoners were concerned, including lieutenant colonels, all Japanese were. One day Dunlop, passing the Japanese bathhouse, did not notice two soldiers bending over buckets, naked and soaped. They called him over and asked him why he had not saluted. He saluted and stood to attention. He expected to be beaten. Okada came up, extricated Dunlop, and, laughing, said: 'Colonel Dunroppo must remember salute Nippon soldier.' Later Dunlop was entering his barracks when he was called by a soldier who was outside the Japanese office about 50 metres away. It was one of the soldiers from the bathhouse. Dunlop stood to attention and saluted. The soldier swung at Dunlop's face with his rifle. Dunlop blocked the blow but then was taken to the guardhouse where the soldier struck him with all his strength with a heavy length of bamboo. Bashed on the arm and leg, Dunlop twice disarmed him. A Japanese officer eventually intervened. When Dunlop complained to the camp commander, he was told, 'You must avoid such incidents with Japanese soldiers'.

Dunlop's relationship with Okada was a complex one. They were a complete mismatch in medical skills, yet Okada had an authority which had to be countered by bluff and stubbornness. In early May, Dunlop pointed out to Okada the many severe ulcer and avitaminosis cases. Okada's answer: 'Now kill pig tomorrow. Fifty men better.' Dunlop's assessment: 'Quite hopeless but good tempered.' Okada's decree on light-duty work in the camp: dysentery, 30 motions no good, 20 motions perhaps work, 10 motions work. Okada did back Dunlop up on some occasions and once attempted to donate a forequarter of beef to the sick from the Japanese kitchen, but lost out in a heated row. It was a relationship affected, as all life was along the line, by the *speedo* period. On June 7, in the monsoon misery, Dunlop's diary note was: 'Notable for the return of those two prize bastards, Osuki and Okada, No. 1 and medical corporal respectively. In general in disgust with life, shaved off my moustaches as a gesture. Feel rather strange without it.' Dunlop was then just coming through a bout of illness, mentally low, 'nearly fifteen wearying interminable months as a POW', and self-diagnosed as having amoebic dysentery. On June 1, he collapsed on one of his many visits to the latrines, reduced to feebly waving his fist at the vultures which had gathered on the branches. He injected himself with emetin and the next day reported with satisfaction that he was improved enough to throw stones at the vultures.

'June 8: Okada down to the hospital early on one of his mad, unreasonable blitzes. Must reduce the hospital to 200! He was savagely ignored.' The next day, Okada came again. He told the medical staff he realised that they had terrific difficulties keeping the men well and at work. He thanked them from the bottom of his heart and from the bottom of his heart it hurt him to see men suffering as these men were suffering. He urged them to try harder for if the sick tally rose, Japanese headquarters would drive sick men to work. Dunlop thought that Okada was 'sincere in the Nipponese fashion'.

The next day Okada was 'howling like a wolf' for 10 more men to go out to work when already 50 men, who were barely about to stand, had gone. Two days later he chased fevered and sick men from the showers, saying, 'Strong men, go work'. Then on June 13, Private R. J. Watson, aged 24, died from dysentery. The cortege was accompanied by a mate who could not control his grief, and by Corporal Okada, of the Imperial Japanese Army. Okada had come to the hospital area and said a prayer over the body. He called for a leaf and water, sprinkling the body, praying and bowing. At the grave side, where Watson was buried with military honours, Okada watched Dunlop carefully, saluting when he did. He said he regretted having been unable to pay his respects at other burials. 'Poor devil,' Dunlop wrote in his diary that night, 'I suppose he has his problems too'.

A little over a fortnight later, Desmond Jackson was on evening parade. The sound of the Last Post came through the jungle. Major Bill Wearne called the men to attention. Funerals were commonplace but this one particularly touched Jackson and Weary Dunlop. They were burying 24-year-old Private Jack Jarvis, a member of Jackson's unit, the 2/3rd Machine Gun Battalion. One of Jarvis's brothers, Harry, was also a prisoner in Hintok Mountain camp; another, Ken, had been killed at Tobruk. Dunlop had fought for Jack Jarvis's life and thought he had won. Admitted to hospital with malaria, an upper respiratory tract infection and cholera symptoms on June 18, Jarvis deteriorated dramatically on June 22. Dunlop had left one ampoule of Ringer's solution (essential body salts) and decided to administer it into the stomach membrane. He used makeshift equipment, including a record needle and a rubber catheter and followed up with kitchen salt and ordinary boiled water. Jarvis showed considerable improvement but at six o'clock on June 29, he died of cholera and uraemia. Dunlop and Jarvis had been winning until the development of uraemia.

The entry in Dunlop's diary is perhaps the most poignant in his remarkable book. Jarvis had been unconscious for two days and his brother had been kept in camp that day, specially admitted to hospital and so was able to attend the funeral service. Because of the possibility of infection, Dunlop was one of the pallbearers.

> ... it was a terrible, sad and dreary little procession, dragging through the rough jungle tracks between the bamboos and dripping rain from a grey sky. The body, roughly sewn in a grey army blanket, sagged between bamboo poles on rice sacks and the dripping under-growth brushed against the stretcher. The brother and a soldier friend, shabbily clad in Dutch oddments of clothing and without boots, picked their way pain-fully in the rear. I saw a bright crimson flower buried among the green jungle undergrowth. I had an impulse to seize it and lay it on the body to add somehow a little touch of beauty and colour. However, being of stolid British upbringing, this impulse was never fulfilled.

Jack Verdun Jarvis, undoubtedly the son of a World War I digger, was 24. He and his younger brother, Harry, 21, enlisted on the same day, both becoming machine-gunners. The oldest of the Jarvis boys, Ken, enlisted a week later and served in the 2/48th Battalion. He was 30 when he was killed.

THE MONSOON WENT on, *speedo* went on, the dying went on.

> Stan Arneil: September 3. Four years today! In the last two days three of the finest chaps in our unit have died, Tucker, Harry and Guy, all from A Coy. Malnutrition and cardiac beri beri is doing most of the killing now. I

worry about the Englishmen under my care. They practically walk to the cremation pyre. They stop eating, lay down and refuse to live. It is incredible. Instead of hanging grimly on to life with both hands they start to criticise their meals and that is the finish. Meals here, particularly breakfast is almost revolting but most of us regard it as a legitimate ticket home and religiously poke it down. I must get home.

The railway line reached Shimo Songkurai where Wally Mulvena lay buried and Harry Weiss lay in the jungle hospital.

Harry Weiss: September 20. A week of terrible beri beri and I find it so hard to eat this food and have even got despondent. Then I think of our workers who have worked night and day lately (five hours sleep) on a little better food, but the Japanese have given them good boiled sweet spuds and tea. Yesterday the railroad truck passed the camp and the light motor skips are already rushing southward, we may get out of here some day. Wish I could eat and feel well. Was the only one given a shot of Vit.B1 today, so the MO couldn't have liked the ticker. We get no treatment except rest.

This is the last entry in Harry Weiss's diary. He died that day. Harry Jarvis had died too. He survived his brother Jack by only one month. Poor old boys.

CHAPTER 20

The Seventh Circle

I had become one of the walking dead who had so frightened me when I first came to Outram Road.

Eric Lomax

There were few ways to get off the railway. One was death. Wally Mulvena, Mickey Hallam, Harry Weiss, the Jarvis brothers and tens of thousands of others took that path. Another was escape. A few tried and were executed when captured. A rarer few succeeded, one of them Desmond Jackson's closest friend, Ken Linford. Another way was to fall into the hands of the *kempeitai*, the Japanese military police, an organisation with the powers and earned reputation of the Gestapo. The *kempeitai* was founded in 1881 as a semi-independent branch of the Japanese army. Its writ was to fight subversion; its chosen weapon was torture; its living victims in South-East Asia were incarcerated in Singapore's Outram Road jail. If Hellfire Pass was at the height of *speedo* a scene from Dante's *Inferno*, then Outram Road jail was the Seventh Circle of Hell where Dante found, guarded by the Minotaur, the beast-man, a place of violence. The prisoners in Outram

328

Road jail, under the eye of the *kempeitai*, were isolated from the outside world and, often, from each other. They were kept at the point of death. Many did die.

On November 22, 1943 Lieutenant Eric Lomax, formerly in charge of the signals section of the 5th British Field Regiment, now prisoner of war, was sentenced by Japanese military court in Kanchanaburi to five years' imprisonment. He was part of a group swept up by the *kempeitai* after an inspection uncovered radios in their camp. Lomax also had in his possession a meticulously drawn map of the Thai–Burma railway. The guilty were profoundly relieved. They had expected death. They were taken by train to Singapore and through the high, grey gates of Outram Road jail. Behind the massive glass-embedded, barbed-wire-topped walls were civilians, Japanese soldiers and prisoners of war who had committed crimes against the Emperor. John Wyett, Australian staff officer was there, with his friend Jack Macalister, RAAF flight lieutenant and Hudson bomber pilot. So was Herb Trackson, who had been shipped to Borneo as part of B Force.

The gods of war have a sense of humour. As a boy growing up in Scotland, a loner, Eric Lomax had an epiphany on an autumn afternoon in 1932. He recorded the precise date: September 12. With his mother he was crossing a long footbridge over railway lines, or, as he puts it, 'a shiny heavy web of iron and wood, dead straight parallel lines of metal suddenly curving and merging smoothly into other sets of tracks; ladders fixed to the earth, climbing into the distance'. He watched shunting engines Nos 9387, and 9388, smoke and steam, all brass and power, as they crashed wagons around a freight yard. Eric Lomax had been born as a railway buff, a fanatic. He was hungry for the sight of engines and trains such as the mighty Atlantics and Pacifics and the fabulous Flying Scotsman, hunting down rare and elusive varieties. In mid-1943, joy! An exotic creature in a strange jungle-siding setting, with cowcatcher and high-waisted steam engine, black boiler and brass trim, a magnificent machine built at the turn of the century by Krauss of Munich. Lomax, a world away from Scotland, was train-spotting still. This was the first locomotive he had seen on this completed section of the Thai–Burma railway. The buff was now a conscripted railway worker, helping repair bogies and engines.

Lomax, a radio expert, became part of a network that built and operated a small set to listen to the progress of the war on All India Radio from New Delhi. 'Stealing back information from our captors,' he called it. This was a dangerous undertaking. But Lomax did something else. He made that map. There was a personal motivation: an old need, as Lomax explains it, to locate himself precisely on a grid, to record, list and categorise the world around him as far as possible. In Kanchanaburi, it was a way of creating certainty in a world robbed of certainty. It would also be important if there were to be an escape. Lomax used as sources prisoner-of-war lorry drivers who had been up the railway trace, and Japanese plans and documents he had seen lying around. This was map as potential death warrant. He hid it rolled up in a bamboo tube at the back of their latrine. When the Japanese soldiers told the radio group they must pack at once and leave the camp, Lomax did something incredibly foolish: he asked to go to the latrine, retrieved his map and took it with him.

I MET TAKASHI Nagase in the Tokyo Station Hotel, a place favoured by old-fashioned Japanese who politely abhor the shining five-star towers. He had travelled four hours on the *shinkansen*, the state-of-the-art bullet train, from his provincial home for a family wedding. He was 85 years old, a wisp wrapped around a core of spiritual intensity, remorse and contentment. Lomax first met Nagase in the *kempeitai* head-quarters in Kanchanaburi. He would not know Nagase's name for decades but Nagase's voice became part of his nightmares. Lomax and his four friends had been delivered to the *kempeitai* bloodied messes. One by one they had been beaten with pickaxe shafts by Japanese and Korean guards. The Dutch doctor who had been told to be ready to treat them listened through the night and counted 900 blows. Both of Lomax's forearms had been broken, several of his ribs cracked and his hip damaged. He had been turned from a white man beaten mostly blue-black. Some days later he was taken from his cage (1.5 metres long, .75 metres wide, 1.5 metres high) to a room where two Japanese waited. One was an NCO, large, broad-shouldered, shaved-headed, thick-necked; a man full of latent and obvious violence, Lomax thought. The other was far smaller, almost delicate, with a good head of very black hair, wide mouth and defined cheek-bones. He looked very unmilitary.

In that first session, the interrogator told Lomax two of the prisoners involved in the radio had made full confessions. Lomax would be killed shortly, whatever happened. Nagase thought Lomax was doomed too. Lomax insisted he was a railway fanatic. He wanted to take the map home as a souvenir. How unconvincing. The route of the railway was a secret, yet Lomax had marked it in great detail. A signature on a protocol of examination, a confession of spying, and exe-cution would be certain. From morning till night for more than a week, 18 hours a day, Lomax was interrogated. About his life before the war, about his training, about where the Allied landings would take place, about how to convert a receiver to a transmitter, about anti-Japanese activities in the camp. The interrogator changed. The constant was the inter-preter, his voice flat, mechanical, repetitive, relentless, demand-ing guilt, promising death. Lomax wanted to kill him.

One day Lomax was trying to explain the arcane romance of engines, boilers and gauges when the interrogator dragged him out of the room. He has no memory of what came next. This was what happened, what Nagase describes as 'the usual torture'. He was placed in a bathtub, laid on his back with a towel loosely covering his mouth and nose. They poured water over his face and the soaking cloth blocked his nose and mouth. He struggled to breathe and when he opened his mouth they poured water down, poured it until he was choking and drowning. Lomax screamed and cried out, 'Mother, mother'. Nagase muttered to himself: 'Mother, do you know what is happening to your son now?' Then there was a beating and the interpreter saying: 'Lomax, you will tell us. Then it will stop.' Lomax did remember thinking once he felt the interpreter's hand on his hand, 'a strange gesture, the obscene contrast between this gesture of almost comfort and the pitiless violence of what they were doing to me'. Actually the interpreter, horrified, trying to control his shaking body, and fearing that Lomax was going to die in front of him, had taken his wrist to feel for a pulse.

Lomax did not break. When he was leaving the *kempeitai* headquarters, the interpreter came close to him, looked carefully around, and said the words he had heard prisoners say to one another: 'Keep your chin up.'

HERB TRACKSON CLOSES his eyes and begins to recite:

> *I want free life and I want fresh air,*
> *I long to canter after cattle . . .*

It is a long poem, 66 lines, about the life of an American cowboy. There is love:

She was as wild as the breezes above.
From her little head to her little foot
She would sway with a suppleness to and fro,
Sway with passion like a sapling pine
That grows on the edge of a canyon's bluff . . .

There is loss. She is killed in a stampede. The cowboy buries her and, of course, his heart lies buried with her.

The rhythms of the Texas plains take Herb Trackson back. It is 1943 and he is 22 years old. He is in a cell in Outram Road jail. The poem, taught him by a cellmate, is one way he leaves behind the dreadfulness of prison for free life and fresh air. Another is to revisit his childhood and adolescence in northern Queensland. He came from a big family, eight children; four boys and four girls. His father was a butcher. All the boys became butchers, all the girls nurses. When he returned from the war, he astonished his family with what he could tell them about themselves.

Trackson first tried to enlist when he was 18. His father wouldn't sign the papers then, but when there were reverses in the Middle East, he said, 'Oh well, I think they'll need you now'. He was 19. He spent his short war delivering ammunition to the beleaguered troops on the Malayan peninsula. The surrender angered him. The nine-day voyage to Borneo as a member of B Force was gruelling, thirsty men packed between decks on the *Yubi Maru* on a layer of six inches of coal dust. They were bound for Sandakan, which was then capital of North Borneo, a town built on one of the world's beautiful harbours. The men landed on July 18, 1942 and were marched about 14 kilometres to newly christened No.1 Prisoner-of-War camp. Trackson was not impressed. 'A bit of a camp in the scrub', he called it. 'There's nothing for us here,' he said. He was right: there was nothing but death for those who stayed.

He was brash enough to say to the officers, 'Why don't we overpower these blokes? We're fit enough. We've had a bit of dysentery, that's all. Take their rifles and then go bush, you know.' Of course that wasn't on. They didn't think much of that. There were guards and barbed wire, but he thought it would be easy enough to get away. After listening to the welcoming speech by the camp commandant, Lieutenant Susumi Hoshijima, with its usual praise of the Emperor and the Greater East Asia Co-Prosperity Sphere, and the promise that Japan would be victorious even if it took 100 years, he said to himself, 'That's it. I'm off.'

On July 31, as a thunder of rain turned the day dark grey, Trackson and his mate Matt Carr escaped from Sandakan. They were followed shortly after by another four from their supply company: Harrington, Allen, Jacka and Shelley. They were in a land of dense jungle, swamps and rubber estates, a land of some friends and many who could be enemies. In general, the Chinese of the Greater East Asia Co-Prosperity Sphere could be counted on. Fear and anger had flowed swiftly from mainland China to the scattered migrant communities after the Japanese atrocities. But the Malay and indigenous populations had been promised by the Japanese the greater reward of liberation from the tuans as well as monetary rewards for helping capture escaped tuan soldiers. The group moved across country and based themselves in a small abandoned hut in the jungle. Hungry, they took the chance of approaching a farmer's house. For three nights Chu Li Tsia fed them. Then they split up. Four went to seek help from Mr Phillips, a British timber company manager, married to a Malay. Phillips, who had not been interned, was part of a fledgling civilian network that assisted the prisoners of war. Going to Phillips's house was not a good move. It was opposite the local headquarters of the *kempeitai*. Locals saw them entering the house. The inevitable followed: to escape certain torture and punishment by the *kempeitai* Phillips handed the men over, with regret, one assumes, and perhaps with understanding on the escapees' part.

Trackson and Carr cut towards the coast. They had visions of native sailing craft, a placid Sulu Sea and an easy leapfrog up the delightful chain of islands to Mindanao, the most southerly of the Filipino provinces. And there they would probably have found, though this was not part of the plan, the Japanese army who had landed on the south-east of the island on December 20, 1941. However, the Australians had less than a month of freedom. They searched for their boat, raiding fish traps and native gardens, surviving not really well, but surviving, until they were betrayed. They woke under a coconut tree on a plantation where Carr had been sleeping and Trackson shivering with severe malaria, surrounded by 50 Japanese soldiers.

For Trackson, it was the softest of interrogations by the *kempeitai*. No bashing, no water torture. There must have been the look of country innocence about him. He couldn't tell them anything about military matters. He had just delivered the ammo. He couldn't tell them about Brisbane or Sydney. That was the Big Smoke. He'd never been there. Reunited, the six were taken by boat to Kuching, the major centre. Trackson, saved by quinine and saline solution given him by the Japanese but sick still, had dim memories of the courtroom where they were tried but none of the sentencing. As he lay collapsed on the floor with another bout of malaria, the interpreter pronounced that the six were to spend four years in solitary confinement in Outram Road jail. Had they tried to escape along the Thai–Burma railway, they almost certainly would have been executed. That was the penalty for the early attempts. Standing beside Trackson was Jeff Shelley, from

Boorowa in New South Wales, one of the four who had knocked on Phillips's door.

For the first nine months Trackson was locked away in his own world, 2.4 metres by 1.5 metres, two planks of wood for a bed, a wooden block for a pillow, a tattered blanket, a pail for a latrine, a bare electric light bulb out of reach on the ceiling that burned night and day, a small hatch in the doorway. As the *kempeitai* gained more clients, cells were shared. Once Shelley joined Trackson. It was Shelley who taught Trackson about the wide Texas range,

> *The green beneath and the blue above,*
> *Dash and danger, life and love and lustre.*

On October 29, 1944 Trackson stood over the body of Jeff Shelley on the cell floor. He had not long before turned 27. He was dead of dysentery.

HANDS BOUND BEHIND his back, Major John Wyett, graduate of His Majesty's Command and Staff College at Quetta, was pushed and pulled across the Padang, the parade and playground of Singapore's tuans. Wyett was a Pathan bearer's nightmare. He had long, unkempt hair down to his shoulders, a wild moustache that joined a beard in a matted mess covering his chest. He was barefoot, wearing crumpled shorts and dirty, short-sleeved shirt. The only clean bit of him, hidden, was a shiny, red, relatively fresh scar from an appendix operation that had been both necessary and unnecessary. Pushed and pulled along with him, similarly elegant, was Flight Lieutenant Jack Macalister. They were being displayed to the Singaporean crowd as trophies before being taken to that grand, colonnaded seat of British colonial justice, the

Supreme Court. Wyett and Macalister were on trial for their lives. Sitting in the Chief Justice's chair, wearing campaign ribbons and samurai sword, was Major General Fukuye, the Japanese commandant. Wyett faced five charges: communicating with the enemy, attempting to escape, plotting to destroy the property of the Emperor, inciting revolt against the Imperial Japanese Army and spying on the operations of the Japanese forces. Presumably, Macalister was charged with attempting to escape. With an inadequate Japanese interpreter, the two men had little knowledge of what was being said in the Singapore Supreme Court.

The *kempeitai* had come for Wyett in Changi on December 31, 1942. The officers had saved food from their thin rations for a dinner to farewell a very bad year, a year of shame and defeat, and welcome, they hoped, a year of victory and release. The celebrations, as sombre as they would have been, did not even begin. Wyett and a pile of his papers were taken away to *kempeitai* headquarters. He knew he had done things that would make him incontestably guilty in Japanese eyes. He did not know what the Japanese knew. Certainly he had been attempting to communicate with the enemy. On Wednesday nights when possible, he and an ordnance private, Stan Elliman, went to the wrecked battery of 15-inch naval guns just outside the camp. They waded neck-deep through the flooded underground tunnel network to a panel behind which was hidden a radio transmitter Elliman had built. Wednesday nights were the window for communications with British forces in India. They sent off messages ending 'Quetta John'. They did not think they had made contact. In fact, their signals had been getting through and had been acknowledged. Guilty as charged. But did the Japanese have proof?

Inciting revolt? There had been discussions at the prisoner-of-war headquarters about what could be done if (when, they hoped) the tide of war turned against the Japanese and if the Japanese turned against the prisoners. Wyett, the senior officer in charge of operations, had to find out how many men were fit enough to resist, work out the organisation of units and select commanding officers. Black Jack Galleghan called a secret, officers-only meeting to outline the proposal. In a broad sense, guilty as charged.

Attempting to escape? Wyett had hidden in mangroves a holed sampan which he tried to repair and, with the help of a friend, Ken Burnside, was attempting to make a sextant. The sampan had been stolen. Still, perhaps technically guilty. And he and Macalister had discussed the possibility of stealing an aircraft, though they realised the difficulty of having the fuel and the navigational aids to reach friendly territory.

Unknown to the Japanese, Macalister had a track record. In March 1942 Macalister had flown a single Hudson from Darwin on a mission to Penfui airfield on Timor, a tactic being used by the RAAF in the hope of catching Japanese bombers on the ground there. Sparrow Force prisoners at Usapa Besar camp on Timor heard Macalister's Hudson fly over. They gave a silent cheer. Then they heard Zeroes take off from Penfui. Macalister was in serious trouble, in a cloudless sky with the Zeroes scrambling in groups of three to different quarters. He was at tree-top level when one of the groups closed. The rear-gunner was killed. Two of the crew bailed out when the Hudson was too low over a ridge top and died. Macalister jumped soon after and was lucky. His parachute opened in time. Captured and brought to Usapa Besar, Macalister one day watched a DC3 fly over to land at Penfui. He said later: 'A few of us got together and had a bit of a fantasy.' It almost became reality. One night a group of nine, including Lieu-tenant Colonel William Leggatt, commanding officer of Sparrow Force, crawled across the airfield towards the silhouetted Dakota. For hours Macalister tried to start the engines. Perhaps the Japanese had removed the batteries. The attempt was abandoned at 5 am. The men got back to Usapa Besar in time for reveille.

Neither Wyett nor Macalister knew what basis the *kempeitai* had for the charge of attempting to escape from Singapore. When the trial began, two thick dossiers had been carried into court. These were the product of interrogation and torture sessions. Wyett had been beaten with fist and flat of sword, given electric shocks, and subjected to water torture. Macalister would have been similarly treated. They had denied everything. But the charge that particularly worried Wyett was that of inciting rebellion. His interrogators seemed to know something. How? Some days when he was being returned to his cell, Wyett had seen Japanese dressed in Dutch Indonesian army uniforms. He was convinced that they were gathering intelligence in Changi and that one had penetrated the prisoner-of-war officers' meeting that had discussed resistance. Galleghan, the Australians' commanding officer, had to be warned.

The chance came two days later when the *kempeitai* brought in a prominent Singaporean Sikh, Ghian Singh, for interrogation. They were overzealous: they extracted nothing incriminating and faced the prospect of his dying on the floor of the group cell in which Wyett was held. Expecting them to send for a doctor, Wyett decided to have acute appendicitis. By the time the doctor arrived, he had worked himself into a sweat. He was lying on the floor, shaking, drawing his right leg up towards his chest as an appendicitis sufferer would do to ease the pain in his right abdomen.

He was convincing. He was taken to Changi hospital where his friend Colonel Charles Osborn, the surgeon-supervisor, knelt beside him and whispered: 'John, is this real or is it a fake?'

'It's a fake, you fool.'

'I'll have to take it out.'

'Well take it out. It's no damn good anyway.'

'OK, cock.'

Wyett lost an appendix; Galleghan got the message to beware of imposters.

Back with the *kempeitai*, Wyett decided the best chance he and Macalister had of escaping execution was to give them the basis for a lesser charge: planning to escape. This meant developing a strategy with Macalister, difficult when they were kept in separate cells and when communication between them was banned. They were lucky. Prisoners in Outram Road jail had found ways out of their solitude. Herb Trackson used more than a poem and memories to enlarge his eight feet by five feet world a little. In the cell next to him was another Australian, Chris Neilson, who had attempted an escape in Singapore. Neilson was a signaller. Trackson knew a little Morse code. Each dug a small stone from their cell wall and tapped simple conversations in the time between guard rounds. In the cell across the passage from Trackson was a British doctor who had been attached to an Indian army regiment. They could see each other through the hatches in their doors. One day the doctor drew an A in the air and made a sign. Trackson learnt, and after a while, across the passage and the silence, they could have what Trackson called 'a bit of a chat'. Wyett and Macalister also learnt sign language. Pre-trial each shared a cell with young Chinese men, members of the Straits Settlements Volunteer Force who had been swept up in the *sook ching* program, the Japanese purge. While they awaited 'purification by elimination' they communicated with sign language.

Wyett and Macalister planned their reluctant confession. On the third day of the trial, Major General Fukuye spoke to the interpreter. The interpreter announced to the court that the defendants Wyett and Macalister had been found guilty. They would be beheaded. They did not know when the sword would fall.

On April 29, nearly a month later, a guard came to their cell doors. It was the Emperor's birthday. They were each given two Imperial gifts: a small rice cake and the news that their death sentence had been commuted to 20 years' solitary confinement.

THE *KEMPEITAI* CAREFULLY calibrated the pain to body and spirit in Outram Road jail. Prisoners were kept barely alive. Those under the shadow of the sword were tormented. Trackson's neighbour, Chris Neilson, called one *kempeitai* Very Special. Very Special often told Neilson he would be very happy to be executed. Very Special was very good. It would be *satu patong*, one cut. Neilson was spared the testing of Very Special's boast when he was given a fixed three-year sentence. Like Eric Lomax, they became skeletal. The skin that stretched over protruding bones itched. Pimples covered the body, pus-filled, bursting to form yellow scabs. Hunger was a constant. Lomax once saw a single grain of rice on a cell doorstep. He picked it up and ate it. There was also the hunger for normal human contact. Guards tried to make silence absolute. People were beaten for talking to themselves.

Once, just the once, both Wyett and Trackson saw a glimmer of humanity from their jailors. Wyett developed beri-beri and pellagra. His skin was covered with scales and those scales were infested with scabies. One day a face appeared fleetingly at the slot in his cell door and through the slot was pushed a small piece of newspaper, half the size of the palm of a hand. On it was a tiny dab of ointment. Wyett never found out who did it.

For Trackson, it was a sip of water. He was accustomed to bashings. Try to keep standing. Best if you could get in a corner because once they got you down they kick and kick you. He hated it particularly when they hit him on the head with the key. The door was thick wood, the key large and cast-iron, kept on a bootlace. He disliked the pain; he hated the degrading casualness. One night the prisoners had been given smoked sardines, cured in salt, but nothing to drink. That night Trackson was in an agony of thirst. He had taken his clothes off and was seeking comfort on the cold cement floor. A guard he had exchanged a few words with looked through the slot. Trackson called for water, expecting nothing. The guard went away. He came back with a dish of water.

Wyett fought time by inventing in his head an internal combustion engine to run on solid fuel and a reliable changer for 78 rpm records. He fed lice to two spiders in the corner of his cell. Trackson coaxed a mouse that came into his cell with precious grains of rice. Then one day, in darker depression, he killed it. Wyett drifted out of his shrunken and diseased body and up, looking down on it lying on the cell floor. Trackson spent hours looking up at the unblinking electric light, trying to think of ways of getting the bulb down because he wanted to smash it and use the sharpness to kill himself.

Wyett lay ill for one week, or perhaps two. In lucid moments he thought of his out-of-body experience. It did seem to demonstrate that there was more to a man than just flesh and blood. The *kempeitai* sent him to Changi. Ruthless and murderous, they would nevertheless send the desperately sick to the camp hospital. This had nothing to do with being humane: the dead could not do their duty to the Emperor by serving out their sentence. Wyett, who had got back to Changi once by faking appendicitis awoke one day in Changi hospital truly ill. Later Macalister, near death too, joined him.

Eric Lomax and Herb Trackson tried trickery. Malnourishment and illness had recruited Lomax to the ranks of the living dead. He felt close to death. He had to get out of Outram Road. To do this he would have to convince his jailers he was about to die, thus cheating them of the time he owed on his sentence. Lomax had discovered that by deep and accelerated breathing he could drive up his pulse rate. With practice he could produce a state of agitated trance. He was carried to the cell for the extremely ill. There he formed a team with an Australian, Stan Davis, who had been a member of a group in Sandakan caught operating a radio set. This was their agreement: when food was brought to the cell, Davis would eat only the rice; Lomax would eat the fragments of soy beans and fish. Over two months Lomax became as close to a skeleton as a man can and still live and breathe. Davis had the sickly bloatedness of wet beri-beri. One last night of spasms caused by accelerating his pulse rate and Lomax was carried out of Outram Road jail on a stretcher. Davis followed him soon after.

Trackson saw his chance when he was one of a party sent out by the Japanese to dig tunnels. He asked two English prisoners to stage a cave-in. They pulled him out of fallen debris and carried him to the guards. He was taken to a hospital in Singapore. He knew he was safe from physical examination; he was covered with scabies. The Japanese doctor asked him to move his legs. He couldn't, he said. They were numb. The doctor sent him to Changi and there the hospital staff nursed him to health. They fed him any leftovers and put flesh on his bones. Gradually his weight rose from 5 stone to 13 stone but he paid a high price for recovery. The *kempeitai* were solicitous. Japanese doctors visited Changi hospital regularly. One day Trackson was judged well enough to return to Outram Road jail. He descended to the Seventh Circle again and he was reduced again to a scabies-covered skeleton. Then the *kempeitai* sent him back to Changi hospital.

CHANGI MEANT THE possibility of life. Men from Outram Road jail fought desperately to stay there, with aid from their friends. Their weapons were their own bodies. Wyett recovered slowly and while he lay in his bed, the nerves controlling his foot muscles had deteriorated. He walked with difficulty. The condition was called dropped foot. His left foot was particularly affected. His friend Charles Osborn gave him medical advice. Hippocrates would not have approved. Wyett should not work to strengthen his foot muscles. Better a man alive and limping than a dead John, Osborn said. So John Wyett dragged his left foot. It would always be smaller and weaker but his aura of frailty protected him from the *kempeitai*. Macalister, however, was increasingly in danger. His RAAF friend Arthur Tinkler pointed out that he was looking too well. Medical officer Charles Huxtable, twice the winner of the Military Cross in World War I, gave him medical advice. Hippocrates would have been horrified. 'Mac,' he said, 'I'm going to bust your foot so you can't walk. Tink can get a sledge-hammer. Charles Osborn has a small quantity of cocaine, not enough to do the job properly, but it might deaden the pain a bit.' Huxtable and Tinkler smuggled Macalister to a concrete-lined anti-malarial drain. The doctor held Macalister's foot in position; his friend swung the sledgehammer. It was only a temporary reprieve.

Lomax too failed the *kempeitai* fitness test and was returned to Outram Road. He found there had been some improvement, the food a little better and the worst of the diseases eradicated. But the existence was still one of physical and psychological brutality. An obsessive about trains, Lomax was now obsessive about escape. He wangled his way onto the squad that collected latrine buckets, giving mobility under the eyes of only one guard. He decided self-injury was the way out. This was the plan he developed: walking up a steep, steel stairway he would trip on the seventeenth step. The fall from there would be enough, he hoped, to harm but not cripple. Then he would lie immobile in the cell he shared with a young Indonesian. For two weeks he would eat only minimal food. Then, one day the guard would find him lying in a pool of his own urine. It worked. This time in Changi hospital he had a real accident. While boiling down sea water to make salt, he tipped near-boiling sludge down his leg.

Lomax, Trackson, Wyett and Macalister survived Outram Road jail and the war. Decades later, in Kanchanaburi, Eric Lomax heard the voice of Takashi Nagase again, and looked into his eyes.

CHAPTER 21

Staying alive, with a little help from their friends

Plumbago, botanical name *Indica coccinea*. Shrub two to four feet high. Shapely flowers, a delicate vermilion. This one grew in Takanun camp, 227 kilometres along the Thai–Burma railway, on the banks of the River Kwai. Takanun was the navigable limit of the Kwai during the dry season. Between Takanun and Tamajao, about 20 kilometres further on, several great cuttings had to be built. In 1943, those men of F Force in Takanun, the fittest frail, arose in the dark at 7 am, marched and worked and suffered for 14 hours and fell into their damp, meagre beds at 11 pm. Robert Hardie, a British doctor who had been attached to the Federated Malay States Volunteer Force, treated the ill and dying. Hardie kept a diary in which he recorded the details of ulcers, putrefaction and filthy men staggering on matchstick legs, faces wasted, eyes glazed with anguish and despair. He also kept a sketchbook: the plumbago has three flowers full-opened, two unfurling, and three buds closed tightly still; an orchid, *Calanthe rosea*, sent by Colonel Johnston from upriver, floats above a thick, furry stem, the trumpet a dusty pink.

The Japanese prisoner-of-war camps were lush with pain, inhumanity and ugliness, killing grounds for bodies and spirit. Colonel Nakamura harangued the prisoners under his command. Health followed will, he told them. But good health was out of their reach. Poor diet, sapping work in atrocious conditions and lack of medicines saw to that. Simply staying alive was a challenge. Staying alive was a matter of luck, discipline, mates and medical people working miracles. It was also a matter of finding sustenance for the spirit, of escaping from the bleakness of daily life and the awful sameness stretching out ahead. Dreams, hopes, poetry, acts of defiance, concerts, beauty of nature, belief in God: all these could help.

Hardie looked at flowers and he looked at stars. On a night of the waxing moon, he watched just after dark Perseus, Andromeda, Auriga and Capella. There was a line of others above the southern horizon. After moonset, and just before dawn he saw A and B Centauri and the Southern Cross in the south, Boötes, the Northern Crown, the Lion, the Crab, and Denebola overhead and Regulus and Arcturus blazing like planets. Hardie, like Herb Trackson in Outram Road jail, who rode the Texas range, memorised poetry. He had read classics at Oxford but the poems he loved were from the nineteenth century: Matthew Arnold's *The Scholar-Gipsy* and Keats's *Ode to a Nightingale*. They are not jolly poems. Like Hardie, the protagonists yearn to escape their world.

Arnold envies the scholar-gipsy . . .

> . . . *we others pine*
> *And wish the long unhappy dream would end,*
> *And waive all claim to bliss, and try to bear,*
> *With close-lipped Patience for our only friend,*
> *Sad Patience, too near neighbour to Despair*

Keats could have been writing about Hardie's Takanun or any of the camps . . .

The weariness, the fever, and the fret
Here, where men sit and hear each other groan;
Where palsy shakes a few, sad, last grey hairs,
Where youth grows pale, and spectre-thin, and dies,
Where but to think is to be full of sorrow
And leaden-eyed despairs . . .

CHILLA GOODCHAP TOOK personal revenge. Goodchap never forgot the coolie trot. Bending slightly forward, shoulders stooped a little under the bamboo pole, move more quickly than a walk, but with no high-knee lift. Keep the loads along either end of the pole balanced and as steady as possible. Go along the 3-kilometre jungle track, G-string flapping. At a safe distance between the camp and the work site, stop. After a minute or so, trot away again. Goodchap had fallen into a good job, delivering food to the Japanese guards. There were seven hooks along each side of his pole for the dixies Goodchap collected from the Japanese kitchen. When he darted off the track, he quickly examined the contents: rice, of course, but one would have some smoked fish, another some omelet. He took a little from each. Then he urinated in each, just a drop or two. He thought it was a fair trade. Once a guard at the work site called Goodchap over and offered him leftovers. No thanks. Crook, Goodchap said, holding his stomach. *Byoki.*

Weary Dunlop found solace in the surroundings of the Hintok prisoner-of-war camp. The jungle had a new coat of multitudinous shades of tender green; the atmosphere appeared to have been washed ineffably clear and pure by the rains, the sky was a serene and fathomless blue. Dunlop recorded in his April 4 entry the light of great cumulus clouds over the mountain rim, radiantly white, and vividness and colour were everywhere. He watched long chains of butterflies, great troops of monkeys, admired beautiful flowering trees, including (here's irony), the Japanese *ranunculus*, a lilac-flowering acacia with a beautiful scent.

Neil Dawson, of the 2/40th, thought of home. He read and reread his single letter from his fiancée, Iris Flight. On the envelope he wrote two lists. One was the record of his path through the diaspora. From Java, where he was captured, to Singapore on January 4, 1943, to the railway camps on January 21, 1943, back to Singapore on June 26, 1944, embarking on July 1, 1944 on '70 days starvation trip' to Japan on the wreck of a ship the prisoners called the *Byoki Maru*, the sick ship. It ends, simply, 'Pitt Street, Sydney'. The other was a wish list: . . . apple pie with cheese, Irish stew with pork suet dumplings, fried pineapple, eggs and bacon, salmon salad, milk, eggs poured over toast with spuds, cauliflower with cheese sauce. And the sandwiches: ham, bean, pork, Belgian, currant jelly, chopped raisins, lettuce, chilli sauce or ketchup, cream cheese and jelly, peanut butter and jelly, grated raw carrots and mayonnaise.

Ray Parkin, *Perth* survivor, drew a rhinoceros beetle lumbering like a tank on the ground, but looking like a grand coat-of-arms with the lace of its wings extended for flight. He drew orange-vermilion vine blossoms, strange, fleshy flowers, growing in cover, 'something seven-dwarfish about them', clouds of butterflies, a leaf insect, pale green, with rust blemishes and a yellow-green underside. One day when he was working on a hammer-and-tap team, he hung his dixie up on a bamboo cane in the shade. He noticed two fungi, each a white phallus 15 to 20 centimetres in height, with a sulphur-green bonnet like a rocket, and a red frill under the brim. He came back for his midday rice. The frill had expanded and dropped to the ground in a delicate and fleshy net like a gas mantle. The red had diluted. The hem on the ground was pink and near the bonnet, the net was a creamy colour. 'There was, perhaps,' Parkin wrote in his diary, 'a maypole effect to it; but to female-starved men, it had something of the allure of a veil dropped from a hat brim.'

Jack Chalker, British artilleryman, had been waiting to take up a scholarship to London Royal College of Art when his call-up papers arrived. Chalker reached Konyu river camp, travelling on the Kwai with an artist's eye through deep, limestone gorges, passing strange masses of water-sculpted rocks topped with large trees. He painted a glorious sunset and, in intricate detail, with annotations, passion flowers, ground orchids and hibiscus.

Along the railway he began a career as a medical illustrator, working closely with Weary Dunlop. He sketched the first of 120 legs to be amputated at Chungkai prison hospital, a limb with the bone exposed from ankle to knee and perhaps two-thirds of the flesh eaten away by the tropical ulcer. He painted Australian prisoners working in Hellfire Pass. In the middle-ground a man has been beaten. He is falling to the ground.

Both Parkin and Chalker drew death as part of the landscape. In Parkin's sketch of the Hintok River camp, there are five rough crosses in the foreground and a sixth lashed as a crucifix between two tall trees. 'Oriental bamboos,' he notes, 'make gothic arches over English dead.' Chalker's watercolour of the Konyu river camp is pastoral: calm river with gentle bends, a collection of thatched huts that look charming enough in the middle distance and mountains, delicately shaded, as a backdrop. Nine crosses, neat, perhaps lashed bamboo, in the foreground are the sign that something terrible is happening here.

Among those sketches and paintings of life and death along the railway, done in secret and smuggled at risk, two stand out. They deserve to be as iconic as the images from New Guinea: Damien Parer's blinded digger and mate and George Silk's fuzzy wuzzy angel helping another wounded digger. Jack Chalker called his drawing, with irony, 'working men'. There is a frail figure in rags. His stick legs disappear into too-large, laceless, battered boots. He may be having trouble seeing. In his right hand is a walking stick, a length of bamboo. His left arm is around the neck of a taller mate in tattered clothes, barefooted. The mate is carrying a pathetic load, the possessions of two men. He is bowed a little towards his companion, not with effort, but with compassion. The Gee family is convinced it is Allan Gee, *Perth*'s bugler, who returned home with impaired sight, but it is an Everyman picture. There were so many men along the railway who needed help and so many who helped them. Ray Parkin's drawing illustrates a particular incident, his heart-tugging description of 'two malarias and a cholera'. Humanity struggles to cope with inhumanity.

TOM UREN, THE socialist warrior, was set on his ideological path when he was on the railway. In his maiden speech to Federal Parliament, he said:

In our camp the officers and medical orderlies paid the greater proportion of their allowance into a central fund. The men who worked did likewise. We were living by the principle of the fit looking after the sick, the young looking after the old, the rich looking after the poor. A few months after we arrived at Hintok Mountain camp, a part of British H Force arrived. They were about 400 strong. As a temporary arrangement, they had tents. The officers selected the best, the non-commissioned officers the next best and the men got the dregs. Soon after they arrived, the wet season set in, bringing with it cholera and dysentery. Six weeks later only fifty men marched out of that camp, and of that number only about twenty-five survived. Only a creek separated our two camps, but on one side the law of the jungle prevailed and on the other the principles of socialism.

It wasn't quite as ideologically determined as that. Thirty per cent of H Force were unfit when they left Changi.

A child of the Depression and of working-class parents, Uren, as under-educated poor boys did, and still do, dreamed of boxing his way onward and upward. He trained at Dunleavy's Gym. He wasn't a street-fighter, a slugger. He really believed boxing was a sweet science, and his heroes were Archie Moore, Gene Tunney, Billy Conn and, in particular, the great Joe Louis. Uren could recite the words of Louis's trainer, Jack Blackburn: punching involves a transference of weight from one foot to the other and a coordination of the momentum and rhythm of the body. Uren was a contender for the heavyweight championship of Australia. He could have been champion, probably would have been champion but for a dose of the flu which started the day before his title fight with Billy Britt, 15 three-minute rounds to the belt, the prize and glory. For five rounds, Uren fought the Louis/Blackburn way. He knocked Britt down in the sixth, the only knockdown of the fight. The referee stopped it in the seventh. An exhausted Uren could not keep his arms up. Billy Britt was the winner, the new heavyweight champion of Australia, on a tko.

As prisoner of war along the railway, Uren found another mentor. Harry Baker was about 20 years older, a former cane-cutter with a couple of fingers missing, a mark of his trade. Baker and Uren were a hammer-and-tap gang. Rhythm was as important in the Konyu cuttings, Baker taught Uren, as it was in the ring. Save your energy with smooth strokes; let the hammer do the work. And another thing, take your time in meeting the darg, the contract. Don't bust your guts. Don't burn yourself out.

This was important for self-preservation of the relatively fit. It was also important to the weak. The Japanese set the workload according to the capabilities of the strongest workers. Do too much too quickly and your mates suffered. Show-offs. That was a serious insult in Uren's language. But there were a couple on the work party, men the Japanese called *ichiban*, Number One. Tiny, a big man of course, was like that.

At the end of one long day, the work party started back to camp, a 6-kilometre trek on a slippery, steep, treacherous track. The prisoners had to carry the tools, the hammers and drills, back. Most of the hammers were eight-pounders. Some were sixteen-pounders. The Japanese engineer distributed them. When Tiny was given an 8-pound hammer to carry, Uren confronted him. Tiny took a 16-pound hammer. The Japanese engineer saw this. He was on a raised bank, holding a length of solid green bamboo. He called Uren across, stood him to attention and swung savagely. Rhythm is important in defence, too. Uren swayed with the force of the blow and fell to the ground. 'It's okay, I rode the punch,' he said to his mates. The engineer stood Uren to attention again, swung again and Uren tried to sway with the blow again. The bamboo caught him heavily on the back of the head. As he lay in the mud he said to his mates: 'It's fair dinkum this time.'

THERE WERE STILL men who dreamed of escape, despite the example of the Tavoy eight and others executed when they were betrayed and brought back to camp. Uren and three mates did: Bill Bedford, the amateur heavyweight boxing champion of Queensland, a Spitfire pilot; Donald (Scorp) Stuart, a machine-gunner (Scorp had been bitten by a scorpion); and Kevin Wylie, a Hurricane pilot. They had heard a rumour that British forces had struck back from their Indian bases and were driving east across Burma to cut the Japanese line of communications between Rangoon and Mandalay. Uren and his mates were from the era when most Australian boys carried a shanghai, a catapult, in the back pockets of their shorts. They carved one each, and when they could, practised in the jungle. Their plan was simple: slip away from the camp and walk through jungles and over mountains and through more jungles, killing wildlife for food with their trusty catapults. After 1400 kilometres, they would join up with the British. The four took their plan to Weary Dunlop and Major Bill Wearne. Dunlop gave them a good hearing. He appeared not unsympathetic. Wearne was the bad cop: it was a fantasy; they had the wrong information; they would endanger other people; the Japanese would take reprisals. What the would-be escapers did not know was that the officers were aware of the real situation in Burma. They had what Dunlop hides as 'X' in his diaries, a secret radio.

Escape had to be a matter of the mind except for a few. Once Uren sat with 800 men at Hintok River camp. Rain during the day had cleared the sky. Stars were bright above the clearings and the path of the River Kwai. The only light was from a log fire. Uren was leaning his back against a tree. He was out of the camp, the jungle and the war, under different stars. He was

> . . . down by Kosciusko, where the pine-clad ridges raise
> Their torn and rugged battlements on high,

Where the air is clear as crystal, and the white stars fairly
  blaze
At midnight in the cold and frosty sky,
And where around the Overflow the reed-beds sweep and
  sway
To the breezes, and the rolling plains are wide . . .

Standing in the flickering firelight, a slouch hat on his head at an angle, was Major Allan Woods. Woods had been part of the prisoner-of-war leadership team since Java. Unlike many in his audience, city boys who could only ride horses and see the bush in their dreams, Woods was from Silver Spur station in Queensland and he had skills to go with the myth of Australian males as bushmen. He was cobbler, tin-smith, carpenter, maker of artificial legs, physiotherapy and medical equipment and a designer of an ingenious theatre light for Dunlop, Coates and other surgeons to work by. At Hintok Mountain camp it was he who dammed the small creek and constructed bamboo pipes on trestles to carry water to bamboo showerheads 200 yards away. Filthy men, dusty or muddy depending on the weather, could shower under running water. He also knew Banjo Paterson's *The Man from Snowy River* by heart.

For Uren, this night riding after the colt from Old Regret was the only entertainment during his time on the railway. Others were luckier. At Kun Knit Kway, a camp 26 kilometres from the Burma terminal, Thanbyuzayat, in February 1943, volunteers began creating a theatre: basically a bamboo-and-atap lean-to and a dirt stage. There was lighting: two big bonfires, not too close to the bamboo. There was an orchestra pit. The Kun Knit Kway theatre was a distant jungle descendant of the Pow Wow theatre founded by Norman Carter at the Bicycle Camp prison in Java. A civilian scriptwriter and producer of newsreels, Carter had arrived in Singapore just before the fall, introduced to the public by the *Straits Times* as a propaganda scriptwriter who would produce anti-Japanese newsreels. He joined the escape armada but his ship was bombed and beached on Banka Island. He hid but was found by Japanese collaborators and handed over to the Japanese.

Carter suggested the Java theatre group to the prisoners' commander, Brigadier Arthur Blackburn, the day after a confrontation between the brigadier and the Japanese commander, Lieutenant Sonai. After a false accusation of showing lack of respect to Private Hansho Shoko, Blackburn VC, hero of Pozières, was ordered to clean out the prisoners' jail latrines with his bare hands. Morale was bad, Carter argued. A theatre would lift it, not an open-air theatre with a few old jokes and community singing, but a converted barn with stage, proscenium, an actual front curtain. And overhead floats! Footlights! Costumes! Greasepaint! There was a problem. Regulations on the prison noticeboard banned, among other things, musical instruments, singing and whistling, but Blackburn got permission from Sonai for rehearsals in the evening and on Sundays.

With a skilled backstage crew at work, Carter had the strange nucleus of an orchestra: a female impersonator, Vilhelm Vanderdeken, who played guitar, a Scot, Jock Milliken, accordion ('guid auld songs wi' real toons'), and another Dutchman, Freddie, who played the flugelhorn. Soon Carter was busy casting. Fred Quick, tall Texan, was the crooner. Jack Coxhead, *Perth*'s bandmaster, was conductor and he enrolled shipmate Vince Brow whose clarinet was at the bottom of the Sunda Strait, but who was carving another one. Doc Clark, of the 2/2nd Pioneers, stocky, auburn-haired, offered gag routines and then auditioned as a dancer, his preliminary shuffle seaming into a snappy tap.

A poster went up announcing that on July 27, 1942, at the

Bicycle Camp Theatre, the POW-WOWS would present the scintillating mirthquake, *Tit Bits*. There had been some discussion of the title. It was provocative, a reminder to the men of a huge emptiness in their lives. Quick said: 'What the hell! In another three months we'll all be impotent anyway. Let's give them a bit of sex before it's too late.' (It seems Quick was right enough. There is rarely a mention of sex in the diaries kept at the time or in the recollections of the survivors. Malnutrition, disease and exhaustion were no aphrodisiacs.)

On the night, Lieutenant Sonai made a grand entrance, a soldier carrying his green upholstered armchair. *Tit Bits* was not Noël Coward but it was a triumph. Vilhelm, the guitar-playing female impersonator, wore a high-slashed cheongsam, and the Beautee Ballet chorus hula skirts from shredded palm leaves, topped with falsies. Doc Clark starred as Rice Belly Nellie and Jock Milliken and his accordion played encore after encore.

By the time Carter started casting for his first production in the minimalist Kun Knit Kway theatre in Burma, a farce called *The Sultan of Sarong*, the illness rate and the death toll were steadily rising. Clark and Milliken were members of a mobile group working punishing hours. There would be no more theatre for them. In real life, their role was to die.

KEITH ROSSI, WORLD War II and Vietnam veteran, talked of the freemasonry of soldiers. There is a freemasonry of prisoners of war too. Some of the survivors say they have no knowledge of acts of selfishness or greed. Perhaps such things happened in other camps, they say. Some want to protect the mateship myth; others want to leave disappointments, anger and bitterness in the jungle and in the past. Some say if you weren't there you can't possibly know what it was like. They are right, of course. Prisoners were tested as few people are, not for hours or days, but for months and years. Ordinary men did do extraordinary things, the definition of the best heroism. Other ordinary men could steal, and not just, as with F Force, in the worst of times, the time of cholera, when they were on the edge of survival.

In his preface to his war diaries, Weary Dunlop said he shrank from publishing them for over 40 years. It seemed that they might add further to the suffering of those bereaved and add to controversy and hatred. He distrusted judgments he made under circumstances he viewed as black and white with no shades of grey. On the one hand he felt that Australians had written something very special in the annals of human suffering. Even the humblest of men had quite a lot of God in them, he said. On the other he had reacted sharply to the few who shed all decency in their preoccupation with self-preservation. 'Also there were those,' Dunlop wrote, 'who bore the badges of leadership, even men of proven valour in action, who reacted to imprisonment with an irritating inertia reflecting suspension of purpose.'

Dunlop watched one of his medical staff, Alan Gibson, near-naked and a skeleton, shivering with chronic malaria and racked with dysentery, lay his blanket, his comfort, over a naked man with cholera. But his diary contains several entries featuring a Private Franklin, embezzler and 'thorough dyed-in-the-wool young scoundrel', who threatened to tell the Japanese about X, Dunlop's radio. Woven through the second book of Ray Parkin's trilogy, *Into the Smother*, is the saga of Izzy. Izzy from Woolloomooloo, fatherless, brought up mainly by the roving gangs; Izzy who, they are sure, has stolen part of the camp's sugar, who they would like to half-kill, who, they think, doesn't really have the power to help himself; Izzy who is caught with a couple of others, skulking in the bush away from his job, bashed and made to hold a 30-pound rock above his head for some time; Izzy, barely 20 years old, with amoebic dysentery, his face wizened and old, a shrivelled relic before he's dead. 'You'll get back to the 'Loo and the sheilas there,' Parkin says.

'This way,' Izzy replies, 'the old lady won't know . . . think I'm a hero . . . better like this.' They often called Izzy a lying, thieving larrikin, but in his last weeks, Parkin said, he had produced from somewhere an endurance and courage he greatly admired. He died better than many.

There was redemption for Izzy in his dying. There were officers who escaped retribution because of the bone-weariness of the prisoners of war: Bill Dunn described one as 'a most dreadful man who had his great tin trunk with him that we had to carry with us, camp to camp, full of cigarettes, food and books. He had his own tent and he just sat in it for the whole 12 weeks of hell. He put a chap, poor devil from New South Wales on a charge. I was escort for him and had to march him in front of the officer who went on and on and then fined him 14 days' pay. He said: "Have you anything to say, Gunner?" The gunner said: "Yes sir. I don't see why a man should go out and slave out his guts all day and then come home and be fined by a big bastard like you who sits on his arse all day and smokes cigarettes." He got disciplined again because he told him the truth. The officer had been high up in a company before the war. Whether he went back to that position, I don't know. The chaps really did want to go to town on him when they got home, but it all died down. Everyone was just so glad to be back.'

Parkin calls some 'frightened self-seekers' and says others, who have got out of touch with their men can only wave the Manual of Military Law at them in an endeavour to intimidate. Chalker reports two British officers selling quinine tablets to outside contacts while men in their camp were dying of cerebral malaria and blackwater fever for lack of them. Kevin Ward talks of an officer who 'when the going got tough, didn't want to lead us any more. Padre Marsden, the Catholic padre, stepped up and said, "I'll lead you spiritually". Dr Fagan stepped up and said, "I'll lead you medically". So this was our assurance that at least we had a chance to survive.'

Only a minority of officers failed, perhaps 10 per cent in the estimate of Don Wall, of F Force. The boundaries of the world of most prisoners were small. Wall was selected by the Japanese as a driver and he knew more about the railway and the camps along it than most. He saw every working party. He saw their crowded cemeteries, and that's what shook him. He knew that in every camp there were officers who stood by their men, who were bashed or tortured in their cause. Ken Dumbrell put it simply: 'I go out to work with the men and I cop the bashings. If anyone was getting stuck into, I'd buy into it. Had to. If you didn't do that you might as well not be there. Then they'd take it out on you, but by then they'd lost a bit of their sting, which sometimes saved you a bit.'

THE RAILWAY TESTED faith in man and in God. Colin Finke-meyer, the boy from the wide Wimmera, had a strict Lutheran faith. As mates died he questioned. Now look, if there's a God, what is He doing? Whose side is He on? What the hell is He doing to look after us? Why is He letting that young fella die like this, that other young fella die like that? What have the fellas done? Finkemeyer was convinced there was no-one looking after him. He'd have to look after himself from now on. He became convinced too that nature was the source of life. On rare days off, he would sit in the jungle, looking at the canopy. He would listen to the quietness, watch for the movements.

Once a wasp stung and paralysed a huge spider. This was the intriguing thing: there was a canal running by and under a bridge and the wasp pushed the spider into it. The spider floated down the water and under the bridge. The wasp flew down, pulled it to the bank, out of the water and to its nest. It laid its eggs in the spider and filled it with mud. The wasp looked after its young. Nature looked after life. (Pity about the spider.)

Stan Arneil, travelling towards the railway in April 1943, as a member of F Force, looked out from the crowded swelter of the rice truck at knobs of rock, a great yellow blob of cloud, walls of jungle aflame with red and yellow vines making a madman's pattern too hard to follow. He thought: 'I would not miss this for the world.' Three months later, in the time of cholera, he wrote in his diary that he could not help being seized by fits of black depression. In August: 'The horrible sight of four to eight corpses being carried away and burnt each day refuses to become a commonplace in my eyes.' In September, having suffered malaria and ulcers on his feet, one down to the bone on his toe: 'Please heaven let the war finish soon. Surely we do not deserve this.' In October: 'It is hard to keep alive the will to live. I can hang on myself but others are falling under the strain every day.' Through all this, Arneil kept his Catholic faith and hungered for Mass and Holy Communion. Back in Changi in May 1944: 'Ascension Thursday. Mass this morning in the little hut we use for a Sgts' Mess. Before joining the army all my Masses had been heard in churches, since then I have heard Mass in the open, with steel helmet and rifle, in native quarters, in a beer garden, ramshackle huts, tents, anywhere at all seems to be fit for a P.O.W. to hear and as for confession, well up North we were allowed to confess any time we saw the padre, mainly because an hour later in those days, even though a man may have been presumably healthy, may have been too late.' In his final diary entry, back in Australia after his reunion with his family: 'Thank you dear God for watching over me and bringing me home. Thank you Holy Mary Mother of God for the protection you have given me.'

Arneil did not know it when he was on the railway but, under the eyes of the Japanese, prisoners were receiving life-saving temporal help.

SUCH A PRETTY girl, so polite, and she speaks a little Japanese and is learning to write it. What a treasure in this town in the depths of Thailand, with its hovels and hen runs, untidiness, tumbledown outer walls, dust in summer, mud in the monsoon. For the Japanese she makes the boat trip down the River Kwai to Kanchanaburi worthwhile. Panee works in her parents' general store, a clutter with an amazing range of goods and clouds of spicy aromas. Though she doesn't help much when the Japanese soldiers come in with the Allied prisoners of war. She talks with the soldiers, smiles at them. To be honest, she flirts, and while she does the prisoners, there to fetch and carry, have quick conversations with her mother, Surat, and her father, Sirivejjabhandu Boonpong. They slip him special shopping lists.

Boonpong is mentioned in Dunlop's preface to his diaries but his name does not appear in the entries, an essential precaution. The camps were often searched for smuggled goods, for radios and for sketches and written material. Boonpong's name in a discovered diary would be a death warrant for him and his family. Instead sprinkled through are asterisks and footnotes, added long after the war: 'There have been some pleasing signs of late as regards medical stores and emetine in particular. Certain gentlemen have supplied some 72 grams and offer a most hopeful avenue for either free supply of drugs or supplying a cheque for medical purposes.* (Boonpong and the underground)'. 'I am at present in the lines sharing a bay with Lt-Col Thomas. The hospital today obtained some most useful drugs and money – 3000.* (By grace of that magnificent man, Boonpong)'.

Outwardly, there was nothing heroic about Boonpong. He was small, bespectacled and always wore a neat white shirt. His family had been in Kanchanaburi for two generations, his mother half Chinese and half Thai, his father a doctor. Built by Rama I early in the nineteenth century as a strategic outpost on the smugglers' and invasion route from Burma across the Three Pagodas Pass, Kanchanaburi was a sleepy river town when the Japanese and their massive slave army arrived to build a railway. Boonpong was one of the traders whose boats supplied the prisoners' canteens in the camps. He built a reputation as a fair man, with the lowest prices and the thinnest profit margins. He advanced loans to prisoners for personal possessions they had managed to keep out of the grasp of the Japanese. He also chanced the lives of himself and his family.

Prisoners lived their days with a gnawing sense of powerlessness and isolation. They received letters from home and Red Cross parcels at the whim of the Japanese. They were indeed the legion of the lost. However, hidden hands were helping them. About 200 British subjects had been interned in Bangkok by the Phibun Government after it declared war on the Allies in 1942. One of them, K. G. Gairdner, started the V Organisation. His Thai wife, Millie, and a Chinese employee, K.S. Hong, had freedom of movement. Through them, Gairdner managed to make contact with prisoner-of-war officers. A two-way traffic to the camps dotted north along the path of the railway began: small packets of drugs and money, as well as reports on the war's progress to the prisoners; news of camp conditions, drug needs and Japanese movements to V.

Boonpong was a friend of a V contact. He also had links with *Seri Thai*, the secret organisation founded by Seni Pramoj, the Thai ambassador in Washington, who had refused to deliver the declaration of war on the United States. It was a perfect match. The Japanese allowed Boonpong's boats access to the camps. They carried vegetables, eggs, whitebait, salt, peanuts, oil, tobacco and sugar. Soon they carried too a precious cargo of money and medicines: emetine (for amoebic dysentery) and hyoscine (for cerebral malaria) to save lives; idoform to save limbs which would have been lost to tropical ulcers. Dunlop smuggled downriver special requests. He wanted *tulle gras*, a special dressing, to perform skin grafts on ulcer patients. These vital medical requirements were purchased by Boonpong's wife, Surat, and the couple packed them in cabbages or packets of tobacco. Surat put herself directly in harm's way as did Millie Gairdner; Surat carried batteries for radios under her arm into camps. Millie gave a bag of tapioca flour to prisoners in front of a guard. Inside it were packets of Thai 20-tical notes.

On Anzac Day eve 1998, at Hellfire Pass, the Australian Prime Minister John Howard presented to the Boonpongs' grandson, Veeravej Subhawat, a posthumous certificate of appreciation for their family's bravery and selflessness. (Australia is often tardy in honouring heroes and recognising debts.) Howard paid tribute to the quiet heroics of the Boonpongs and to the simple deeds of Thai people who would leave hard-boiled eggs on river banks to be found by starving prisoners. 'This sacred place', he called Hellfire Pass, a memorial that did not seek to magnify tragedy but to commemorate triumph.

In those days of 1943, the triumph was to stay alive. Lieutenant Usuki, commandant of Konyu 2 camp, told the prisoners: 'The Japanese are prepared to work: you must be prepared to work. The Japanese are prepared to eat less: you must eat less. The Japanese are prepared to die: you must be prepared to die.' A convenient belief in suffering shared has persisted decades after the truth of the railway was exposed. It cloaks the guilt or duality of the Japanese towards the suffering inflicted. Senior engineer Renichi Sugano, leader of the Japanese ex-servicemen who served in Burma and along the railway, at one point in our conversation in Tokyo said that at the time he had not been informed of the conditions in the camps where a lot of people had died. Engineers, Japanese soldiers and prisoners of war were living separately.

But when he went along the railway, hadn't he seen gangs of prisoners, emaciated and ill?

Yes, many, but he could see the ribs of Japanese soldiers too. A lot of soldiers and engineers got sick too, and were sent to hospital. The food and living conditions were extremely bad. They were eating only rice and salt because there were no food supplies; rice and salt and, in the mountains, bamboo shoots.

While the Japanese at times subsisted on thin rations, there was a life-and-death difference between nutrition and health care for the Japanese and for the prisoners. Captors and captives also regarded one another across a psychological chasm. But they were all men at war in an alien land. Engineer Futamatsu wrote: 'When a man spends a long time in the jungle, he realises his way of life is to keep alive.' Japanese soldiers carved chessmen and mahjong tiles out of bamboo. As night fell over the jungle greenness, 'everyone felt homesickness and yearned for his homeland. Its fields and mountains floated under their eyelids and in dreams they saw the dream-faces of their family and friends.' On sleepless nights they looked up at the same stars Robert Hardie gazed at and wondered when they would return home. Increasingly, they scanned the daytime sky anxiously. They had doubts about the progress of the war.

THE LIBERATOR HEAVY bomber was the most expensive and complicated aircraft of its time, a handful for a pilot, less stable than its rival, the B-17 Flying Fortress, but with a longer range. It was a prime example of the overwhelming power of the American war production machine. Nearly 20,000 were built and they flew in every theatre of World War II. Late in 1942, Liberators flying out of Assam in India were attacking Rangoon, Mandalay and other targets in Burma. In November eight flew a round trip of 4440 kilometres to bomb Bangkok's oil refinery and power plant. Clearly, the whole of the railway would be in their reach and vulnerable. Futamatsu was the designer of the steel bridge over the Mae Klong, the bridge transformed by David Lean's artistic licence into the wooden structure over the Kwai. Three hundred metres long, with 11 spans of 22 metres crossing the waterway and comb-shaped steel trusses brought from Java, the bridge was (and is) impressive. It was a prime target. Futamatsu records the spreading of camouflage netting along it and the positioning of anti-aircraft guns.

In March 1943, Allied aircraft had made their first strikes on the railway project, bombing marshalling yards and workshops at the Burma terminus, Thanbyuzayat. Neighbouring these targets were Japanese barracks and stores and indistinguishable among them, 14 long hospital huts containing 3000 prisoners. The Japanese guards, a prisoner of war recorded, 'became very excited, rushed about in all directions, shouting, fixing bayonets, loading rifles; nobody was allowed outside the huts on penalty of being shot, and we were not allowed to use slit trenches . . . The Japanese remained in their slit trenches for about half an hour after the planes had gone.' Afterwards Brigadier Varley got permission from the Japanese to dig slit trenches. He also wanted to lay out a cross of red gravel on white sand. The Japanese could not supply material for this and they refused to allow the prisoners to construct a white triangle on a blue base, a symbol showing a prisoner-of-war camp.

For powerless prisoners, the sight of Allied planes was wonderful for morale. In May big four-engined plans flew over Thanbyuzayat camp on the way to some unknown target to the south. Patients who could walk came out of the hospital huts to wave. Australian Bob Skelton and Englishman Les Bullock, members of Norman Carter's concert troupe, composed a song to the tune of *Comin' Round the Mountain*:

> *They'll be dropping thousand pounders*
> *When they come.*
> *They'll be dropping thousand pounders*
> *When they come.*
> *They'll be laying hard-boiled eggs*
> *Around the yellow bastards' legs*
> *Cos they'll be dropping thousand pounders*
> *When they come.*

On June 12 the Liberators came again, six of them. The gods of war have in their ranks the god of irony. Rohan Rivett came out of the hospital hut where an American orderly was treating sores on his back and down his legs. Cheered by the sight he went inside again then heard someone outside say that the aircraft had broken into two formations of three and were wheeling around. A wave of sound blasted through the bamboo and atap hospital. They were dropping 250-pounders and 500-pounders. They did not target the camp and the hospital, but one bomb scored a direct hit on the well, 45 metres from the fence. Rivett's theory was that it looked like a gun emplacement from the air. The well party, 12 prisoners who had gone to draw water, died.

Three days later Liberators came again, probably the same six. This time they hit the camp, source of small-arms fire during the first attack. The Japanese had established machine-gun posts. They had no impact. For an hour, the Liberators bombed and strafed. Rivett and a friend, Don Capron, RAAF flying officer, shared their slit trench with a small bullfrog. Capron had an expert's eye: 'Hell! The blighter's coming straight in again. Here come the eggs. They'll be close this time!' The two men and the frog survived. Seventeen prisoners died. Next day the Thanbyuzayat hospital was evacuated, a forced march of almost 3000 sick men to abandoned and derelict work camps along the railway. More prisoners died.

In the following months, the monsoon provided cover and protection for prisoners of war and the railway from the Liberators. Nothing protected the prisoners of war from the demands of the engineers, though at least even the fanatics realised that the completion date had to be put back. The weather was against them, and the terrain. They were driving too many of their slave workers to death. Major General Eiguma Ishida took total control. This is recorded in the Official Japanese report thus: 'Major General Ishida was newly appointed director of construction for perfect realisation of the scheme. He aimed at completion of the work by the end of October, renewed the organisation of the staff and endeavoured to stimulate morale . . . He cherished the slogan "Prisoners of war and labourers are the fathers of construction" and corrected the erroneous idea of "Mastership" prevailing among officers and men.'

These were great times to be Japanese. The 5th Railway Regiment was pushing the track from Burma across the Three

Pagodas Pass. The 9th Railway Regiment was conquering rugged Thailand. They would meet at Konkoita, 262 kilometres from the Thai terminus. Engineer Futamatsu wrote: 'In a day we crossed one valley, took the top of a hill in the evening. The next day we pulverised solid rock and plugged up a deep ravine, each day extending the railroad towards the joining up point.' In the real railway world 'we', of course, were a relative handful of Japanese and a vast army of prisoners and Asians, emaciated, ulcerated, malaria-ridden and hosts to a variety of other diseases.

At the end of August, the gap was 100 kilometres. The final race came for the joining-up point and (this is Futamatsu again) the jungle shook with their efforts. However, side by side with triumphalism, is the acknowledgment that the labourers, 'without distinction of day or night, were plunged into continuous labour without sleep or rest'. He did cold calculations of cause and effect. During the monsoon when supply lines were hard to maintain rations were reduced by half; malnourishment reduced efficiency at work and in the long run increased the number of sick which further reduced efficiency. Nippon very sorry. Many men must die.

THE MONSOON ENDED. The sun ruled the sky, beating straight down. Cicadas were shrill and insistent. So much noise from a small insect. At Konkoita the railway trace cut a straight line through the jungle. The roadbed had been completed and at the chosen joining point the embankment was low. It was October 17, 1943. One hundred metres to the south was the 9th Railway Regiment squad. They had chosen the rugged look, naked from the waist up. To the north were troops of the 5th Railway Regiment. They were in formal dress with cavalry carbines slung across their backs. A small

number of prisoners of war and Asian labourers, the worker
ants of the railway, were bit players in this choreographed
event. The eyewitness was railway official Hatamaru from the
4th Special Bridging Unit. At 11 am the signal was given. Rail-
tractors pushed forward flatbed cars carrying rails. As sleepers
were lined up, the rails were dropped down and spiked. North
met south at the 262.53 mark from the Nong Pladuk starting
point. *Banzai!* One thousand years! Hatamaru wept.

On October 25, Robert Hardie watched an engine chuff
past Takanun camp, decorated with the crossed flags of Japan
and Thailand. This was engine C5631, which in time resided
proudly in the Yushukan museum, next to the Yasukuni
Shrine. Then it was pulling several flatcars on which frames
had been erected to protect senior Japanese officers from the
sun. They were also protected from the sight of the squalor of
the coolie camp a kilometre along the track. A high bamboo
screen had been built. They might have wondered though
about the stench. Awaiting engine C5631 and the special
guests headed by Southern Army Chief of Staff Kiyomina,
were the Southern Army's military band, a Japanese film crew
and a group of prisoners of war, including Chilla Goodchap.
The eyewitness was Futamatsu, one of the architects of the
railway. At the joining point the commanders of the two construction units hammered gunmetal spikes into a special ebony
sleeper. To the chorus of cicadas, the band played the Japanese
national anthem.

The film crew captured blue of sky, green of jungle, swing
of hammers. The camera panned along a line of prisoners of
war. There was Chilla Goodchap. Out of a group of about 200
prisoners of war, 40 had been selected. Goodchap, who had
been living life naked except for his three G-strings, found
himself wearing shorts, shirt and large sunhat and even boots.
He shook hands with a Japanese officer and the camera

followed him into a tent. He was given a tray piled with bananas, pawpaws and jackfruit and on top a packet of cigarettes. Goodchap smiled and stepped off-camera. The Japanese took away his uniform (they only had 10) and they took away his tray. As the band played on, its repertoire including selections from *Carmen* and *The Merry Widow*, Chilla Goodchap resumed his usual full dress, his G-string.

Hardie recorded in his diary for October 25: 'To celebrate the junction of the rails, the Japanese have given the workers a whole holiday for one day and have made a special issue of extra food – Japanese tinned milk, margarine and fish.'

Stan Arneil records in his diary: 'Stinny died last night in awful circumstances. God rest his soul, he died hard.'

COLONEL NAGATOMO, WHO had greeted prisoners of war under his command in Burma with the exhortation to work cheerful, ordered ceremonies to mark the completion of the railway. On November 20, prisoners watched Japanese soldiers lay wreaths at wooden crosses specially erected in camp cemeteries. At one Nagatomo read out a 'Letter of condolence on the occasion of the memorial service for deceased POWs'. His officers repeated it at others.

As this first stage of the railway construction has now been completed I have on this day of commemoration the honour of taking this opportunity of consoling the souls of the POWs of the 3rd Branch, numbering 665, who have died in this district during the past year. In my opinion it is a virtue since ancient times to pay homage to the souls who have died in war, even though they be enemies. Moreover you were under my command and have endeavoured to work diligently in obedience to my orders while always longing for repatriation to your own country once the war is over and peace restored. I have always done my utmost to discharge my duty conscientiously taking responsibility for all of you as your commander.

Now you have passed on to the other world, owing to the unavoidable prevailing diseases and indiscriminate bombing, I cannot see you in this world any more.

Visualising your situation and that of your relatives and families, I cannot help shedding tears sympathising with your unfortunate circumstances.

This tragedy is the result of war. However it is owing to fate that you are in this condition and I consider that God has called you here. However today I try to console your souls and pray for you in my capacity of your commander, together with other members of my staff by dedicating a cross and placing a wreath in your cemetery.

In the very near future your comrades will be leaving this district. Consequently it may be impossible to offer prayers and lay a wreath in your cemetery for some time to come. But undoubtedly some of your comrades will come here again after the war to pay sincere homage to your memory.

Please accept my deepest sympathy and regards and may you sleep peacefully and eternally.

Given on the 20th day of November, in the 18th year of Showa.

Rohan Rivett listened in anger. It was one of the most nauseating displays of Japanese hypocrisy. It was an insult. But, he thought, so limited and obsessive was the Japanese mind that it probably was not intended as such. Indeed it was not unusual for Japanese to treat the dead as soldiers when in life they had been regarded as shamed for being taken prisoner.

While those ceremonies were taking place, the survivors of F Force and H Force were beginning the journey back to Singapore. They reached Changi on December 21. David Griffin watched. His name had been on the F Force list but a staff sergeant from another unit asked to take his place. His great mate, with whom he had enlisted, was going and they wanted to stay together. Griffin and the other men of Changi were gaunt, but the F Force survivors were slowly moving skeletons emaciated almost beyond belief, many with dreadful sores and peeling skin, some unable to move and some so light that a Changi prisoner had no difficulty lifting them. Griffin knew the exchange had probably saved his life.

There was shock and there was sympathy and there was love. Stan Arneil should tell the story:

It was a moonlight night and Changi with the tropical waters round the island was so beautiful. I can still hear the squeal of the brakes as the trucks lined up. The people from Changi knew we were coming, and they came over to see us, to look for old friends and to see how we were. We got out of the trucks, a couple were dead and we laid them on the ground and we lined up on the road. We were not ashamed because we were soldiers and we wanted to look like soldiers. The people from Changi stood back and uttered not a word. It was really quite strange. We lined up on the road as best we could and stood up as straight as we could. Those who couldn't stand up straight were on sticks. And those who couldn't stop shaking with malaria were held by their friends. We thought that this was what we should do as soldiers to show we were not beaten. The sergeant-major dressed us off and we stood in a straight line as he went over and reported to Colonel Johnston. Johnston went over to

HELLFIRE

Black Jack Galleghan and he said, 'Your 2/30th all present and correct, sir'. And Galleghan said, 'Where are the rest?' [Johnston] said, 'They're all here, sir.' And we were. Black Jack Galleghan, the iron man, broke down and cried. It was an incredible scene. We wanted to show them we were soldiers.

Men at Changi had been saving scraps of food for Christmas dinner: salt, red-palm oil and a little sweet *gula malacca*. They gave it to the survivors of F Force. On Christmas night Arneil went to Midnight Mass sung by a Dutch, an English and an Australian priest. He took communion. Perfect.

But the war had 20 months to run. Many more men would die, and imprisoned nurses. There would be, as usual, death from disease. There would be death from bombs and death at sea. The struggle to stay alive continued until war's end and beyond.

CHAPTER 22

Friendly fire

Early in the morning of October 25, 1944, Richard O'Kane, commander of the American submarine *Tang*, was on the bridge, peering over the Formosa Strait. The *Tang* was in the last minutes of its fifth war patrol, on a mission to sink Japanese shipping. It was in the last minutes of its existence. The Japanese dream of the Greater East Asia Co-Prosperity Sphere could only have been turned into reality if its boundaries could be defended and its resources exploited. Command of the sea lanes and a strong merchant fleet were essential. Japan began its audacious war without adequate shipping: the merchant fleet was capable of carrying only 65 per cent of the nation's peacetime imports. By the end of 1942, the Imperial Japanese Navy was on the defensive and more and more of the merchant fleet was being blown out of the water. By August 1943, when *Tang* was launched, more than one million tons of Japanese shipping had been destroyed. By mid-1944, hundreds more ships had been sunk. The ability to supply troops, particularly the 15th Army in Burma, was crucial. An offensive against the British had been crushed and the Thai–Burma railway, built at such cost in slave-labour blood and Japanese morality, could, under constant air attack, deliver only a fraction of supplies needed.

Tang (named after a small, tropical fighting fish with needled fins) was one of the most successful of the American submarines that tormented the Japanese. The skipper and the submarine were made for each other. O'Kane, who had proved himself an aggressive, resourceful and successful officer on the submarine *Wahoo* under his mentor, Dudley (Mush) Morton, was chosen to command *Tang* while it was being built. He was even more successful on *Tang*. For its fifth patrol, *Tang* loaded 24 Mark 18 electric torpedoes. By that October morning, 22 had been fired to devastating effect, only one missing its target. Now O'Kane was stalking again a tanker that had already been hit, its mainmast the point of aim. *Tang* was on the surface, silently closing at 6 knots. At 900 yards O'Kane called 'fire' and the twenty-third torpedo arrowed away. He immediately repeated the order. In the forward torpedo room, Pete Narowanski said: 'Hot dog. Course zero-nine-zero, head her for the Golden Gate.' As Narowanski's thoughts turned to home, O'Kane and his party on the bridge were watching with horror the twenty-fourth torpedo. In his official report, written in September 1945, O'Kane said: 'This torpedo curved sharply to the left, broaching during the first part of its turn and then porpoising during the remainder. Emergency speed was called for and answered immediately on firing and a fishtail manoeuvre partially completed in an attempt to get clear of the torpedo's turning circle. This resulted only in the torpedo striking the stern abreast the after torpedo room instead of amidships.' *Tang* sank by the stern in seconds. There was no time to clear the bridge. There was no time to obey O'Kane's order to close the hatch. The torpedo's rudder had jammed as it sped along at 27 knots. *Tang*, ultra-efficient killer submarine, killed itself. Only nine members of the crew, including O'Kane and Pete Narowanski, survived.

O'KANE LEFT THE navy and the sea in 1957. He was a cer-
tified all-American hero, winner of the Congressional Medal of
Honor 'for conspicuous gallantry and intrepidity in combat'.
In 1977 he had retired from business to his ranch in Sonoma
County, California. It was only then, more than three decades
later, he felt he could write in detail about the triumphs and
the tragedy of *Tang*. He still did not find it easy. *Clear the
Bridge! The War Patrols of the U.S.S.* Tang, begins:

> Forgive me for writing here to the relatives of all men
> who served in *Tang* and especially to the kin of those
> who sailed on her last patrol. As you may know, I
> attempted to reach some parents and relatives after
> repat-riation and later following final survey to duty in
> 1946. It was too early and perhaps will ever be so, for
> no matter how one views the loss of *Tang*, a thought of
> *Titanic* will always be present in a situation wherein the
> captain returns and shipmates are left behind. Believe
> me, on that fateful night I became physically exhausted
> in trying to reach my ship and men, then so close
> ahead.

O'Kane said that as he wrote the account it became necessary
time and again to saddle up his buckskin and ride into the hills
so that, on his return he might continue with a clear eye.

The book was a reaching-out as well as an exercise in
exorcism by O'Kane, haunted by the loss of his men and by
the tradition that captains went down with their ships. He
hoped the relatives reading the account would in spirit patrol
with *Tang* and think of it and their kin with utmost pride. He
was proud himself, pointing to *Tang*'s five Presidential Unit
citations and saying that sinking a convoy of four ships with a
single salvo of six torpedoes (which the *Tang* had achieved on

its third patrol in June 1944), must rank as the most devastating submarine salvo in history.

On his property in north central Victoria, Lance Gibson, former lieutenant in the 2/3rd Machine Gun Battalion and former prisoner of war of the Japanese, read O'Kane's book with particular interest. Gibson had been on a Japanese transport, the *Tamahoko Maru*, sunk by the *Tang* on an earlier patrol. In the Indonesian prisoner-of-war camp Gibson formed a lasting bond with Desmond Jackson; 30 years on, he and his wife Mary formed a bond with Dick O'Kane and his wife Ernestine. Gibson wrote to O'Kane in 1979. O'Kane replied in January 1980, apologising for the delay. He told of his recovery from a tumour operation, of going on a hiking and fishing trip with Ernestine in an old VW camper: 18 days and 113 trout. He told of his abandoned attempt at ranching.

Gibson was born to the land. His family had settled their property in 1869; O'Kane was born in Dover, a sea-coast town in New Hampshire. The family lived on a hobby farm not far from the Portsmouth Navy Yard, which built submarines. At 19 O'Kane entered the US Naval Academy. In this first of many letters, O'Kane rambled on about overseas travel, the virtues of the VW camper and the pleasures of riding Dusty, his buckskin. He discussed his attitude to the Japanese, one he shared with Gibson. But he did not specifically address the point of Gibson's letter, though he thanked him 'for supplying information on the numbers of surviving prisoners of war from the *Tamahoko Maru*'. 'Actually, from the moment of firing,' he said, 'the seas were clear in such a short time (seven minutes – probably a bit less, as we did not check the time until we steadied in the clear) that it's a wonder that anyone survived.' This sounds cryptic, but what Gibson had told O'Kane was that he had been on board one of the four ships sunk in that six-torpedo salvo. He told of his and his mates' struggle in the sea off Nagasaki and how many had drowned. He and O'Kane had both been victims of a *Tang* torpedo.

LIKE JOHN CURTIN'S Australia, wartime Japan was ordered by its government to embrace austerity. No evening wear for Australian women; a kimono for Japanese women with shortened sleeves and cloak, the material khaki, the National Defence Colour, and not even one single line of gold-embroidered thread. Encouraging such symbolism were the slogans: 'Let's send even one more plane to the front', 'Deny one's self and serve the nation', 'Serve the nation with one death'. The substance of Japanese life was seriously affected. Bad harvests at home, the difficulties in importing food and the shrinking waters available to fishing fleets saw a steady deterioration in the Japanese diet in both quantity and quality. As the nutrition value decreased, the incidence of beri-beri, one of the signature illnesses in the prison camps, increased. Manpower was a growing problem. Japan, with a population of around 72 million, had more than six million in the armed forces. Labour was sucked from agriculture and peacetime industries into the war machine.

Japan turned to its young, students like 15-year-old Tetsuko Tanaka, who, when the war started, was dreaming the girls' dream of becoming a ballerina. As the war demanded more men, classes at her school, Yamaguchi Girls' High School, gave way to volunteer work: planting rice, weeding paddy fields, harvesting, carrying charcoal down from the mountains. In 1944, the students of Yamaguchi were visited by an army officer who told them they would be making a 'secret weapon'. They went to an area, a prime military target, wearing white headbands with the characters 'Student Special Attack Force' on them. Their mission was to make balloons which, filled with hydrogen, would be slung with a 15-kilogram anti-personnel bomb and two 2.2-kilogram incendiary bombs. Riding the jet stream, they would sail across the Pacific to North America. (Some of the 9000 or so launched did reach the enemy. Forty years on Tanaka learnt that a woman and five children on a picnic had been killed when a fallen bomb exploded. She was stunned and remorseful.)

Japan also turned to its colony, Korea. While women were impressed as 'comfort women', prostitutes for the military, in the Greater East Asia Co-Prosperity Sphere, men – perhaps as many as one million – were brought to labour in Japan. Some had no choice; others, like the 'liberated' Malays and Burmese who worked on the Thai–Burma railway, were lured with promises of high wages and good working conditions. Like the Malays and Burmese, they were atrociously treated. On one estimate, as many as 64,000 died.

And Japan turned to its spoils of victory, Allied prisoners of war. The shuffling of groups around the empire began in 1942. They were transported to Formosa, Korea and the home islands. Some were being sent to hard labour and some to interrogation centres. One cargo was made up of the major prizes of the Malayan campaign, Generals Percival and Callaghan and all the senior officers in Changi down to full colonels. What all the various contingents faced was a voyage in deplorable conditions. They also faced danger as they ran the gauntlet of Allied aircraft and submarines. The seas became increasingly unsafe for Japanese ships and all who sailed in them, but even in 1942 it was a lottery.

The *Natuno Maru* sailed from Rabual on July 6. On board were the officers of Lark Force, and 19 women, including six army nurses. The nurses had a difficult three years in Japan. Their clothing issue was a four-yard length of warm material, a pair of briefs and a singlet, tennis socks but no shoes. At times they worked digging air-raid shelters, carrying bundles of wood and cutting down trees. However, they were lucky compared to their fellow nurses on Sumatra. There was little violence from the guards and the civilians were well disposed. None died. They were lucky too compared with Norris Kennedy, the soldier they tried to help escape the invading Japanese by covering in boot black, and compared with the other 'hostages to fortune' of Lark Force taken prisoner.

On June 22, Kennedy was among 1050 troops and 200 civilians who boarded the *Montevideo Maru*. They were headed for a rendezvous with the American submarine *Sturgeon* off the Philippines. *Sturgeon*'s skipper, Lieutenant Commander Wright, reported in his log for June 30:

> At 2216 sighted a darkened ship to the southward . . . Put on all engines and worked up to full power, proceeding westward in an attempt to get ahead of him. For an hour and a half we couldn't make a nickel. This fellow was really going, making at least 17 knots, and probably a bit more, as he appeared to be zig-zagging. At this time it looked a bit hopeless, but determined to hang on in the hope he would slow or change course towards us. His range at the time was estimated at around 18,000 yards. Sure enough, about midnight he slowed to about 12 knots. After that it was easy.

Sturgeon fired four torpedoes. The log records, matter-of-factly: 'At 0240 observed ship sink stern first . . . his bow was well up in the air in six minutes. Dove at dawn. No further contacts.' About 20 Japanese survived. The hostages to fortune disappeared and for more than three years their relatives and loved ones lived in that particular agony of hoping, of not knowing whether they were alive or dead. On October 20,

1945 the Australian Government was informed by the Japanese that the *Montevideo Maru*, port of departure Rabaul, carrying a considerable number of prisoners, had been sunk.

IN 1944, DESPERATE for labour for its wharves, factories and mines, Japan ordered the drafting of 10,000 of the fittest prisoners from camps in the diaspora. From the Bicycle Camp in Java they took Lance Gibson and other members of the 2/3rd Machine Gun Battalion, members of Sparrow Force and other Allied prisoners, a total of about 770. The party of 268 Australians included Allan Chick. It transited through Singapore and in May set off on the *Bijou Maru*, a freighter loaded with bauxite. Gibson went on board with a hangover. The group had been lucky in its interpreter, an American-educated Korean, Minni Sam, who was not much for the Japanese. He had smuggled five officers out of River Valley camp to a Chinese house. They dined on roast suckling pig; they toasted China, Korea, Australia, America and each other with Chinese brandy.

The voyage did not begin auspiciously. An escort was torpedoed the first night out of Singapore. After three days in Manila, the convoy sailed into a typhoon. The *Bijou Maru* limped out the other side, one engine shut down and the cookhouse washed away. At Takao, on Formosa, the prisoners were transferred to a larger, newer vessel, the *Tamahoko Maru*. They were pleased: more space, and a cargo of sugar and pumpkin, which they proceeded to eat their way through. But everyone travelled in tension until Japanese land was in sight, the home island of Kyushu. The next day they were due to berth in Nagasaki. One of the relieved guards organised a concert on a hatch cover. He sang and a Dutchman played his piano accordion. 'Nearer My God to Thee' would have been appropriate.

The night of June 24 was black and *Tang* was waiting. At 9.45 the alert came over *Tang*'s bridge speaker: 'Radar contact, bearing one five zero, range twenty thousand yards.' In half an hour the pretty tune 'The Bells of St Mary's' chimed over the address system, the signal that *Tang* was going about its business of sinking ships and, in what has become known in modern warfare as collateral damage, drowning men. *Tang* stalked the convoy, snaked its way through the escort screen until dead ahead lay, as O'Kane described them, 'the great, fat sterns of the main body'. Nagasaki and safety were only 25 miles away.

This is the way ships die, as described by O'Kane. All six torpedoes were under way. The torpedo run was one minute and 48 seconds, he was told. He watched from the bridge while the seconds were counted down. Then: 'A whack, a flash, and a tremendous rumble came from the freighter's stern. Then from amidships, and her whole side was ripped out. The countdown was resumed only to be smothered by two more explosions. The second ship's stern was a mass of flames, and her super-structure aft crumbled with the second hit. More explosions and accompanying flashes followed, not timed as our tor-pedoes, and within minutes escorts were racing through the holocaust, dropping depth charges singly and in patterns. *Tang* was racing too, for the nearest deep water.'

Gibson was in the forward hold of the *Tamahoko Maru* when the torpedo hit. Around 80 men had been on the hatch cover to escape the stifle. The cover was blown off, they all died and the water rushed into the hold. Gibson jumped over-board, reached the surface in slow seconds, grabbed a breath and saw the tail-end of the ship disappearing towards what O'Kane persisted in calling Davy Jones's locker. A tangle of cables dragged him down again. He struggled back to the surface of a rough sea in a pitch-black night. At dawn

Japanese boats arrived in the area to pick up survivors, Japanese survivors. Prisoners who tried to climb aboard were kicked back into the sea. It was only, Gibson says, when Minni San, the Korean interpreter, argued their case with the Japanese that prisoners were picked up by a boat. 'They also rescued civilians,' Gibson recalled later, 'and one poor little Japanese girl had a little baby which she had managed to hang on to – it was dead of course – and when we were on the way in one of the Jap sailors took a look at it, saw it was dead, took it from her and heaved it over'. Also down in Davy Jones's locker were 560 of the 772 prisoners of war who had sailed on the *Tamahoko Maru*. Allan Chick was among the survivors.

THE MEN WHO walked up the gangway of *Tamahoko Maru* in Formosa had been relieved to leave the shabby *Bijou Maru* behind; the 1250 Australians who boarded the *Rashin Maru* at Singapore on July 4 were appalled by the condition of their rusted, battered vessel. It was about the size of a Sydney Harbour ferry. There was a gaping hole where the bridge should have been and the Japanese captain, a merchant seaman, skippered from a jury-rigged box-like structure on the poop deck. There were no forward hatch covers. Two great steel girders ran the length of the ship, welded to the decking which had dropped 40 centimetres. Apparently they were all that prevented the *Rashin Maru* breaking in two. Its armament was a brass, wheeled, bell-mouthed, muzzle-loading cannon and the ammunition, iron cannon balls. Built in 1912, the *Rashin Maru* began life regally under the name *Canadian Princess*, became the *Potomac*, was sold to Japan for scrap in 1923 but sailed on as a tramp steamer. In Febuary 1942 it was bombed and burnt out in the Java Sea, towed to Singapore, and patched up. *Rashin* means compass needle. Petty Officer Horry Abbott of *Perth* looked at it with a sailor's eye. It had to be called *Byoki*; it was a bloody sick ship, he said. And so, finally, the *Canadian Princess* became the *Byoki Maru*, the sick ship.

The *Byoki Maru* sailed from Singapore as part of a 14-ship convoy. It carried as cargo a small load of baled rubber and the Australian prisoners, including *Perth*'s Ray Parkin and Sparrow Force's Neil Dawson and Tom Uren, under the command of the redoubtable Roaring Reg Newton, as well as myriad lice, bugs and flies. The cautious convoy made a quick run east to Borneo, hugged the coast and then stayed in the shadow of a chain of islands on the way to Manila. There was the usual rice pap with additions of maggoty, rotten dried fish and there was the usual stench in the cramped holds. Sometimes, the way cruise ships do, the *Byoki Maru* and its companions anchored in idyllic bays. Then for three weeks the *Byoki Maru* hove to in Manila Bay. The men's health declined and the clouds of flies thickened. The Japanese response was to order each man to kill 10 flies a day. Tom Uren's boxer's reflexes came in handy.

The *Byoki Maru* sailed again in a convoy of about 30. One day out, on a calm sea where even a battered tramp could behave like a princess, the *Byoki Maru*, riding high in the water, was actually leading one of the two columns, a proud position, but exposed. American submarines struck. They torpedoed two plump tankers astern. Amid a flurry of the escorts and a salvo of depth charges, the convoy sailed on in fear. What happened two days later was terrifying. The *Byoki Maru* bucked, tossed and pitched in giant waves sucked up by a typhoon. At times the men in the uncovered holds could look out horizontally at walls of water. Welds holding the girders to the deck came apart. Parkin, who knew too much about the sea, was convinced after a series of five violent rolls that the ship was about to turn straight over. While prisoners struggled to the engine room with coal to keep the boilers going, the captain managed to steer the *Byoki Maru* to the shelter of the Mabudis islets.

Seventy days after leaving Singapore, the *Byoki Maru* reached Moji, on Kyushu. Parkin delivered a sailor's highest praise: this sick ship had a soul. What started out as derision became a term of affection. Among Neil Dawson's souvenirs, along with Miss Iris Flight's letter, is an impressive piece of parchment. 'Blue water certificate', it is headed. 'This is to certify,' it says, 'that TX3395 Dawson N.T. was on the Singapore-Japan tourist cruise of the Good Derelict *Byoki Maru*, July 1944.' At an international prisoner-of-war reunion in 1986, a former American submarine commander told of an attack on a convoy off the Philippines in August 1944. He had looked at the leading ship. It was a wreck, he thought, and he told his men not to waste a torpedo on it. It became folklore among those who sailed on the *Byoki Maru* that the sick ship was a lucky ship.

The *Rokyu Maru* and the *Kachidoki Maru* weren't. On September 6, 2300 men under the command of Arthur Varley, the skilled, pragmatic leader of A Force on the railway, were formed up to march to the docks. It was a straggle, really, men thin to the point of emaciation carrying their small bundles of possessions. Some wrapped the little they had in blankets, swagmen prisoners. Ray Wheeler was among them, and Bob Collins of *Perth*. Chinese and Malays along the streets watched them in silence and in pity.

About 1000 British troops boarded the *Kachidoki Maru*. About 1250 Australians and British, including Varley, boarded the *Rokyu Maru*, pushed into the forward hold which in normal times carried a maximum of 187 steerage passengers.

The Japanese had divided the hold horizontally into two decks with a ceiling height of no more than 22 centimetres. These were typical hell ships. Those survivors of A Force remembered without fondness the *Mayebassi Maru* which had carried them to Burma and work on the railway. But the *Kachidoki Maru* and the *Rokyu Maru* were heading into perilous seas. The men knew by now of submarine strikes. Before embarkation, Varley buried his diary in Changi. With his usual attention to the welfare of his men, he organised former *Perth* sailors and former merchant mariners to assist army officers if they had to abandon ship. A premonition, perhaps.

The convoy took its own precautions. The two transports, two other passenger-cargo vessels and two fully-laden tankers were escorted by a destroyer, *Shikinani*, and three escorts. Overhead flew two float planes. Every seven minutes the convoy changed directions. It was zigging and zagging towards a wolf pack.

In 1942 American intelligence and communications officers at Pearl Harbor opened a gold mine of information. They broke a Japanese naval code. The decoded Japanese messages were given the top-secret designation, 'Ultra'. As the Japanese and American fleets shaped up for what was to be the crucial Battle of Midway in June, the American admirals had intelligence on the timing of Japanese actions and approach paths of their carriers. It was a lucky failure of Japanese intelligence that kept such vital information flowing for the rest of the war. Even as dive-bombers from the *Enterprise* and the *Yorktown* were devastating the Japanese flagship *Akagi* and its sister ship *Kaga*, the secret of the breaking of the code was being revealed. A Japanese agent in America only had to go to a newsstand and buy a copy of the *Chicago Tribune* to read on the front page 'Navy Had Word of Jap Plan to Strike at Sea'. Loose navy lips and a foolish journalist informed the public that the navy had learnt 'of the gathering of the powerful naval units soon after they put forth from their bases'. While the White House and the navy were trying to keep attention away from the revelation, a congressman went on the attack over 'this unthinking and wicked misusing of freedom of the press', helpfully emphasising that 'somehow our Navy had secured and broken the secret code of the Japanese Navy'.

The code-breakers held their breath. But nothing changed. So in September 1944 the skippers of the American submarines *Growler*, *Pampanito* and *Sealion* received Ultras alerting them to the approach of the *Shikinani*-led convoy. Would they have known that there were prisoners of war on board? Don Wall, in his book *Heroes at Sea*, argues that as the code-breakers in most cases knew what cargoes the freighters were carrying, it is reasonable to assume they would know whether they were also carrying troops or prisoners of war. But, he continues, it is unlikely that ComSubPac (the Commander of Submarine Forces in the Pacific) would have disclosed this information to the skippers; their job was to sink ships.

Early on September 12 the convoy was in the South China Sea. The *Shikinani* was leading the middle of three columns, with three frigates on each flank. Ray Wheeler was in the hold of the *Rokyu Maru*, hunched head on knees, trying to sleep. *Growler* struck. The *Shikinani* sank. Wheeler knew they were in desperate trouble. The remaining escorts did what they could, dashing about and dropping depth charges. The transports zigged and zagged. A few hours later, the pack attacked. There was an explosion, a glare that penetrated the gloom of the hold, and screaming and shouting on deck. *Sealion* had fired six torpedoes at a tanker and then hit another transport. Some of the prisoners who tried to force their way out of the hold were beaten back by Japanese with the butts of their rifles. They threatened to shoot. The *Rokyu Maru*, in the brightness of burning ships, had nowhere to hide. It lifted from the water when the first torpedo hit near amidships. The second holed the bow. The *Rokyu Maru* wallowed and the Japanese began abandoning ship. This was the time of Frank McGrath's revenge. A member of the tough 2/2nd Pioneers that had fought in Syria and Java, McGrath was bitter towards the Japanese. A tall man, he had been a target for their bashings. Once along the railway a Japanese guard stood on a box to hit him. He told his mates he would get square. As the Japanese came down from the bridge, he belted them and when a mate looked back as he was going overboard, McGrath was still punching. Perhaps it was sweet, but McGrath himself sank beneath the South China Sea two days later.

Ray Wheeler, wounded by debris, hauled himself out of the hold by a steel cable. He looked over the stern and saw two tankers burning and spewing oil into the sea. He watched a Japanese crewman jump into the flames and disappear. Also to the stern was an American passenger ship that had been captured in Shanghai. Wheeler had seen it close up as they left Singapore, with a happy group of Japanese women, children and officers on board returning home. It too was burning and 44-gallon drums on the deck were exploding, firing themselves into the air, landing on the oil-slicked water and sending blue flames skipping across the waves. He and two mates, Snowy Walker and Bobby Dart, decided to stay on board for a while.

Bob Collins also saw the sense in not jumping too soon. He was arguing with an Allied lieutenant who was shouting to abandon ship that they shouldn't go over the side unprepared. This is where experience comes in handy. When the officer ordered him to obey, he said: 'Look sir, I've been sunk before.' Collins had left the *Perth* cradling Redlead, the ship's cat; he eventually went over the side of the *Rokyu Maru* with Burke and John Cobon, 26-year-old identical twins from Crows Nest, Queensland, who always stuck together.

Around midday when the *Rokyu Maru* had only a few feet of freeboard left and was making death groans, Wheeler, Walker and Dart threw a hatch cover over, dropped quietly into the water and pushed it on a twisting path through patches of burning oil. The sea was speckled with wreckage. Men clung to planks, rafts and flotsam. They watched and hoped as Japanese boats picked a way among them. Arthur (Blood) Bancroft, another *Perth* veteran of sinkings, was in a group with a Japanese officer in their midst. There had been some discussion about whether they should drown him but they decided he might be a ticket to ride. When a destroyer approached, they got him to stand up and wave. The destroyer dropped a boat which rowed across. While the prisoners were fended off, their ticket was taken on board. The destroyer steamed off and then did a sweep towards them then veered away, the crew jeering. 'We gave back just as good as we got,' Blood Bancroft has recounted, '[calling out to the Japanese] "You'll get yours, you yella bastard!" Things like that. And we started singing *Rule Britannia*.'

Ray Wheeler had joined about 200 in a loose cluster. A Japanese launch off a destroyer worked its way back and forward as it picked up its own. An officer armed with a Luger stood in the bow. 'Goodbye,' he said, 'you all die. Goodbye, you all die.' 'Hope the bloody sub gets you,' Wheeler thought. He watched as the destroyer sailed towards another Japanese warship. They were exchanging signals. Blink. Blink. Blink. BANG. The torpedo hit amidships, the superstructure of the frigate went up in the air, and Wheeler, his wish granted, watched matchstick figures fall to the sea, watched the frigate break in two and watched the halves disappear.

The Japanese ships dropped their last depth charges and picked up their last survivors. Gradually the sea became silent, except for the murmur of men and occasional screams. Life and death became a matter of chance. Groups sometimes coalesced, sometimes fragmented. Currents in the water and whims took men in different directions. Luck put some men on lifeboats abandoned by rescued Japanese while others crowded on makeshift rafts that rode beneath the surface. Some had swum back to the *Royku Maru* as it took its time to sink and found food, water and wonderful cigarettes. Most had no food and no water. The water bottles they carried were three or four years old and the salt water seeped through porous corks in an hour. Over the horizon, *Pampanito* was still hunting the fleeing remnants of the convoy. At 10.40 that night, it fired three torpedoes at the *Kachidoki Maru*. Nine hundred British prisoners of war were cast upon the waters.

Many men died that first day, survivors of the *Perth* sinking, survivors of the railway and its brutality and survivors of disease. Among them were the Cobon twins, who had become separated from Bob Collins. Ian MacDiarmid, a mate from their 2/10th Field Regiment, was in one of the abandoned Japanese boats. Light was fading, a storm coming, the sea chopping up and currents clashing. MacDiarmid threw a rope towards the Cobons. It was not long enough. They weren't seen again.

Those in the boats cooeed and rowed towards answering cooees. Sometimes they found people; sometimes they didn't. Overnight in the darkness men just slipped away from rafts and life. The next day the boats had come together in two groups. They rowed in different directions. The men in the boats under the leadership of Chief Petty Officer Vic Duncan of *Perth* were picked up by a Japanese frigate. Two other frigates appeared on the horizon where the other group had last been seen. Men from one of the boats in Duncan's group heard machine-gun fire. What happened is not positively known but the indications are a massacre. Brigadier Arthur

Varley and the men he was travelling with disappeared without trace.

Ray Wheeler and his mates Snowy Walker and Bobby Dart stayed close together on one of the semi-submerged rafts through the burning days. On the third night Walker and Dart died a mercifully quiet death. They had been drinking sea water. They wouldn't listen to anyone. They were gutted on sea water. All Wheeler could do was close their eyes and push them off. At daylight he saw Blood Bancroft and several others on some flotsam and jetsam but they seemed to be sitting out of the water as they drifted towards the horizon. He shouted that he would try to catch them up. Two hours, he thought, he could do it in that, but he got more and more tired and had only closed the distance a little. He saw another, small raft, with two men on it. He swam over to have a break. They were British, Poms, and they were drinking sea water and urine. 'You're pinching our water,' they said. Both of them had a whack at him and he swam away after Bancroft. Five hours, swimming and drifting, then someone had hold of him through the slipperiness of the oil that coated him. Someone lashed him to a raft. Then there were five. Another drifted up, Phil Beilby. The sea had brought together six men who had got to know one another working on the railway.

The fourth day was a doldrums day for the hundreds paddling or drifting across calm, blue-copper water. There was more dying, and the living eased themselves now and again into the water for passing coolness. They talked of haircuts and menus, of preferring not to be picked up by the Japs. They floated among illusions and delusions. In one group sitting on a raft chest-deep in water, Bill Cunneen, big, tough, a sergeant, said: 'I'm responsible for you men. Hand me that bucket. There's a camp over behind that hill and I'll go and get you a bucket of water.' They shouted: 'Oh, sit down Cunneen.' Sometime later Cunneen said: 'I can hear a motor.'

CAPTAIN'S LOG, USS *Pampanito*:

While patrolling on the surface on an easterly heading from Hainan Island in the South China Sea, Latitude 189°42'N, Longitude 114°00'E, the OOD and bridge lookouts sighted a lifeboat and a large quantity of debris floating on the surface of a calm sea. This spot was a little to the north of where an enemy convoy had been intercepted and attacked by our wolf pack on the night of 11-12 September 1944. There was the possibility of the lifeboat being occupied so course was altered only to find it abandoned. At this time, 1610(I), a lookout reported that there were two rafts on the horizon with men on them. It was naturally believed that they were Japanese, so small arms were broken out and preparations made for taking prisoners.

On the approach to the first raft, which was a makeshift affair of hatch covers and timbers, it was noted that the fifteen men it contained were thickly covered with crude oil and were clothed very scantily, though some had nondescript hats and a few wore the regulation Japanese soldier's caps. They were waving frantically and all shouting at will so that no words could be distinguished, although one voice was finally heard to speak distinctly in English. While getting the raft alongside, orders were given to bring aboard the English-speaking man, and by the time the first line was over the amazing announcement came to the bridge: 'They are British and Australian prisoner-of-war shipwreck survivors'.

Pampanito radioed *Sealion* for assistance. *Pampanito* moved towards a second raft and took bearings on three more. It passed a small raft carrying a dead man, picked up 11 men in another group, gathered in another man on a small raft, almost blind and semi-conscious (he died the following evening, the captain reported), followed at high speed the bearing of a raft which had disappeared over the horizon to the south and rescued in the dark another 13 men. *Pampanito* had gathered 73 men from the sea.

At just after 6.30 that evening, about an hour before sunset, *Sealion* made its first sighting of survivors. It formed a rescue team of three swimmers, a hauling-out party and a delivery and stripping party to get the oil-covered men on board. *Sealion*'s log records: 'When darkness came, fifty-four survivors had been rescued. How many of the thirteen hundred prisoners still lived among the bales and boxes cannot be estimated. Even if daylight had lingered, only a very few more could have been taken on board. The fortunate ones whom we saved required nursing, care, medicine and hospitalisation.' Bob Collins of *Perth* was fortunate; still adrift on their set of rafts were Bancroft, Wheeler and their four companions. They had watched a submarine moving back and forward across the sea, sometimes stopping, sometimes heading towards them, then turning away. Bill Smith, Regimental Sergeant Major with the 10th Field Artillery, had tied his shirt to an oar. He was waving it and shouting: 'Over here, you silly buggers. We're over here.' The others called out too but they heard the diesel engines increase power. The submarine disappeared into the darkness, leaving a silent group of men on the silent sea.

RAY WHEELER CAN see an island. It has a jetty on it. He drifts towards it. His father Fred (who is fighting the Japanese in Borneo) is standing there. Fred calls out: 'Ray, would you like a beer?' He is holding something in his hand, maybe a bunch of bananas. He calls out again: 'Ray, can the Japs hurt me?'

Ray shouts back: 'No, they will never hurt you, Pop.'

Wheeler woke to the tossing of the raft and the shaking of one of his mates who asked whom he was speaking to.

A few days after Wheeler was reunited with his family, his mother Florence showed him a letter. Fred Wheeler had written it from Labuan on Borneo. He told Florence he had talked to Ray the night before. Florence had taken the letter down to her Methodist church in Richmond and shown it to the minister. After the war, when he heard Ray Wheeler had returned, he asked him to come down and deliver a sermon on the strange ways in which God moved.

THE SIXTH DAY the waves were building up and the men lashed themselves to the rafts. Then, above the whine of the wind they heard the steady, powerful beat of a diesel engine. A voice called: 'Hi. Can any of you guys catch?' *Queenfish* had found them. Five hundred and forty-three Australian prisoners of war on the *Rokyu Maru* were lost, including 33 men from *Perth* who had faced double jeopardy. The submariners were shocked at the condition of the survivors. They had expected them to be wretched: the effects of the depth charges sown by the Japanese escorts, oil, sun, lack of food, lack of water would have sapped the strongest. But all the survivors showed signs of long, sustained suffering. They were emaciated. They bore the marks of, or still had a bewildering range of tropical diseases: beri-beri, ulcers, malaria, pellagra. Some were near blind. Most carried the scars of beatings. They told their rescuers the story of three terrible lost years and the deaths of thousands. The world was about to find out the truth of the Japanese and their treatment of prisoners of war.

The earliest report to the Australian Government on life in a prison camp had given false comfort. Lieutenant Bill Jinkins, of Gull Force, escaped with six other Australians from Ambon after six weeks in captivity. Stealing a *prau*, the group island-hopped to Australia. Like some other Australians, Jinkins had personal experience of the true spirit of *bushido*. The Dutch officer who commanded Allied forces on Ambon, Lieutenant Colonel Kapitz, had been taken prisoner on February 1, 1942. Jinkins, getting word that Kapitz had written a note on the Dutch surrender to Gull Force commander William Scott, rode a bicycle to a Japanese roadblock. He asked to see a 'shogun' and was taken to Major Harikawa who arranged a meeting with Kapitz. Harikawa drove Jinkins, with the note, to the Japanese front-line. He gave him a captured AIF motorcycle to use, shook his hand and said: 'If you do not come back, I hope we shall meet in the field.'

Back in Australia Jinkins delivered the good news: 'The treatment by the Japs was as fair as it could be.' The day began with physical training. The men played sport and did courses including law, motor mechanics and English literature while the battalion band practised.

The escape of Jinkins's group was a catalyst for a hardening of Japanese attitudes. The penalty for escape and concealing escape would be death. If escapers were not recaptured an equal number of prisoners of equivalent rank would be executed. The Ambon camp became one of the worst of places. The Allied governments would not discover this until after the war, but they would have known in 1943 from secret sources such as Boonpong and the V organisation that something bad was happening along the Thai–Burma railway. With the rescue by the American submarines of survivors of their attacks, the governments now had the detailed testimony of those who had been victims of brutality and eyewitnesses to atrocities.

On November 17, 1944 the British Secretary of State for War, Sir James Grigg, and Australia's Acting Prime Minister, Frank Forde, made coordinated statements to their parliaments. For those tens of thousand who lived in hope for their missing there was a new certainty and an inescapable, painful uncertainty. No more could they take any comfort in postcards like the one Doris Mulvena received from Wally: 'I am well. We have concerts.' They were forced lies, mockeries.

In Canberra, Forde went to the Dispatch Box and moved the adjournment motion. He gave details of the last voyage of the *Rokyu Maru*, the sinking and the rescues. 'After the men had been accommodated in a convalescent home in Australia,' Forde said, 'opportunity was taken to have them compile lists of their comrades who had been on board the sunken transport and also to obtain a first-hand story of how the Japanese have treated Allied prisoners of war in Burma and Thailand.' Detail followed detail, a steady drumbeat that fed anger and fear: many of the men wore only loincloths; food consisted of a pannikin of rice and about a pint of watery stew a day; sick men ordered to work; doctors did their best but sickness and deaths were inevitable; amputations of limbs by local anaesthetic; work shifts increased from 12 hours to 18 hours a day, sometimes exceeding 24 hours of continuous work.

Then the inevitable, logical conclusion: 'It is deeply regretted that, at this stage, it cannot be stated how many Australians have died. An early estimate places the death toll in Burma and Thailand at about 2000 out of approximately 10,000 Australians. It is hoped that this estimate will prove too high, but unfortunately it may turn out to be an understatement.' Forde spoke of the matchless courage of the men. They had shown themselves undaunted in the face of death. 'The many others who have survived privations and disease in the jungle have developed spiritual and physical powers to triumph over adversity and over their captors. Let us look forward to the day of their release.' In the House of Commons, at the end of Grigg's statement a member asked that it be sent 'to Dublin for the benefit of the Japanese consul-general who is residing in that city'. Perhaps the parliamentarian thought the Japanese would be moved by shame or by pragmatic concern about their international reputation to change their ways. If so, he was mistaken. Mistreatment would continue and there were atrocities to come.

However, the Australian Government kept to itself news of one of the worst atrocities of the war. The story of the massacre of the nurses on Banka Island in 1942 had spread, in secret anger, through the prison camps along the railway. The survivors of the *Rokyu Maru* brought it home with them. But obviously the government realised, as the surviving nurses and their fellow prisoners did, that witnesses to that horror would be in mortal danger from the Japanese.

RICHARD O'KANE, WHO retired from the navy with the rank of rear admiral, died in February 1994 of pneumonia and was given a hero's funeral at Arlington National Cemetery, burial place of America's military dead. His last years had been hard. The old submariner was lost in the fog of Alzheimer's disease. His wife Ernestine had to lock the doors and windows because he often tried to get out of the house. He was Captain O'Kane again and he had to reach his men and the sinking *Tang*.

CHAPTER 23

Things do taste better from silver spoons

The body weighs perhaps 35 kilograms. The living are much like the dead, skin and bones, and 20 of them carry the coffin. This is how they do it. Three poles are placed underneath and, three women to each end, 18 lift them. One person walks ahead, holding her hands behind her to steady the coffin and to watch the track ahead. The twentieth steadies it from behind. Australian nurses, prisoners of the Japanese at a derelict rubber plantation in Sumatra, are burying their own.

Sixty-five had escaped from Singapore two days before the fall; at war's end there would be 24 survivors, barely enough for a burial party. In mid-April 1945, they helped bury Margaret Dryburgh, a pioneer Scottish missionary in China and Malaya, gifted musician and composer. She wrote 'The Captives' Hymn'.

Father, in captivity, we
Would lift our prayer to Thee
Keep us ever in Thy love,
Grant that daily we may prove
Those who place their trust in Thee,
More than conquerors may be.

Give us patience to endure,
Keep our hearts serene and pure
Grant us courage, charity,
Greater faith, humility,
Readiness to own Thy will,
Be we free or captives still.

The story of the 24 surviving nurses, like the story of most prisoners of war in the diaspora, is one of endurance. Their friends died in different ways: drowning, cold massacre, casual brutality, and from a variety of diseases. Beri-beri, dysentery, malaria and fevers flourished among the malnourished. Then there were the small, puzzling acts of inhumanity. Why dump a meagre supply of vegetables on the road outside the camp gate and not allow collection for two days or so while they rotted in the sun? Captivity stretched on: adequate food and clean water denied; adequate medicine denied; adequate cooking fuel denied; in 1944, skeletal figures, hammering for eight hours a day at rock-hard earth with *chunkels,* heavy hoes, to try to turn the parade ground into a garden to supply their own food; the 'strong' ill, who could barely lift a *chunkel,* digging graves for the internees.

These were the possible fates awaiting Pat Gunther and her best friend, Kath Neuss, as they sailed through Sydney Heads on the *Queen Mary*, assured by Lady Gowrie, the Governor-General's wife, that they were part of the luckiest group of nurses to leave Australia. In this saga of misfortune, Pat was the luckier of the two, though at times she would wish she could change places with dead Kath.

They went in style on the old *Queen*. Gunther remembers nurses bubbling with excitement and the dazzle and dance with officers in uniform in the grand saloon. The *Queen Mary* docked in Singapore naval base, home of the phantom force that was supposed to be the might of the British navy in the Far East. It was February 18, 1941.

The nurses crossed the causeway between Singapore and the Malayan mainland by train bound for Malacca. Lady Gowrie was right so far. Malacca is on the west coast, a fabled spice port with a charming river squiggling inland. Down the centuries Malacca had been the home of a Chinese princess, of Portuguese St Francis Xavier and then his tomb for a time, and of Armenians escaping one of their early and endless persecutions. The centre of the town is old Dutch, stolidly colourful, painted ochre-red. In Malacca and the other straits settlements, Penang and Singapore, Chinese migrants married Malay women, and produced, along with tribes of children, the distinctive Nonya cuisine, hot, spicy and pungently aromatic.

The nurses were welcome strangers, single women usually with a sense of fun, but respectable. They were the daughters, mostly, of the Australian middle class and lower middle class, but they were also the daughters of Florence Nightingale. They were guests in the almost-best homes. Gunther remembers a dinner party given by a Chinese millionaire. He had first come to Malaya as a coolie. Now he owned tin mines. His daughter, slender and elegant, would have graced any saloon, Gunther thought, innocent then of colour bars. After dinner the host played the violin, with a beatific expression on his face.

They went to the Spotted Dog at the Selangor Club, favourite nightspot for planter society, sipped stingahs and watched one of life's little melodramas/tragedies play out. A beautiful Eurasian frequently accompanied a young British officer. What a fine couple, grace on the dance floor, almost made for each other. A whisper to Pat and Kath: 'Such a shame. If they married, there would be no further promotion for him.' That was the rule, you see. Eurasians were not socially acceptable to the British or to the Asians.

After the Japanese landed in the north on December 8, life changed for everyone: millionaires, star-crossed couples and nurses. Soldiers were relentlessly pushed back down the Malaya peninsula. The nurses were trucked back to Singapore, often among the retreating troops. Gunther's hospital set up in Manor House and Oldham Hall, on the north side of the city. She was in charge of a makeshift ward: two concrete tennis courts covered by a huge marquee, not exactly bomb-proof. There Gunther nursed soldiers wounded by the Japanese and dazed by the force of the onslaught. She asked a 19-year-old how he had crossed the Muar River during one of the few stand-and-fight battles. 'Sister, we were walking on dead bodies,' he said.

On February 11, 1942 the matron called Gunther's unit, the 10th Australian General Hospital, together. She had been ordered to send half the nurses back to Australia. Would those who were prepared to stay move to her side? Every one of the nurses did. Gunther and Neuss were among those who were picked to stay, and this was definitely bad luck. The 65 departing nurses were told to board the *Empire Star*, a large transport. Despite wave attacks by 50 bombers, and two hits, the *Empire Star* reached Australia. Two nurses who treated wounded during attacks were decorated for bravery. Only one nurse died, of amoebic dysentery.

The Singapore hospital was reorganised and Gunther took over two houses. That night big defending guns blasted nearby, plaster fell onto the wounded, windows rattled and a piano tinkled. A group of soldiers was sheltering in one of the rooms, among them a pianist from Mario's nightclub in Melbourne, playing and replaying popular tunes.

The day after the *Empire Star* sailed, a complete evacuation was ordered. It was one of the worst moments of her life, Gunther said, leaving her patients. Gunther, Neuss and their group made their slow way through the rack and ruin of the city to the *Vyner Brooke*. The former pleasure yacht of the White Rajah of Sarawak was designed to carry 12; 300 men, women and children scrambled on board. Slow, old and armed with one 2-inch gun, the *Vyner Brooke* had no chance. The captain hid her in mangroves overnight and tried to keep to the cover of islands during the day. On February 14, having been strafed once and losing several lifeboats, she was bombed. Jessie Simons counted 27 explosions. Sylvia Muir remembered shrapnel flying: '. . . the poor old fellow right beside me had his stomach ripped open. He was sitting there. I can still see him, hanging on and singing "Britons never never will be slaves". So it must be something we British, or ex-British, do.'

The stricken *Vyner Brooke* listed to starboard. Passengers jumped into the sea or slid down ropes. Kath Neuss was bleeding from her left hip. Pat Gunther helped her down a ladder to a lifeboat that was filling quickly with women and children. Gunther gave Neuss the tin hat she was carrying with her. Perhaps she would need it to bail the boat. With another friend, Win Davis, Gunther swam away. The *Vyner Brooke* sank quickly leaving on the oily surface bodies, bobbing heads and small groups in the remaining lifeboats or clinging to wreckage and rafts. Gunther and Davis drifted to a raft already heavily laden with two British women, a sailor, a badly burned gunner, the ship's radio operator and Jessie Simons. Simons slipped out of her dress and draped it round the gunner, whose uniform had been burned away, to protect him from the sun. Gunther gave him some morphine tables but he drifted off sometime during the night. The rest on the raft would reach land but Gunther would never see Kath Neuss again. When she returned to Australia after the war, Gunther wanted to see Neuss's mother. She hadn't met her before. The mother refused. 'The girls were always together,' she told friends. 'Why didn't they stay together? Why wasn't Kath on the raft?'

Through that night, the raft drifted and swirled in the current. Once out of the darkness swept an elderly man lying back in his lifebelt, his unlit pipe stuck jauntily, Simons recalled, between his teeth. Shortly after, the current took him into the darkness again. For a time they bumped and weaved among the Japanese ships invading Sumatra. Later they saw a bonfire on the beach at Banka Island, a large island just off the coast. These were surely *Vyner Brooke* survivors, and so they tried to swim and tow the raft towards welcoming flames but the current dragged them out and away: this time Pat Gunther was lucky.

The people round the fire on Banka Island were Kath Neuss, Vivian Bulwinkel, 20 other nurses, some women with children and a number of wounded men from the lifeboat. Others had swum ashore. A day later it was decided that a naval officer would walk into the town of Muntok to ask the Japanese for help with the wounded. As the day grew hotter, the women with children left to look for a village and food, water and shelter. The nurses stayed with the wounded men. When the officer returned with a Japanese patrol, the men were separated from the nurses and taken round a bluff. The Japanese returned alone, wiping their bayonets. The nurses were then told to line up facing the sea and walk towards it. They were machine-gunned from behind. A bullet passed through Vivian Bulwinkel's hip and she was hurled headlong into the water. She floated until the Japanese lost interest and then crawled into the jungle. Kath Neuss's body rocked in the waves.

Gunther and the group on the raft were still within tantalising sight of the Sumatran shore, kept out by the current, when they were taken aboard a small Japanese landing craft. The Japanese soldier in charge picked up a *parang*, a heavy, long-bladed knife. He reached to the bottom of the boat for a coconut, sliced the top off and passed it to the women. On shore they were taken to an abandoned house where they scavenged odds and ends of clothing. As Win Davis and Gunther sat on a log, a young Japanese pilot walked by. He stopped, took off his long leather flying boots, then his socks. He gave his socks to Gunther.

The Australian nurses, fleeing civilians and captured military personnel, Dutch, British Commonwealth and a scattering of Americans, joined 70,000 Dutch women and children as captives of the Japanese throughout Dutch Indonesia. The Japanese coming had been foretold in 1160 AD by Joyoboyo, King of Kediri, in east Java:

> For ten generations a great white buffalo will plough the rice fields of Ismoyo (Java). This will be a time of suffering and deep sorrow. When the people have finally accepted the Divine Will as their own, God, in his mercy, will send them an ally. A little yellow monkey from the island of Tembini will rule over Ismoyo for the life of one maize plant. Only then will Ismoyo return to its people, to its right rulers, to the sons of the earth.

Shirley Fenton Huie, who quotes this prophecy in her study, *The Forgotten Ones,* says it was used to rally support for Indonesian independence in the struggle against Dutch colonialism. The interpretation is simple, up to a point. The great white buffalo is, of course, the Dutch. Nice image. The little yellow monkey is the Japanese. They would not have liked that. The difficulty is interpreting 'the life of one maize plant'. The time from planting to harvesting is three and a half months. Certainly not long enough. Perhaps it meant the span from one planting to the next, about eight months. But the Japanese were still there, and growing increasingly unpopular with their 'younger brothers'. With lateral thinking, the interpreters decided that it referred to the length of time a corncob could be stored and retain its vitality: three years, close enough to the three-and-half years the Japanese had the country in their grasp.

One of the younger brothers was Bambang Soemardjo, who after Indonesian independence was active in the trade union movement and an opponent of the Suharto regime. In 1942 Soemardjo, a 19-year-old senior high school student, was conscripted to the Dutch civil air defence. His post was 12 kilometres from one of the Japanese invasion points. As instructed he destroyed his transmitter then fled. He was sheltered by an Indonesian family in a nearby town for a month. But it was a time of hope. He was a fledgling nationalist, opposed to the Dutch tuans. His people were poor and oppressed. At school, children had to learn Dutch and were forbidden to speak their native language. Propagandists had spread the message that the Japanese big brothers would come as liberators.

Soemardjo got a job in the railway system and trained as a service regulator. Doubts about the Japanese soon grew. Every day he saw prisoners passing through his station, Dutch women and children, packed into goods wagons in appalling conditions, treated inhumanely. Indonesian officials were appointed as administrators and the language blossomed, but the maltreatment began and arrogance replaced brotherly love. In 1943, his mother became ill with malaria and fell into a coma for nearly a month. There was no medical treatment available and for this Soemardjo blamed the Japanese.

Those three and a half years were long ones for Soemardjo, who felt one coloniser had been replaced by another. They were an eternity for the prisoners struggling to survive.

IF THE SEARCH for an explanation for the Japanese treatment of prisoners of war leads to the perversion of the spirit of *bushido*, the belief that soldiers who surrendered had forfeited their right to live, in what dark place lies the explanation for the treatment of non-combatant civilians, especially women?

George Brouwer finished his professional life as a senior public servant, head of the Victorian Premier's Department but came out of retirement to serve as Ombudsman. We met for coffee at a Melbourne sidewalk café. Brouwer began life on a coffee and rubber plantation in Indonesia. 'The Japanese simply treated men and women with equal brutality,' Brouwer said. His father Jan, who managed the plantation, had migrated from Holland when he was 18. His mother Josephine was born in the Indies of Irish-German parents. Jan Brouwer was interned soon after the Japanese invasion, leaving Josephine on the plantation with George, then four and a half, and his brother Robbert, who was 10. One day the Japanese caught a Dutch soldier on the plantation. His mother hadn't known he was there in the jungle, George Brouwer said, but the Japanese accused her of hiding him. They took her away and they tortured her for two weeks. They put their thumbs on her eyes, pushing deeper and deeper, saying she would be blinded. They had noticed a piano in her home. 'She was very musical,' George Brouwer said. They smashed the piano and then smashed her fingers so she would never play the piano again. They interned her with George but, and this was cruelty too, sent 10-year-old Robbert to a different camp. Robbert almost died in captivity. He was desperately ill at the time of liberation. George should have died. In the camp he used to sleep packed between his cousins, Donald and Goldie. Cholera stalked the camp, highly contagious. It took nine-year-old Donald from one side of George and then, quickly, 17-year-old Goldie from the other.

After the war, Jan Brouwer was most unforgiving; 'a Friesian,' George Brouwer said, 'in the Calvanist tradition'. Yet Josephine Brouwer did not hate. She would say there were good Japanese and bad Japanese, like everyone. The torturers were Korean Japanese, brought in for the job, but some camp guards would smuggle in lollies and leave them under her mat as a comfort. George Brouwer himself looks back on the Japanese with some gratitude. 'They did have a sense of duty, you know. At war's end, our camp was under attack from Indonesian nationalists who wanted to drive the Dutch from their country at last. They had rifles and hand grenades. The Japanese were prepared to defend us with their lives.' Little yellow monkey comes to the aid of white buffalo; not in the prophecy.

LIKE THE MEN in many camps throughout the diaspora, women lived to a pattern of grind and endurance, with sudden, unpredictable acts of violence. Shirley Huie tells the story of Dr Engel, one of three doctors caring for 4000 Dutch women and children in Solo camp in Central Java. She is described as tiny, looking a little like Madame Curie, with light grey, almost white curly hair, pulled back from her ears into a tight knot at the nape of her neck. One day she stood face to face with a high-ranking Japanese officer. She had moved past him to attend a fainting woman. She had not bowed, a terrible offence. The officer slapped Dr Engel's face; she slapped him back. The officer drew his sword; she grabbed it and pulled it from his hands. He ordered her locked up in a small cage, with no sanitary arrangements. She was beaten, kicked around head and body.

For months the women heard only vague rumours that she was still alive. Then on the birthday of *Tenno Heika* (Heavenly

Father, the Emperor of Japan) they were allowed to make a wish. Anneke, Huie's source and witness, said: 'The Japs expected us to ask for extra food but almost without exception we requested that Dr Engel be brought back to us. To our great surprise, our wish was granted. She was a broken old woman in body but not broken in mind by any means.' Later dysentery killed her.

THE 32 NURSES had washed up on Sumatra in February 1942 with nothing but their wits and spirit. They were taken to a coolie camp, dirty and basic, and there the survivors tried to find out about family and friends. 'You were on the *Vyner Brooke*,' they would say to Gunther. 'Do you remember a woman . . . ?' and they would describe her. Gunther could only remember one. She held on to her for so long that she couldn't hold on any longer, and she was frothing at the mouth anyway and she was unconscious. So she would say, 'I do remember a lady. She was fair and plump and middle-aged with slightly buck teeth. But she just drifted away.'

Stragglers came to the coolie camp. After the sinking, Betty Jeffrey and Iole Harper had joined a raft crowded with two Malay sailors, five or so women and two children, five nurses, and the popular Matron Paschke. Three times they approached the shore and three times they were swept out again. During the night they too were caught up in the invasion fleet. Japanese soldiers in the surrounding boats, chatting away, looked hard at them and then continued towards Muntok. After daylight, Jeffrey, Harper and the two Malays swam beside the raft and again the party got close to the shore. Again the current gripped the raft. It was carried away. The women and children, the other nurses, and Matron Paschke were never seen again. Jeffrey and Harper lost contact with the Japanese and for three days swam or sheltered among mangroves until they reached a fishing village where they waited for their captors.

A week later Vivian Bulwinkel, back from the dead, was escorted in. The nurses clustered around her. She told of the massacre and of finding Private Kingsley, an English soldier who had been bayoneted by the Japanese. For 10 days Bulwinkel kept Kingsley and herself alive with the help of village women, but they decided it was hopeless and gave themselves up. On the advice of captured members of a British intelligence section, the massacre at Banka Island was only spoken of with caution during the war. It was not a story the troops of God would want spread. There is pain when Pat Gunther tells it now: 'Of course, you see, I still miss Kath Neuss.'

Early one morning they were marched to the Muntok pier, and men and women put on separate boats, the women's a filthy cattle boat, to cross the strait from Banka Island and sail up the Moesi River to the provincial centre, Palembang. There were sunken ships, oil slicks, the debris of war, and a perfect rainbow. Gunther thought it a good omen; Margaret Dryburgh was later moved to poetry.

> *We captives left the pier before dawn*
> *To meet a future dark with threatening fear.*
> *'What lies ahead?' our anxious spirits sighed.*
> *A wondrous rainbow arch with vivid gloss*
> *Proclaimed the answer. 'Hope on, hope on' it cried.*
> *'Hope on' reflected colours echoed low.*

Moral: Do not trust rainbows.

At Palembang they were trucked past jeering Indonesians to abandoned Dutch houses, and crowded into two of them. The houses had been stripped of furniture but in one were three tea chests packed with silver, much of it hallmarked. The nurses picked out spoons to eat with. Gunther chose a small jam spoon, 'hall-marked, of course, as things do taste better from silver spoons'. She kept it throughout captivity. It is now in the Australian War Memorial.

For a week or so the Japanese paid little attention to them. Then they were moved out of their houses, which the Japanese said were to be used as a club for 'entertainment'. The senior Japanese officers wanted the nurses to serve as comfort women. According to Simons, 'geishas' was the term used by the British woman, a mother of two and a survivor of the *Vyner Brooke,* who canvassed the camp for volunteers. When there were none, the Japanese instructed that some Australian nurses attend the club's opening night to entertain the six officers. Twenty-seven of them did. They left behind the sick and, to look after them, the most glamorous of the group. They dressed as carefully as they would for a Saturday night out in Australia, but with a difference. Those with a choice put on their drabbest dress. Some rubbed ash into their faces. They tugged hair back or up or forward, whatever style suited them least. Betty Jeffrey watched Pat Gunther and laughed: the more she plastered her curly hair back, the prettier she looked. One nurse clumped into the club in men's boots, one in football boots. They nibbled at the refreshments, pocketing what biscuits and cakes they could. All declined alcohol. Australian girls drank milk at Saturday night parties, they said. Conversation faltered and all the would-be geishas finally escaped. There was a price to pay. For several days they were given no food and allowed to buy none so they ate tapioca root growing in the yard. But virtue had triumphed.

They had established that they would only nurse and they worked alongside British sisters and Dutch nuns, caring for the ill. But they had to do more to subsist. Many of the Dutch

women came into internment with possessions in their suitcases and guilders in their purses. The nurses cooked and
cleaned for them, and did their laundry. They made sweets,
removed rat droppings from *gula java* (a mixture of palm
sugar, sago and coconut milk) and added assorted native con-
coctions for flavouring. They cut hair. Pat Gunther, having had
lessons from a Dutch nun, Sister Paula, painted. They were
small, delicate works, on the skilled side of naïve, of camp
houses and camp life; kitchens, women pounding and sifting
tapioca flour. She called them 'almost an egg'. She sold them
for 40 cents, almost the cost of an invaluable egg on the black
market.

Some women did leave the camp to live among the
Japanese. They were called 'The Girl Friends'. When they
returned, they were well fed and well dressed. They were
shunned until one of the older British women lectured the
nurses and the other younger women: 'You look down on
them, but they are your protection.' The British woman who
tried to procure nurses as geishas said she was doing it for
the sake of her children, not a claim the nurses accepted. But
if she had, it would be understandable, perhaps admirable. In
war commandments are suspended; in camps, moral precepts
may seem dispensable.

Hunger and malnourishment were ever-present enemies. In
Muntok camp in 1944, the nurses were burying sometimes
three women a day from their circle of acquaintances. And the
mothers, the mothers who for two and a half years had sacrificed their rations to their children, were steadily losing the
battle. One watched four of her five die in the one week.

Drudgery, boredom and squalor lived in the camps too,
killing spirits. The camp had received helpful advice and an
analysis of Western culture from a Japanese guard. Jessie
Simons jotted it down. 'I want pay attention to you,' he said.

'You all people have individualism; you are having the collective life now. Important conditions of the collective life have two things. They are comradeship and order. If you cannot be having them we shall not say that you are the foremost nation. And we shall give you them compulsorily.' The nurses needed no lessons in comradeship. They hated being separated even temporarily when they were being shuttled from camp to camp and even though, as Pat Gunther puts it, undoubtedly mildly, they didn't always agree.

FOR THE CAMP as a whole Margaret Drysburgh and another skilled musician, Norah Chambers, provided solace. Norah Chambers formed a 'vocal' orchestra, a version of *a capella*. Betty Jeffrey joined them. They practised the *largo* from the *New World Symphony*, 'Morning' from the *Peer Gynt* suite, Percy Grainger's *Country Gardens*, and Ravel's *Bolero*. The orchestra was divided into first, seconds, thirds and fourths. For the first performance in front of their captive public was added, fittingly, Mendelssohn's 'Song without Words'. The prisoners loved the concerts. So did the Japanese.

There was also a famous mannequin parade, presented by Paula of Palembang, stage persona of Jean Ashton, with orchestral accompaniment. 'Camp possibilities' featured curtains and other available materials turned into a fetching twin set, 'snappy sunsuit', 'something practical for every-day tasks', which were their work shorts. This was in 1943. Paula of Palembang, as a style clairvoyant, and perhaps as a pessimistic prisoner, unveiled 'Likely fashions for 1945'. The lights were dimmed and then came up briefly on three girls clad only in three pawpaw leaves.

The first death among the surviving nurses came out of petty brutality. In September 1944 Wilhelmina 'Ray' Raymont who earned a little money making pretty little handkerchiefs, was sitting on her bed sewing. The guard the nurses called Rasputin came in and began shouting. There was a knob of wood missing from the wood boarding behind her bed; Raymont had damaged Japanese property, he claimed. She was ill, but he made her stand in the sun, a popular punishment. A nurse gave her a hat. Rasputin knocked it away and punched Raymont to the ground. He refused pleas from a doctor to end the punishment. Eventually she collapsed, desperately ill, and never recovered.

WHEN 1945 DID come, it met Paula of Palembang's predictions. The women had been moved to Banka Island in November 1944. All the nurses had some illness and 31 of the 32 suffered malaria attacks. Four made a living as 'nightmen'. They had two kerosene tins, two half coconut shells nailed on sticks for scoops and a long pole to help carry the tins away. At dawn they began scooping out the latrines and made six long trips into the jungle before breakfast. For this they got 80 cents a day from the camp's pooled money.

In January 1943, the nurses had received a message from a Japanese official, sent, he said, through a neutral channel by Australian Prime Minister John Curtin. 'Keep smiling', it said. In January 1945, Iole Harper told her friends she had a terrific idea: ask the Japanese for permission to send a cable to Mr Curtin saying, 'Can we take the grins off our faces now?'

Some of the women in the camp were so weak and so thin that they slipped through the narrow aperture over which they squatted in the latrine. They fell into the pit below. Screams brought rescuers and the women were washed down with buckets of water and taken to hospital. They didn't have long to live. The Japanese charted the physical decline. Captain Siki, who took over as military commandant in 1944, ordered a monthly weighing. The graph went steadily downward. Over the next six months, Jessie Simons shrank from 8 stone to about 6 stone, and this was typical. Gunther was only 5 stone at the last weighing in February 1945. The nurses came to regard Siki as a nasty piece of work. 'Mean-souled scoundrel', Jessie Simons called him: tiny, one hard staring brown eye and the other bloodshot and apparently useless, given to speeches on the glory of the Japanese empire and seeming to take sadistic pleasure in delivering bad news. Yet Siki did order the dispensing of injections against typhoid, dysentery and cholera. Some lives were saved but the death rate rose remorselessly.

One of the women who died was Ruth Russell-Roberts, the former Hartnell model who had spent her last day in falling Singapore with her husband Denis in true style. Pat Gunther had become friendly with her and they would walk in the evenings round the perimeter. Russell-Roberts had heard that her child had reached England safely; she had heard that Denis was in Changi, a prisoner, but safe. She had everything to live for, Gunther said. After the war, Denis went to Singapore's Alexandra hospital when he got news that women from the Sumatra and Java camps were about to arrive. He looked at them, ill, weary, unkempt and thin. 'Then I saw Christine (Bundy) and she saw me. She was overcome and found it difficult to say anything. She squeezed my hand and whispered in my ears, "I'm so sorry, Denis." It was just like that.' Molly Ismail, who went shopping for her engagement ring during an air raid, did survive, but it was not a fairytale ending. When she and her fiancé met again in England, feelings had faded. She married someone else.

The women were moved again in March 1945, to Muntok pier and by slow boats up the Moesi River to Palembang once again, bound for Lubuk Linggau. The dying died quickly on the boat carrying the very ill. The bodies had to be simply rolled overboard, wrapped but unweighted. For a while seven corpses floated along in the wake of the ship.

The trip took three days by boat and train to Lubuk Linggau and then by truck to the rubber plantation. In this last camp, the last battle of about 600 women and children began against sickness and starvation. The cemetery, up on a hill among trees, ferns and wildflowers, filled. There were no concerts now. The survivors of the vocal orchestra were too ill to perform. Then one day there was an announcement: a Japanese military band was waiting on a rise at the far end of the camp. The women were tired, ill, and didn't move. Gold Teeth, the interpreter, shouting angrily *lekas*, hurry, and swinging a stick above their heads, herded them up. The music of *Poet and Peasant* drifted towards them through the rubber trees. The band was immaculately uniformed, clean-shaven. They played mostly German music, overtures and waltzes. Among the prisoner-audience were German women. The Japanese had interred all Europeans, allies or not. They were particularly moved by the music. Gunther was too. She wept silently. This really was a pretty area, she thought, gentle grassed slopes, a bubbling creek and a small streamlet joining it after passing under the barbed wire, dragonflies floating on quivering, delicately coloured transparent wings.

Another day a nun took a group of small children outside the barbed wire to collect wood. A Japanese guard caught them. While the young children ran down the ridge like a flight of birds, to the point where the barbed wire crossed the creek, the guard beat the nun's upper arms with his baton. The nurses knew she would have difficulty getting back into camp because her arms would be useless for some time. They also knew that any attempt to help her would only worsen things. Gunther wept again.

WHEN I MET Pat Darling (nee Gunther), she had just turned 89, curly hair grey, of course. She lived in an apartment, immaculately tasteful, in Sydney. How had they coped with the endless time in the camps? I asked. 'Ah, bridge,' she said. 'I had played bridge since I was a child. So had Pat Blake. Jessie Simons borrowed some cutting instrument from the nuns and she made two packs of cards out of photograph albums the Dutch had left. We drew suit colours with crayons on one side and on the other were the photographs of chubby Dutch children. Jessie and Win hadn't played before, so we taught them. Win was my partner. For a while we weren't very good. But we played every moment we could, whenever we had a bit of spare time. We played through lunch. In the evenings we would only put the cards down when we had to go down for *tenko,* to be counted. Once when Pat was weak, she said after the first hand, "Make me dummy, I'll have to lie down".

'We kept a tab, a score and Jessie and Pat were miles ahead of us. But we got the hang of it. Win and I were getting on top of them, but they weren't going to let us. Eventually we did. But we said, "That's all right, when we get back to Australia we will all fly down to Melbourne and we'll shout you two strawberry shortcake at the Wattle", because that is what Melburnians talked about, this wonderful shortcake they had at the Wattle Café. So you see, you filled in your time.'

'Did you ever get to have strawberry shortcake at the Wattle?' I asked.

'No, you see, Win died,' Pat Darling said. And sat silent for a while.

DYSENTERY KILLED WIN Davis on July 19, 1945, just short of her thirtieth birthday. She had become convinced she would not live to see it. Another needless, avoidable death.

Gunther looked at her dead friend. At least she wouldn't suffer any more. The dead prisoners were at peace; the drowned nurses were at peace; Kath Neuss, massacred on the beach, was at peace. Gunther turned away and went to where she and Win had slept and began sewing her thin rice-sack mattress to Win's. That had been the agreement: the one who lived longer would have a more comfortable mattress.

Gunther was weary. In the previous camp the nurses had made wills, leaving their possessions to friends. Without wills, the Japanese took the articles, and the nurses had to buy them back. They wrote letters to their family. Gunther's said:

Dear family,
Please don't worry about me. I enlisted of my own free will, knowing I could be going into a war zone. We nurses have been interned with a lot of other women. We have always managed to stay together. I have not been raped, bashed or tortured. If I die, it will be due to malnutrition or malaria. I am still me.
All my love, Pat.

Each night when she settled down to sleep, she said: 'Please God, don't let me wake up tomorrow.'

One night she had a dream. She had died and was walking up a hill to a place where she knew she had to go. A young air force officer helped her the last few metres. He was so clean and healthy. She laughed and said, 'Well, you died in the full flush of beautiful youth.' He, looking at her gaunt, ragged appearance, said: 'And you died in a prison camp.' . . . She walked towards a raised, curved dais, surrounded by graceful columns. There a group of women, dressed in Grecian clothes, stood, Kath Neuss and Win Davis among them. Kath smiled her crooked smile and said, 'You're older than I am now.' The difference in their ages had always irked Kath. Win said, as Gunther knew she would, 'We knew you'd be late.' As they stretched their hands out to one another, Gunther woke up. She couldn't believe she was still in the camp. She preferred the fantasy of death to the reality of her life. She treasured the dream. It sustained her in the dragging months ahead.

CHAPTER 24

Then there were none

From walking in the footsteps of the dead,
Feeling their presence in a rotten boot,
A blaze upon a tree that marks a grave,
A scrap of webbing and an earth-stained badge,
A falling bamboo hut, a giant tree
They rested at; this creek,
This climb that runs sweat into your eyes –
Though you aren't laden, fevered, starved . . .
You tell yourself you know how they went by.

Colin Simpson

When Owen Campbell returned from the river there was a stillness in the North Borneo jungle. Ted Skinner was dead. His throat was cut. Beside his hand lay the jagged lid of an empty tin of salmon. Campbell knew what had happened, and why. For three days Skinner, a skeleton weakened further by dysentery, had urged Campbell to leave him, to catch up with the others. He was a dead man, he said. On June 16, 1945 Skinner gave Campbell no choice. Sapped himself by beri-beri, Campbell dug a shallow grave, rolled Skinner's body in and piled on logs and stones. He struck out to the north-east, after his mates. Ted Skinner's bones lie somewhere in the North Borneo jungle. His elder brother John is buried in the Labuan war cemetery.

The Skinner brothers were from Tenterfield, on the northern tablelands of New South Wales. John was older by four years, but they were close and they enlisted together on August 1, 1941. Their serial numbers were NX41647 and NX41648. Both joined the 2/10th Field Ambulance. When the Japanese made their thrust across the Johore Strait to Singapore they were in the north-west sector where the Australians took the brunt. On July 18, 1942 the brothers, members of B Force, disembarked at Sandakan, on Borneo's north-east coast. Among the filthy, hungry cargo stumbling with them off the *Yubi Maru* was Herb Trackson. Thirteen days later Trackson made his break for freedom. Captured, he was sent to Outram Road jail. But he lived. Of the 2434 prisoners in the camp at Sandakan in 1944 – 1793 Australians and 641 British – only six survived, all Australians. They escaped in the final weeks and days of the war. Brutality and disease killed many. Others died or were murdered on marches through the jungle from Sandakan to Ranau, 266 kilometres away. Those who survived were massacred. John Skinner was the last to die of the hundreds of ill left at Sandakan.

AUGUST 15, 1945 was a momentous day in world history: turmoil in Tokyo, young militant Japanese officers trying to prevent Emperor Hirohito bringing the war to an end and the lives of millions in the balance. In the Sandakan prisoners' compound, Warrant Officer Hisao Murozumi had his sword raised. It would be the last atrocity in this camp in this backwater of war. Terrible things happen in battle. In the heat and smoke of it, morality enters a strange world. Killing is survival.

What Murozumi was about to do was barbarism. A prisoner, tall, thin, wearing only a loincloth was pushed down to kneel beside a slit trench. A black cloth was tied around his eyes. His hands were free because he was too weak to struggle. Murozumi carefully took his stance. It was a matter of pride to do this properly. He stood legs apart, arms above his head, the blade in a two-hand grip pointing directly backward, eyes fixed on the bare, supremely vulnerable back of neck. The sword flashed, John Skinner was beheaded and guards shovelled earth into the trench.

The Japanese walked away, thinking the truth about the last days at Sandakan lay buried with John Skinner, but there was a witness to the execution of the thin man. Wong Hiong was a 15-year-old Chinese boy. For two years he had worked in the Japanese cookhouse. Small, he was called *kodomo*, child, by the Japanese and was something of a mascot. He saw and heard more than he should. He had been told by Murozumi not to leave the barracks but he had followed the Japanese towards the prisoners' compound and climbed a rubber tree. He watched as the man was punched and kicked towards the trench. He watched the lonely death of John Skinner. Five hours later Japanese people heard the announcement of the end of the war, but it was already over for the Skinner brothers.

NORTHERN BORNEO, NOW the Malaysian states of Sarawak and Sabah, was an exotic corner of the British Empire. Pirates roamed the seas and head-hunters the land. For a time Sarawak was ruled by private companies and white rajahs. The first, James Brooke, was more enlightened than most colonisers. In 1842 he wrote: 'I hate the idea of a Utopian government, with laws cut and ready for the natives,

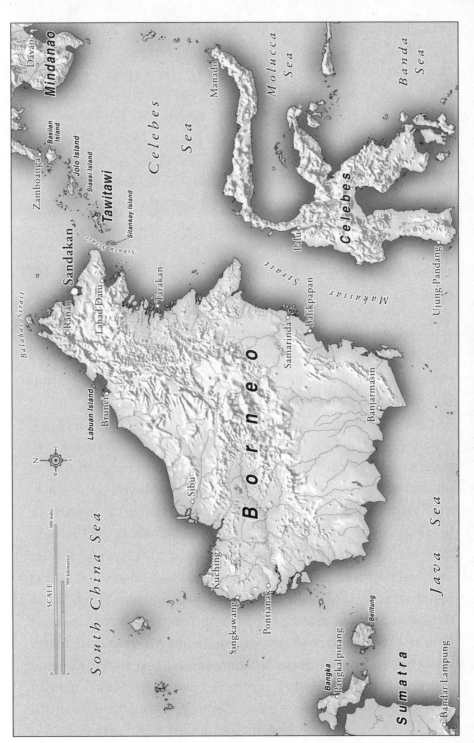

Locality map showing Sandakan and Tawitawi

being introduced . . . I am going on slowly and surely, basing everything on their own laws, consulting the headmen at every stage, instilling what I think is right – separating the abuses from the customs.' Sandakan was the capital of North Borneo, the region which became Sabah, where the largest of the indigenous groupings was the Kadazans or Dusans. The arm of the Empire here was the British North Borneo Company, cousin of the East India Company. The Dusans lived in isolated villages and practised swidden agriculture, clearing jungle for their gardens and moving a short distance every few years from site to site as the soil lost fertility. In the nineteenth century, they paid little attention to the coming of the company. During World War II, the majority remained loyal to the British and some were violently antagonistic towards the Japanese. This was a blessing for Owen Campbell. The Murats, another tribal group, also took no delight in the fall of the tuans. This was a blessing for an exclusive group of prisoners, the Dit Club.

Campbell was tough, hardened by years on the land. He was brought up on his family's selection at Goondiwindi, worked on his uncle's farm and then became head stockman on a cattle property running Herefords. He loved the mustering, the dipping and the branding. He loved being on horseback. When he stood in line to enlist, a bloke said to him: 'Never join the infantry. You've got to walk everywhere. Get into the artillery, where you ride.' At the end he was going on foot towards death. Campbell joined the 2/10th Field Regiment and sailed for Malaya on February 2, 1941. It was a long wait for a short, sharp war: action at Mersing on January 22, 1942 and the spiking of the guns on February 15. After capture, Campbell worked on the Singapore wharves. One day in March 1943 an officer came. 'You, you, you, you, you,' he said. 'Pack your kit. You're going on that ship there.' He was pointing to the *de Klerk*, an aged steamer. E Force was being drafted to follow B Force to Borneo. The *de Klerk* transported 1000 men, 500 of them Australians, to Kuching, in Sarawak. First impressions were of another of the fleet of hell ships. But the good ship *de Klerk* carried a cargo of tins of pork and baked beans and cartons of cigarettes. The prisoners ate well and, by one account, smoked 30,000 cigarettes in the three days to Kuching. There they first unloaded a freighter, the *Taka Maru*, then boarded it for the voyage to Sandakan.

When the *Taka Maru* docked at Sandakan, the men were ferried across to temporary accommodation on Berhala Island, a quarantine station and leper colony in the harbour. There they were met by the commandant, Captain Susumi Hoshijima, a graduate of Osaka University, tall and impressive, except when he mounted his white horse to make inspections of the mainland camp. To a bushman like Campbell, he was ugly in the saddle. Hoshijima welcomed E Force much as he had welcomed B Force: exhorted them to work hard building an airstrip; warned them that death was the penalty of trying to escape and that if the Japanese did not kill them, the jungle would; said that Japan would be victorious if it took 100 years.

Listening were a group of men who, like Herb Trackson and his mate Matt Carr, were not going to wait around that long. They were members of what had become known in Singapore as the Dit Club, formed in the early days of captivity by men determined to escape. Dit was Morse for E and E stood for escape. Two of them, Rex Blow and Miles Gillon, were lieutenants in Campbell's 2/10th Field Regiment. The third was Captain Ray Steele of the 2/15th Field Regiment. On the voyage from Singapore, Steele had unsuccessfully urged that they hijack the *de Klerk* and sail it to Australia. An enthusiast, he also suggested taking over the *Taka Maru* between Kuching and Sandakan.

As it turned out, Berhala Island was a dream headquarters for the Dit Club. It was lush and the Japanese, regarding sea as moat, were lax in supervision. The lepers, who had established gardens, had two dugout canoes. Most important, on Berhala the Dit Club had contact with Koram bin Anduar, and Koram who had one small vice, smoking foul black cheroots, had valuable connections.

One day he had been fishing in his *prau* when the sea heaved and a submarine surfaced. The conning tower hatch opened and a Filipino working with the American forces waved Koram across and handed him a letter. Give it to any white man, he said. The Americans were offering help to escape. They wanted to inform any white man that *kompits*, the traditional sailing craft of traders, smugglers and fishermen, were making regular trips between Sandakan and Tawitawi island, where guerillas were operating. Tawitawi, the first of the stepping stones of the Sulu islands between northeast Borneo and the southern Philippines province, Mindanao, was less than 250 kilometres of comparatively sheltered sea away, an easy voyage on a *kompit*.

Koram was a lucky choice by the Americans. A Murat tribesman, he had been a corporal in the British North Borneo Constabulary. He was a poor choice by the Japanese as a guard on Berhala, with instructions to spy on E Force. Koram had already been arrested twice on suspicion of carrying messages for prisoners and threatened with death. He was indeed a link between the camps, the civilian detainees and a network of people willing to help them. It wasn't long before the Dit Club, now expanded to seven, and Koram were working together.

The question of escape is a vexed one for officers from generals down. Should your prime duty be to stay with your men? Will the people you leave behind feel the wrath and pay a heavy price? So worried was E Force commander, Captain Rod Richardson, about repercussions that he considered telling the Japanese of the plans. He relented. Campbell was impressed by Rex Blow: nice man, a daredevil. Good luck to them, he thought, but the odds were against them. He was staying behind the wire.

The Dit Club literally went into training, swimming up and down the beach to build fitness. Koram smuggled in supplies. Then they received sobering news. Three men had escaped from a mainland camp. Hoshijima had been right about the jungle. It defeated them. Two were betrayed by Malays and summarily executed; a third, Sergeant Walter Wallace, was eventually rowed on a small boat by members of the underground to Berhala to await the escape of the Dit Club. That happened suddenly on the night of June 4 when Koram delivered news that E Force would the next day be moved to the mainland. After dark the men walked along the decking to the latrines on stilts above the tidal flats, dropped down and made their way to a rendezvous point. Three paddled out to sea in one of the lepers' canoes and reached Tawitawi nine days later. The remaining five hid from the Japanese on Berhala for 21 days waiting for a promised *kompit*. On the night of June 26 they heard a boat off the beach. They gave the signal, puffing to the point of sickness on Koram's black cheroots. Four days later they were on Tawitawi. On July 1, the Dit Club eight formally became members of the 125th Regiment of the United States forces in the Philippines, known on Tawitawi as the Filipino Guerilla Army.

KORAM BIN ANDUAR was the living stuff of myth. He was soon caught up in a wave of arrests and welter of torture by the *kempeitai*. The Sandakan underground was the victim of an act of spite. A man who felt cheated in a business deal betrayed a key figure to the Japanese. Searches of the camp unearthed maps, arms and radio parts; sweeps gathered in prisoners, civilians and members of the constabulary, including Koram. Some withstood days of pain and would not be broken. Some told little, but enough to keep the dogs running. Lepers provided information that Koram had been seen with the E Force escapees. Badly beaten by *kempeitai* interrogators, he escaped through a lavatory window. He hid at first under their noses. He ate apples he stole from their larder. After a fortnight, when he had recovered from his injuries, he went to the Sandakan jetty. An oil store and a fuel lighter burst into flames, with Koram's help. He made his way upcountry to the settlement of Beluran and paid a courtesy call to Japanese headquarters. He had been sent, he told the Japanese, to take a census of civilians in the region. When they waved him off he was leading three coolies instructed to carry his belongings, which now included food and cigarettes. Eventually he arrived at Kota Belud on the north-west coast, a three-week walk, where friends in the constabulary invited him to join the Kinabalu guerillas.

There he took part in a bloody, abortive uprising, torching with his friends the main jetty and dockside godowns. Thirteen hundred guerillas and 1900 Japanese died, five guerilla leaders were beheaded and 176 civilians executed by firing squad. Koram escaped the post-rebellion carnage of October 1943: he had become ill and returned to his father's home. You might think that Koram would now melt in among the Murat, perhaps try a little swidden farming for a while. But he went to a Japanese post and confessed that he had helped eight prisoners of war escape from Berhala Island. He wished to atone, he explained. He would track them down. A huge gamble, but it worked. For months he chased phantoms around Borneo, happening to visit Japanese troop centres, noting movements and sketching installations. In May 1945 his luck ran out. He was betrayed and arrested by his masters. Of course he escaped again and crossed to Tawitawi, bearing valuable information. He saw the war out working with Australia's undercover organisation, the Services Reconnaissance Department, back in North Borneo again. He was a member of a spy team, Agas IV (*agas* is Malay for gnat or sandfly). He had at last found the man he had told the *kempeitai* he would search for: Agas IV's leader was Rex Blow.

Koram was awarded the MBE. His contact in the Sandakan camp, Lionel Matthews, was also decorated. To the Military Cross he had been awarded for bravery in action during the Malayan campaign was added the George Cross for gallantry. It was posthumous. The citation said Matthews had directed an underground intelligence organisation and arranged delivery of sorely needed medical supplies, food and money to the prisoners of war. He had been instrumental in arranging a radio link with the outside world and was also responsible for organising the British North Borneo Constabulary and the loyal natives in Sandakan into readiness for an armed uprising against the Japanese. He successfully organised escape parties. Arrested by the *kempeitai*, he was subjected to brutal treatment and starvation but steadfastly refused to implicate his associates. Even at the time of his execution he remained defiant.

After a 40-minute trial, Matthews and fellow officer Rod Wells had been found guilty of, among other things, espionage and rebellion. As they were being marched, handcuffed together, to hear their punishment, Matthews said to Wells: 'Rod, you'll get home. Give my love to Lorna and to my son.' Wells was sentenced to 15 years' solitary confinement. He did get home, though he had to survive Outram Road jail first.

Matthews was sentenced to death by firing squad. He was put into a van with eight Asian civilian members of the underground also condemned to death and he called out through the grill: 'Keep your chin up boys. What the Japs do to me doesn't matter. They can't win.' He died game, refusing a blindfold and shouting: 'My King and God forever. My King and God forever.'

In the aftermath of the Sandakan purge, the Japanese shipped most of the prisoner-of-war officers from Sandakan south to Kuching, the capital of Sarawak. The sad fact is that nothing could help or save all but six of those left behind.

ON TAWITAWI THE Dit Club became fighting men again. In August 1943 they carried out a successful raid on a Japanese submarine-chaser that had put in on the south of the island but a fortnight later suffered in an ambush by pro-Japanese Moro tribesmen. Rex Butler, one of those who had paddled the dugout canoe from Berhala, was killed and decapitated. Miles Gillon was wounded. Later, surviving members of the Dit Club, men who had been powerless as prisoners of the Japanese, found themselves in a position of power over Japanese prisoners. They found themselves in a moral dilemma. This was the context: war on Tawitawi was messy and vicious, as guerilla war in particular can be; the people were divided and many were starving; the Japanese knew the guerillas were there, bombed their camps and raided and razed villages that supported them.

One day about 30 Japanese drifted to shore in lifeboats. Their ship had been torpedoed. Long after war had turned into peace Ray Steele grappled with what happened. He was brutally honest about it. He described the Japanese as an embarrassment to the Australian guerillas. Under normal conditions, he said, and according to the Geneva Convention, they should have been fed and housed and made prisoners of war. Leaving aside just how 'normal conditions' in war can be defined, there is no doubt conditions on Tawitawi were difficult and hazardous for the guerillas. Steele acknowledged the personal dimension: he and his mates and all prisoners of war had been badly treated; no Geneva Convention or Red Cross for them. There was an argument about what to do with the Japanese. They had nowhere to keep them and they couldn't feed them. Letting them go would risk providing the Japanese army with dangerous information. The decision was to dispose of them. As senior officer, Steele himself took action. He and some Filipinos took the Japanese back to sea. They pushed them overboard and cleaved their skulls with *parangs*. Steele shot the wounded and those attempting to get back into the boats. 'What else could we do with them?' he asked decades later.

WAR RAISES MANY questions. The prime one is: Why? Is it for a just cause, or national survival, or territorial ambitions, or to cement an alliance? There are questions about grand strategies and battle tactics. Inspired or foolish or flawed? Then there are myriad questions about actions, the morality of them and the necessity for them. Why did the Japanese on Banka Island slaughter the nurses? Ray Steele examined his conscience about what happened in the sea off Tawitawi and concluded the guerillas had no choice.

The Japanese certainly had a choice about the fate of the men of Sandakan. They were on the verge of starvation but the Japanese commandant had 90 tonnes of rice stored under his house and there were at least another 54 tonnes in the camp. Many of the prisoners were desperately ill. The Japanese had almost one million quinine tablets, 19,600 vitamin A and D tablets, quantities of vitamin B and C tablets, hundreds of Red Cross parcels and stockpiles of medical supplies and surgical equipment. Why were the prisoners denied these things that would have saved their lives? There is a simple answer to that. It is the same as the answer to the question of why prisoners were forced on the marches to Ranau. The Japanese wanted them dead.

As the war worsened there must have been a growing realisation in Tokyo that there would be a reckoning for the treatment of prisoners of war. General Douglas MacArthur's headquarters had intercepted among Japanese signals one on August 1, 1944 to Formosan POW headquarters clarifying 'emergency measures' to be taken against prisoners of war.

Although the basic aim is to act under superior orders, individual applications may be made in the following circumstances:

When an uprising cannot be suppressed without the use of firearms or when escapes from the camp may turn into a hostile fighting force.

Whether they are destroyed individually or in groups, or however it is done, with mass bombings, poisonous smoke, poisons, drowning, decapitation, or what, dispose of them as the situation dictates. *In any case it is the aim not to allow the escape of a single one, to annihilate them all, and not to leave any traces.* [Emphasis added]

In November 1944, armed with the graphic eyewitness accounts of the horrors of the Thai–Burma railway by prisoners of war rescued by American submarines, Australia and Britain had exposed and condemned Japan to the world. In December, Japanese soldiers had taken 'emergency measures' as American troops attempted to free prisoners of war on the Philippines island of Palawan. The 150 Americans who had been ordered into air-raid shelters were doused with petrol, set alight and attacked when they tried to get out. Only four survived. But the Americans were later successful in two bold strikes at Santo Thomas University in Manila and at Los Banos, to the south, the first by a heavily armoured flying column and the second by paratroopers.

Sandakan was a logical North Borneo invasion point for the Allies. Perhaps that is why the Japanese began moving the prisoners to Ranau in January 1945. What quickly became apparent was that marching the men through mud and slush and swamps and over mountains was an efficient way of taking 'extreme measures'. The first group, 455 men, were sent out in nine parties. They were supposedly the fittest. That was relative. Most were emaciated, ulcerated, with rags for clothes. Most were soon barefooted as they lost their Japanese-issue rubber slip-on shoes. They were carrying almost 30-kilo loads of rice, ammunition and Japanese officers' gear. They fed on a small amount of watery rice and fern tips, or anything they could garner from the jungle, snails and frogs if they were lucky. At night the fortunate managed to shelter under leaves of banana palms. It was an ordeal that could and did kill fit men. Captain Ryoichi Mizuto was in charge of the fourth party. His unit was fresh. They had only arrived in Borneo three months before and while most had endemic malaria, they were, according to Mizuto, well-conditioned. Of his party 10 prisoners of war died. So did four Japanese soldiers. One hundred and fourteen of the 455 did not reach Ranau. Those who were not dead when they fell to the jungle track were finished off with bashing, bayonet or bullet.

Bill Moxham, one of the six to survive Sandakan, was in one of the later parties.

The guards kept us going at full pace all the time and along the track we smelt and saw bodies. They were Australian soldiers' bodies from the previous march. We could recognise them. Some of them we knew personally . . . On the way I suppose I saw or smelt between 20 and 30 Australian bodies; there could have been a lot more. Men from my own party could not go on. Boto was the first place where we had to actually leave anyone; we had to leave four as they could not proceed. At the next place, at the bottom of a bog hill, we left two more men and later heard shots. In all my dealings with the Japanese I have never seen any of our chaps after they have left with the Japs. Once you stopped, you stopped for good. The Japs had no time for the sick, they would not even feed them.

On March 17 the Japanese War Minister, Shibayama Keneshito, sent a telegram to all commands. It confirmed previous directives on 'emergency measures'. There was an element of double-speak about it, but in essence it was a death warrant for the men of Sandakan.

Prisoners of war must be prevented by all means available from falling into enemy hands. They should either be relocated away from the front or collected at suitable points and times with an eye to enemy raids, shore bombardments etc. They should be kept alive to the last wherever their labour is needed. In desperate circumstances, where there is no time to move them, they may, as a last resort, be set free. Then emergency measures should be carried out against those with an antagonistic attitude and utmost precautions should be taken to ensure no harm is done to the public. In executing emergency measures, care should be had not to provoke enemy propaganda or retaliation. Prisoners should be fed at the end.

ORANG TUA KULANG realised he had made a mistake. *Orang Tua* means headman. Kulang was headman of the Dusan people at Muanad River, deep in the North Borneo jungle. The Japanese asked him to cut a section of the new track between Sandakan and Ranau. It was a good choice. Slight, lithe, with the toughness of a liane vine, Kulang was a great hunter and the jungle was his element. So why did he trace the track through marshy ground, at a steep slant up hill-sides and through the darkest, densest, dankest thickets? He was waging what he called a little war of his own in revenge for Japanese depredations among the Dusan. He killed them in ambush when he could. His personal tally was 96, 50 shot and the rest decapitated with his *parang*. He did not know that much of the tragic traffic along the track he was making as difficult as possible would be prisoners of war.

On May 27, Australian and American troops, wrongly informed by an Agas unit that all prisoners of war had been evacuated to Ranau, attacked Sandakan by air and from the sea. Two days later the Japanese ordered all prisoners who could walk (or partly walk) to get ready to leave. Five hundred and thirty-six set off in groups on the second march; 288, including John Skinner, were too weak and ill to go. The Japanese burnt the camp. It must have been a wrenching leave-taking for Ted Skinner, who was with Owen Campbell in the fifth party.

Campbell was weak when they set out. On June 6, he was exhausted. He had walked through stench, heard the shots as his mates who could not go on had been killed. He had struggled knee-deep in mud along the path chosen by Kulang. They had only reached the ration and staging post at the 48-mile peg. The Japanese issued them with 10 days' rations to take them to the next staging post. Campbell knew he could not make it. He talked to Skinner, Sid Webber, Ted Emmett and Keith Costin about escape.

On the second day out from Sandakan, Allied aircraft had swooped overhead and the guards had scattered and hidden. Campbell took note. On June 7, planes came over again. The guards dropped their packs and hid in the jungle. The five prisoners grabbed rice and tins of salmon from the packs and slid down a steep, 60-metre bank. They lay among bracken until the column moved on. They were deep in North Borneo's jungle heart.

After Skinner killed himself, Campbell pushed on to find his mates. He caught crabs and once a small jungle creature he ate raw. He followed the Muanad River downstream. When he caught up with the others, Costin was in a lean-to, ill with dysentery and malaria. Webber and Emmett, who had been fishing, said they would hail one of the passing boats and get help. Not a good idea, argued Campbell, who stayed back. As a boat paddled by a Malay approached them, a Japanese soldier suddenly stood up and killed Webber and Emmett with a burst of fire. They fell into the river.

For three days Costin and Campbell lived on fish and fungus, then Costin died. Once again Campbell buried a mate in a shallow grave. He was alone and he had beri-beri. It was, as best he could remember, June 21. For the next 11 days, he walked in and out of delirium. Once he was wounded in the wrist by a Japanese soldier as he tried to float across the river on a log. Often his dead mates came to talk to him. Finally, on July 3, as he was trying to steal fish from a trap, he saw two Dusan in a canoe. 'Abang,' he called, the polite Malay greeting which means older brother. Lap and Galunting took him to their village where he was fed, nursed and when necessary, hidden by the acting *Orang Tua*, Saliam. Some time later the *Orang Tua* returned. It was Kulang, who had been on a mission with an Agas party. Kulang took over care of Campbell, still with scabies, matted hair and long beard. He shaved him with an old (and blunt) cutthroat razor. On July 19, Kulang and the Dusan, well-armed, took Campbell downriver to the Agas camp. On July 23, Campbell was evacuated by sea plane to Tawitawi.

As Campbell was making his escape, the killing continued. In July, only between 80 and 90 prisoners were still alive in the ashes of the Sandakan camp. Many of the 288 had died. Seventy-five pathetic figures had been marched off in the direction of Ranau. They did not get far and their bones marked their progress. On July 13, 23 of those left at Sandakan died. This is what happened in the words of a Japanese guard, Yashitoro Goto, when he was interviewed by war crimes investigators:

> It was Takakua's [Captain Takuo Takakua] order so we could not disobey. It would be a disgrace to my parents so we carried out the orders. Taking the PWs to the airport near the old house on the drome, all those who could walk. There were 23 PWs and under Murozumi's [Warrant Officer Hisao Murozumi] order we lined them up and shot them. The firing party kept firing until there were no more signs of life. Then we dragged the bodies into a nearby air-raid shelter and filled it in.

Takakua was hanged as a war criminal. Murozumi, who gave the order to fire and who, according to Wong Hiong, beheaded John Skinner, was sentenced to life imprisonment. Goto, who was only following orders, was sentenced to 15 years' imprisonment. None of the convicted Japanese who were sent to prison served longer than 13 years.

Five other prisoners of war escaped and lived to return to Australia: Keith Botterill, Nelson Short, Bill Moxham, Bill Sticpewich and Dick Braithwaite. The last of those who survived the Sandakan–Ranau marches were murdered by the Japanese on August 27, five days after surrender leaflets had been dropped in the area.

Only six survivors. Surely, given the might and power of the Allied forces at this stage in the war, these sick and powerless men were not beyond the reach of rescue. We know the military leadership could be blithe about lives chewed up as part of a grand design, or by mistake. There was Major General Sidney Rowell's epitaph for the men of Lark Force on Rabaul: 'It's not the first time a few thousand men have been thrown away and it won't be the last.' But that was in the desperate days of the Japanese blitzkrieg in 1942 when the fear was that it would overrun Australia. In 1945 the Allies were driving towards the Japanese homeland. At Manila's Santo Tomas University on February 6 the Americans freed 5000 prisoners. On February 23, 200 American paratroopers were dropped 100 kilometres behind enemy lines in an area defended by 6000 Japanese troops. In 17 minutes, 2135 internees and 12 US navy nurses were freed and taken to evacuation craft.

Why didn't Australian diggers storm into Sandakan? As the official version puts it mildly in the Department of Veterans' Affairs *Laden, Fevered, Starved*, the issue is contentious. In April 1945, Rex Blow and Jock McLaren, two of the Dit Club members who had been fighting as guerillas on Tawitawi, were summoned to the Morotai island base to meet the Australian commander, General Thomas Blamey. McLaren raised the question: 'What about the blokes behind the barbed wire in Sandakan, can we help them?'

Blamey replied: 'I think we can.' At the end of the meeting he said: 'If it could be fitted in with other operations we'll do it, and you two will be in it.' What Blamey didn't tell Blow and McLaren was that a rescue mission, Project Kingfisher, had been planned and only days before it had been aborted.

Whose fault was that? I spoke with Owen Campbell in June 2003, then the last living survivor of Sandakan. He was emphatic: Blamey and MacArthur. MacArthur bypassed Borneo to get to the Philippines, Campbell said. All he thought of was his 'I shall return' pledge. He wouldn't give Blamey the aircraft needed for a paratroop drop. Blamey should have stood up to him. Blamey was weak, Campbell said.

The source for the story that MacArthur blocked the supply of aircraft was Blamey himself, in a speech to an army association conference in 1947. 'We had high hopes of being able to use Australian parachute troops,' he said. 'We had complete plans for them. Our spies were in Japanese-held territory. We had established the necessary contacts with prisoners at Sandakan, and our parachute troops were going to relieve them. The parachute regiment didn't know what was planned, of course. But at the moment we wanted to act, we couldn't get the necessary aircraft to take them in. The operation would certainly have saved the death march of Sandakan. Destiny didn't permit us to carry it out.'

Neither destiny nor MacArthur was to blame. MacArthur had given his approval for Project Kingfisher and there was no difficulty with the availability of C-47 aircraft. The RAAF had 71 in their pool. According to Lynette Silver in her book *Sandakan: A Conspiracy of Silence*, Blamey lied. MacArthur was the scapegoat for the bungling of the SRD, Blamey's intelligence creation. On April 3, 1945 Agas agents had wrongly reported that all the prisoners of war had been moved from Sandakan, out of reach of Project Kingfisher.

On June 19, 1945, military intelligence produced another assessment of the situation in the Sandakan area. After the PT boat attacks on May 27, 1000 to 1500 Japanese troops had been evacuated westward, leaving only 200 to 300 men in the area; about 200 were members of a naval unit guarding suicide boats hidden in caves; between 100 and 150 prisoners of war had been left behind, too ill to be moved to Ranau; it was impossible to say how many Japanese were left to guard them; it might be as low as 10, probably as great as 100; they were also in poor physical condition.

In part the assessment was based on the debriefing of Dick Braithwaite, who escaped from the second death march two days after Owen Campbell and his group. For five days he followed elephant and wild pig tracks through the jungle and struggled through moss morasses. On the point of surrender he hailed an old river fisherman. He was taken by canoe to a PT boat and on June 15 reached Tawitawi. He told officers about the treatment of the prisoners of war at Sandakan and about the death marches. Braithwaite knew they were going towards the foothills of Mount Kinabalu and suggested this was a point where they could start their search. The officers said they would take action straightaway.

For a week Braithwaite lay in hospital being treated for malnutrition and a leg poisoned by ant bites. He was, he said later, coming good. But then he was devastated. A colonel came in, asked him how he was and said: 'We're going in now to look for your friends.' Braithwaite rolled on his side in the bunk, faced the wall and cried like a baby and said: 'You'll be too late.'

When the full crime and tragedy of the death marches became public in 1947, critics of the Labor Government and Prime Minister Ben Chifley attacked them for not caring about the fate of a few prisoners of war. This time the politicians weren't to blame. A minute paper from the Department of Defence to the Prime Minister says there is no record of any official request being made to General MacArthur or RAAF Headquarters for the provision of aircraft or an airborne operation for a rescue attempt. It says the possibility of a rescue had been examined at Advanced Headquarters, Allied Land Forces, and found to be quite impracticable from all aspects. General Blamey had made no report on the matter to the Prime Minister or the Advisory War Council. Then Chifley was given the sort of advice any politician likes to hear. He was reminded that in 1946 the government had decided that it did not favour holding inquiries into past operations 'as no good purpose would be served by seeking to allocate blame for the reverses sustained during the early part of the war'. Just as there was no investigation into how Lark Force, Gull Force and Sparrow Force came to be left hostages to fortune in 1942, there was no investigation into why on August 15, 1945, John Skinner was kneeling beside a ditch in Sandakan, waiting for Warrant Officer Murozumi's sword to fall.

BE SURE TO wear a nice hat, the newspaper photographer told Evelyn Campbell. It was January 1946. He had just told her that Owen Campbell had returned to Australia and was at an army hospital. She had been notified years ago that Owen was missing believed dead. Evelyn believed he was alive. She chose her hat, a gay one with a long coloured feather, and the photographer took her and Owen's son, seven-year-old Alan, to Greenslopes hospital. They found Owen on a back verandah, wrapped in blankets in the summer heat. Evelyn threw herself on him, and bounced off. It was strange. His stomach was huge, still bloated with beri-beri.

When he first came back, Campbell worked as a demobil-iser at an ammunition dump, but he wanted the calm of the country again. They farmed. He went to church on Sundays to keep Evelyn company. Religion had not been that important to him, though he went to church with Evelyn when they were courting. She was a true believer and always answered the telephone by saying: 'Jesus loves you.' He did, however, have a feeling in Sandakan that somebody was looking after him. One Sunday at the Pentecostal church, the Lord was with him and he became a minister and put the horror behind him.

Bill Moxham couldn't. He committed suicide in 1961. Bill Sticpewich was run down by a car when he was crossing a road in 1977. Dick Braithwaite died of cancer in 1986. Nelson Short died of a heart attack in 1995 and Keith Botterill of emphysema in 1997.

On July 3, 2003 Owen Campbell died of cancer.

Then there were none.

CHAPTER 25

It was the first time I'd seen a Nip cry

Des Moloney was tall and fading to the thinness of a prisoner of war. He was ravaged, as anyone who underwent interrogation by the Japanese would be. But he was dancing round this barracks building in the Bicycle Camp in Batavia, formerly the capital of Dutch Indonesia. His left hand was upraised, holding the phantom hand of a woman. His right arm was round her phantom waist. He swayed and spun and he sang:

> *Mairzy doats and dozy doats*
> *And liddle lamzy divey,*
> *A kiddlely divey too, wouldn't you?*
> *Mairzy doats and dozy doats*
> *And liddle lamzy divey,*
> *A kiddlely divey too, wouldn't you?*

Sol Henderson and his mates looked at one another, partly amused, partly bemused. Moloney danced and sang on:

> *If the words sound queer and funny to your ear,*
> *A little bit jumbled and jivey,*

Sing 'mares eat oats and does eat oats
And little lambs eat ivy'.

Of course the words sounded queer to Sol Henderson and his mates, and dancing with a woman was something they had long since stopped dreaming about. Des Moloney had literally dropped down from another planet, one they had left more than three years before. It was 1945. Moloney was RAAF, a crew member of a Liberator bomber that had flown out of north-west Australia on a mission to Indonesia. It had been shot down over Lombok. Captured, Moloney was eventually pushed by guards in among the ragged time-servers at the Bicycle Camp. Then began his second interrogation: How was the war going? How were the people back home responding? What were they doing, thinking? Were there Yanks in Australia? What about the Yanks and the Aussie women? What was the latest music? What were the latest songs? What were the latest dances?

Mairzy doats and dozy doats . . .

SOL HENDERSON WAS a member of the 2/40th, the core of Sparrow Force on Timor. The battalion began its war 920-strong. In battle, it lost 53 men, killed in action or dead of wounds. During captivity, it was scattered across the Greater East Asia Co-Prosperity Sphere. At war's end men were surviving in Thailand, Japan, Singapore, Sumatra, Java, Saigon, Mukden and Borneo. A total of 264, 29 per cent of the battalion, died, including 11 per cent on voyages to Japan.

For Henderson time was the enemy. It fought him for his mind. That's how it was for most prisoners of war. Over by Christmas, many had thought in 1942. By April 1944, Weary

Dunlop who, a year before had found solace in shades of the jungle, clear and pure skies, chains of butterflies and troops of monkeys, wrote in his diary that he seemed to have lost all emotional depths; his sense of beauty and his appreciation of it seemed to have suffered; he couldn't react very much to physical suffering or death. In November, he recalled the appalling days of *speedo* and the time of cholera when most had descended into a desolate place, a valley of dry bones. 'Life is too sweet, too transient not to grudge the dragging years. How full they might have been of service, of lovely things and loving, compared to this vegetable death in life.'

In Java, Henderson knew little about the progress of the war and the end games being played. His 2/40th Battalion mate, Clyde McKay, at least was aware that things had gone terribly wrong for the Japanese in Burma. McKay had been part of a Sparrow Force draft sent to Thailand under the command of Weary Dunlop. He was a hammer-and-tap man on the railway and after it was completed he worked as a general rouseabout on maintenance. The railway was a supply line to Burma. McKay saw arms and men and ammunition chuffing and creaking north through the jungle. Then one day in 1945 he was with a gang at a wayside station and a train slowly pulled in, three truckloads behind. The Japanese guards looked in and then looked away. McKay looked in and said: 'My God. Poor buggers.' They were wounded Japanese soldiers, the wreckage of the Burma campaign. The prisoners pulled them out. There were three or four dead in each truck, and the living were lying in maggots and filth. The prisoners washed them and washed out the trucks. They filled their water bottles. They burnt the dead. One of the wounded Japanese began crying. 'It was the first time I'd seen a Nip cry,' McKay told me. 'In those circumstance, they weren't enemy. They were wounded soldiers and their own had just ignored them.'

In 1942, the Japanese blitzkrieg had rolled across Burma towards the giant prize of India but the defeated British forces regrouped in Assam on the plateau around the city of Imphal. A profoundly relieved Churchill later wrote: 'The road to India was barred.' Early in 1943, a force of 3000 Chindits under Colonel Orde Wingate penetrated 320 kilometres into Burma. It was a costly exercise in terms of casualties and loomed larger in legend than effect, but it did worry the Japanese. They feared a major British offensive. In August 1943 the Southern Army, under the urgings of the 15th Army commander, General Renya Mutaguchi, gave instructions for preparations for *U-Go*, a pre-emptive strike. The order was to 'advance to Imphal before enemy preparations for a counter offensive could be completed. After crushing the enemy at Imphal, our forces will seize the Arakan Mountain range and establish the defence line there. Upon the occupation of Imphal, the provisional government of Free India will be established there in order to accelerate the political campaign in India.' It looked great on paper.

During the Malayan campaign, units under Mutaguchi's command had won imperial citations for the initial landing at Kota Bharu and for the invasion of Singapore. Mutaguchi had been described as 'distinguished and resolute'. In Burma he presided over a massive defeat and a disastrous retreat. *U-Go* was launched on March 15, 1944. A Japanese force of 115,000 headed into the mountains, its equipment carried by 12,000 horses (including some mules), 30,000 oxen and 1030 elephants. The oxen were Mutaguchi's idea, borrowed from Genghis Khan. When the food they were carrying was consumed, they would be next on the menu. One symptomatic problem: Burmese oxen were bred to pull carts not carry loads on their backs; when tired they simply dug their hooves in.

Near his house Mutaguchi had a special place built for

Shinto worship, a square covered with white sand marked by four bamboo poles on the corners. As the Japanese advance was halted, he spent more and more time there praying for God's help and victory. God did not intervene. After three months of intense battle, the Japanese were thrust back. There were 65,000 casualties. All the horses died but most of the elephants and a few mules survived. There is no record of what happened to the oxen.

The retreat through Burma was a death march, but it was not a Sandakan. It was not an extermination of the helpless by the enemy. Staff Sergeant Yumasa Nishiji, one of the survivors, said Japanese soldiers called the route the 'Human Remains Highway'. It was a vision of hell, he said, men in their twenties struggling along stooped like old men. 'Many enemy soldiers were deterred from pursuing us along this road; they did not wish to witness such an atrocious scene; they made a detour instead.' After the war, Nishiji felt he did not have the proper words to cage the horror. He made minimalist drawings of men barely crawling, of a soldier standing among dead men holding the pair of boots he had taken from one, of couples in a close embrace, the hand grenade with which they would kill themselves nursed between them. Death before the disgrace of capture. More than 305,000 Japanese soldiers fought on the Burma front; 180,000 of them perished.

AS THE JAPANESE soldiers withdrew from Burma, the Allies were island-hopping closer to their homeland, putting it in reach of land-based B-29 bombers. Saipan, in the Mariana group, was a key objective. In the carve-up of colonies after World War I, the Japanese wanted the Marianas the way Billy Hughes wanted New Guinea. The island group became the outer edge of the homeland defensive perimeter. Prime Minister

Tojo declared Saipan 'an impregnable fortress'. People never learn, do they? However, the Americans did buy Saipan dearly in blood, 14,000 out of 70,000 invaders suffering casualties. Here the concept of *gyoskusai* was put into practice: fight to the last man; strive to die in a final attack. On Japanese figures, 41,244 of the 43,683 military defenders died. Squad Leader Takeo Yamauchi was one of three of his regiment of 250 men to survive. He did because he decided to surrender and risk eternal shame. Once he hid in a cave on the northern tip of the island with a Japanese sergeant, some soldiers and some Japanese women with their babies. When the babies cried, the sergeant said the Americans would hear them. 'Kill them yourselves,' he said, 'or I'll order my men to do it.' Several mothers killed their own children. It was the behaviour of the Japanese civilians on Saipan that shocked and alarmed the Allies. Near the cave where Yamauchi hid was a cliff. It became known as Suicide Bluff. Here women threw children over, or jumped, holding their hands, driven by fear of Americans, pressure by the military and devotion to the Emperor.

The fighting had lasted 30 days and on July 10, two Marines, Al Perry and Paul Scanlon, who during that time had not washed or changed their clothes, decided to bathe in the ocean. They were close to the cliff-edge when they were confronted by a Japanese family – a young woman, a small boy and an elderly couple. The woman opened the suitcase she was carrying and showed the Marines, who spoke no Japanese, a black and white photograph of a soldier, probably her husband. She tapped Perry's canteen. Perry realised the family had been drinking sea water. As the Marines shared their water, more Japanese, including soldiers, formed a line in front of them. Scanlon went back to company headquarters to get more supplies and as Perry waited he noticed for the first time bobbing heads in the water, people swimming out to sea. He went to the cliff-edge and looked down on broken bodies, most of them women and children. Those who had survived the fall were swimming towards death.

Scanlon and Perry distributed another 10 gallons of water then walked away from a nightmare. Other Marines had arrived and some were shooting at the swimmers. Leave them, let them die with dignity, Perry argued. Four days earlier Perry had himself single-handedly killed 27 Japanese. With his unit under a heavy counter-attack, he stood up and walked forward firing his automatic rifle. For this he was awarded the Silver Star 'for conspicuous gallantry and intrepidity'. Perry looked back on Saipan as the most obscene experience he had encountered in his lifetime. 'War is crazy,' he wrote in a personal memoir. 'One day we are killing each other and the next day we are trying to save them.'

The loss of Saipan brought down the Tojo Government. For the Americans the victory carried a grim message: in an invasion the Japanese homeland would be soaked not just with soldiers' blood, but with the blood of Japanese civilians, of men, women and children.

In Tokyo, newspapers presented the death leaps as proof of the pride of Japanese women and one carried a comment by an academic that 'our courage will be buoyed by this one hundred times, one thousand times'.

ON NOVEMBER 24, 1944 the first B-29s flew off from the Marianas to strike at Japan. Children had been prepared for the raids. They danced to a special civil-defence song:

Air raid. Air raid. Here comes an air raid!
Red! Red! Incendiary bomb!
Run! Run! Get mattress and sand!

Air raid. Air raid. Here comes an air raid!
Black! Black! Here come the bombs!
Cover your ears! Close your eyes!

The air did burn red over Tokyo on March 9, 1945. That night 334 B-29s dropped around half a million jellied-petroleum incendiary bombs in clusters. Neat bamboo and wood houses became perfect fuel and there was little the people could do but cover their ears and close their eyes and hope that somehow they would not be seared. Babies being carried on their mothers' backs were burned off, about 80,000 people died and one million lost their homes. It was an atrocity to match Britain's fire-bombing of Dresden or the Japanese Rape of Nanking. Churchill, calling up memories of the Blitz and pointing to the 'cruelties and tyrannies' inflicted by Germans, at first defended the tactic as the sword of justice. He had second thoughts. The destruction of Dresden remained a serious query against the conduct of Allied bombing, he said, and urged more precise concentration on military objectives. America put moral distance between itself and Dresden. Secretary of War Henry Stimson said: 'Our policy never has been to inflict terror bombing on civilian populations . . . Our efforts still are confined to the attack on military objectives.' The skimpy American air force justification for the fire-bombings of Japanese cities was that small-scale war production sites were scattered through residential areas.

THE THAI–BURMA RAILWAY was a military objective. Liberators continued about their legitimate work, bombing and strafing bridges, marshalling yards and camps along its length. Unfortunately, the 500-pounders and the bullets did not discriminate between Japanese and prisoners of war. Desmond

Jackson listened subconsciously for the distinctive four-engine drone. Aerial attacks were powerlessness multiplied and too much for his closest mate, Ken Linford. 'It's the feeling of not being able to hit back that gets me,' Linford told Jackson, 'and my nerve just goes.' Jackson was 13 when he first met 10-year-old Linford in a small Tasmanian seaside town. They went in different directions when they enlisted, Jackson the machine-gunner to the Middle East, Linford to Timor with the 2/40th. The vagaries of war brought them together as prisoners on the *Usu Maru* carrying Dunlop Force from Java towards Singapore and the railway. Their paths crossed several times and in May 1945 they were sheltering from the same intensive attack by six Liberators on Ratburi, a small centre on the main Thai railway line. When a Thai agent, Ja Ray, who had access to their prison camp, offered to help prisoners escape and join the guerilla movement, Linford and two others accepted. He preferred the risk of recapture and probable execution to the danger from the sky. On July 28, the three pushed through the high bamboo fence and eventually joined Allied commandos and Thai guerillas. It was a rare successful escape.

In Ratburi and in many camps throughout the prisoner-of-war diaspora there was a new and dangerous uncertainty. Through secret radio or rumour there was a growing conviction that soon the Allies would be victorious. There was still the day-to-day risk of death by disease or random brutality. Ray Parkin, having survived the sinking of the *Perth*, the railway and the voyage to Japan, was in a camp near the village of Neshi Ohama on the main island, Honshu. What really hit him there, he remembered, was that he had a good chance of not being alive tomorrow, that these people had the power of life and death over him. There would be no post-mortem. One Japanese could have him dead in a few minutes, just because he lost his temper.

That was the everyday reality. But what would happen on the day when the troops of God had to face the bitter shame of defeat? In August, Clyde McKay was at Nakom Nayok camp, 150 kilometres north-west of Bangkok. A Japanese soldier who spoke reasonable English had made a practice of walking beside him on the way to the work site. One day the Japanese talked about the end of the war. He made a sign across his throat with his finger: Australians kill Japanese. 'No,' said McKay and held out his hand. 'When war finished, you Nippon, us Australia.' It reassured the Japanese who brought McKay half a dozen bananas the next day. But McKay himself was uneasy. The prisoners had been digging tunnels into hills. What were they to be used for? At Kanchanaburi, Ken Dumbrell looked at the big ditch the Japanese had ordered dug and the four towers and the machine guns. You don't have to be a Rhodes Scholar, he thought. They had a stockpile of stones hidden in the dirt. No good going like sheep. At Nakom Nayok the machine guns also faced inwards and Weary Dunlop had received alarming information from a Korean guard. Called Z in the diaries, the guard was pessimistic that any prisoner of war would survive the peace. There would be massacres and death marches. Dunlop organised resistance. The men were to arm themselves with weapons that were liter-ally stone-age; Dunlop himself had made two of what would become known as Molotov cocktails, saki bottles filled with petrol stolen from trucks; and according to one source, a Korean (possibly Dunlop's Z), offered to give the prisoners the Koreans' weapons.

The danger was real. Already bodies were mouldering along the track between Sandakan and Ranau, and at Ambon prison-ers were being starved and worked to death. All commands had received War Minister Keneshito's directive on emergency measures to prevent prisoners falling into enemy hands and there is the suggestion that the Commander-in-Chief of the Southern Army, Field Marshal Count Terauchi, had ordered all prisoners in the region to be killed if the Allies invaded South-East Asia.

And what of the thousands of prisoners of war in Japan, living in the heart of the enemy? After the incendiary bombing of Tokyo, B-29s sowed firestorms over five more cities. Tens of thousands more died and millions upon millions were left homeless. Surely rage would burn fiercely in the people?

ONE AUGUST MORNING, Desmond Jackson was on a work party loading barges near Ratburi. The men had left their hats on the ground and as a Chinese man walked past, he stooped and quickly put a package under one, saying quietly 'Important news for you'. Back at the camp for lunchbreak, the men opened it. There was a single-page newspaper, the *Bangkok Chronicle*, a Japanese propaganda sheet printed in English. The banner headline was 'Russia Invades Manchuria' and this was important news indeed. After three bloody months of battle, ranging from artillery barrages to the flushing-out of individual Japanese soldiers from foxholes by flamethrowers, the Americans had captured Okinawa as a forward base for invasion of the homeland. Now, to the rear, the Japanese had to fight their old Russian enemy on a new front. There was only one other item on the *Chronicle*'s page, a small one headed 'New Weapon'. It gave little detail: the weapon was barbarous, the newspaper said. It had caused considerable loss of life but nothing could defeat the fighting spirit of the Japanese.

The world had changed. On August 6, at 8.15 am, an American B-29 flying out of the Marianas released an atom bomb over Hiroshima. It fell for 45 seconds, then exploded, delivering to the Japanese people, as President Harry Truman had threatened, 'a rain of ruin from the air, the like of which has never been seen on this earth'.

Three days later, Neil Dawson of the 2/40th was working, clearing away the wreckage of a zinc factory at Omuta that had been destroyed in an air raid. Over a range of hills and across a bay was Nagasaki where another 2/40th man, Allan Chick, was at Camp 14, near the city centre. An aircraft flew over and Dawson glanced up. Minutes later there was a blast, the air shuddered and rising up swiftly over the range of hills was a mushroom-shaped cloud.

CHAPTER 26

The Fat Man sings; the Crane speaks

We have discovered the most terrible bomb in the history of the world. It may be the fire destruction prophesied in the Euphrates Valley era, after Noah and his fabulous Ark.

President Harry Truman's diary, July 25, 1945

Blinding blue-white light was followed by blackness. Allan Chick, 25-year-old cray-fisherman from tiny St Helens, on the east coast of Tasmania, stood stunned within the framework of a partly completed building in Nagasaki. Day returned. Chick looked up at a sky purple-brown with dust and smoke. The roof beam on which he had been sitting an instant before had vanished. It was not long after eleven o'clock on August 9 and for the second time in four days parachutes had gently wafted down the most terrible bomb in the history of the world to explode over a Japanese city. Prison Camp 14 housed 169 men, including 24 Australians, and it was only 1700 metres from the hypocentre, the point at which a free-falling bomb would have hit the ground. The 24 Australians had no right to survive, and particularly not Allan Chick, perched up in the path of death. There was devastation between Camp 14 and the hypocentre, there was devastation beyond and in Nagasaki perhaps 75,000 people were dead or dying.

Above the city rose the most sinister shape in the history of the world, a mushroom that bulged and bloomed, sibling of the one that marked the death or dying of perhaps 140,000 in Hiroshima. The warped winds returned to normal and blew the clouds away; but the moral doubts have remained ever since. The source of the bombs' power was, Harry Truman remarked, the source from which the sun draws its power. The Sun sustains life but the coyly code-named Little Boy, dropped over Hiroshima, and Fat Man, dropped over Nagasaki, were pure destruction. Still, a baby burned off its mother's back in the fire-bombing of Tokyo or a baby crushed in a London house during the Blitz is just as dead as a baby disembowelled in an atomic blast. Jellied petroleum and TNT can do dreadful things, but those early atomic bombs, though now dwarfed in potency, were awesome. In 1946 the United States Strategic Bombing Survey, a group of civilians appointed to examine the impact of bombing on Japan, produced this comparison: the damage and casualties caused at Hiroshima by the one atomic bomb dropped from a single plane would have required 220 B-29s carrying 1200 incendiary bombs, 400 tons of high-explosive bombs and 500 tons of anti-personnel fragmentation bombs.

The birth of the age of atomic terror can be traced back to a memorandum written in Britain in March 1940 by two scientists, Otto Frisch, a refugee from Nazi Germany, and German-educated Rudolf Peieris on the properties of a radio-active 'super-bomb' using the rare isotope uranium 235. The energy to be used was stored in atomic nuclei.

The energy liberated in the explosion of such a super-bomb is about the same as that produced by the explosion of 1000 tons of dynamite. This energy is liberated in a small volume, in which it will, for an instant, produce a temperature comparable to that in the interior of the Sun. The blast from such an explosion would destroy life in a wide area . . . In addition, some part of the energy set free by the bomb goes to produce radioactive substances, and these will emit very powerful and dangerous radiations . . . Some of this radioactivity will be carried along with the wind and will spread the contamination; several miles downwind this may kill people.

The two scientists described another very attractive attribute of the super-bomb: the cost of producing it would certainly not be prohibitive. Then, having declared that they did not feel competent to discuss its strategic value, they made an accurate prophecy: 'As a weapon, the super-bomb would be practically irresistible.'

In his diary entry of July 25, Truman said the bomb would be used against Japan before August 10.

I have told the Sec. of War, Mr Stimson, to use it so that military objectives and soldiers and sailors are the target and not women and children. Even if the Japs are savages, ruthless, merciless and fanatic, we as leader of the world for the common welfare cannot drop that terrible bomb on the old capital or the new. He and I are in accord. The target will be a purely military one and we will issue a warning statement asking the Japs to surrender and save lives. I'm sure they will not do that, but we will have to give them the chance.

That day an order went out to General Carl Spaatz, the commanding general of the Army Strategic Air Forces: 'The 509 Composite Group, 20th Air Force will deliver its first special bomb as soon as weather will permit visual bombing after about 3 August on one of the targets: Hiroshima, Kokura, Niigata and Nagasaki . . . Additional bombs will be delivered on the above targets as soon as made ready by the project staff.' There was no mention of 'military targets'.

The next day, July 26, Truman and Clement Attlee, the Labour leader who had replaced Churchill as Prime Minister, issued the Potsdam Declaration. It warned that 'the might that now converges on Japan is immeasurably greater than that which, when applied to the resisting Nazis, necessarily laid waste to the lands, the industry and the method of life of the whole German people. The full application of our military power, backed by our resolve, will mean the inevitable and complete destruction of the Japanese armed forces and just as inevitably, the utter destruction of the Japanese homeland.' The declaration demanded the elimination from authority of the militarists and said 'we do not intend that the Japanese shall be enslaved as a race or destroyed as a nation, but stern justice shall be meted out to all war criminals, including those who have visited cruelties upon our prisoners'. Truman and Attlee called for unconditional surrender. They would brook no delay, they said. There was no mention of the fate of the Emperor.

On July 28, the Japanese Prime Minister, Kantaro Suzuki, announced that the government would ignore the Potsdam Declaration. The Frisch-Peieris prophecy was about to be fulfilled. As Truman had noted in his diary, the old and new capitals, Kyoto and Tokyo, were spared a rain of atomic ruin from the sky. As it happened, the civilian men, women and children of Hiroshima and Nagasaki were not.

AS THE WOUNDED and the walking dead, skin and flesh hanging off, drifted among the fires, the flattened buildings and human wreckage of Nagasaki, a guard came up to Chick and a small group of prisoners standing stupified in Camp 14. 'Go, go, go,' he said. They discovered some Red Cross parcels that had been kept from them by the Japanese, took them and walked along a road that led into the hills. They found an abandoned horse and cart and made their way out of the grievously wounded city.

At about this time, the news of Nagasaki and the second atomic bomb was delivered to Japan's Supreme War Council as it discussed acceptance or rejection of the terms of the Potsdam Declaration. Council members were Prime Minister Suzuki; Foreign Minister Shigenori Togo; the Minister for the Army, General Korechika Anami; the Minister for the Navy, Admiral Mitsumasa Yonai; the Chief of Army Staff, General Yoshijiro Umezu; and the Chief of Naval Staff, Admiral Soemu Toyoda. They were agreed on one thing: the imperial structure must be preserved. Suzuki, Yonai and Togo wanted to accept the declaration, with the proviso about the Emperor. The other three argued for insertion of other conditions, and in effect for the continuing of the war.

The six carried their differences into the meeting of the Japanese Cabinet that afternoon. Admiral Yonai put the argument for acceptance: 'We might win the first battle for Japan but we won't win the second. The war is lost to us. Therefore we must forget about "face", we must surrender as quickly as we can and we must begin to consider how best to preserve our country.' General Anami spoke for rejection: 'We cannot pretend to claim that victory is certain, but it is far too early to say that the war is lost. That we will inflict severe losses on the enemy when he invades Japan is certain, and it is by no means impossible that we may be able to reverse the situation in our favour, pulling victory out of defeat.'

The Japanese militarists lived in a parallel universe, where the spirit of *bushido* was protection against the power of America and of the atom. Twice the hammer blow of the universe had fallen on Japanese cities. Bombers spewing fire and explosives roamed the skies at will. The population was fading further into malnutrition. Russia had declared war. A year after the war, the US Strategic Bombing Survey noted that 'it seems clear that even without the atomic bombing attacks, air supremacy over Japan could have exerted sufficient pressure to bring about unconditional surrender and obviate the need for invasion'. Yet on August 9 Anami listened impatiently in the Cabinet meeting to the dire plight of the nation then said: 'Yes, yes! Everyone understands the situation . . . but we must fight through to the end no matter how great the odds are against us.'

Sometime after the war, a group of young Japanese scholars, journalists and writers made an attempt to understand the Japanese military mind and the actions of the militarists in that turbulent period when the nation was on the cusp of almost complete destruction. They formed the Pacific War Research Society and after eight years produced a study, *Japan's Longest Day*. It is a fascinating account of assassinations, a coup attempt, the isolation of the Imperial Palace and a desperate search for the Emperor's recording of the Rescript to end the war. The plotters were determined to save the Emperor from his advisers and from himself by preventing surrender. If the military mind defied penetration, the Pacific War Research Society did create a marvellous metaphor for Ichigaya, the War Ministry, and its denizens: 'a huge, disturbed ant-hill, with hundreds of warrior ants scurrying back and forth through the long corridors, their antennae raised to receive whatever emanations might serve to solve their dilemma; they were driven almost by instinct to defend the ant-hill and the nest that sustained it, though this might mean the destruction of hundreds of millions.'

Anami held the line at the Cabinet meeting. There was deadlock. Tradition was that the Emperor would be presented with the considered and unanimous decision of the government. Now the Supreme Council went to the Emperor for a decision. They waited for the descendant of the Amaterasu O-Mikami, the Sun Goddess, in the underground bomb shelter of the Imperial Palace. He sat in a plain, straight-backed chair while the two sides argued.

Early on the morning of August 10, Emperor Hirohito said continuing the war could only result in the annihilation of the Japanese people. 'That it is unbearable to me to see my loyal troops disarmed goes without saying . . . But the time has come to bear the unbearable.' So a message went out to the Allied powers: the Japanese Government would accept the terms of the Potsdam Declaration, with the understanding that none of the demands prejudiced the prerogatives of the Emperor as sovereign ruler.

The American response was not what either of the Japanese parties wanted. It said: 'The authority of the Emperor and the Japanese Government to rule the state shall be subject to the Supreme Commander of the Allied powers.' However, senior Japanese advisers decided that 'subject to' ought to be translated in the sense of 'controlled by' rather than 'obedient to'. Emperor Hirohito agreed with Foreign Minister Togo's advice to accept the Allied terms.

On the morning of August 14, the Cabinet and the Supreme War Council waited again in the underground bunker in the Imperial Palace. Emperor Hirohito entered, wearing a simple military uniform, and listened again to the arguments for war and for peace. When Hirohito himself spoke, it was of pain, sorrow and the imperative of avoiding Japan's annihilation.

Particularly concerned at the reaction of the troops, he said he would make the announcement of the acceptance of the Potsdam Declaration personally. He instructed the Cabinet to prepare an Imperial Rescript.

General Anami returned to Ichigaya now determined to obey his Emperor and bear the unbearable. Japan's military forces, which had shaped the nation and shaken the world, and still six million strong, would accept defeat and dismemberment. Confronted by middle-rank officers, Anami said that the Emperor had made his decision. Anyone who disagreed 'will have to do so over my dead body'. Anami had already begun planning his death by *seppuku*, ritual suicide. But some of the young officers began planning the deaths of the peace advocates, Prime Minister Suzuki, Foreign Minister Togo and the Emperor's closest confidant, Marquis Koichi, Lord Keeper of the Privy Seal. They would rescue the Emperor from his advisers. They would stop the broadcast. The army would rise up behind them and reject surrender.

Cabinet crafted the Rescript, incorporating parts of the Emperor's addresses to the two conferences. The Emperor made minor changes and then recorded the Rescript for broadcast at noon the next day. Where to keep the recordings? Two chamberlains decided to place them in a small safe in the office of a member of the Emperor's retinue. This was fortuitous.

Not long after midnight, two of the plotters, Major Kenji Hatanaka and Lieutenant Colonel Jiro Shiizaki, went to the office of Lieutenant General Takeshi Mori, commander of the 1st Imperial Guards Division. They shot Mori and decapitated his brother-in-law, Lieutenant Colonel Michinori Shiraishi, who was with him. From Mori's desk they took his personal seal and fixed it to a forged order, 'Strategic Order 584'. The division was to 'protect the Emperor and preserve the national polity'. The Emperor and his family were to be 'guarded' at the Imperial Palace; the Tokyo Broadcasting Station was to be occupied and broadcasts prohibited.

For a few chaotic hours, the plotters believed the coup would succeed. A detachment of misled guards surrounded and isolated the Imperial Palace and the Prime Minister's residence was attacked. But a search of the Imperial Household Ministry overlooked the small safe and its precious recordings, and the army did not rise up. As noon on August 15 neared, Hatanaka and Shiizaki killed themselves in front of the Imperial Palace and Anami committed *seppuku* in his house, facing towards the Imperial Palace. Anami left a death note: 'For my supreme crime, I beg forgiveness through the act of death.' He was taking responsibility for Japan's defeat. Hatanaka left a death poem: 'I have nothing to regret now that the dark clouds have disappeared from the reign of the Emperor.' That was nothing to do with the plotters, of course. America had decided to preserve the descendant of the Sun Goddess as a human being in the cause of reconstruction of Japan.

TRADITIONALLY, THE PRONOUNCEMENT of an Imperial command was known as the Voice of the Crane. The crane is an imperial symbol and the belief is that the sound of the crane can be heard in the sky when the bird is hidden from view. On December 8, 1941 the Japanese had read the words of their Emperor in an Imperial Rescript published in the evening newspapers. It was a declaration of the war on America and Britain that had already begun with the strikes on Pearl Harbor, Hong Kong and Malaya. The Rescript began: 'We, by grace of heaven, Emperor of Japan, seated on the throne of a line unbroken for ages eternal, enjoin upon ye, Our loyal and grave subjects . . .' It claimed that 'it has been truly unavoidable and far from Our wishes that Our empire has been brought to cross swords with America and Britain' and concluded: 'The hallowed spirits of Our Imperial Ancestors guarding Us from above, We rely on the loyalty and courage of Our subjects in Our confident expectation that the task bequeathed by Our forefathers will be carried forward and that the sources of evil will be speedily eradicated and an enduring peace immutably established in East Asia, preserving thereby the glory of Our Empire.'

At noon on August 15, 1945 the Voice of the Crane was heard in Japan. The Japanese people in shock and sorrow listened to the human voice of their divine ruler, high-pitched, uncertain, speaking in courtly phrases. Hirohito did not use the word 'surrender', but said, 'We have decided to effect a settlement of the present situation by resorting to an extraordinary measure'. With Japan's forces being overwhelmed on land, sea and in the air throughout the Greater East Asia Co-Prosperity Sphere and swathes of its cities smouldering ruins, Hirohito said the war situation had developed 'not necessarily to Japan's advantage, while the general trends of the world have all turned against her interest'. (This form of words had been insisted on by Anami in an empty attempt to save military face.) The enemy had begun to employ a 'new and most cruel bomb, the power of which to do damage is indeed incalculable, taking the toll of many innocent lives'. The Emperor told his people he had ordered the acceptance of the Potsdam Declaration.

There was an expression in the Rescript of the deepest sense of regret to the Allied nations of East Asia 'who have consistently cooperated with the Empire towards the emancipation of East Asia'. There was solicitude for the military fallen of Japan and the people who had suffered. There was a warning of hardships ahead and the statement that 'we have resolved to pave the way for a grand peace for all the generations to come by enduring the unendurable and suffering what is insufferable'. Nowhere was there an admission of Japanese arrogance towards the people of East Asia at least equal to that of the colonial powers they sought to drive out. Nowhere was there an apology for the havoc and death they caused throughout the region. Nowhere was there an expression of shame for the treatment of the Allied prisoners of war and the Asian slaves.

THE NEWS RIPPLED out in August through the prison camps where men and women had been enduring the unendurable for years: something awesome had happened in Japan. In Kobe in early 1945, prisoners had been locked indoors and forbidden to look upwards when the first American reconnaissance planes appeared in the sky. On the August day after the bomb fell on Hiroshima, Snowy Marsh watched an old steam engine haul carriages through Kobe carrying women and children, the flesh burned from their faces and arms. The day after the bomb fell on Nagasaki, in Sendyru camp a deaf Japanese civilian motioned Chilla Goodchap across and drew two strange shapes in the dirt. He could not speak properly, but he said 'boom, boom'.

For Allan Chick, down from the hills around Nagasaki, life among the ruins was unreality. One day the commandant of the camp addressed the prisoners through an interpreter. As the commandant spoke on, the interpreter said: 'I will not tell you everything he is saying but his message really is that the war is over. You can all go home.' Chick didn't know what to make of it. When he had thought of this day, he thought there would be shouting and hollering and carrying on. There was nothing. They just stood there, dumb.

Spud Spurgeon, Hudson bomber pilot, and Lance Gibson, survivor of the *Tang* attack, spent the last months of the war in an officers' camp at Mukden, Manchuria. One day Spurgeon was walking around the quadrangle with Air Vice-Marshal Sir Paul Maltby, who had commanded British and Australian air units. Spurgeon saw out of the corner of his eye something above the airfield about 4 kilometres away. 'Sir, I don't know if you can see that far, but that's a Liberator and there are nine parachutes that have dropped out of it.' There was another sign at Mukden that the war was over. A canal flowed by and down it came a constant stream of bodies. It was in this area that Japan had staged the 'incident' in 1931 that was the excuse for Japanese aggression. The Chinese were taking revenge. Several days later there was a roar and flourish of tanks at the gates of Mukden camp. An officer called out: 'I am pleased to announce to you that by courtesy of the Russian army you are now free men.'

First, the Russians wanted to shoot all the Japanese guards. The Allied officers objected. 'Doesn't matter,' the Russians said, 'you use them for whatever you like now and we will fix them after you go.' Second, the Russians wanted to toast. They had gallons of vodka. Gibson spent nights toasting Roosevelt, Churchill, Stalin, Truman, wives and mothers, the draining of glasses punctuated by bursts of submachine-gun fire into the floor and through the ceiling. Liberation by the Russians was not safe.

At Nakom Paton in Thailand on August 16, a Japanese guard pedalled past Bill Dunn on his bicycle. 'You master now,' he said, 'you master now.' Ken Dumbrell was in Kanchanaburi camp. It was over, people were saying. Dumbrell wanted to test this. He went to the Japanese headquarters where the soldiers were sitting around a table. 'I want some sugar,' he told the interpreter, an unthinkable action for so long. He got his sugar but the interpreter said: 'Dumbrellsan, you think we're finished. One year, five year, ten year, hundred year, Japan number one, you number two.'

On August 16 at Ratburi, Desmond Jackson was still working on the railway. He breakfasted, as he had for years, on rice gruel and then marched out with his party to build an engine shelter shed. At 3.30 pm a Japanese corporal ran up to the officer in charge who listened, stood still for some seconds then rushed towards headquarters, hanging onto his sword as he went. Work continued, but an hour later the men were marched towards their camp. Watching them from the embankment was the Thai Ja Ray, who had not been seen since he had organised the escape of Ken Linford and the two others to join the guerillas. Ja Ray, a showman, suddenly burst into song. Jackson recognised the tune as an approximation of 'God Save the King'. The words were:

Please listen to me now.
I have to let you know.
The war is done.
England victorious.
America victorious.
Japan has surrendered.
The war is done.

David Manning was attached to a Japanese battalion based on an isolated rubber plantation in southern Thailand. On August 20, the prisoners were called on parade. There was no interpreter. The commander addressed them. He was sombre, but what was he saying? At the end, he looked at them, then bowed. Manning thought: 'He's trying to tell us the war is over. I'll never have to bow to another Japanese.'

AT LAST, ELEVEN days after the Voice of the Crane was heard in Japan, the news reached the Australian nurses and civilian women and children in Lubuk Linggua camp on Sumatra. There had been indications. Children under 12 were allowed to visit their Dutch fathers in the nearby men's camp. As they lined up, some were told there was no need to go. Their fathers were dead. All were emaciated but some children were too malnourished to walk across. Four from the one family went bearing bad news. When they returned they said: 'Daddy couldn't speak to us. He was crying all the time about Mummy.'

On August 24, 1945 Captain Siki, the 'mean-souled scoundrel', stood on a table to make a promised important announcement: 'Now there is peace, and we will all soon be leaving Sumatra. If we have made any mistakes in the past we hope you will forgive us, and now we will be friends,' he said.

It took three weeks for an Allied search party to locate the nurses. The Japanese had not been helpful. On September 15 the nurses stood on the verge of an airport at Lahat, watching a speck of silver turn into a Douglas transport. The door opened and an Australian major emerged, followed by two women in safari jackets, slacks (Slacks! The nurses were stunned), gaiters and boots and pips on their shoulders.

This is how Pat Gunther remembered the occasion. The major says: 'Where are the Australian nurses?' The nurses, in the faded remnants of their uniforms, laugh. 'We're here.' Someone says to the women who have come down the steps of the plane: 'Who are you?' The senior one says: 'I am the mother of you all.' She is Matron Annie Sage, head of the nursing service. Matron Sage says: 'Where are the rest of you?' There is a silence for a moment, then a voice says: 'They're all dead.'

CHAPTER 27

Crime and punishment

A rainbow
In every dew-drop
On a rotten wooden cross

Takashi Nagase

Lieutenant Eiji Hirota bowed to the three men looking down at him from the bench. 'I wish to thank the court and its members,' Hirota said, 'for all they have done for me during the three days' trial. During the trial I have come to recall the past days when I dined and talked with the prisoners of war. I have mingled with the prisoners of war more as a neighbor than enemies on the battlefield. Due to the fact that I was not in actual battle, I have mingled with them as neighbors.'

Major Sydney Hodgens, Major Norman Quinton and Captain Hubert Vallenburg, the Australian Military Tribunal sitting in Singapore, listened impassively. It was September 21, 1946. That afternoon they retired briefly and then delivered their verdict. What Lieutenant Hirota had actually done, they found, was to commit 'a war crime in that at Hintok-Kanu area, Siam, between May 1943 and August 1943 in the supervision of the work of prisoners of war employed in the construction of the Burma–Siam railway he inhumanely treated the said prisoners of war, contributing to deaths, bodily injury, damage to health and mental suffering'.

The tribunal directed that 28-year-old Hirota be hanged. As he stood on the scaffold on January 21, 1947 did he think of Weary Dunlop? Did he remember that March day in 1943, when Dunlop said: 'I have taken steps to have you hanged, for you are a black-hearted bastard'? The hangman, a very busy person, went about his work, and justice was done. Or was it an act of revenge, as Hirota's engineer friend and mentor, Renichi Sugano, has claimed? In war, to the victors the spoils; in peace, to the victors the opportunity to try the enemy as war criminals.

Allan Chick, already a witness to history at Nagasaki, had a seat at the International Military Tribunal where Japanese leaders were being tried for 'crimes against peace'. Not ready to return to life on a Tasmanian cray boat, Chick went back to Japan as a member of the occupation forces. When officers learnt he had been a prisoner of war, they arranged for him to go to the hearings. So there he was, a corporal in a hall full of braid and badges of rank, watching General Hideki Tojo, architect of the war and once the most powerful man in Japan, taking his place in the dock before 11 judges from the Allied powers, headed by Australian Sir William Webb. Chick knew he had been lucky to survive the war, first the bomb and second, the likely annihilation of prisoners of war had the Allies invaded Japan. But he felt no particular, personal satisfaction in watching Tojo fight for his life.

For General Tomoyuki Yamashita, the Tiger of Malaya, defeat brought double punishment. Yamashita appeared to be magnanimous in victory, perhaps to a fault, to the humiliated Allied commander, General Arthur Percival. As he was leaving

Singapore, his great prize, in July 1942, Yamashita sent a note to Percival accompanying 'a small token of my personal interest in your welfare', 30 tins of butter, 30 tins of cheese, 150 bottles of beer and two bottles of sherry. Percival was freed in Manchuria; Yamashita was captured in the Philippines. MacArthur delighted Percival by inviting him not just to attend the Japanese surrender ceremony on Tokyo Bay, but to stand in a place of honour directly behind him. The golden moment for Percival came at another ceremony at Baguio, in the Philippines, when his old adversary formally surrendered. 'As Yamashita entered the room,' Percival recorded, 'I saw one eyebrow lifted and a look of surprise cross his face – but only for a moment. His face quickly resumed that sphinx-like mask common to all Japanese, and he showed no further interest.' In fact the sphinx was in anguish. Yamashita thought Percival's presence was an act of revenge, humiliation for humiliation. He told a chaplain just before his execution as a war criminal that the thought of committing suicide crossed his mind for a moment when he saw Percival. His death poem was: 'The world I knew is now a shameful place / There will never come a better time / For me to die.'

DUNLOP'S FIRST DIARY reference to Hirota (spelt Hiroda) was on March 19, 1943. It began 'dreadful news in the evening'. Hirota was demanding 600 men to work on the railway. This meant no work on sanitation and malaria prevention. Worst of all, it meant light-duty and no-duty men and all men without boots would have to work. 'This is the next best thing to murder,' Dunlop wrote.

The diary entries were damning and so were Exhibits 5, 8 and 10, Dunlop's work tendered by the prosecution at Hirota's trial. Exhibit 5 was a Q form, filled out by prisoners of war to record brutality: 'Lt Hirota attacked a party of "light sick" who were really very ill men, stating that each man must carry one log up a slope. Cpl Cully AIF (Timor Btn) defended the party and was then felled by Hirota who struck him on the neck with a large sapling. I attended to him when he was dazed and vomiting.' Exhibit 8: 'Lt Hirota in a violent rage. As a result of this incident it was instructed by Lt Hirota that I should be punished for my interference and I was called to the guard tent and struck several times by two Japanese privates in the presence of Captain Rees. I also received orders that I would not be again allowed to approach Lt Hirota personally.'

By Exhibit 10, Hirota must have felt the terrible lightness of the noose on his neck: 'He was a man-killer, pure and simple. He personally entered my hospital and drove sick men to work without food or water . . .'

JAPANESE PRISONER-OF-WAR CAMPS, with their flies, filth, maggots, bred disease. They also bred hate among men who lived with brutality, hunger and humiliation, who watched their mates die and who felt their own lives slipping away. In the Potsdam Declaration, the Allies had promised stern justice to Japanese war criminals. Forewarned, the Tokyo authorities on August 20 sent a telegram to all prisoner-of-war camps:

Personnel who have ill-treated POWs and internees or who are very much hated by them should at once be transferred elsewhere, or steps taken to conceal their whereabouts. Moreover, documents which it could not do to have fall into enemy hands should at all costs be destroyed after use.

In those first days when prisoners were regaining their old personas as free individuals, there were acts of revenge. Some were rage-driven and indiscriminate. On the banks of a river in Bangkok, Ray Myors watched a man who had been drinking with his mates swim out to a canoe carrying a party of Japanese. He tipped it over and, one by one, held the heads of the Japanese under water until they drowned. Some were a deliberate hunting-down. Ray Wheeler, survivor of the long drift after the sinking of the *Rokyu Maru*, in 1946 got a message that a mate of his was in Heidelberg hospital in Melbourne and would like to see him. Let's call him Tom. Wheeler went out, stopping at Penny Ryan's pub to buy a couple of bottles of beer to smuggle in his greatcoat pocket. He saw this bloke at the end of the surgical ward, waving his arm. It was Tom. As Wheeler got closer, Tom continued to wave his arm and then pointed to a watch. 'What the bloody hell's going on?' Wheeler asked. 'So you've got a watch.'

'You know that watch, don't you?' Tom said.

'No.'

'That's Lubralips's watch'. Lubralips, the Boy Bastard and the Boy Bastard's Cobber were the nicknames for a trio of vicious guards in the Burma-side camps. Often Lubralips kicked Tom on his ulcerated shins. The story as related by Tom's mates is that he heard Lubralips was being held in a Bangkok prison. He pinched a military policeman's red-banded cap, a badge and an armband. He went to the jail, said he was going to interview the prisoner and didn't want to be disturbed. He killed Lubralips and took his watch.

There was also restraint, and a weariness about the war and everything to do with it. Bill Dunn and Arthur Foley just turned to each other, shook hands and said: 'We made it, mate.' One night in Bangkok, an American paratrooper invited Dunn out for a ride in a Jeep, the first he'd seen. They drove into a Japanese camp. Along the railway, Dunn had beri-beri and malaria. He had dysentery so badly that Weary Dunlop operated as a last resort. Dunn was given an epidural, which helped, but not enough. 'Oh sir,' he said to Dunlop, 'this must be how a rabbit feels when it's being gutted.' When he slaved at Hellfire Pass, his work party going out of camp and going in filed past the guard they called the Silent Basher who hit each man on the right of the jaw, then on the left. Now Dunn stood among the defeated enemy and one small Japanese laughed. 'I just went like that,' Dunn recalled, 'with the back of my hand and I felt disgusting and said to myself' "Well, you're just bringing yourself down to his level".'

And there were all those tens of thousands of silent witnesses, the dead. But some of them could speak from the grave.

In September 1945, Takashi Nagase, interpreter for the *kempeitei* and aide to a torturer, received a new assignment. The Allies had asked for a Japanese interpreter to accompany a party, including released prisoners of war, along the railway. Its mission was to find and record graves. The party travelled by train, over the bridges and embankments, through the cuttings. The price of a ticket to ride had been paid in lives. The search started near Thanbyuzayat, the Burma terminus. In two years since it had received its last body, the stark, bare cemetery had been cloaked in green. Japanese soldiers cleared the growth. There were the graves, shallow depressions, some still marked by decaying wooden crosses. The sun played on them again and on the morning dew. Takashi composed his haiku.

Some days later at the site of the 100-kilo camp, Nagase watched as Captain Athol White of the 2/26th Battalion, a former prisoner of war, stood by the large cross in the camp cemetery, holding a compass. White walked slowly, deliberately until he reached the base of a tall tree. He told the

Japanese work party to dig there. They unearthed a wooden box and in it was a sealed bottle which contained records of camp life and of the deaths of men, material which would be valuable as evidence. White had followed a compass bearing of 11 degrees from the cross to the spot where his superior, Major John Stringer, had buried the box when the camp had been emptied two years before.

AS MEN LIKE Tom became executioners and men like Dunn struggled with emotions and conscience, the Allied nations began preparations for formal war crimes trials. Earl Mountbatten, Supreme Allied Commander, South East Asia Command, warned that 'nothing would diminish our prestige more than if we appeared to be instigating vindictive trials against individuals of a beaten enemy nation'. He realised, Mountbatten said, that the trial of war criminals might prove to be a source of difficulties. This was some understatement. The first, complex problem is to establish just what is criminal in the conduct of war when all the machines are destructive, soldiers are trained to kill and obedience to the orders of superiors is relentlessly instilled. Should the deaths of some civilians be regarded as merely unfortunate collateral damage in attacks of military objectives? Is the wholesale slaughter of populations with the intent of shortening the war and preventing even more deaths acceptable? In World War II, the boundaries of the battlefield were extended deep into the suburbs by waves of bombers as part of grand strategy. Surely the deaths of hundreds of thousands of civilians raise great moral questions.

In the prisoner-of-war camps hidden in the Asian jungles wrongs were done too, individual wrongs, one man brutalising another. Mountbatten pointed out the difficulty of fixing the blame. It was important that a chain of responsibility should be established, he said, for this was the only way in which individual brutalities could be with logic and justice laid at the door of those who had not personally committed them, but who had certainly authorised and encouraged, if not connived at their perpetration. Charges of petty brutality, Mountbatten said, must therefore be laid against individual perpetrators; then, ascending in the hierarchy, those responsible for definite orders which had given rise to those acts should be tried; and finally, those whose overall policy had been implemented by the orders given, and by the acts themselves.

It was decided that three classes of war criminals should be prosecuted: A class, Japan's military and political elite, who planned and oversaw the conduct of the war; B class, who committed conventional war crimes or breached the laws and customs of war; and C class, who committed crimes against humanity, especially non-combatant civilians. Australia was enthusiastic in the pursuit of alleged war criminals and in executing them. Plans for a gallows were sent to Rabaul, where 87 were sentenced to death and for a period up to seven a day were hanged. Detailed 'Notes for guidance in carrying into effect sentence of death by shooting' were distributed. There would be 10 in the firing party; they would be informed that one of the rifles would be loaded with a cartridge from which the bullet had been extracted; the medical officer would fix a white disc over the man's heart; the order 'fire' would be given in a low voice; if the medical officer is unable to certify death, the officer in charge would shoot the man with his own pistol. Unfortunately, there is evidence that the same attention to process was not demonstrated in all the trials of war-crimes suspects.

HISTORIAN GAVAN McCORMACK examined the case of Im Yong-Jun. This is a precis: Im, 25 years old, third son of a

Korean farmer, known by his Japanese name Hayashi Eishun. Charge: inhumanely treating prisoner of war Lance Sergeant L. E. Whitfield. The facts: Whitfield had been discharged from hospital after a bout of dysentery. Very short-sighted, he failed to rise and salute a guard who had entered his dimly lit hut and was kicked in the stomach. Died 12 days later. Cause of death on death certificate, dysentery. Evidence was presented by affidavit and there was no opportunity for the defence to cross-examine. Key witness: Major Sydney Krantz, army doctor, who according to evidence, examined Whitfield immediately after the assault and said death had been caused by kicking. Whitfield referred to a guard known as the Maggot, 'a particularly nasty piece of work . . . harsh and brutal'. The flaws, both extremely damaging to the prosection: Krantz insisted he did not at the time know a Whitfield; there was serious doubt whether Im was the Maggot. Moreover, Im had previously been tried on the very same charges but the Judge Advocate General refused to confirm the sentence of the court. Im was hanged at Changi jail on June 27, 1947. To the end, McCormack summed up, this case was marked by irregularities.

Then there was the case of Yi Hak-Nae, another lowly ranked Korean, first found guilty of being responsible for the death of over 100 Australian prisoners and sentenced to death. He was reprieved and the sentence commuted to 20 years' imprisonment. His trial had lasted an effective 80 minutes. The evidence was thin and ambiguous, McCormack found, and this case alone was sufficient to raise doubts about the quality of justice dispensed in Australian war crimes trials.

McCormack levels one charge at the tribunals: 'They failed signally to understand either the structure of military command or the extent to which the moral vortex of Japanese militarism worked to suck up all autonomy and responsibility from the lower levels and concentrate it at the top.' His broad criticism of the war-crime trial process is that 'it was the lowest ranks of the Japanese system, particularly the Korean guards, upon whom the heaviest retribution was visited. Ironically, therefore, judicial responsibility increased as actual power in the Japanese hierarchy diminished. Those responsible for scripting and directing the tragedy – the planners, politicians, engineers and officers – by and large escaped responsibility.' At the Tokyo trials of class A criminals there was a limited sheeting home of responsibility for the treatment of prisoners of war, while the matter of responsibility at the Daihonei (imperial headquarters) in Tokyo, of Southern Expeditionary Force headquarters and of the Railway Regiment headquarters was only inadequately pursued.

Patriotism is the last refuge of the scoundrel; 'I was only obeying orders' is the first line of defence of soldiers charged with war crimes. Lieutenant Colonel Yoshitada Nagatomo, who was responsible for 10,000 prisoners of war working on the Burma end of the railway, was convicted on two sets of charges. One was being a party to the mistreatment of prisoners of war, causing death, injury, damage to health and physical suffering. In the petition to the Advocate General against Nagatomo's conviction, his Japanese lawyer submitted that Nagatomo had in fact managed to save lives of prisoners of war under his command when the death rates of the Burma section and the Thai section of the railways were compared. The lawyer pointed to evidence given at the trial by Lieutenant Colonel F. Hazengerg, a leader of a group of Dutch prisoners of war: 'The Colonel was always very interested in things, he is not a bad man. I think he did his best.' He submitted that Brigadier Varley, who had commanded the Allied prisoners of war in Burma 'who later met his untimely death (may his soul rest in peace) en route to Japan by an Allied torpedo attack, would surely have testified in just the same way as the Dutch representative of behalf of Nagatomo'.

Perhaps Varley would have, had his flotilla of lifeboats not sailed off towards the guns of Japanese ships. The death rate was lower on the Burma sections, partly because the terrain in general was not as harsh and partly because the doomed, sick men of F Force worked in Thailand. Australia's official historian, Lionel Wigmore, adds another factor: the better relations between Varley and the Japanese. 'This was partly due,' Wigmore says, 'to Varley's perspicacity in keeping the maximum number of men at work, and his continued efforts to improve conditions, but also because Nagatomo (hamstrung though he may have been in some respects by higher authority) and most of his officers were reasonable to a degree that would have astonished senior officers charged with liaison between their troops and the Japanese at other times and places.' Varley himself wrote that when a Japanese NCO 'blitzed' a sick parade to get more workmen, claiming it was on Nagatomo's orders, he disbelieved this, ordered a sick parade and asked Nagatomo himself to make an inspection. 'The sick included hundreds with tropical ulcers varying in size up to a small saucer,' Varley noted. 'Nagatomo was astonished. He ordered that numbers going to work be left to doctors and he asked what medicines and drugs . . . were required.' At Varley's urgings, Nagatomo also asked the railway commander to reduce the hours the men had to work. 'Unfortunately, he has done this before,' Varley commented, 'and the railway commander had not agreed.' Nagatomo agreed to issue orders forbidding guards from striking prisoners, while he asked Varley to instruct prisoners not to treat the guards with disdain (probably from a pragmatic point of view a reasonable request). Striking did continue. Perhaps these words from the dead Varley may have helped Nagatomo's case. But the official history was not published until 1957, a decade after he had been hanged.

Nagatomo was found guilty of two other charges: 'In violation of the laws and usages of war', he had ordered the execution of Gunner K. J. Dickinson and Sapper A. J. Bell. In February 1943 Dickinson, Bell and Major A. Mull escaped from Thetkaw camp in Burma. Mull, who had served with British forces in India and who knew the jungle, planned to lead the party across the border to Assam. After three days, Dickinson came down with malaria and, as the men had agreed, was left to fend for himself. He was recaptured and executed. Mull and Bell had cleared the heavy jungle when they were challenged by a Burmese police patrol. Mull died in the gunfight and Bell was wounded. Bell was another of those Australians to die game before the firing squad. Japanese guards presented arms to him as he lay dead on the ground.

At his trial, Nagatomo said he had received a standing order for the execution of escaped prisoners. 'The orders in general to all camps and the camp staff that run-away prisoners should be shot to death – that was issued by myself in a general way.' However, when Varley had protested about the planned execution of Bell, Nagatomo had gone to seek definite instructions from Major General Saba at the Thai headquarters. Saba had been adamant on the execution.

Where does blame start? Where does it stop? In the face of the dreadful toll of prisoners of war and Asian labourers in the 1943 cholera epidemic, there was a reluctant acknowledgment of group guilt by engineer Yoshihiko Futamatsu: 'There had been no reason to suppose that there would be epidemics of such ferocity: such violence was beyond anticipation but it is true that the Japanese Army did not take sufficient counter measures in time. There were too many victims and the army, I think, did not do enough and deserves criticism.' Individuals, of course, dodged blame. Hirota's lawyer argued: 'Surely the large number of casualties suffered by the prisoners of war working on the railway should be the responsibility of those who organised the project and those who were in command of the forces detailed to carry it through. They alone could have stopped it, and they alone should die because of it . . . I must beg you to consider your humble petitioner among the vast number of helpless victims of a horrible mistake.' Nagatomo's lawyer drew a distinction between the military men in charge of the camps and the engineers who demanded the turning out of sick men from hospitals to work: 'Every work-camp commandant was troubled by the forcible demands from the Railway Corps . . . In my view it is the Railway Corps that should be held responsible for this great disaster.' Hisokazu Suzuki, representing a group of Nagatomo's co-accused, including Captain Shizuo Wakamatsu, argued for the over-turning of the convictions. 'Will it not sound rather strange to say that the person who was charged and punished with responsibility . . . is only a captain, a keeper of the prisoners?' Suzuki said. 'There are other persons than the captain who should be held responsible for the high death-rate. They are General Tojo, Field Marshal Sugiyama [Chief of the General Staff], and Field Marshal Terauchi [Commander in Chief of the Southern Armies].'

Tojo and 27 other military and political leaders were tried as A class war criminals before the International Military Tribunal. Tojo and six others were executed. Sixteen were sentenced to life imprisonment, but paroled in 1955. The conduct of the trials has been criticised. Historians Meirion and Susie Harries say the Manila trial of Yamashita reflects 'extraordinary discredit' on MacArthur. They point to deficiencies of the Tokyo tribunal: no solid foundation in established law, lofty and impractical aims, curious choice of some defendants, controversial choice of judges (only India and China represented of the Asian nations and no neutral representation).

There was still a long queue of potential defendants when the Tokyo trials were halted in 1949. Winston Churchill said: 'Revenge is, of all satisfactions, the most costly and long drawn out; retributive persecution is, of all policies, the most pernicious. Our policy . . . should henceforth be to draw the sponge across the crimes and horrors of the past – hard as that may be – and look, for the sake of all our salvation, towards the future.' But Australia continued to look back in anger. There was a series of trials on Manus Island between June 1950 and April 1951, the major quarry being General Takuma Nishimura, accused of responsibility for the Parit Sulong massacre. Fourteen defendants were sentenced to death and 15 to life imprisonment.

After analysing the outcome of trials over the suffering of F Force, McCormack concludes that responsibility for the actions and inactions that contributed to the appalling death rate was at a level of authority that began only where the indictments and trial stopped. He quotes a Japanese study of 'execution eve' statements by condemned B and C class war criminals: without exception they believed themselves victims of injustice, even martyrs.

The wider problem is how the Japanese people viewed the war-crimes process. Professor Aiko Utsumi of Keisen University has made a detailed study of the mistreatment of prisoners of war and the weight of public opinion against a national apology. Utsumi says: 'The POW atrocities and the B and C trials that resulted produced hardly any reflection by Japanese on the war. On the contrary, resentment against the judgments created the climate for the growth of self-justification.'

Japan's refusal to apologise, and to face up to its history and teach that history to its children has meant lingering pain to prisoner-of-war survivors and disquiet in the region. Lee Kuan Yew, creator of modern Singapore, had a harsh lesson in the importance of heritage in the early days of occupation. A child of the British Empire, he had to get a friend to translate the Chinese characters on a placard beside the severed head of a Chinese on a pole. He then learnt Chinese. Decades after the war, Lee remained concerned about the Japanese psyche. There was a sub-stratum of the culture, he thought, that led them to carry every-thing they did to extremes. They practised unbelievable cruelty and systemic brutalisation. 'Are they still like that, the present generation? No. Can they be re-indoctrinated? Yes, it's part of their culture. I do believe they can be re-indoctrinated especially when they have refused, as the Germans have done, to openly declare that their war was stupid and wrong. But I think the emergence of a nuclear China has put paid to future ambitions.'

NEIL AND IRIS Dawson walk past the statue of Simpson and his donkey along the path to the granite presence of the Aus-tralian War Memorial. Iris Dawson always feels she is entering a cathedral. The flame burns. There are all those names and memories. There is the sense of loss. This day on the steps is a group of young Japanese tourists. They laugh, jostle, change places as they pose for photographs. Neil Dawson stares ahead and walks stiffly past. He still has nightmares. There are still things he can't talk about, even to Iris. She stands in front of the Japanese. 'This is a sacred place,' she says. 'It's no place for fun and games. We'd take off our shoes if we were entering a place like this in your country.' She knows they haven't been told much about the war and anyway she doesn't think a culture as old as Japan's can be changed in a couple of generations.

IN 1992, TWO men sat beside the river in Kanchanaburi, downstream from the River Kwai bridge. They talked and they laughed and once one reached out to touch the other's hand. Then they went together to the site of a building where they had last met. This had been a house of pain and now there was a healing. Eric Lomax and Takashi Nagase had met again. Nagase had returned to Japan after the war, carrying his personal burden of guilt and convinced that blame travelled up and up until it settled on the once-divine shoulders of the Emperor. The Emperor should abdicate.

When the Japanese Government lifted travel restrictions in 1963, Nagase returned to Thailand. The bodies he had helped locate along the southern half of the railway had been brought for reburial at Kanchanaburi. He walked along the long rows of graves and then went to the large white cross and laid a wreath. He wanted to make peace with the dead. He also wanted reconciliation with the living and in 1976 arranged a meeting of former prisoners of war and former Japanese soldiers at Kanchanaburi. He wrote about his war in a confessional book, *Crosses and Tigers*, in 1990. A year later Lomax, a man who still thought of revenge, was reading of the torture of an unnamed prisoner. It was his torture, his beatings, his screaming. He read of Nagase's visit to Kanchanaburi cemetery, and of Nagase standing before the cross, of Nagase's spiritual catharsis there and of Nagase's sense of guilt vanishing. Lomax's wife, Patricia, wrote to Nagase. 'How can you feel "forgiven", Mr Nagase,' she asked, 'if this particular former Far Eastern prisoner of war has not forgiven you?' Eventually the Kanchanaburi meeting was arranged, and then the Lomaxes flew with Nagase and his wife to Japan. They went to Yasukuni shrine, where war criminals are honoured. On the final day, Lomax met Nagase and read to him a letter he had written. Lomax wanted this to be a deliberate, formal occasion. The letter said Nagase had been most courageous and brave in arguing against militarism and working for reconciliation. It said that while Lomax could not forget what had happened in Kanchanaburi in 1943, Nagase had his total forgiveness.

When I met Nagase, who lived the history, he was concerned with the lack of knowledge of young Japanese about it. They should know what was done in the Emperor's name and be aware of the dangers of the cult of obedience. Academic Yuki Tanaka, who has studied Japanese war crimes, is worried too. He writes:

> Those who fought in the Asia-Pacific war were in reality mostly ordinary Japanese men. They were our fathers and grandfathers. We need to face up to the fact we could easily become this 'other' in changed circumstances . . . We Japanese need to re-experience the crimes of our fathers and grandfathers as deeply and as viscerally as the Germans have re-experienced their past. It is not enough for us to gain a purely intellectual understanding of them. In doing so though it is important to ask the question: under what circumstance did (and do) human beings conduct themselves as war criminals?

JAPANESE AND KOREANS, guards and generals, politicians and military planners, were not the only ones to face trial after the war. H. Gordon Bennett, hero at Gallipoli and commander of the 8th Division in Malaya, the man who wanted Monash's mantle as Australia's greatest general, was fighting not for his life but for his reputation. The ugly charge levelled by his accusers, General Percival and General Blamey, was that Bennett, who had escaped from a hospital ship to rejoin his men at Gallipoli, had deserted his command at Singapore. Blamey referred the matter to the army's legal branch and a military court of inquiry sat in judgment. Bennett made a tactical retreat from it, his counsel arguing the hearings should be open to the public. The court found it had been Bennett's duty to remain with his command, that he had issued an order to AIF officers and other ranks to remain in their positions and that he had been the only general officer not to go into captivity with his men. 'The Court is of the opinion, on the evidence, that Lieut-General H. G. Bennett was not justified in handing over his command or in leaving Singapore.'

Bennett had his allies, and they came from the ranks of the men he had allegedly deserted. A meeting of the 8th Division Association dismissed the court of inquiry finding and called for a Royal Commission into the 'whole, ill-fated Malayan campaign, including the escape of Lieut-General Gordon Bennett'. Then there were the welcome words: 'Further this association wholeheartedly supports General Bennett's actions in successfully escaping from Singapore.'

Bennett had his days in court. Little good they did him. The Royal Commissioner, Mr Justice Ligertwood, agreed with Percival, Blamey and the court of inquiry: 'At the time General Bennett left Singapore he was not a prisoner of war in the sense of being a soldier who was under a duty to escape. He was in the position of a soldier whose commanding officer had agreed to surrender him and to submit him to directions which would make him a prisoner of war.'

There was, however, a sweetener for Bennett. Ligertwood said: 'I can say at once that in coming to his decision to escape and in putting it into effect, General Bennett was not conscious that he was committing a breach of his legal or military duty, nor was he actuated by a desire to secure his own safety and avoid the hardships and inconveniences of imprisonment. I think that he acted from a high sense of patriotism, and according to what he conceived to be his duty to his country.'

Among those who gave evidence at the Royal Commission

was 8th Division staff officer John Wyett. It was not favourable. Wyett thought Bennett should have stayed and that Bennett had seen that his only chance of realising his dream of supreme command was to escape.

Wyett was there for the final act, the military funeral for Henry Gordon Bennett in 1962. He was moved as he watched the flag-draped coffin, bearing the general's cap, his sword and an impressive array of medals; he was moved as the gun carriage left, to the slow rhythm of the Dead March. He was not moved to change his judgment of Bennett. 'This was a nation's tribute of forgiveness of a brave patriot and most controversial general; but a man fated to be remembered as the one who had "voluntarily and without permission deserted his command and abandoned his troops",' Wyett wrote.

That is not how Bennett was remembered by many 8th Division survivors. In October 1945, as the thunder of legal battles filled the air, the hospital ship *Manunda* moved towards the dock in Sydney harbour with a cargo of 8th Division ex-prisoners of war. Waiting for them was a spare figure wearing a suit and a homburg. He looked up at the waving men. There, slung on the ship's side, was a sheet and on it was scrawled:

WE WANT
BENNETT
8TH DIV

Note that the 'WE' was underlined.

Bennett and his wife were first up the gangway. Gilbert Mant, who had enlisted in the 8th Division before serving as a war correspondent during the Malaya campaign, wrote this report:

As they clustered around him and grasped his hand on the deck of the hospital ship, some said there were tears in the eyes of the tough, pugnacious general the Japs had tried so hard to kill . . .

. . . The emotional moment on the hospital ship was perhaps the greatest moment of Bennett's life. It was the vindication he wanted most of all: the faith of the rank and file . . .

. . . In the three years of frustration after his escape from Singapore, he had been the victim of a smear campaign and had developed almost a persecution complex. The knowledge that most of his men, who had had plenty of time to brood over the matter, were behind him was a heart-warming experience.

On Anzac Days in Sydney, Bennett, wearing his homburg and World War I and World War II campaign medals, marched in front of his men.

It is understandable if many of the 8th Division survivors did not want their leader taken away from them in disgrace. They were coming out of a world of suffering and uncertainty where each day could bring death. They were returning to uncertainty. Would they be regarded as Australian soldiers or as slaves of the Japanese? Had their wives, their fiancées, their girlfriends waited for them through the long and mostly silent years?

CHAPTER 28

Home

Small scraps of a small photograph fluttered down into the wake of the hospital ship carrying released prisoners of war back to Australia. Victor Ryan was conducting a personal ceremony to consign the memory of his fiancée to the deep. Ryan had just learnt he had been Thompsoned. He had begun his war doomed to lose, an observer in the three-man crew of a Vildebeeste bomber in No. 100 Squadron. Obsolescent was too polite a word for this biplane. A war correspondent noted that the Vildebeeste flew so slowly that it gave the impression of being suspended motionless in the air. Ryan's friend, Ivor Jones, a gunner-wireless operator in No. 36 Squadron, thought this was just a little harsh. The Vildebeeste could be used as a torpedo bomber. Jones remembered clinging white-knuckled to his Lewis gun (World War I vintage), when pilot Buck Buchanan put their kite into a shuddering dive. It could reach 225 kilometres an hour dragged down by the torpedo. In level flight its top speed could match that of a reasonable family motor car. Early in the Malayan campaign, Vildebeestes were used as night bombers. Darkness was their only real protection. On January 26, 1942 they lost that. Early in the morning, a Japanese invasion convoy of one aircraft carrier, four cruisers, six destroyers, two transports and 13 smaller craft was spotted 32 kilometres off the coast heading for Endau, in north-east Johore state. The Allies only had 36 fighters and bombers available, including the 21 Vildebeestes of No. 36 and No. 100 squadrons.

'The Zeros were up there licking their lips,' Jones told me. Victor Ryan's No. 100 squadron went in first at around three in the afternoon. They at least had some cloud cover, but they lost five out of 12. Jones and No. 36 Squadron flew through a clear blue sky at about 5 pm, ahead of their fighter escorts, which were refuelling. They were bombing the landing zone and the Japanese fighters were strafing them. Five of the nine Vildebeestes went down. Jones's was tattered by bullets and Buck Buchanan told him to bail out. He jumped. And hung there. He had forgotten to unhook his monkey strap. He looked down at the battle over the beach. He didn't want to go there and hauled himself back to his cockpit. The fighters arrived. Stay in, Buchanan said, and the Vildebeeste made its slow way back to base not much over ground level. Victor Ryan had returned too, but wounded through the foot. He was on the list for repatriation to Australia, but he was enveloped by the surrender and disappeared from the world and his fiancée's sight.

For many prisoners of war and for many of their families, the silence was absolute. Desmond Jackson was an exception with his 70 letters. Neil Dawson received that one letter, two years in passage, signed 'still your fiancée, Iris'. In Victor Ryan's camp, Norman Thompson, a 2/3rd machine-gunner, belatedly received bad news: his fiancée had married another man. This news, like all news, was shared among the men. Similar letters arrived and calls went round the camp: 'I've been Thompsoned.' Victor Ryan was told by his sister, a physiotherapist on the hospital ship he thought was sailing him to a reunion. 'God, I've been carrying the photograph of another man's wife in my pocket for two years,' he said.

FROM JUNGLE CAMPS and squalid jails, from the outskirts of pretty Japanese villages and the atomic wasteland of Nagasaki, from Manchuria and other parts of the ruins of the Greater East Asia Co-Prosperity Sphere, they were coming home. But to what sort of welcome? This had been given some thought by the Australian authorities in mid-1945 when eventual victory was ensured. The Minister for the Army, Frank Forde, was an advocate of a public welcoming, of parades and reassurances of the people's regard and sympathy. Forde received contrary advice from the army's Adjutant General, Major General C. E. M. Lloyd, a desk officer, who wrote:

> The actual meetings of the repatriates with their next-of-kin is marked by emotions which have to be seen to be believed. My own personal view is that these reunions should be had in the homes of the people . . . such a course would avoid the contagious emotionalism approaching hysteria. The participation of the Commonwealth government [in a public reception] should be carefully considered. There is a feeling in the Army, and I think in the country generally, that the flap concerning the repatriated prisoners is a bit exaggerated. The great bulk of them are fit and well, provided with large sums of money from their enforced period with no expenses, and now granted discharge from the Army. On the other hand the soldier who has borne the whole load comes from the still continuing battle in New Guinea, tired, diseased and NOT discharged and nobody but his next of kin are really very interested in him as an individual.

An army instruction urged that no more publicity than 'inevitable' be given to the ex-prisoners' experience and deprivation. They should not be encouraged to believe they were entitled to any special privileges.

Lloyd's letter is breathtakingly mean-spirited. It is an example of the military mind at its worst. It lacks intelligence, intuition and a basic humanity. Lloyd, Forde and the country had known since late 1944, when American submarines had rescued from the sea the men whose Japanese transports they had sunk, that dreadful things were happening in the world of the prisoners of war. Out of captivity, the skeletons quickly put on weight, but many had been damaged by disease and the psychological scarring was often hidden deep. Apparently Lloyd witnessed some happy, exuberant reunions. Many weren't. For some homeward-bound men like Victor Ryan, there was no-one to be reunited with. Anyway, the reunion only marked the start of long struggles to rebuild lives.

LATE IN 1945, Mary Everard received her first letter of the war from Lance Gibson. After being liberated in Manchuria by the Russians, Gibson had made a slow way back to his family farm in north central Victoria. An army nurse, Everard could not get leave from her hospital in Brisbane. It was short-staffed and crowded. For some the physical wounds took a long time to heal in the peace, and the psychological ones longer. The beginning of the letter alarmed her. 'Dear,' Gibson said, 'I've changed'. She rang her favourite relative, her aunt Elsie. 'What am I going to do? Has he got one arm, one leg, one eye, or what?' Ring him, Elsie said. It's only five bob for the army on a Sunday. Mary Everard did. She could have skinned him. Gibson wanted to warn her that he had a moustache.

Mary and Lance had met in Adelaide in 1941. Gibson was a young 2/3rd Machine Gun Battalion officer, training a platoon of raw recruits. He was officer of the guard one night when Mary Everard walked past. She caught his eye. A perky walk, he thought. Mary was what was called in those days a bit of a bolter. She and Lance went out a couple of times and she liked him, but Adelaide was full of young army and RAAF men. The night before embarking on the *Queen Elizabeth* for the Middle East, she partied. Too many prawns, oysters and gin slings. She fainted. Her friend Ginnie got her to their cabin, went to dinner and then came bounding back with the news that Gibson was on board. They became close, and luck kept them close. Both of their units went to Palestine. There Lance gave her a half-sovereign with a hole bored through. This Mary turned into what she called her 'dead-meat ticket', her identification disc. In Jerusalem, he gave her a ring. They didn't become officially engaged. That would have meant Mary returning to Australia, but there was an understanding. Then Gibson sailed off towards Java and the Japanese.

In his letter, Gibson was undoubtedly warning Mary about more than his moustache. As an officer, he had escaped much of the brutality and the possibility of being worked to death. But he had lost years of his life, came close to dying and malnourishment had taken away half his weight. By the time he reached home, he was 12 stone again, and would have looked well in Major General Lloyd's eyes. It was flab though. Gibson always thought he was one of the lucky ones. There was Mary waiting and there was the familiar farm, with its far horizons. He did, however, have three attacks over a year or so. They frightened Mary. She didn't know what they were. Worse than any malaria she had nursed, or anything else. A high temperature, the bed shook, he poured sweat. 'And was very unhappy,' Lance said. He wasn't troubled much by nightmares except year after year, decade after decade, around about June 24. That was the night in 1944 when Dick O'Kane's *Tang* torpedoed the *Tamahoko Maru*.

BILL DUNN, WITH a childhood of abandonment, always wanted a family. He married the night before he sailed for Malaya with the anti-tank unit. His first months in captivity were tolerable. One day a Japanese guard picked him out. He wanted his motorcycle repainted. For three days Dunn stayed at one of the former Raj homes. The Japanese listened to Tokyo Rose, but, as it turned out, her message was in a way a personal one for Dunn: 'Oh boy, you really should be home you know. The Americans are giving your wives and girl-friends a wonderful time. You really should be home looking after them. Boy, why don't you go home?' Dunn went to the Thai–Burma railway and he survived Hellfire Pass. When he returned home, his wife, his uncle and his sister were waiting for him on the wharf. They had a day out in Melbourne, a good meal and his sister presented him with two tickets for the best show in town at the Tivoli. Afterwards Dunn and his wife went to the house in suburban Heidelberg where she was living. She made a cup of tea and then went and stood on the other side of the kitchen. She said: 'Well, I'm living here with someone else. You can stay the night if you want to.'

SNOWY MARSH WAS staging through Manila on his way back from Japan. There he received a letter from his father telling him that his fiancée Heather, who thought he was dead, had married someone else. He couldn't settle back in Cairns. He went south, keeping moving, always searching for his prisoner-of-war mates. They were everything to him, better than a family. Eventually Marsh did marry. Edna had been a friend of Heather's; they went to school together, went to the same church, learned piano together. Snowy Marsh and Edna had a good life and three daughters. She died in 2000. Heather's husband had died a year before. Heather and Snowy Marsh married. 'At 82 and 85, you didn't want to hang around too long,' Marsh said. 'Anyway, it had already been a 64-year engagement.'

CORPORAL ALLAN CHICK of the British Commonwealth Occupation Forces did not come home to Australia until 1953. He brought his wife Haruko with him. 'Haruko' has perhaps 17 different meanings. One of them is spring. Haruko was a spring baby. Every Japanese surname represents something. Hers was Kojima, meaning small island. Haruko and Allan Chick were helping to make history and change a nation. They were sailing to the land of White Australia. Billy Hughes at the end of World War I had called up the regiments of the dead to defend the White Australia policy at the Paris Peace Conference and blocked Japan's attempt to lift restrictions on Japanese immigration; John Curtin, at the outbreak of World War II had declared: 'This country shall remain forever the home of those people who came here in peace in order to establish in the South Seas an outpost of the British race.'

There was an innocence about Chick, the boy from the Tasmanian fishing village, when he enlisted on June 17, 1940. He wrote his first letter to St Helens from the 2/40th Battalion training camp at Brighton, Tasmania, three days later.

> Dear Mother,
> It's like a big city with over 2000 men here. The camp covers more ground than St Helens and has about ten times as many street lights. It's all laid out like a city with its streets and a bloke can get lost if he goes about half asleep.

As the battalion moved north across the Australian mainland there were letters (all addressed to his mother) about training.

February 2, 1941: 'We're supposed to be pursuing the fleeing Italians in the direction of Bengasia [Libya]'. There was a letter about a girl he had left behind: he was worried about Edna, who had just turned 16, 'stewing her brains about him'. She was too young for that.

But there was one from Katherine in the Northern Territory that indicated he was not a typical child of his times. It was Easter Monday and he wrote about the camp, the frontier town with its few whites, and about the Aborigines.

> Some of our troops treat them with contempt, call them Jacky. They don't seem to realise that those who work for the whites are perhaps more intelligent than some of themselves.

Chick sailed to Timor, a member of Sparrow Force. His last letter before captivity was written to his brother Col, who was in the RAAF.

> 12/2/42
> I've had little time to write until now owing to Jap raiders and excessive amount of work to be done . . . At present I am quartered in a native hut which local historians say is the morgue, along with ants, bees and mossies and occasional fowl. Occasionally we live pretty well here, having chicken and beer at a belated supper, topped off with tinned frankfurts and tomato sauce . . .

Next there was a postcard, written later that year.

> I am now in a Japanese prisoner of war camp, in Java.
> My health is excellent.
> I am constantly thinking of you. It will be wonderful

when we meet again.
Love and best regards to you all.
Coming home soon.
Allan.

Then, written in 1944:

Dear Mother,
I am now in Japan. I am still looking forward to a letter
from you. I am well; hoping same all of you, and may the
New Year bring realisation of our hopes.

In October 1945 Evelyn Chick received a letter in an envelope
marked LIBERATED AUSTRALIAN PW.

18/9/45
Dear Mother,
Received a short note from dad last night, dated 22nd Aug,
first word I have received in three and a half years, but it
made no mention of yourself which I thought rather
strange. Would you please write, giving a resume of what
has happened since your last letter which was dated Jan
26th and received Feb 19th coinciding with Jap landing
on Timor . . . I would like to know who is dead, who is
married, and if there is anyone there old enough to marry.

Marriage was something of a preoccupation for Chick, now
aged 25 and having lived three and a half wasted years, but he
mixed seriousness with banter. From Manila on the repatriation voyage to Australia he wrote:

. . . I guess I'll have some trouble dodging would-be
brides when I get home, so it may be a good idea to

spread a yarn about me getting mixed up with some dusky tropical maiden. I guess there are plenty of adventuresses around now . . .

Chick escaped the adventuresses of St Helens and returned to Japan as a member of the occupation forces, first of all searching for arms caches. He found a nation devastated.

14/6/46
. . . Don't worry about a cake, haven't the inclination for some when you see millions facing starvation. It gives me a guilty feeling . . .

He found Haruko, daughter of a high-ranking police officer who had been cashiered. Her mother had died in the world flu epidemic in 1920. Chick quickly made up his mind that they would marry but he was aware both of the longstanding wall of prejudice around White Australia and of the still-fresh pain and hatred spawned by the war. He was not a racist but racism was part of the nation's social fabric; he had been a prisoner of war, but had not suffered the torment of the railway or of the other hearts of darkness. A collection of his letters home about Haruko are in the Australian War Memorial. The replies from his mother are not. They don't need to be. As he heads steadily towards marriage, Chick manoeuvres, advances and retreats in reaction to her reactions.

2/7/46
. . . This non-fraternisation order here is a real farce. You can look out the window and see a Yank or two go by with a Nip girl, do it in front of the officers and military police and nothing is said so long as you don't actually touch the girl, but it is nothing to see a Yank

holding hands or even with an arm around her . . . Also a lot of our girls around, but no one takes the least notice of them . . . Don't ask me why as it has me beat, or perhaps as an Aust remarked 'I'd crawl over a dozen of their kind to get to my little Nip sort' sums up the situation pretty well . . .

23/7/46

. . . Haven't got the least desire to bash Tojo or anyone else. It's a funny thing but the people back home who never actually contacted the Nips are more hostile than the chaps who fought them . . . So you wouldn't like a Jap girl as a daughter-in-law. Well, I guess you know I have a girl friend in Japan . . . My particular friend is not by any means beautiful, is a decent girl and has modern ideas. It is their custom to have their husbands chosen for them when they are 22 or 23 and she is already dreading the day. So I might be part of a long-range plan she had but just whether she will ever beat the old established family control system would be interesting to know . . . Will send you a photo of the future daughter-in-law when I get a good one . . .

6/9/46

. . . Excuse crack about daughter-in-law as I have no intention of marrying her . . .

18/9/46

. . . Got a new [girlfriend] now. Sacked the old one, as she wouldn't move outside the door . . . Girlfriend is a twenty-year-old schoolteacher, perfectly respectable, has no mother and lives with her 18-year-old sister at a friend's house. Incidentally, their friend was in the army and fought against the 2/40th btn in Timor so he knows as much about Timor as I do . . .

Chick enclosed a photograph of two young Japanese women wearing traditional clothes. 'Let me know which one you would like for a daughter-in-law,' he wrote, 'and I'll see what can be done about it.' It seems the letter was passed around the family, and the initial reaction was shock. On the envelope is written in one hand that the letter 'should be destroyed' and in another 'tell him to wake up'.

26/11/46
. . . Sorry I said you were as mad as a meat axe over me having a Nip girlfriend, but I got that impression from one of your letters. If I should ever marry a Nip girl I would never be silly enough to take her anywhere near St Helens as people round there are too one-eyed for that sort of thing. If you want to get rid of that snap, send it back to me. Will not send any more or even mention them again . . .

19/11/48
. . . As for marrying a Jap girl, I still intend to do so but it cannot be done at present, but if you should happen to get a letter with a civilian address on it you can pretty well say I'll be married within three months. I have never met a finer girl than this and hardly expect I ever will. Have no intention of living in Aust with her . . . will stay in Japan or go to England . . .

14/3/49
. . . If I ever marry here will keep it to myself . . .

2/6/52

. . . I married the girlfriend here last December. Ceremony was performed at half past two on the thirtieth of December last in the Methodist Church at Hiroshima. The ceremony was both in English and Japanese. So far no one knows, not the army even. My wife sends her best wishes, not without certain misgivings, however . . .

11/8/52

. . . Her right name is Haruko, but when I use a name at all I call her Juanita. There are no Nip wives in Tassie yet. I should be able to get her to Aust now provided Labor does not get into power in the near future . . . She was extremely pleased to hear of your best wishes as she had an idea you didn't actually approve of a Japanese d-in-law. It is the same girl I used to talk about. I first met her on Sept 8th 1946 . . .

In March 1952 the defences of the citadel were breached. The government gave permission for Australian servicemen to bring their Japanese brides home. The women had to be approved by the Australian Embassy and screened by the Japanese police: no communists, prostitutes, holders of criminal records, no sign of hereditary insanity in their families. Six hundred and fifty came. Twelfth to register had been Allan Chick. He had decided to bring Haruko back to St Helens. The RSL, which would become one of the most conservative organisations in the nation, while saying in the magazine *Mufti* that the question of a ban on the brides' entry was a matter for discussion, came to their support in the meantime. Those wives who did come 'lawfully and at the invitation of their Australian husbands should be treated decently,' the RSL said, 'with a special effort on the part of returned men to make them feel comfortable if only to offset the inevitable hostility from a small group of people in the community who, in addition to not having travelled beyond their own shores, have a way of attacking any person who does not conform to their own pattern and way of life'. It was a generous and surprisingly socially progressive appeal.

Allan and Haruko Chick came to St Helens in trepidation. Haruko always remembered with gratitude the warmth of the welcome. 'The family was so kind and there was this big party. It was easier than I expected. Perhaps it was because it was such a small place and because I was not a young girl. I was 36 when I came.' She never went back to Japan. She was home.

FOR MANY OF the prisoners of war, world peace and the return home did not mean personal peace. Historian Michael McKernan's study of them and their treatment by authorities, military and civil, is properly titled *This War Never Ends*. Those I interviewed said they received minimal or no support. They were advised not to talk about their experiences with their wives; their wives were advised not to raise the matter. Many of them were left alone with their hurt and their hate.

Some of the prisoners of war themselves wanted to deny the prisoner-of-war experience. John Wyett, the man who signed the captivity order in Singapore and suffered terribly in Outram Road jail for longer than he had fought as a soldier, opposed the formation of prisoner-of-war associations. There should have simply been an 8th Division Association, he argued. But there were different needs. The prisoners of war represented four per cent of Australians on active service but

30 per cent of those who died. Between 1945 and 1959 they continued to die at four times the rate of other veterans. From 1959 on, they died at a 20 per cent higher rate. This was hidden. The *Australian Medical Journal* only published the evidence in April 1989.

The men and their families struggled as best they could.

Herb Trackson: 'I didn't talk to my wife about it, but if it wasn't for her, I'd have been in real trouble. I had a young bloke and he was just toddling but I got pretty bad. At night time I couldn't read a book with murder in it. I couldn't just lie and think because the blackness came. She would come in where I was lying on the bed and she knew I was going down and down. She used to say to me, "Oh, don't be such a sook," you know, and "Get hold of yourself." Then I used to get cranky and once I got cranky it was right, whereas if she had come in and said, "Oh dear, never mind", that would have been the end of me. But she stirred me up and got my dander up and started me fighting again.'

George Bell: 'I slept on an open verandah when I got back. Somehow I didn't want walls around me. The neighbours complained about me screaming at night so I had to move into a bedroom so they couldn't hear me scream. When Wanda and I married she got the shock of her life. We'd be asleep and suddenly I'd be in the air, straight up in bed. I'd been beaten again for not bowing low enough. I had blood running out of both my ears for not bowing low enough. All I could feel about the Japanese was hate, hate, hate.'

When I met George Bell in 2002, he said he had no love for the Japanese but he didn't hate them as he had when he first returned. 'I have a lovely wife, I have got four children, seven grandchildren and one great-grandchild and I am still alive today which I thought I never would be.' Bell died some months later, aged 83.

For some the hating never stopped. Others, even during the war, were learning to separate some individuals from the system. Ray Parkin records one day in May 1943 along the railway, not long before the start of *speedo*. The work party had only one Japanese with them. There was no common language but much arm-waving. The prisoners had a little Malay and less Japanese. He had a little English and some Malay. Parkin described him as a pleasant little bloke whose heart was not made for hate. He led the party back to camp at the end of the day, singing them most of Bing Crosby's songs. As a finale Parkin join him in a duet of 'When Irish Eyes Are Smiling' and 'Home Sweet Home'.

On Christmas Day 1944, at Saganoseki camp in Japan, Tom Uren was beaten with an iron bar for insubordination to a Japanese NCO. He was fortunate not to be crippled. But his hatred of all Japanese was healed there. He worked three shifts a day beside older Japanese and then they shared a communal bath in the traditional manner. Again there was no common language but they communicated, as Uren put it, through the eyes, the hands and the heart. All wanted the war to end and the old Japanese workers showed compassion for those who were weak or ill. Uren thought he grew as a person. It wasn't the Japanese he hated, but militarism and fascism. In life there was no progress in hate.

Desmond Jackson struggled with the concept of forgiving but not forgetting. Wasn't forgiving a betrayal of his mates who had died? Then in 1966 a young friend of his, David Stynes, brought to Australia the woman he hoped to marry, Yoshiko Kobashi. She and Jackson met and talked and he found for her the hatred and contempt vanished. In 1967, Yoshiko Kobashi walked down the aisle of St John's Anglican Church in Toorak on the arm of former prisoner of war Desmond Jackson. He was giving the bride away.

What continued to concern Jackson was that Yoshiko had no knowledge of Japanese militarism, the dark side of war and the treatment of prisoners of war. Japanese history is distorted, as Australia's history was for so long through omission and commission: the failure to face up to the brutality of Aboriginal dispossession and the cloaking of it with the legal doctrine of *terra nullius*, Australia as land belonging to no-one before European colonisation. Nations must know their pasts.

Prisoners of war deserve a rightful place in the history of World War II, different from but equal to the front-line soldiers. Like the Anzacs, they are the stuff of legend.

In 1992, a play was produced in Hobart. Author Richard Davies took the title, *A Bright and Crimson Flower*, from Weary Dunlop's account of the jungle burial of Private Jack Verdun Jarvis. The cast have names like Spud and Blue and Wag, but the play is real and true. It is no *Bridge on the River Kwai* or fact-and-fiction television. There are the words of the prisoners of war, their humour, their suffering, their mateship, their dying. In the audience at the premiere there were prisoners of war who were each given a red carnation. As the curtain fell, a young woman reached towards Desmond Jackson and said: 'May I touch you?'

DURING THE *SPEEDO*, the killing time on the Thai–Burma railway, Cyril Gilbert and Ronnie Ferguson, two young mates from Brisbane, would talk about life after the war. Freedom and beer and football and girls and food and family. Ferguson died on Christmas Day, 1943, of beri-beri and starvation. He is buried in Kanchanaburi cemetery. Gilbert walks along the long, serried rows. There are inscriptions of love and loss: 'In undying memory of Alf, who never returned to see his son.' There are inscriptions of love and pride: 'Rest with Australia's brave, my beloved.' On Ferguson's, his family has written: 'His name liveth for evermore'. Gilbert remembers the dead as they were. Ronnie Ferguson is forever 28. Gilbert says he can't picture him as an 80-year-old white-haired bastard. He cries.

Surely they were soldiers.

Endnotes

Chapter 1 A different courage
Page
1   '[Men] will sacrifice': A. B. Lodge, *The Fall of General Gordon Bennett*, p. 41.
4   'During the operations': Citation for Victoria Cross, Charles Anderson, AWM.
5   'I watched them go': Ray Parkin, *Wartime Trilogy*, p. 542.
6   'In 1942 Doris Mulvena received': Doris Mulvena, personal interview.
7   'A day wouldn't pass': Kevin Ward, personal interview.
7   'I will take you from an older Australia': Lodge, p. 311.
8   'You have in the past spoken': Queensland Ex-POW Reparation Committee, *Nippon Very Sorry – Many Men Must Die*, p. 36.
9   'Savagery of the Japanese': Lionel Wigmore, *The Japanese Thrust*, p. 485.
9   'The taking of that ridge': Tom Uren, *Straight Left*, p. 21.
10 'I still squirm': Peter Henning, *Doomed Battalion*, p. 103.
10 '*In a white cot*': poem, AWM.
10 'There are also official records': Mark Johnston, *Fighting the Enemy: Australian Soldiers and their Adversaries in World War II*, p. 80.
11 'My regard for Tony': Mark Johnston, 'Yet they're just as human as we are', Seminar paper, Australia–Japan Research Project.
12 'I do it every time I go back': Kevin Ward, personal interview.
12 'I invited him': E. E. Dunlop, *The War Diaries of Weary Dunlop*, p. 195.
12 ' "No, no, no," Sugano says': Renichi Sugano, personal interview.
13 'Some were shot': Charles Bean quoted in Patsy Adam-Smith, *Prisoners of War, from Gallipoli to Korea*, p. 31.

13   'Leslie Duncan Richardson': Adam-Smith, p. 36.

14   'The spectacle of this Eastern nation': Meirion and Susie Harries, *Soldiers of the Sun*, p. 52.

14   'We were soldiers': Kevin Ward, personal interview.

Chapter 2 A pestiferous varmint
Page

16   'An illusionist, an orator': Donald Horne, *Billy Hughes*, p. 15.

16   'The world be made safe': Woodrow Wilson's 14 points, WWI Document Archive, Yale Law School website.

17   'Whoever controls the islands': W. J. Hudson, *Billy Hughes in Paris: The Birth of Australian Diplomacy*, p. 15.

17   'It showed the hemisphere': Hudson, p. 20.

17   'Perhaps the most important document': Kiyoshi Kawakami, *Japan and World Peace*, pp. 45–62.

17   'He was a *genro*': Harries, p. 48 and p. 124.

17   'The people's unique, divine origins': Harries, p. 12.

18   'The *Lady Rowena* was leaking': Neville Meaney, *Towards a New Vision: Australia and Japan through 100 Years*, pp. 39–42.

18   'There was one edict': Des Sissons in J. A. A. Stockwin (ed.), *Japan and Australia in the Seventies*, p. 193.

19   'He was an acrobat': T. B. Millar, *Australia in Peace and War*, p. 90.

19   'The unity of Australia is nothing': Paul Kelly, *The End of Certainty: The Story of the 1980s*, p. 3.

20   'The population problem': Kawakami, pp. 45–62.

21   'Mr Hughes listened': Lloyd George, quote in Episode 5, '100 years, The Australian Story', Australian Broadcasting Commission.

22   'I would walk into the Seine': Hudson, p. 54, 57, 127.

22   'A pestiferous varmint': Stephen Bonsal, *Suitors and Suppliants: The Little Nations at Versailles*, March 16 entry.

23   'The doctrine that all men': Fitzhardinge, Vol. 2, pp. 401–402, quoted on ABC *Federation Story*.

23   'Following a grand ball': Horne, p. 192.

23   'We went into this conflict': Hudson, pp. 127–128.

24   'The Far Eastern peoples': Kawakami, p. 62.

24   'The modern riddle': Wigmore, pp. 1–2.

25   'John Curtin predicted': David Day, *John Curtin: A Life*, pp. 432–433.

Chapter 3 Troops of God
Page

26   'Corpses drifting swollen': Masanobu Tsuji, *Singapore 1941–1942*, p. 314.

28   'I saw the contents': Keith Rossi, personal interview.

30   'Handy little men': Rudyard Kipling in Harries, p. 79.

30   'Your enemy is a curious race': John Dower, *War without Mercy: Race and Power in the Pacific War*, p. 67.

30   'Japanese soldiers were similarly reassured': Tsuji, pp. 323, 330.

30   'We are fighting for the emancipation': Wigmore, p. 631.

31   'At the hand of a samurai outraged': Harries, p. 15.

31   'Introduced to guns': Jared Diamond, *Guns, Germs and Steel*, pp. 257–258.

32   'Tall, stiff-backed': Harries, pp. 32–33.

32   'More of these piteous deaths': Harries, p. 51.

33   'Every man likes': Yoshida Kenko, *Essays in Idleness*, pp. 35–36.

34   'The first is righteousness': S. Adachi, quoted in *Nippon Very Sorry – Many Men Must Die*, p. 18.

35   'To be incited': Harries, p. 18.

36   'Meet the expectations': H. T. and C. F. Cook, *Japan at War: An Oral History*, p. 264.

36   'Among Allied troops': Harries, p. vii.

36   'Heads should be cut off': Cook, pp. 41–42.

37   'In the olden days': Harries, p. 35.

37   'He was born in a small village': Takashi Nagase, personal interview.

37   'Know ye, our subjects': Imperial Rescript on Education.

38   'His body belonged': Nagase, personal interview.

39   'He was an engineer': Renichi Sugano, personal interview.

40   'Read only this': Tsuji, pp. 295–349.

40   'My body': A. Swinson, *Four Samurai*, p. 162, quoted in Harries, p. 292.

41   'A war criminal': charge made by Alan Warren, *Singapore 1942*, p. 278, and Ian Ward, *Snaring the Other Tiger*, p. 78.

41   'Period of penance': Tsuji, p. 264.

41   'The great aim': Tsuji, pp. 348–349.

42   'The field service code': Dower, pp. 206–207.

42   'We were against': Tsuji, p. 21.

43   'The Peace Preservation Law': Cook, pp. 221–222.

43   'Tadasu Hayashi': Harries, pp. 54–55.

44   'Why should we forgive': Harries, pp. 157–161.

46   'He remembered the shock': Cook, p. 452.

46   'Terumichi the priest': Cook, p. 451.

46   'Isn't it a fact': Kenji Ueda, Yasukuni shrine website.

47   'Japan's victory in the Russo-Japanese war': Wall panel, Yushukan museum.

48   'When you encounter': Tsuji, p. 330.

Chapter 4 Heirs of the Anzacs
Page

50   'A land where books': Judah Waten, *Australia since the Camera: The Depression Years, 1929–1939*.

50   '*They call her a young country*': A. D. Hope, 'Australia', in Harry Heseltine (ed.), *The Penguin Book of Australian Verse*, p. 190.

51   'Finkemeyer lived a good and simple life': Colin Finkemeyer, personal interview.

51   'There were unemployed dances': Waten.

52   'Australia's Bill Woodfull was struck': C. M. H. Clark, *A History of Australia*, VI, pp. 429–430.

52   'A left-winger, Egon Kisch': F. K. Crowley, *Modern Australia in Documents*, p. 587.

53   'A day of mourning': S. Alomes and C. Jones, *Australian Nationalism*, p. 242.

55   'Until recent years': *Argus*, January 1, 1939.

56   'Fellow Australians': Robert Menzies, Menzies Virtual Museum.

56   'War was inevitable': Desmond Jackson, personal interview.

57   'Hello Australians': Jackson, personal interview.

57   'To learn a bit': Lance Gibson, personal interview.

58   'His father Percy': Bill Dunn, personal interview.

59   'For a while the Goodchaps': Chilla Goodchap, personal interview.

60   'Don Wall's father': Don Wall, personal interview.

60   'David Manning's father' : David Manning, personal interview.

60   'Ray Wheeler's father': Ray Wheeler, personal interview.

61   'Nursing was a delight': Pat Darling, personal interview.

61   'For Ron Wells': Ron Wells, personal interview.

62   'Wally Mulvena was': Doris Mulvena, personal interview.

62   'For Allan Chick': Allan Chick, personal interview.

Chapter 5 John Curtin and the Former Naval Person
Page

63   'His Vickers machine gun': Jackson, personal interview.

64   'British intelligence summaries warning': Gavin Long, *Greece, Crete and Syria*, p. xvii.

65   'The British slaughtered the Matabele': John Bellair, *From Snow to Jungle: A History of the 2/3rd Australian Machine Gun Battalion*, p. 264.

65   'At 7 pm on June 17': Bellair, p. 55.

66   'In the crowd cheering like mad': Bellair, p. 59.

67   'Descent into poverty': Day, p. 52.

68   'Ye shall be one nation': Day, p. 151.

68   'Stand upright, proud of yourself': Clark, p. 11.

69   'However, he often broke': Day, p. 397.

69   'If you kill a man': Day, footnote 30, p. 195.

69   'This horrible business of war': Day, pp. 195–196.

69   'The hope, however little': Paul Hasluck, *The Government and the People, 1939–41*, pp. 39–41.

70   'We have to concentrate': Hasluck, pp. 42–45.

70   'You ask, what is our aim?': Winston Churchill, Churchill Centre website. 'The call is for your courage': report in *Sydney Morning Herald*, December 9, 1941, quoted in Day, p. 433.

71   'President to Former Naval Person': Winston S. Churchill, *The Hinge of Fate*, p. 100.

71   'Deterioration in our position': Wigmore, p. 182.

72   'We refuse to accept the dictum': Curtin writing in the *Melbourne Herald*, December 27, 1941.

73   'It will always be deemed remarkable': Churchill, p. 20.

74   'Panic and disloyalty': David Day, *The Great Betrayal*, pp. 228–229.

74   'Suicidal and dangerous': Billy Hughes, quoted in Churchill, p. 23.

74   'If the Malay peninsula': Churchill, p. 23.

74   'If the power of Britain': Raymond Callahan in Brian Farrell and Sandy Hunter (eds), *Sixty Years On: The Fall of Singapore Revisited*, p. 156.

75   'Now, suddenly, all this vanished away': Churchill, p. 55.

75   'In Curtin's absence': Warren, p. 181.

Chapter 6 Twilight of the tuans
Page

78   'The superior status of the British': Lee Kuan Yew, *The Singapore Story*, pp. 51, 52.

79   ' "Harry" was suggested by': Lee, p. 28.

80   'His wife Kwa Geok Choo': Lee, p. 13.

80   'The Prophet Muhammad': C. Mary Turnbull, *A History of Malaysia, Singapore and Brunei*, p. 21.

81   'There is a very rich merchandise': Turnbull, p. 41.

81   'It was the home of': Turnbull, p. 10.

81   'A pre-eminent pivot': Turnbull, p. 101.

81   'The worst disaster': Churchill, p. 88.

82   'It would be all too hard': Farrell and Hunter (eds), p. vii.

82   'Churchill was emphatic': Churchill, p. 28.

82   'Reflected on an enduring theme': Malcolm H. Murfett in Brian Farrell and Sandy Hunter (eds), *Sixty Years On: The Fall of Singapore Revisited*, p. 9.

83   '[W]hile I am not quite clear': Farrell and Hunter, p. 30.

83 'He had been commissioned by the Chiefs of the General Staff': Farrell and Hunter, pp. 32, 33.

84 'Upon the competence': Day, p. 351.

85 'The Japanese would never attempt': Alan Warren, *Singapore 1942: Britain's Greatest Defeat*, p. 23.

85 'The snobbish but decent Warburton': W. Somerset Maugham, *The Casuarina Tree*, pp. 103–105.

86 'The English wife says': Maugham, p. 195.

86 'A historian of the decline and fall': W. Somerset Maugham, *The Gentleman in the Parlour*, pp. 9–11.

87 'Newcomers left visiting cards': Lavina Warner and John Sandilands, *Women Beyond the Wire*, p. 18.

87 'Lee Kuan Yew had been asleep': Lee, p. 45.

87 'A small number of Asiatics': Lee, pp. 51–53.

88 'Ruth was a beautiful': Warner and Sandilands, p. 41.

89 'She had beauty and she had status': Molly Ismail's story is told by Warner and Sandilands.

90 'It was about the master race': Lee Kuan Yew, personal interview.

Chapter 7 Officers and gentlemen
Page

91 'There is no limit': quoted in John Wyett, *Staff Wallah at the Fall of Singapore*, p. 31.

91 'While John Wyett takes his bath': Wyett, p. 29, and John Wyett, personal interview.

92 'To the newcomer, the jungle': Gordon Bennett, pp. 8–9.

94 'One of nature's gentlemen': Kinvig, *Scapegoat: General Percival of Singapore*, p. 226.

94 'Streak of the impresario': Kinvig in Farrell and Hunter (eds), p. 260.

94 'Ruthless, brilliant': Kinvig, *Scapegoat*, p. 225.

95 'He fixed me with his pale blue eyes': Wyett, p. 12.

96 'Percival was a prisoner of war in Formosa': Lodge, pp. 247–248.

96 'Condemned by photography': Kinvig in Farrell and Hunter (eds), p. 241.

97 'His father was a schoolteacher': Frank Legg, *The Gordon Bennett Story*, pp. 5–6.

98 'McNicoll called an officers' meeting': Legg, pp. 33–35.

99 'From in front, through the shrapnel fire': Staniforth Ricketson quoted in Legg, pp. 49–50.

100 'A large group of Turks appeared on the ridgeline': Legg, pp. 51–54.

101 'Lieutenant Dallas Moor won the Victoria Cross': Les Carlyon, *Gallipoli*, p. 308.

101 'Charles Bean, war correspondent': Carlyon, p. 164.

102 'Now I found that my dreadful experience': Gordon Bennett in Legg, pp. 75–76.

103 'I have become a fatalist': Legg, p. 87.

103 'Experience has proved': Legg, p. 151.

104 'He went to the elite Rugby School': Kinvig, *Scapegoat*, pp. 5–6.

104 'The only bag I have made is one rat': Percival's early military career is detailed in Kinvig, *Scapegoat*, pp. 29–112.

104 'Hop and caper': Kinvig, *Scapegoat*, pp. 49–51.

105 'The nasty little guerilla war': Kinvig, p. 90.

105 'In London he received a briefing note': Kinvig, p. 49.

105 'He warned a volunteer unit': Kinvig, *Scapegoat*, p. 106.

105 'Burgle Malaya,': Kinvig, p. 106.

106 'Far from being impregnable': Kinvig, *Scapegoat*, p. 112.

106 'I had expected to be a person of some consequence': Arthur Percial, *The War in Malaya*, p. 14.

107 'I wish you bloody soldiers': Peter Elphick, *Singapore: The Pregnable Fortress*, p. 222.

108 'Liveries of ostentatious gold': Lady Diana Cooper quoted in Warren, p. 136.

108 'He is also the mouthpiece': Elphick, p. 225.

108 'A rotten judge': Warren, p. 320.

108 'Yamashita, bulky, tall': Yoji, in Farrell and Hunter (eds), p. 187.

108 'A veteran of the China wars': Yoji, pp. 198–205.

109 'After receiving a report': Warren, p. 279.

110 'He had tolerance': Tsuji, p. 196.

110 'They are all stupid': Yoji, p. 202.

Chapter 8 A toast to you, dear pals
Page

112 'Curtains of rain': Spud Spurgeon, personal interview.

113 'At a November conference in Tokyo': Warren, pp. 47–48.

113 'I am looking to you': Callahan, in Farrell and Hunter (eds), p. 159.

113 'The sleep of the saved': Wigmore, p. 136.

114 'Japan would be concentrating': Wigmore, pp. 93–94.

115 'The naval escort bombarded': Tsuji, pp. 93–96.

116 'I do hope, sir': Warren, p. 60.

116 'Admiral Tom Phillips': Elphick, p. 247.

116 'Force Z, in a foray': Warren, p. 66.

117 'He had been in bed': Wigmore, p. 145.

117 'In all the war': Wigmore, p. 145.

117 'It was under pressure from Churchill': Warren, p. 43.

117 'Three small and outdated': Wigmore, p. 103.
118 'Promoted out of turn': Warren, pp. 43–44.
118 'What on earth': Elphick, p. 247.
118 'Bert Harris exploded': Elphick, p. 248.
119 'However, historian Alan Warren': Warren, p. 65.
119 'Phillips had flown': Wigmore, p. 122.
119 'He said to his son': Warren, p. 67.
120 'Below them was a majestic sight': Tsuji, p. 99.
121 'I have seen a show of spirit': Wigmore, p. 144.
121 'More cynical commentators': Warren, p. 76.
121 'A large bouquet of flowers': Tsuji, pp. 100–101.
121 'Beautiful. It's an airliner': Spud Spurgeon, personal interview.
122 'The power who commands': John R. Ferris in Farrell and Hunter (eds), p. 95.
123 'You departing members': Ferris, in Farrell and Hunter (eds), p. 98.
123 'One came out of the cloud': Spurgeon, personal interview.

Chapter 9 Triumph of the two-pounders
Page

125 'Here Lieutenant Harry Head's 12 Platoon': A. W. Penfold, W. C. Bayliss and R. E. Crispin, *Galleghan's Greyhounds*, p. 88.
125 'Shortly before 4 pm': Penfold, Bayliss and Crispin, p. 87.
126 'Gordon Bennett wrote in his diary': H. Gordon Bennett, *Why Singapore Fell*, p. 111.
126 'Percival, during his earlier tour': Kinvig, *Scapegoat*, p. 140.
127 'British and Japanese officers': Wigmore, p. 92.
127 'Damaging 40 per cent': Kinvig, *Scapegoat*, p. 132.
127 'They've now made you responsible': Kinvig, *Scapegoat*, p. 141.
127 'Habit of falling asleep': Elphick, p. 232.
127 'Verge of nervous collapse': Kinvig, *Scapegoat*, p. 180.
128 'Because of a delay': Warren, p. 79.
128 'The Japanese did not have one accurate map': Tsuji, p. 120.
128 'Almost uncanny sense': Kinvig, *Scapegoat*, p. 154.
129 'The "mystery" of 10 guns': Tsuji, p. 118.
130 'We are ready': Wigmore, p. 140.
130 'If we had judged': Tsuji, p. 125.
130 'In this anti-climactic manner': Kinvig, *Scapegoat*, pp. 156–158.
131 'Ordering *kirimoni sakusen*': Akashi Yoji in Farrell and Hunter (eds), p. 191.
131 'While enemy bullets fall': Tsuji, pp. 171–175.
132 'The moral effect of meeting tanks': quoted in Warren, p. 133 and p. 144.

132   'It is now clear': Wigmore, pp. 166–167.

133   'All Saturday and Sunday': Ian Morrison quoted in Wigmore, p. 209.

134   'A huge force of matchless Australians': Warren, p. 36.

134   'It is naturally disturbing': Wigmore, p. 209.

134   'I do not see': Wigmore, pp. 209–210.

135   'Black Jack may be an old': Penfold, Bayliss and Crispin, p. 84.

136   'Permission is grudgingly given': Kenneth Harrison, *The Brave Japanese*, pp. 20–22.

136   'Captain Duffy had let one column': Penfold, Bayliss and Crispin, p. 88.

138   'This time there was no mistake': Harrison, p. 26.

138   'At fifteen minutes to one o'clock': Sergeant Stan Arneil, quoted in Wigmore, p. 218.

139   'Thus ended the first action': Penfold, Bayliss and Crispin, p. 134.

139   'Fought with a bravery': Tsuji, p. 193.

140   'An excited commentator': Wigmore, p. 223.

140   'I have the impression': Legg, p. 208.

140   'He had misread many enemy intentions': Lodge, p. 113.

141   'He watched aghast': Lodge, p. 109.

141   'Enthusiasm for ambushing the enemy': Wigmore, p. 222.

143   'The use of the 45th Brigade was a crime': Anderson quoted in Lodge, p. 110.

143   'The Japanese took small boats': Wigmore, p. 224.

143   'A desperate fight': Tsuji, pp. 203–204.

144   'For all I care, Mr McCure': Harrison, p. 41.

144   'Bill, I was wrong': Harrison, pp. 46–47.

144   'Halt. Who's there?': Harrison, p. 50.

145   'Nasty little incidents': Charles Warden in Ward, p. 205.

145   'The company charged, singing': Wigmore, p. 237.

146   'He stopped, looked at his hand': Harrison, p. 55.

146   'Shoot me, Jim': Harrison, pp. 57–58.

146   'Pressed by ground troops': Wigmore, pp. 243–244.

Chapter 10 Fall of the fortress

Page

148   'An inferior troop': Winston Churchill quoted in Farrell and Hunter (eds), p. 160.

148   'An Australian major was pointing his revolver': Wyett, p. 81.

149   'Wyett nodded towards the pipers': Wyett, p. 82.

149   'I toured slowly through Johore Bahru': Bennett, p. 161.

150   'Tears rolled down his rugged cheeks': Bennett, p. 156.

151 'But they won't get me': Legg, p. 222.
152 'They were a fine body of men': Wigmore, p. 226n.
152 'It goes BANG': Kevin Ward, personal interview.
152 'The top floor was a glassed-in': Tsuji, pp. 227–229.
153 'Australian and British officers': Warren, p. 217.
153 'Percival's inability': Warren, p. 172.
153 'The general effect': Wigmore, p. 290.
153 'Greatly exaggerated estimates': Warren, p. 231.
154 'In the Green Palace, Tsuji': Tsuji, pp. 220–222.
154 'In December 1945 Percival wrote': Warren, p. 214.
156 'A scraggy waste of stunted rubber': Wigmore, p. 302.
157 'General Percival again expressed': Bennett, p. 170.
157 'My deduction': Wigmore, p. 288.
157 'Fed the fiction': Warren, p. 219.
158 'He was a doctor in civil life': Warren, p. 233.
158 'No question of surrender': Warren, p. 180.
158 'Churchill questioned': Churchill, p. 60.
159 'The defenders must greatly outnumber': Churchill, pp. 93–94.
159 'No weakness must be shown': Wigmore, p. 341.
159 'In some units': Wigmore, p. 341.
159 'Holding the paper delicately': Wyett, personal interview.
160 'I could smell the blast': Bennett, pp. 186–187.
161 'It's over, here, take this': Lee Kuan Yew, *The Singapore Story: Memoirs of Lee Kuan Yew*, p. 46.
161 'It was a strange sensation': Wigmore, p. 352.
162 '29 wooden boxes': Wigmore, p. 353.
163 'We pulled up near a building': Wigmore, p. 370.
163 'There must come a stage': Wigmore, p. 372.
164 'It is always right': Churchill, pp. 97–99.
164 'So long as you are in a position': Wigmore, p. 378.
164 'I have my honour to consider': Kinvig, *Scapegoat*, p. 213.
165 'Owing to the losses': Kinvig, *Scapegoat*, p. 217.

Chapter 11 The great escape

Page
166 'There is honour': George Harding' in the diary of Colin Brien, 'Notes and Reminiscences—Malaya Campaign and Prisoner of War Days'.
167 'Evacuees were pushing up': Fred Ransome Smith, personal interview.
168 'He was carrying a large Japanese flag': Warren, p. 264.
168 'The painful events': Percival, *The War in Malaya*, p. 294.

169 'In the Japanese Defence Agency': Kinvig, *Scapegoat*, p. 219.

170 'The officers filled their cups': Tsuji, p. 269.

170 'That night Yamashita was sleepless': Yoji, in Farrell and Hunter (eds), p. 198.

170 'Smith felt shame': Ransome Smith, interview.

171 'The "bad hats", the black sheep': Bennett, p. 213.

171 'His mind was elsewhere': Wyett, p. 88.

171 'You're a coward': Wyett, p. 99.

172 'On the morning of February 15': Wigmore, p. 378.

172 'One has Thyer': Elphick, p. 259.

172 'Bennett knew he would disapprove': Legg, p. 253.

172 'Early that evening': Frederick Howard, *Wilfred Kent Hughes: A Biography*, p. 103.

173 'I must at all costs': Bennett, p. 198.

173 'He flew into Broome': Bennett, p. 199 and p. 217.

174 'Was this belief': Legg, p. 299.

174 'Their war was over': Bennett, p. 197.

175 'John, I can't': Wyett, p. 106.

175 'The route was lined': Wilfred Kent Hughes, 'Slaves of the Samurai', in Howard, p. 115.

175 'Sadness, anger, shame': Kevin Ward, Bill Dunn and Colin Finkemeyer, personal interviews.

176 'The British soldiers looked like men': Tsuji, p. 273.

176 'Erect, unbroken': Lee Kuan Yew, p. 55.

176 'The Mildura Pipe Band': Neil C. Smith, *Tid-Apa: The History of the 4th Anti-Tank Regiment*, pp. 80–81.

Chapter 12 Birds in a cage
Page

178 'It's not the first time': Sidney Rowell quoted in D. M. Horner, *Crisis of Command, Australian Generalship and the Japanese Threat 1941–43*, p. 36.

179 'My dearest Neil': Iris and Neil Dawson, personal interview.

180 'The considered opinion of the Chiefs of Staff': Wigmore, p. 41.

181 'With reluctance': Wigmore, p. 59.

181 'The enemy should be made to fight': Wigmore, p. 397.

182 'Before taking off': Peter Stanley, *The defence of the 'Malay barrier': Rabaul and Ambon, January 1942*.

182 'We could see dimly the shapes': Wigmore, p. 403.

184 'They then stabbed us in the back': Wigmore, p. 668.

185 'An air alarm as we were about to move': John Ballantyne, personal diary.

186 'Boat belong Japan-e stop': J. T. Moyle, *Escape from Rabaul*, personal diary, p. 31.

187 'They lined up and sang "Silent Night" ': Moyle, pp. 38–40.

189 'Lind told his superiors': Wigmore, p. 416.

189 'Present combined army forces inadequate': Wigmore, p. 422.

189 'Additional requested': Wigmore, p. 423.

190 'So far as I can judge': Wigmore, p. 424.

191 'A record of blasting through forbidding mountains': Wigmore, p. 437.

191 'Gull Force lost 309': Wigmore, p. 347.

192 'The people of Albury': *Border Morning Mail*, quoted in Henning, p. 24.

192 'Purely suicidal': Henning, p. 37.

193 'We are looking at': Wigmore, p. 473.

193 'They dropped 600 paratroopers': Neil Dawson, personal interview.

194 'Major Campbell was attracted': Henning, p. 106.

195 'McKay was confident': Clyde McKay, personal interview.

196 'Only a third of Gull Force': Hank Nelson, *Prisoners of War: Australians under Nippon*, p. 97.

197 'So far in this war': Wigmore, p. 675.

198 'Wavell said he considered the risk': Wigmore, pp. 446–447.

198 'A patchwork of villages': Bellair, p. 96.

198 'No Japanese landings': Wigmore, p. 501.

199 'Is everything all right, corporal?': Jackson, personal interview.

200 'Blackburn, with the monsoon starting': Wigmore, p. 503.

200 'They found Dutch officers': Bellair, pp. 101–102.

200 'To die standing': Wigmore, p. 152.

201 'We did not have trained': Henning, pp. 118–119.

202 'Many thanks for the article': Letter in Ballantyne's diary.

Chapter 13 Sea-dog and ship's cat

Page

203 'Bob Collins is on wrecked raft': Margaret Gee, *A Long Way from Silver Creek*, pp. 213–214.

203 'Chilla Goodchap is being tumbled': Chilla Goodchap, personal interview.

204 'It contented itself': Alan Payne, *H.M.A.S. Perth*, in Acknowledgments.

205 'I name this ship *Perth*': Payne, p. 3.

205 'He stuffed it, wriggling': Gee, pp. 148–149.

206 'One small, shell-torn': G. Hermon Gill, *Royal Australian Navy, 1939–1942*, p. 453.

207   'It sank its first victim': Gill, p. 448.

207   'His capacity to grasp': Gill, p. 451.

207   'He lacked that experience': Gill, p. 457.

209   'As the executive signal was made': Gill, p. 312.

210   'They are leaving us alone': Payne, pp. 51–53.

210   'The Japanese navy's firepower': Gill, pp. 468–469.

211   'Soldier were taught': Nicholas Tarling, *A Sudden Rampage*, p. 253.

211   'Maximum of three to four': Payne, p. 67.

211   'He arrived in Java tired and ill': Gill, fn p. 556.

212   'Sighed, listed': Gill, pp. 612–616.

213   'I now had under my orders': Gill, p. 615

213   'Strictly speaking': Gill, p. 616.

214   'The hope ended': Payne, p. 83.

215   'The temperature is over 110 degrees': Ernie Toovey, 'For the Duration', personal diary, pp. 18–19.

216   'I'll see you in Young and Jacksons': Gee, p. 160.

216   'Toovey lands nearby': Ern Toovey, personal interview.

218   'Rode the waves in Bondi style': The story of the aftermath of the battle is told in Payne, pp. 91–98, and the story of Mary and Robin, in Parkin, pp. 36–42.

219   'He then pointed to my left': Payne, p. 104.

220   'David Manning was wearing only a money belt': David Manning, personal interview.

221   'We've had no food all day': Rohan Rivett, *Behind Bamboo*, pp. 75–76.

222   'Who's the Aussie Rules fan?': Manning, interview.

222   'Thirty hours after': Goodchap, interview.

224   'Admiral Helfrick': Gill, pp. 616–624.

227   'For five days he was given no food': Wigmore, p. 535.

228   'It started with a soft hit': Toovey, pp. 49–50.

Chapter 14 Getting to know you

Page

230   'Lieutenant Okasaka arranged': Official reports, correspondence Bryan J, Galleghan F, National Archives of Australia 144/14/65.

231   'Two days before': Wigmore, p. 523.

232   'Play the *King*': Nelson, p. 31.

232   'Galleghan stood': George Aspinall, *Changi Photographer*, p. 90.

232   'Just to be sure': Cyril Gilbert, personal interview.

233   'The Japanese set up bureaucracies': Aiko Utsumi in AWM Australia-Japan Research Project seminar paper, p. 1.

234   'Yamaguchi: Is it wise': Wigmore, pp. 521–522.

235   'Tom Dowling of the 4th Anti-Tank': Colin Finkemeyer, *It Happened to Us – Mark II*, p. 61.

236 'The Brown Bomber': Finkemeyer, pp. 112–113.

237 'Galleghan is short': Stan Arneil, *Black Jack: The Life and Times of Brigadier Sir Frederick Galleghan*, p. 112.

238 'You could hop into it': Gilbert, personal interview.

238 'On the day after the surrender': Arneil, p. 106.

239 'Arneil was a magnet': Stan Arneil, *One Man's War*, pp. 32, 33.

240 'It's the fashion now': Wigmore, p. 511n.

241 'Within 40 or so words': Russell Braddon quoted in Nelson, p. 34.

241 'That bloody mongrel': Clyde McKay, personal interview.

241 'A big martinet of a man': Warren, p. 38.

243 'He was so strict': Stan Arneil, *Black Jack: The Life and Times of Brigadier Sir Frederick Galleghan*, pp. 23–27.

244 'It is requested that permission': Arneil, *Black Jack: The Life and Times of Brigadier Sir Frederick Galleghan*, p. 32.

244 'Don't worry about me, sir': Sue Ebury, *Weary: The Life of Sir Edward Dunlop*', p. 311.

244 'How passionately British,': Ebury, p. 24.

244 'In my boyhood': Ebury, pp. 36–37.

245 'Tom Uren saw': Tom Uren, personal interview.

245 'I *shoko*': Ebury, p. 317.

247 'Nakazawa looked at Griffiths': Dunlop, p. 7, and Ebury, p. 322.

247 'I left this melancholy affair': Dunlop, p. 103.

248 'A kind of golden prison age': Laurens van der Post, in Dunlop, pp. viii–xi.

249 'She is the only stable thing': Dunlop, p. 119.

249 'As the Japanese fleet withdrew': Churchill, pp. 215–216.

250 'To my astonishment': Dunlop, pp. 141–143.

250 'The Japs had taken our colonel': Clyde McKay, personal interview.

251 'He tucked a note from Blackburn': Ebury, p. 371.

251 'More blustering nonsense': Dunlop, p. 147.

Chapter 15 Across the Three Pagodas Pass

Page

252 'How could we get into that jungle': Yoshihiko Futamatsu, *Across the Three Pagodas Pass* (translated and annotated by C. E. Escritt, 1987, IWM, p. 91).

252 'The Siamese twins': Kinvig, *River Kwai Railway*, p. 24.

252 'Burmese king Hsinbyushin': Charles Kimball, *A Guide to Thailand*.

255 'The Thai Foreign Minister': Wigmore, p. 141n.

255 'I would like you to know': Elphick, p. 157.

256 'As a strategic object': Churchill, pp. 58, 127.

256 'The Total War Institute': Tarling, pp. 127–128.

257 'One renews his decision': Futamatsu, p. 99.

258 'The Japanese came and went': U Kok, personal interview.

258 'How can the present generation': Futamatsu, p. 37.

259 'The youthful survey unit commander': Futamatsu, pp. 171–172.

259 'Spread out like a white cloth': Futamatsu, p. 91.

261 'To Bum Tham': Bum Tham, personal interview.

261 'It had the air': Futamatsu, p. 128.

261 'From April to August 490 inches': Kinvig, *River Kwai Railway*, p. 49.

262 'Even today in my memory': Futamatsu, p. 173.

263 'The job involved blasting': Futamatsu, p. 123.

263 'He drove men': Kinvig, *River Kwai Railway*, p. 83.

263 'Seventy per cent of the terrain': Wigmore, p. 588.

264 'In one of the two holds': Rivett, pp. 135–139.

265 'Many men were murdered': Rivett, p. 141.

266 'He had the best body': Goodchap, personal interview.

266 'More disciplined': Wigmore, p. 543.

267 'He pointed over the fence': Ken Dunmbrell, personal interview.

267 'The spirit of these eight': Wigmore, fn p. 544.

Chapter 16 The race that stops a nation
Page

269 'Work cheerfully': Rivett, p. 123.

269 'Breakfast had been brought to them': Jim Osborne, personal interview.

270 'You are only a few remaining skeletons': Rivett, pp. 122–123.

270 'The three of them loved horses': Osborne, personal interview.

272 'Do you know it's the bloody Melbourne Cup': Ron Wells, personal interview.

273 'I ask you to reconcile yourselves': Curtin quoted in Hasluck, *The Government and the People 1942–45*, pp. 270–272.

274 'Fashions for Victory': Hasluck, p. 277.

275 'Health follows will': Dunlop, p. 259.

275 'Ray Wheeler was lucky': Wheeler, personal interview.

277 'How strange is': A. E. Coates, *The Volunteer*, p. 186.

278 'The good Kumada': Albert Coates and Newman Rosenthal, *The Albert Coates Story*, p. 108.

Chapter 17 Hearts of darkness
Page

281 'Purely amoral coolie vermin': Wigmore, p. 547.

281 'A land of milk and honey': McKay, personal interview.

282 'In 30 hours': Dunlop, p. 154 and Desmond Jackson, *What Price Surrender?*, pp. 40–45.

283 'They had them stand out': Panaotie, Devenish and van Nooten, in Nelson, p. 88.

283 'Ando then rose': Wigmore, pp. 605–608.

284 'A scandalous state of affairs': Wigmore, p. 609.

284 'Five men had died': Report on Ambon and Hainan, appendix, AWM.

285 'He was belted across the back': Tom Uren, personal interview.

287 'Was talking to Johnnie': Rivett, p. 248.

288 'It was in this camp': Ern Toovey, *For the duration*.

288 'Ken Dumbrell, who as an officer': Ken Dumbrell, personal interview.

289 'Long after the war': Chilla Goodchap, personal interview.

289 'He was rotten with dysentery': Gee, pp. 189–190.

290 'I am going to die tonight': Gee, pp. 187–188.

291 'Coates was grateful': Coates and Rosenthal, p. 112.

293 'The route home is inscribed': Wigmore, p. 550n.

294 'We had a big element of malaria': Coates and Rosenthal, pp. 177–178.

297 'Gottschell attacked': Coates and Rosenthal, p. 117.

Chapter 18 A day in the life of Desmond Jackson

Page
298 'In Hintok Mountain camp': Desmond Jackson, personal interview.

303 'Contusion of the heart': Dunlop, p. 251.

Chapter 19 In the time of cholera

Page
306 'Kevin Ward fought': Kevin Ward, interview.

307 'We have been told': Don Wall, *Heroes of F Force*, p. vii. (All Wall quotes in chapter from this book.)

309 'Harry Weiss': Harry Weiss's diary entries are recorded in Wall's *Heroes of F Force*.

310 'A frightful night march': Arneil, *One Man's War*, p. 75.

311 'The mud was treacherous': Cyril Gilbert, personal interview.

311 'The Japanese officer put this in writing': Wigmore, p. 573.

312 'The corporal's only reply'; Wigmore, p. 573.

314 'Cholera broke out': Wigmore, p. 547.

315 'George Harding, bushman-poet': Di Elliott, personal interview.

315 'Gentlemen, things are grim': Hunt quoted by R. H. S. Kelsey in Wall, p. 137.

316 'Four more cholera suspects': Arneil, *One Man's War*, p. 95.

316 'Poor old boy': Kelsey in Wall, p. 139.

317 'When thieving threatened'; Wall, p. 131.

317 'Such crises produce': C. H. Kappe and A. Curlewis, 'The Story of F Force', *Mufti*, p. 25.

318 'He gave up taking names': Wall, p. ix.

319 'Ns now say': Dunlop, p. 177.

320 'Nippon very sorry': Parkin, p. 524.

321 'Sulphur ointment, sir': Wall, p. 101.

322 'The so-called doctor': Robert Hardie, *The Siam–Burma Railway: The Secret Diary of Dr Robert Hardie*, p. 101.

322 'The log-sitting game': Dunlop, pp. 239–242.

326 'It was a terrible, sad and dreary': Dunlop, p. 253.

326 'Four years today!': Arneil, *One Man's War*, p. 124.

Chapter 20 The Seventh Circle
Page

328 'I had become': Eric Lomax, *The Railway Man*, p. 167.

328 'The *kempeitai* was founded': Tarling, p. 14.

329 'A shiny heavy web': Lomax, p. 13.

331 'Lomax and his four friends': Lomax, pp. 119–125.

332 'Mother, do you know': Lomax, p. 142, and Nagase, *Crosses and Tigers*, p. 16.

332 'Herb Trackson closes his eyes': Herb Trackson, personal interview.

337 'Wyett faced five charges': Wyett, pp. 138–140.

337 'He and an ordnance private': Wyett, p. 123.

338 'Macalister had flown': Henning, p. 138.

339 'A prominent Singaporean Sikh': Wyett, pp. 144–145.

341 'Those under the shadow': Nelson, p. 165.

344 'Better a man alive': Wyett, p. 174.

Chapter 21 Staying alive, with a little help from their friends
Page

346 'Plumbago, botanical name': Hardie, p. 118.

347 'On a night of the waxing moon': Hardie, p. 60.

348 'Goodchap never forgot the coolie trot': Goodchap, personal interview.

349 'The light of great cumulus clouds': Dunlop, p. 202.

349 'He noticed two fungi': Parkin, pp. 469–470.

351 'In our camp': Uren, pp. 36–37.

352 'Punching involves a transference': Uren, p. 13.

352 'Uren found another mentor': Uren, p. 34.

353 'At the end of one long day': Uren, personal interview.

354 'Bill Bedford, the amateur heavyweight': Uren, pp. 32–33.

355 'He was cobbler': Dunlop, p. 361.

356 'Morale was bad': Norman Carter, *G-String Jesters*, p. 18.

357 'What the hell': Carter, p. 36.

358 'Even the humblest of men': Dunlop, pp. xv–xvii.

359 'A most dreadful man': Bill Dunn, personal interview.

359 'Frightened self-seekers': Parkin, p. 427.

359 'Two British officers selling': Jack Chalker, *Burma Railway Artist: The War Drawings of Jack Chalker*, p. 114.

361 'Knobs of rock': Arneil, p. 72.

361 'Mass this morning': Arneil, p. 177.

362 'Such a pretty girl': Subhawat Amornsri, granddaughter of Boonpong, personal interview.

362 'Hovels and hen runs': Hardie, p. 41.

363 'About 200 British subjects': Kinvig, *River Kwai Railway*, pp. 150–152.

364 'The Japanese are prepared to work': Kinvig, dust jacket, *River Kwai Railway*.

365 'He could see the ribs of Japanese soldiers': Sugano, personal interview.

365 'When a man spends': Futamatsu, pp. 213–214.

366 'In November eight flew': Kinvig, *River Kwai Railway*, p. 62.

366 'Neighbouring these targets': Kinvig, *River Kwai Railway*, p. 155.

366 'Became very excited': Wigmore, p. 554.

367 'Patients who could walk': Rivett, pp. 199–203.

367 'They'll be dropping thousand pounders': Carter, p. 125.

368 'He cherished the slogan': SEATIC Bulletin No. 246, p. 8.

369 'The jungle shook with their efforts': Futamatsu, pp. 184–185.

369 'The monsoon ended': Futamatsu, pp. 237–238.

371 'Letter of condolence': Rivett, pp. 249–250.

373 'It was a moonlight night': Arneil, quoted in Nelson, p. 68.

Chapter 22 Friendly fire
Page

375 'The merchant fleet was capable': Kinvig, *River Kwai Railway*, p. 17.

375 'Hundreds more ships': Kinvig, *River Kwai Railway*, p. 178.

376 'In the forward torpedo room': William Tuohy, *The Bravest Man*, p. 319.

376 'This torpedo curved sharply': Richard O'Kane, *Clear the Bridge! The War Patrols of the U.S.S. Tang*, pp. 457–462.

378 'On his property': Lance Gibson, personal interview.

379 'A kimono for Japanese women': Cook, p. 185.

379   'Bad harvests at home': United States Strategic Bombing Survey, *Summary Report*, pp. 18–19.

379   'As the war demanded more': Cook, p. 188.

380   'Some had no choice': Cook, p. 173.

380   'Their clothing issue': Wigmore, p. 618.

381   'They were headed for a rendezvous': Don Wall, *Heroes at Sea*, pp. 135–136.

383   'Radar contact, bearing one five zero': O'Kane, pp. 226–227.

384   'Gibson recalled later': Lance Gibson, personal interview.

385   'It was a bloody sick ship': Nelson, p. 140.

385   'Myriad lice, bugs and flies': Uren, pp. 44–45.

386   'After a series of five violent rolls': Nelson, p. 143.

387   'The convoy took its own precautions': Wall, p. 18.

387   'They broke a Japanese naval code': Tuohy, pp. 62–65.

388   'The code-breakers in most cases': Wall, p. 18.

389   'Frank McGrath's revenge': Wall, p. 29.

389   'Look sir, I've been sunk before': Wall, p. 22.

390   'We gave back': Wall, p. 35.

390   'Ray Wheeler had joined about 200': Wheeler, personal interview.

391   'MacDiarmid threw a rope': Wall, p. 40.

392   'I'm responsible for you men': Wall, p. 64.

393   'While patrolling on the surface': Wall, p. 67.

394   'When darkness came': Wall, pp. 76–77.

396   'Stealing a *prau*': Wigmore, pp. 434–435.

396   'The treatment by Japs': Nelson, p. 87.

397   'In Canberra, Forde': *Parliamentary Debates, House of Representatives, Vol. 180*, pp. 121–124.

398   'In the House of Commons': Kinvig, *River Kwai Railway*, p. 189.

398   'The story of the massacre': Hank Nelson, 'A Map to Paradise Road: A Guide for Historians', *Journal of the Australian War Memorial*, Issue 32, March 1999.

Chapter 23 Things do taste better from silver spoons

Page

399   'Three poles are placed underneath': Pat Darling (nee Gunther), *Portrait of a Nurse*, p. 78.

399   'Margaret Dryburgh, a pioneer': Jessie Elizabeth Simons, *While History Passed*, p. 52.

401   'They were the daughters': Hank Nelson, *Prisoners of War: Australians under Nippon*, p. 69.

401   'A dinner party given by a Chinese millionaire': Darling, p. 10.

402   'Walking on dead bodies': Darling, p. 16.

403 'The poor old fellow': Nelson, p. 73.

403 'Kath Neuss was bleeding': Pat Darling, personal interview.

404 'Out of the darkness swept': Simons, p. 18.

405 'The Japanese soldier in charge': Darling, pp. 24–25.

405 'For ten generations a great white buffalo': Shirley Fenton Huie, *The Forgotten Ones*, p. 6.

407 'The Japanese simply treated men': George Brouwer, personal interview.

409 'Tiny, looking a little like Madame Curie': Huie, pp. 32–33.

411 'The nurses picked out spoons': Darling, p. 34.

411 ' "Geishas" was the term': Simons, p. 36.

411 'Betty Jeffrey watched': Jeffrey, *White Coolies*, p. 29.

412 'Almost an egg': Darling, personal interview.

414 'The guard the nurses called Rasputin': Jeffrey, p. 101.

414 'Four made a living as "nightmen" ': Jeffrey, p. 119.

414 'Keep smiling': Simons, p. 61.

414 'Can we take the grins off': Darling, p. 88.

415 'Mean-souled scoundrel': Simons, p. 91.

415 'One hard, staring brown eye': Huie, p. 112.

415 'After the war, Denis went': Warner and Sandilands, p. 263.

416 'Gold Teeth, the interpreter': Jeffrey, p. 131.

416 'She wept silently': Darling, p. 86.

416 'Like a flight of birds': Darling, pp. 88–89.

418 'Gunther turned away': Darling, personal interview.

418 'Gunther was weary': Darling, pp. 89–90.

Chapter 24 Then there were none

Page

420 '*From walking in the footsteps*': Colin Simpson, *Six from Borneo*, Australian Broadcasting Commission.

420 'When Owen Campbell returned': Owen Campbell, personal interview.

422 'A prisoner, tall, thin': Silver, pp. 234–237.

422 'John Skinner was beheaded': Author Lynette Silver, the 8th Division Association's official historian from 1995 to 2002, is responsible for the detective work which led to the identification of John Skinner's skeleton. See Silver, *Sandakan: A Conspiracy of Silence*, Chapter 13, note 4, p. 394.

422 'Something of a mascot': Don Wall, *Sandakan: The Last March*, p. 118.

422 'I hate the idea': Turnbull, p. 160.

425 '*de Klerk* carried a cargo': Silver, p. 105.

426 'The conning tower hatch opened': Silver, p. 108 and Wall, p. 125.

427 'After dark the men walked': Silver, pp. 114–116.

428   'Lepers provided information': Silver, pp. 125, 299.
428   'He wished to atone': Silver, p. 299.
430   'Keep your chin up': Silver, pp. 154–155.
430   'Ray Steele grappled': Nelson, pp. 116–117.
431   'They were on the verge of starvation': Silver, p. 219.
432   'Emergency measures': Silver, pp. 180–181.
433   'His unit was fresh': Wall, p. 62.
434   'The guards kept us going': Wall, pp. 73–74.
434   'Prisoners of war': Silver, p. 218.
435   'Orang Tua Kulang realised': Wall, pp. 55, 64.
437   'It was Takakua's': Department of Veterans' Affairs, Laden, Fevered, Starved.
438   'At Manila's Santo Tomas University': Silver, p. 181.
438   'What about the blokes': Wall, pp. 57–58.
439   'We had complete plans': Silver, p. 302.
440   'After the PT boat attacks': AWM 54 1010/1/2.
440   'He followed elephant': Wall, pp. 97–98.
441   'A minute paper': Papers of Athol Moffitt, AWM 7/2.

Chapter 25 It was the first time I'd seen a Nip cry
Page

443   'Des Moloney was tall': Sol Henderson, personal interview.
444   'In battle, it lost 53 men': details of battalion history from Henning.
445   'Life is too sweet': Dunlop, p. 364.
445   'McKay saw arms and men': Clyde McKay, personal interview.
446   'In August 1943 the Southern Army': Tarling, p. 111.
446   'During the Malayan campaign': Tsuji, p. 284.
446   'The oxen were Mutaguchi's idea': Kazuo Tamayama and John Nunneley, Tales by Japanese Soldiers, p. 189.
446   'Near his house Mutaguchi': Tamayama and Nunneley, p. 191.
447   'It was a vision of hell': Tamayama and Nunneley, p. 197.
447   'Prime Minister Tojo declared': Cook and Cook, p. 281.
448   'When the babies cried': Cook and Cook, p. 289.
448   'They were close to the cliff-edge': Al Perry, The Men of 'A' Company: A Personal History of the Fourth Marine Division, pp. 3–6.
449   'Our courage will be buoyed': Cook and Cook, pp. 337–339.
449   'Air raid. Air raid': Cook and Cook, p. 337.
450   'Churchill, calling up memories': R. A. C. Parker, Struggle for Survival: The History of the Second World War, pp.164–170.
451   'It's the feeling of not being able': Jackson tells the story of Linford and Ja Ray in pp. 107–136.

452   'He made a sign across his throat': Clyde McKay, personal interview.

452   'Called Z in the diaries': Dunlop, pp. 378–379.

453   'The Commander-in-Chief of the Southern Army': Kinvig, *River Kwai Railway*, p. 191.

453   'One August morning': Jackson, pp. 184–185.

454   'A rain of ruin': Parker, p. 241.

454   'Neil Dawson, of the 2/40th': Neil Dawson, personal interview.

Chapter 26 The Fat Man sings; the Crane speaks

Page

455   'We have discovered': Truman quoted in Robert H. Ferrell, *Off the Record: The Private Papers of Harry S. Truman*, Harper & Row, New York, pp. 55–56.

455   'Blinding blue-white light': Allan Chick, personal interview.

456   'The damage and casualties caused': United States Strategic Bombing Survey, *Summary Report* (Pacific War), p. 24.

457   'The energy liberated in the explosion': Stanford website.

457   'I have told': Farrell, pp. 55–56.

458   'The 509 Composite Group': US National Archives.

458   'The might that now converges': UCLA Asia Institute website.

459   'As the wounded': Chick, personal interview.

459   'They were agreed on one thing': Pacific War Research Society, *Japan's Longest Day*, pp. 25–27.

460   'Yes, yes!': Pacific War Research Society, p. 27.

460   'A huge, disturbed ant-hill': Pacific War Research Society, p. 53.

462   'Over my dead body': Pacific War Research Society, p. 91.

462   'Not long after midnight': Pacific War Research Society, pp. 223–226.

463   'For my supreme crime': Pacific War Research Society, p. 237.

463   'I have nothing to regret': Pacific War Research Society, p. 334.

463   'The crane is': Pacific War Research Society, p. 34.

463   'We, by grace of heaven': Harvard Education website.

464   'High-pitched, uncertain': Harries and Harries, p. 387.

465   'An old steam engine': Snowy Marsh, personal interview.

465   'Boom, boom': Chilla Goodchap, personal interview.

466   'One day Spurgeon was walking': Spud Spurgeon, personal interview.

466   'The Russians wanted to shoot': Lance Gibson, personal interview.

466   'You master now': Bill Dunn, personal interview.

466   'I want some sugar': Ken Dumbrell, personal interview.

467   'At 3.30 pm a Japanese corporal': Jackson, pp. 192–193.

467   'He was sombre': David Manning, personal interview.

468   'Their fathers were dead': Simons, pp. 110–111.

468   'Where are the Australian nurses?': Darling, p. 93.

Chapter 27 Crime and punishment

Page

469 '*A rainbow*': Takashi Nagase, *Crosses and Tigers*, p. 35.

469 'I wish to thank the court': War Crimes, Proceedings of Military Tribunal, Lt Hirota Eiji, National Archives of Australia.

471 'A small token of my personal interest': Kinvig, *Scapegoat*, p. 230.

471 'MacArthur delighted Percival': Kinvig, *Scapegoat*, pp. 234–235.

471 'He told a chaplain': Yoji, in Farrell and Hunter (eds), p. 201.

471 'The world I knew': Harries, p. 394.

472 'Lt Hirota attacked': War Crimes, proceedings of Military Tribunal, NAA.

472 'Personnel who have ill-treated': Aiko Utsumi in Gavan McCormack and Hank Nelson, *The Burma-Thailand Railway*, p. 77.

473 'Ray Myors watched a man': Nelson, p. 198.

473 'What the bloody hell's going on': Wheeler, personal interview.

473 'We made it, mate': Dunn, personal interview.

475 'The Allies had asked for': Nagase, p. 23.

475 'Nothing would diminish': Earl Mountbatten, quoted in the Papers of Athol Randolph Moffitt.

476 'Historian Gavan McCormack': McCormack and Nelson, pp. 85–114.

479 'This was partly due': Wigmore, p. 551.

479 'The sick included hundreds': Wigmore, p. 555.

480 'After three days, Dickinson': Leslie Hall, *The Blue Haze*, p. 112; Wigmore, p. 550.

480 'Surely the large number of casualties': War Crimes: Proceedings of Military Tribunal, Lt Hirota Eiji.

481 'Every work-camp commandant': Trial of Yoshitada Nagatomo and others, AWM.

481 'No solid foundation in established law': Harries, pp. 394–395.

482 'Revenge is, of all satisfactions': Harries, p. 393.

482 'The wider problem': McCormack and Nelson, p. 113.

482 'The POW atrocities': McCormack and Nelson, p. 78.

483 'There was a sub-stratum of the culture': Lee Kuan Yew, personal interview.

485 'Those who fought in the Asia-Pacific': Yuki Tanaka, *Hidden Horrors: Japanese War Crimes in World War II*, p. 6.

486 'The Court is of the opinion': Lodge, p. 261.

486 'A meeting of the 8th Division': *Age*, October 10, 1972.

486 'The Royal Commissioner, Mr Justice Ligertwood': Lodge, p. 287.

487 'He watched the flag-draped': Wyett, p. 216.

487 'As they clustered around him': Legg, p. 276.

Chapter 28 Home

Interviews

PRISONERS OF WAR AND RELATIVES

George Bell, Graham Bourke, George Brouwer, Evelyn Campbell, Owen Campbell, Jack Chalker, Allan Chick, Haruko Chick, Pat Darling, Iris Dawson, Neil Dawson, Ken Dumbrell, Bill Dunn, Russ Durrant, Colin Finkemeyer, Lance Gibson, Mary Gibson, Cyril Gilbert, Chilla Goodchap, Sol Henderson, Desmond Jackson, Pat Jackson, Ivor Jones, Clyde McKay, David Manning, Snowy Marsh, Doris Mulvena, Jim Osborne, Ray Parkin, Fred Ransome Smith, Spud Spurgeon, Ern Toovey, Herb Trackson, Tom Uren, Don Wall, Kevin Ward, Ron Wells, Ray Wheeler, John Wyett.

SINGAPORE

Lee Kuan Yew

JAPAN

Renichi Sugano, Takashi Nagase, Toshiyuki Tanaka, Aiko Utsumi.

THAILAND

Subhawat Amornsri, Bum Tham

BURMA

U Kok, U Than Kuang

OTHERS

Bambang Soemardjo, Keith Rossi

Select bibliography

BOOKS

Adam-Smith, Patsy, *Prisoners of War: From Gallipoli to Korea*, Penguin Books, Melbourne, 1992.

Alomes, S. and Jones, C., *Australian Nationalism*, Angus & Robertson, Sydney, 1991.

Arneil, Stan, *Black Jack: The Life and Times of Brigadier Sir Frederick Galleghan*, Macmillan, Sydney, 1983.

—— *One Man's War*, Sun Books, South Melbourne, 1980.

Bellair, John, *From Snow to Jungle: A History of the 2/3rd Australian Machine Gun Battalion*, Allen & Unwin, Sydney, 1987.

Bennett, H. Gordon, *Why Singapore Fell*, Angus & Robertson, Sydney, 1944.

Blair, Joan and Clay, *Return from the River Kwai*, Futura Publications, London, 1980.

Bowden, Tim, *Changi Photographer: George Aspinall's Record of Captivity*, ABC Books, Sydney, 1993.

Carlyon, Les, *Gallipoli*, Pan Macmillan, Sydney, 2001.

Carter, Norman, *G-String Jesters*, Currawong Publishing Company, Sydney, 1966.

Cassels, Vic, *For Those in Peril: A Comprehensive Listing of the Ships and Men of the Royal Australian Navy who have Paid the Supreme Sacrifice in the Wars of the Twentieth Century*, Kangaroo Press, Sydney, 1995.

Chalker, Jack Bridge, *Burma Railway Artist: The War Drawings of Jack Chalker*, Leo Cooper, London, 1994.

Churchill, Winston S., *The Second World War IV: The Hinge of Fate*, The Reprint Society, 1954.

Clark, C. M. H., *A History of Australia VI*, Melbourne University Press, Melbourne, 1987.

Clarke, Hugh V., *Last Stop Nagasaki!* Allen & Unwin, Sydney, 1984.

—— *A Life for Every Sleeper: A Pictorial Record of the Burma-Thailand Railway*, Allen & Unwin, Sydney, 1986.

—— *Twilight Liberation: Australian Prisoners of War between Hiroshima and Home*, Allen & Unwin, Sydney, 1985.

Coates, Albert, *The Volunteer: The Diaries and Letters of Albert E. Coates, No. 23 – 7th Btn., 1st A.I.F., First World War 1914–1918*, Winifred & Walter Gherardin (family), 1995.

Coates, Albert and Rosenthal, Newman, *The Albert Coates Story: The Will that Found the Way*, Hyland House, Melbourne, 1977.

Cook, Haruko Taya and Cook, Theodore F., *Japan at War: An Oral History*, Phoenix Press, London, 2000.

Crowley, F. K., *Modern Australia in Documents, Vol. 1, 1901–1939*, Wren, Melbourne, 1973.

Darling, Pat, *Portrait of a Nurse*, Don Wall, Mona Vale, 2001.

Day, David, *The Great Betrayal*, Angus & Robertson, Sydney, 1988.

—— *John Curtin: A Life*, HarperCollins Publishers, Sydney, 1999.

Dean, Penrod V., *Singapore Samurai*, Kangaroo Press, Sydney, 1998.

Diamond, Jared, *Guns, Germs and Steel*, Vintage, London, 1998.

Dower, John, *War without Mercy: Race and Power in the Pacific War*, Faber & Faber, London, 1986.

Dunlop, E. E., *The War Diaries of Weary Dunlop: Japan and the Burma-Thailand Railway 1942–1945*, Nelson, Melbourne, 1986.

Ebury, Sue, *Weary: The Life of Sir Edward Dunlop*, Viking Australia, Melbourne, 1994.

Elphick, Peter, *Singapore: The Pregnable Fortress*, Hodder & Stoughton, London, 1995.

Farrell, Brian and Hunter, Sandy (eds), *Sixty Years On: The Fall of Singapore Revisited*, Eastern Universities Press, Singapore, 2003.

Finkemeyer, Gunner, *It Happened to Us – Mark II*, C. E. and D. J. Finkemeyer, 1998.

Gee, Margaret, *A Long Way from Silver Creek: A Family Memoir*, Margaret Gee, Sydney, 2000.

Gill, G. Hermon, *Royal Australian Navy 1939–1942*, Australian War Memorial, Canberra, 1957.

Hall, Leslie, *The Blue Haze*, National Library of Australia, Canberra, 1985.

Hardie, Dr Robert, *The Burma–Siam Railway: The Secret Diary Of Dr Robert Hardie 1942–45*, Quadrant Books, London, 1984.

Harries, Meirion and Harries, Susie, *Soldiers of the Sun: The Rise and Fall of the Imperial Japanese Army 1868–1945*, Heinemann, London, 1991.

Harrison, Kenneth, *The Brave Japanese*, Rigby, Sydney, 1966.

Hasluck, Paul, *The Government and the People, 1939–41*, Australian War Memorial, Canberra, 1952.

—— *The Government and the People, 1942–45*, Australian War Memorial, Canberra, 1952.

Henning, Peter, *Doomed Battalion: Mateship and Leadership in War and Captivity*, Allen & Unwin, Sydney, 1995.

Heseltine, Harry (ed.), *The Penguin Book of Australian Verse*, Penguin Books, Melbourne, 1976.

Horne, Donald, *Billy Hughes*, Black Inc., Melbourne, 1983.

Horner, D. M., *Crisis of Command: Australian Generalship and the Japanese Threat 1941–43*, ANU Press, Canberra, 1978.

Howard, Frederick, *Kent Hughes: A Biography*, The Macmillan Company of Australia, Melbourne, 1972.

Hudson, W. J., *Billy Hughes in Paris: The Birth of Australian Diplomacy*, Nelson, Melbourne, 1978.

Huie, Shirley Fenton, *The Forgotten Ones: Women and Children under Nippon*, Angus & Robertson, Sydney, 1992.

Jackson, D., *What Price Surrender? A Story of the Will to Survive*, Allen & Unwin, Sydney, 1989.

Jeffrey, Betty, *White Coolies*, Panther, London, 1967.

Johnston, Mark, *Fighting the Enemy: Australian Soldiers and their Adversaries in World War II*, Cambridge University Press, Melbourne, 2000.

Kawakami, Kiyoshi Kari, *Japan and World Peace*, Macmillan, New York, 1919.

Kelly, Paul, *The End of Certainty: The Story of the 1980s*, Allen & Unwin, Sydney, 1992.

Kenko, Yoshida, *Essays in Idleness*, Wordsworth Classics, Hertfordshire, 1998.

Kinvig, Clifford, *River Kwai Railway*, Brassey's London, UK, 1992.

—— *Scapegoat: General Percival of Singapore*, Brassey's London, UK, 1996.

Lee, Kuan Yew, *The Singapore Story: Memoirs of Lee Kuan Yew*, Times Editions, 1998.

—— *From Third World to First: The Singapore Story 1965–2000*, Times Media Private Limited and The Straits Times Press, Singapore, 2000.

Legg, Frank, *The Gordon Bennett Story*, Angus & Robertson, Sydney, 1965.

Lodge, A. B., *The Fall of General Gordon Bennett*, Allen & Unwin, Sydney, 1986.

Lomax, Eric, *The Railway Man*, Vintage, Random House Group Limited, London, 1995.

Long, Gavin, *Greece, Crete and Syria*, Australian War Memorial, Canberra, 1986.

McCormack, G. and Nelson, H., *The Burma-Thailand Railway*, Allen & Unwin, Sydney, NSW, 1993.

McKernan, Michael, *This War Never Ends: The Pain of Separation and Return*, University of Queensland Press, St Lucia, 2001.

Maugham, Somerset, *The Casaurina Tree*, Mandarin, London, 1994.

—— *The Gentleman in the Parlour*, Mandarin, London, 1994.

Meaney, Neville, *Towards a New Vision: Australia and Japan through 100 Years*, Kangaroo Press, Sydney, 1999.

Millar, T. B., *Australia in Peace and War*, ANU Press, Canberra, 1978.

Moyle, J. T., *Escape from Rabaul*, Jack and Thelma Moyle, Tallangatta, 2000.

Nagase, Takashi and Masaru Watase (trans.), *Crosses and Tigers*, Allied Printers, Bangkok, 1990.

Nelson, H., *P.O.W. Prisoners of War: Australians Under Nippon*, ABC Enterprises, Sydney, 1985.

O'Kane, Richard H., *Clear the Bridge!: The War Patrols of the U.S.S. Tang*, Presidio Press, California, 1989.

Orwell, George, *Burmese Days*, Martin, Secker & Warburg, London, 1986.

Pacific War Research Society, The, *Japan's Longest Day*, Kodansha International, Tokyo, & Kodansha America Inc., New York, 1968.

Parker, R. A. C., *Struggle for Survival: The History of the Second World War*, Oxford University Press, New York, 1989.

Parkin, Ray, *Wartime Trilogy*, Melbourne University Press, Melbourne, 1999.

Payne, Alan, *H.M.A.S. Perth: The Story of the 6 inch Cruiser 1936–1942*, The Naval Historical Society of Australia, New South Wales, 1978.

Peek, Ian Denys, *One Fourteenth of an Elephant: A Memoir of Life and Death on the Burma-Thailand Railway*, Pan Macmillan, Sydney, 2003.

Penfold, A. W., Bayliss, W. C., Crispin, R. E., *Galleghan's Greyhounds*, 2/30th Btn AIF Association, Sydney, 1979.

Percival, Arthur, *The War in Malaya*, Eyre & Spottiswoode, London, 1949.

Queensland Ex-POW Reparation Committee, *Nippon Very Sorry – Many Men Must Die*, Boolarong Publications, Brisbane, 1990.

Rivett, Rohan, *Behind Bamboo*, Angus & Robertson, Sydney, 1952.

Russell, Lord, *The Knights of Bushido*, Cassell & Co., London, 1958.

Silver, L. R., *Sandakan: A Conspiracy of Silence*, Sally Milner Publishing, Bowral, 3rd Ed., 2000.

Simons, Jessie Elizabeth, *While History Passed*, Heinemann, Melbourne, 1954.

Smith, Lieutenant Colonel N. C., *Tid-Apa: The History of the 4th Anti-Tank Regiment 1940–1945*, Mostly Unsung Military History Research and Publications, 1992.

Stockwin, J. A. A. (ed.), *Japan and Australia in the Seventies*, Angus & Robertson, Sydney, 1972.

Takeyama, Michio, *Harp of Burma*, Charles E. Tuttle Co., Tokyo, 1966.

Tamayama, Kazuo and Nunneley, John, *Tales by Japanese Soldiers*, Cassell & Co., London, 2000.

Tarling, Nicholas, *A Sudden Rampage: The Japanese Occupation of Southeast Asia, 1941–1945*, Horizon Books, Singapore, 2001.

Tsuji, Masanobu, *Singapore 1941–1942: The Japanese Version of the Malayan Campaign of World War II*, Oxford University Press, Singapore, 1988.

Tuohy, William, *The Bravest Man: The Story of Richard O'Kane & U.S. Submariners in the Pacific War*, Sutton Publishing, Gloucestershire, 2001.

Turnbull, C. Mary, *A History of Malaysia, Singapore and Brunei*, Allen & Unwin, Sydney, 1989.

United States Strategic Bombing Survey, *Summary Report*, Government Printing Office, Washington, 1946.

Uren, Tom, *Straight Left*, Random House Australia, Sydney, 1994.

Wade, Tom Henling, *Prisoner of the Japanese: From Changi to Tokyo*, Kangaroo Press, Sydney, 1994.

Wall, Don, *Heroes of F Force*, D. Wall, Mona Vale, 1993.

—— *Heroes at Sea*, D. Wall, Mona Vale, 1991.

—— *Kill the Prisoners!*, D. Wall, Mona Vale, 1994.

—— *Sandakan: The Last March*, D. Wall, Mona Vale, 1989.

Ward, Ian, *Snaring the Other Tiger*, Media Masters, Singapore, 1996.

Warner, Lavina and Sandilands, John, *Women beyond the Wire: A Story of Prisoners of the Japanese, 1942–45*, Michael Joseph, London, 1982.

Warren, Alan, *Singapore 1942: Britain's Greatest Defeat*, Talisman, Singapore, 2002.

Waten, Judah, *Australia since the Camera: The Depression Years, 1929–1939*, Cheshire, Melbourne, 1971.

Wigmore, Lionel, *The Japanese Thrust*, Australian War Memorial, Canberra, 1957.

Wyett, J., *Staff Wallah: At The Fall of Singapore*, Allen & Unwin, Sydney, NSW, 1996.

Tanaka, Yuki, *Hidden Horrors: Japanese War Crimes in World War II*, Westview Press, Colorado, 1996.

AUSTRALIAN WAR MEMORIAL

Brett, Lieutenant C. C., *SEATIC Bulletin, South East Asian Theatre, No. 246.*

Chick, Allan, personal papers, PR85/189.

Campbell, Owen, 'A' interrogation No. 1, 1010/4/27.

Campbell, Owen, 1010/1/2.

Execution of Japanese War Criminals, 54 807/2/1.

Executions of Breavington and Gale, 144/14/65.

Imperial Rescripts, propaganda, 82 1/3/18.

Johnston, Mark, 'Yet they're just as human as we are', Seminar Paper, Australia–Japan Research Project.

Papers of Athol Randolph Moffitt, PRO1378.

Report on Ambon and Hainan, Lt Col. J. R. Scott, 573/6/1A.

Report on employment of prisoners of war in Siam–Burma railway construction, 54 1010/3/10.

Report on the situation in the Sandakan area, 54 1010/2.

Report on the Directorate of Prisoners of War and Internees, 54 780/1/6.

Trial of Yoshitada Nagatomo and others, barcode 5419694, control 849, series B5563 AWM.

Utsumi, Aiko, 'The Japanese Army and its Prisoners', seminar paper, Australia–Japan Research Project.

NATIONAL ARCHIVES

Defence of Rabaul, 16/401/493, MP 729/6.

Trial of Yoshitada Nagatomo and others, 1046277.

War Crimes: Proceedings of Military Tribunal Lt Hirota Eiji, Singapore 18, 19, 21, 1946, A471 81301.

IMPERIAL WAR MUSEUM

Futamatsu, Yoshihiko, *Across the Three Pagodas Pass: The story of the Thai–Burma Railway* (translated by C. E. Escritt, 1987).

WEBSITES

Donsal, Stephen, *Suitors and Supplicants: The Little Nations at Versailles*, Historical Text Archive, historicaltextarchive.com

Kimball, Charles, *A Guide to Thailand*, www.guidetothailand.com

Perry, A., *The Men of 'A' Company: A personal history of the Fourth Marine Division in WWII*, mysite.version.net/res71z3x

VIDEO, PLAYS, TRANSCRIPTS

Davies, Richard, *A Bright and Crimson Flower*.
Federation Story: Immigration and Nation Building, executive producer-Dave Lane, Australian Broadcasting Commission.
100 Years, The Australian Story, Farewell to Great and Powerful Friends, executive producer Dave Lane, Australian Broadcasting Commission.
Simpson, Colin, *Six From Borneo*, Australian Broadcasting Commission.

NEWSPAPERS AND ARTICLES

Argus, 1939–1941.
Kappe, C. H. and Curlewis, A., 'The Story of F Force,' *Mufti*, 1951–53.
Nelson, Hank, 'A Map to Paradise Road: A Guide for Historians', *Journal of the Australian War Memorial*, Issue 32, March 1999.
Stanley, Peter, *The defence of the 'Malay Barrier': Rabual and Ambon, January 1942*, Australian War Memorial.
Warner, Denis, 'They saw the Fat Man and lived to tell the tale', *The Australian Magazine*, July 1–2, 1995.

UNPUBLISHED

Ballantyne, John Stuart, Diary.
Toovey, Ernie, *For the duration*.

Acknowledgements

Not long after we began talking about the death throes of the Australian cruiser *Perth* in the Battle of Sunda Strait, Chilla Goodchap wept. He was describing his feelings as he was being slowly tumbled under water by the ship's propellers. 'Why am I talking about this?' he said. Goodchap almost lost his life. He lost many of his mates in the battle and its aftermath; he lost many more along the Thai–Burma railway.

This book has been a journey, gruelling and saddening, and Chilla Goodchap has been one of my guides. Each of the survivors I spoke with took me into the prisoner-of-war world at great cost. They relived their own pain and the suffering and deaths of people who had made their continued existence in a singular sort of hell possible and tolerable. But the journey became a celebration of the spirit of remarkable men and women. In one of the great, hidden battles of World War II, brutality and inhumanity lost to caring, courage, humour, sharing and strength of will. I thank all I had the privilege of meeting. I owe a particular debt to Pat Darling, Colin Finkemeyer, Cyril Gilbert, Clyde McKay and Kevin Ward, and to Desmond Jackson and his wife Pat, Allan Chick and his wife Haruko, Neil Dawson and his wife Iris, and Lance Gibson and his wife Mary.

Margaret Gee, old journalistic acquaintance and now my agent, was catalyst for this book. Like Chilla Goodchap, her father Allan Gee survived the sinking of *Perth* and the Thai–Burma railway. Margaret cares deeply about her father's story and the stories of all the prisoners of war. She took to Tom Gilliatt, director, non-fiction publishing, Pan Macmillan, a book proposal with the working title 'The Thai–Burma Railway'. Tom Gilliatt took me on trust and encouraged my intent both to broaden the scope of the book and to tell through individuals the story of the prisoners' war, Australia's relationship with Japan and its strategic shift. He helped, advised, dealt with angst and was unfailingly cheerful and supportive.

I travelled in time, examining the relationship and the making of the soldier enemies. What was also essential was the physical journey. The book simply would not have a sense of place without the generosity and knowledge of Rod Beattie of the Thailand-Burma Railway Centre in Kanchanaburi. Rod has looked at the railway with an engineer's eye and with deep sympathy for the prisoners of war. He and his wife Thuy, as a personal mission, reclaimed Hellfire Pass from the jungle and cleared, over two years, six kilometres of the path of the railway. Rod and I have travelled as close as possible to the track from Kanchanaburi to Three Pagodas Pass. He guided me to Cholera Hill at Shimo Songkurai, where Wally Mulvena died. My thanks also go to Dr Paul Gorman. In Burma he organised a convoy which travelled further along the path of the railway towards Three Pagodas Pass than Europeans had been since 1946. In Japan, Hiroshi Osedo, as a friend, arranged interviews, translated, advised and gave insights. I must thank also Lee Kuan Yew, maker of modern Singapore, for giving his time and sharing his perceptions.

The official histories of Long, Wigmore, Hasluck and Gill are essential resources. Another generation of historians has been generous: Hank Nelson, Gavan McCormack, Mark Johnston, Michael McKernan and Alan Warren. I owe a special debt to Warren, author of the excellent *Singapore 1942*, who read relevant chapters of the manuscript. Garrie Hutchinson read the whole of the work in progress. I am grateful for his volunteer copyediting. Karen Ward edited the final work meticulously. Staff at the Australian War Memorial and the National Archives of Australia (both in Canberra and Melbourne) cheerfully went down vague paths I indicated interest in. Don Wall, former prisoner of war, gave me access to his vast trove of research. Brian Farrell, of the National University of Singapore, pointed me towards valuable sources. Lynette Silver's *Sandakan: A Conspiracy of Silence* is necessary reading on that tragedy.

An extract from A. D. Hope's poem 'Australia' is reproduced with permission of Curtis Brown. Mrs R. Escritt kindly gave permission for the reproduction of extracts from Yoshihiko Futamatsu's *Across the Three Pagodas Pass*, part of the Escritt Collection in the Imperial War Museum. Extracts from the following books are reproduced with permission: Patsy Adam-Smith, *Prisoners of War: From Gallipoli to Korea*, E. E. Dunlop, *The War Diaries of Weary Dunlop*, and Sue Ebury, *Weary: The Life of Sir Edward Dunlop*, with permission of Penguin Group Australia Ltd; Stan Arneil, *One Man's War*, with permission of Pan Macmillan Australia Pty Ltd; Winston Churchill, *The Hinge of Fate*, and *The Grand Alliance*, with permission of Curtis Brown Ltd, London, on behalf of the Estate of Sir Winston Churchill; Churchill's cables and his communications with Wavell and Ismay, and other crown copyright material, are reproduced with permission of the Controller of HMSO and the Queen's Printer for Scotland; Haruko Taya Cook and Theodore F. Cook, *Japan at War: An Oral History*, with permission of The New Press; David Day, *John Curtin: A Life*, with permission of HarperCollins; Peter Elphick, *The Pregnable Fortress*, with permission of Hodder & Stoughton; Meirion and Susie Harries, *Soldiers of the Sun*, with permission of Curtis Brown Group Ltd, on behalf of Meirion and Susie Harries © Meirion and Susie Harries 1991; Clifford Kinvig, *Scapegoat*, and *River Kwai Railway*, with permission of Brassey's UK; Eric Lomax, *The Railwayman*, published by Jonathan Cape, and W. Somerset Maugham, *The Casuarina Tree* and *The Gentleman in the Parlour*, with permission of The Random House Group Ltd; The Pacific War Research Society, *Japan's Longest Day*, with permission of Kodansha International Ltd; 'Mairzy Doats' (Drake/Hoffman/Livingston) reproduced with permission of J. Albert & Son Australia Pty Ltd.

Anyone foolhardy enough to embark on a project like this knows the importance of sympathetic ears. Les Carlyon, who trod the path in *Gallipoli*, was always available and wise. His wife Denise assisted with the arcane mysteries of copyright. My thanks to Lorelle Slingsby, who transcribed many of the interviews and became immersed in the stories. Karen Penning, editor at Pan Macmillan, helped me, with good humour and good sense, through the final, nervous weeks. Peter Cole-Adams, Stuart Rintoul and the floating members of the gentlemen's discussion group at Bimbo's learnt more than they wanted or needed to know of progress.

My deepest gratitude, as always, goes to my wife, Anne. She read sources and the manuscript (many times). She travelled with me, when possible, and was my constant companion in the writing process.

However, the book owes its existence to the survivors who shared their stories. Some are now my friends and it pains me when, asked how they are, they say without complaint, 'I'm fading'. But what they suffered, how they carried themselves, how they served their country, should never fade from Australia's memory.

Index